The Dilemma of Style

Architectural Ideas from the Picturesque to the Post-Modern

J. MORDAUNT CROOK

The Dilemma of Style

Architectural Ideas from the Picturesque
to the Post-Modern

The University of Chicago Press

The University of Chicago Press, Chicago 60637
John Murray, London

Printed in Great Britain

96 95 94 93 92 91 90 89 88 87   54321

Library of Congress Cataloging-in-Publication Data

Crook, J. Mordaunt (Joseph Mordaunt), 1937–
    The dilemma of style.

    Bibliography: p.
    Includes index.
    1. Architecture, Modern—England—Themes, motives.
2. Architecture—England—Themes, motives.
3. Eclecticism in architecture—England.   I. Title.
NA975.C7   1987   720′.942   87-10821
ISBN 0-226-12119-4

Contents

List of Illustrations

Abbreviations

List of Illustrations

8

List of Illustrations

Preface

'If the historian of architecture does not take style dead-seriously, he stops being a historian.' (Nikolaus Pevsner, 1961).[1]

IS ARCHITECTURE IN A STATE OF CRISIS? Or are critics simply in a state of confusion? Architectural criticism is scarcely an exact science. In fact our perception of architecture – our idea of good and bad, beautiful and ugly; our very notion of architectural style – has been fairly confused since man first built himself a shelter, then wondered if it pleased his eye. This book sets out to unravel a little of that confusion, at least as regards English architecture during the last two hundred years. It tries to explain – in an English context and without too much jargon – the development of architectural ideas since the eighteenth century.

The Dilemma of Style is not a simple book. But its argument can be stated simply. Style in architecture is a way of building codified in imagistic form. Since the Renaissance – which left us the notion of individual style – architects have often been perplexed by the twofold nature of their calling: building as service and building as art – the eternal tension between form and function. But it was the eighteenth-century philosophy of the Picturesque which turned perplexity into dilemma by multiplying the range of stylistic options. Pugin, Ruskin and Viollet-le-Duc – in different ways – compounded that dilemma by giving it a moral dimension. During the late nineteenth and early twentieth century, the problems created by the need to choose a style – Gothic, Renaissance or some sort of vernacular – accelerated two complementary trends: the cult of eclecticism and the concept of modernity. The Modern Movement tried – and failed – to abolish style by abolishing choice. Post-Modernism – or rather Post-Functionalism – has recreated the dilemma by resuscitating choice. Today the wheel of taste has turned full circle. The twentieth century has had to rediscover what the nineteenth century learned so painfully: eclecticism is the vernacular of sophisticated societies; architecture begins where function ends.

So *The Dilemma of Style* is not another history of English architecture: it is a book about architectural ideas. It is not a study of architectural practice. Its theme is not the process of design – the art of organising a plan in three dimensions – but the way in which that process has been conceptualised during the last two hundred years: conceptualised and codified as style. One further caveat. This book has some hard things to say about the Modern Movement. But it is not an attack on modern architecture. Indeed it ends on an optimistic note. It tries to explain recent confusion, not condemn it. It grew out of two series of Oxford lectures: the Slade Lectures of 1979–80 and the Waynflete Lectures of 1985. Several were repeated at Cambridge, and at the Architectural Association in London. These lectures were thematic rather than chronological; episodic in structure and heavily dependent on slides. They made no attempt at full-scale topographical coverage. They concentrated on ideas. I tried to let architects, critics and theorists speak for themselves.

What were the pundits saying in 1794? What did the Victorians think of Victorian architecture? What did the Edwardians themselves have to say? How did Modernists – and anti-Modernists – justify their own position? What did they all mean by style? And why, at times, did they seem to talk of nothing else? To answer these questions, I went back, wherever possible, to original sources. Hence the density of quotation. I know no other way of measuring opinion.

When Kenneth Clark presented his Slade Lectures of 1945–6 as *Landscape into Art* (1949), he noted that publishing lectures was a well known form of literary suicide. But publish he did, and rightly: if a scholar never takes risks, his subject will never advance. Anybody rash enough to survey two centuries of architectural history must inevitably rely on the work of others. In references and bibliography, I have tried to indicate my debt to the many specialists now working in this field. Not all of them will agree with me. But then it would be a dull lecture which did not provoke debate.

Several people helped me in preparing and checking the text: Hester Whitlock Blundell, Christopher Lennox-Boyd, Susan Mayor, Robin Middleton, John Paul Primiano, Margaret Rose, Sheelagh Taylor and Alan Powers. I am most grateful to all of them, as I am to Camellia Investments for most generous assistance. As Slade Professor, Waynflete Lecturer and Visiting Fellow, I joined the common rooms of a quartet of colleges: All Souls, Brasenose and Magdalen in Oxford; and Gonville and Caius in Cambridge. I also visited the Humanities Research Centre at the Australian National University, Canberra. In return for their congenial company, this book is dedicated to the Fellows of all five.

J.M.C.

1 The Consequences of the Picturesque

'It is the business of an architect to understand all styles, and to be prejudiced in favour of none' (Thomas Hopper, 1830).

DILEMMAS INVOLVE CHOICE: no choice, no dilemma. And choice lies at the root of architectural style – that is, style as understood since the Renaissance: a conscious system of design, a visual code based on tectonic preference, a post-vernacular language of forms.[1] Between the eighteenth century and the twentieth century, architects were perplexed by one overriding concern: the search for a style which was both aesthetically and functionally valid, a style which satisfied traditional canons of beauty and was, at the same time, appropriate to their own age. That generalised statement is not just an historian's method of looking at history: it simply reflects the way in which architects – especially Victorian architects – saw themselves. We know because they said so, again and again and again. One of the few points on which Gilbert Scott and William Morris were in complete agreement, for example, was the belief that the Victorians had no style of their own.[2] Instead they had a choice of styles. So between the disintegration of the classical tradition and the rise of the Modern Movement, architects were faced with a choice – in many cases a multiple choice – between alternative systems of design. Their dilemma was the dilemma of style.

How did this come about? In brief, it was the product first of the Renaissance, and then – more particularly – of Romanticism. Style in architecture is simply a way of building codified by time. But the idea of an individual style is in origin a Renaissance concept, a product of historical awareness and artistic autonomy.[3] Before that, stylistic progression was basically linear: one style led into another over the centuries. After that, there was always an element of decision. But it is only with the arrival of that congeries of attitudes which we label Romantic that this liberation of the creative ego coincides with plurality of choice. During the eighteenth century romantic attitudes transformed architectural composition. Picturesque values (that is, architecture as scenery) and associationist aesthetics (that is, architecture as embodied memory) broke up the canonical harmonies of classicism. Diversified patronage encouraged the pursuit of novelty. And the progress of architectural archaeology multiplied the range of available options. The nineteenth-century idea of 'the styles' replaces the eighteenth-century concept of 'taste', which in turn had replaced the sixteenth-century notion of 'manner'. Or as today's architectural metaphysicians would say, stylistic synchronicity succeeds diachronic evolution. Anyway, from that state of affairs emerged the welter of styles which characterised the Regency; and from that stemmed the two antiphonal themes which dominate Victorian and Edwardian architectural debate: the cult of eclecticism and the idea of modernity. After brief suppression by the 'functional' values of the Modern Movement, atectonic criteria are once again at the centre of architectural thinking. Post-Modernism – or rather, Post-Functionalism – has revived the dilemma of style.[4] The Picturesque is back on the architectural agenda.

The word 'picturesque' derives from the Italian *Pittoresco*, meaning 'after the manner of painters'. The formation of the word is itself an explanation. A group of seventeenth-century French and Italian masters, chiefly Claude Lorrain, Salvator Rosa and Gaspard and Nicolas Poussin, so impressed the susceptibilities of early eighteenth-century Grand Tourists that they conditioned the Englishman's way of seeing for more than one hundred years. By the time 'Picturesque' assumed its capital letter in the second half of the eighteenth century – in the writings of William Gilpin, Uvedale Price, Richard Payne Knight and Humphry Repton – this

1 Stourhead, Wiltshire (1740s–60s). Picturesque landscape.

2 Shugborough, Staffordshire (1747 onwards). Landscape buildings in various styles.

way of looking at nature as though it were a series of pictures had been elevated into a visual philosophy, and its products – the landscape garden, the cottage orné, the suburban villa – had begun a triumphal progress around the world.

So much is familiar. The landscape at Stourhead, Wilts (1740s–60s)[1] has become a synonym for the Claudian ideal.[5] But what part did the Picturesque play in the dilemma of style?

We must start with the idea of appropriate form. The idea of appropriateness in architecture has a long history. Vitruvius endowed the different orders with distinct characters.[6] The classical tradition of decorum, leading to variation and thus to stylistic differentiation, was developed in Italy and France. Blondel explained the appropriate use of style as a kind of 'colouration', 'the poetry of architecture'. 'In a word', he suggests, 'style ... enables the architect to create a sacred genre, a heroic one, a pastoral one'.[7] Ledoux takes such ideas of stylistic expression a good deal further, designing buildings like his notorious phallic-shaped brothel, or his bizarre house for a cooper in the shape of a barrel – buildings which are themselves three-dimensional metaphors.[8] Architecture thus becomes a symbolic language. In England, where neo-Palladianism was, by definition, a conscious stylistic choice,[9] associationist thinking never developed in such a literal way. But the range of stylistic reference became wider as part of the furniture of the Romantic landscape. At Shugborough, Staffs,[2] for example, from 1747 onwards, a Rococo setting by Wright of Durham was decorated with a Chinese summer house, Chinese bridges and Chinese pagoda, a Palladian bridge, a Grecian Tower of the Winds, Hadrianic Arch and Shepherd's Monument, as well as a Gothic pigeon-house and ruins. Such geo-

15

graphical and stylistic diversity seemed appropriate in a garden designed to honour Admiral Anson, circumnavigator of the globe.[10]

In effect, the Rococo, or Poetic or Emblematic garden had revived in Augustan England the apparatus of the ancient Roman garden, via surviving Renaissance examples.[11] This apparatus was then turned into pictorial form and naturalised by absorption into a different climate and a different agricultural context. The Romantic garden was not just a paratactic art – that is a sequence of stage sets designed for peripatetic spectators. It was also a kinetic art in four dimensions: the mobile spectator not only experienced the three-dimensionality of landscape; he was also carried back through time on a magic carpet of associations. As at Duncombe Park, Yorks, where a sinuous walk between classical temples (*c.*1718, 1730, 1758) overlooks the ruins of Rievaulx Abbey: 'Space-Time', by association.

'The principal source of grandeur in architecture', wrote Alexander Gerard in 1759, 'is association, by which ... columns suggest ideas of strength and durability, and the whole structure introduces ... ideas of the riches and magnificence of the owner.'[12] In his *Observations on Modern Gardening* (1770, 1777, 1793), Thomas Whateley explained how such buildings operate in a landscape setting, either as allegory or as metaphor. As allegory, they act as emblems, signposts or symbols. As metaphors their function is expressive: they 'raise and enforce character already marked; [for example] a temple adds dignity to the noblest, a cottage simplicity to the most ... rural scenes.'[13] William Kent's landscape buildings – the Praeneste Monument (1739) at Rousham, for instance – are chiefly informational, that is emblematic. They require explanation; their allusions have to be *read*. 'Capability' Brown's are chiefly affective and expressive. His landscape settings at Stowe, for example, where he smoothed down the work of Bridgeman and Kent: here the forms are naturalistic, and the temples less obtrusively allusive. As Whateley put it, Brown's landscapes have 'the force of a metaphor, free from the details of an allegory'.[14] Repton's garden buildings – the Camellia House at Woburn, Beds (*c.*1806), for instance – are rather different: they do furnish a landscape, but they also make concessions to utility, or at least amenity.[15]

Still, one way or another, the landscape buildings of Kent, Brown and Repton all convey messages. Hence their emphasis on style. A building can conjure up a memory; it can reinforce a mood; it can express its purpose or ownership; or it can simply focus a landscape and create a sense of place. In other words, in the Romantic landscape – whether emblematic with Kent, expressive with Brown, or utilitarian with

Repton – stylistic choices act as triggers to the imagination. In this way, the notion of appropriate character in architecture – the idea of a style for each mood, and a mood for each style – eventually emerged full-blown as the theory of architectural association.

The philosophy of association can be traced back at least to the seventeenth century, to Thomas Hobbes' *Human Nature* (1640) and, more especially, to John Locke's explanation of mental processes in his *Essay Concerning Human Understanding* (1690; 4th edn. 1700).[16] Locke's theories were popularised by Joseph Addison in *The Spectator* of 1712,[17] and refined in David Hartley's *Observations* (1749). But it was the Scottish school – Hume and Hutcheson; Gerard, Kames, Dugald Stewart and Archibald Alison – who built on Locke's psychology and developed a consistent theory of associationist aesthetics. 'All beauty', noted Hutcheson in 1726, 'is relative to the sense of some mind perceiving it.'[18] 'Beauty', Hume concluded in 1757, 'is no quality in things themselves; it exists merely in the mind which contemplates them.... Each mind perceives a different beauty.'[19] That – despite equivocation – was the basis of Burke's view in 1757. His definitions of Sublimity and Beauty were essentially sensationist: 'mathematical ideas', he wrote, 'are not the true measure of beauty'.[20] That was a view put forward, half a century previously, by Claude Perrault.[21] But whereas Perrault preferred fitness to proportion, the Scottish school preferred association to either. Burke had denied that architectural beauty was eternally related to the proportions of the human body. Alison went further. 'What we mean by proportion', he wrote, 'is merely fitness for the ends of stability and support.'[22] In other words, proportion was a variable, not a constant. What counted was not proportion but association. Our awareness of the beauty of proportion is due not to mathematics but to a mental association of the relationship between form and function: certain proportions are thought to be good because they have been known to work. 'When any object, either of sublimity or beauty, is presented to the mind', Alison explained in 1790, 'I believe every man is conscious of a train of thought being immediately awakened in his imagination, analogous to the character or expression of the original object.'[23] Now that psychology of association – what Alison called 'the constant connection ... between the sign and the thing signified'[24] – is surely sound. Cicero expected to find pediments in heaven. Pugin would have been horrified to find anything but pointed arches. Habit and association – just as much as instinct or training – will always lie at the root of aesthetic judgement.[25] Coleridge derided it as mere mechanical fancy.[26] But Hume thought it as inevitable as gravitational thrust.[27]

3 Sanderson Miller, Gothic Ruin, Hagley Hall, Worcestershire (1747–8).
'The true rust of the Barons' Wars'.

Take one famous, near contemporary, comparison. At Hagley Hall, Worcs, stand Gothic[3] and Grecian[4] landscape features, 1747–8 and 1758–9, by Sanderson Miller and Athenian Stuart respectively. These ornaments are not simply signposts to some future Battle of the Styles: Walpole's 'true rust of the Barons' Wars' versus the Arcadian Vision. They are really products of the same mental process, symptoms of associationist thinking. When Joseph Heely visited the Gothic Ruin, he noted: 'in reality, it is nothing but a deception'.[28] In fact it is nothing but a symbol.

It was with such monuments as these that the tradition of a canonical language in architecture – an ultimate standard of taste, however diluted, however vernacularised – was broken, and replaced by the idea of aesthetic relativism.[29] The old aesthetic absolutes dissolved in a haze of association. 'In different climates', wrote Adam Smith in 1759, 'and where different customs and ways of living take place ... different ideas of beauty prevail. The beauty of a Moorish is not exactly the same as that of an English house.'[30] 'If you judge Gothic architecture by Grecian rules', wrote Bishop Hurd in 1765, 'you find nothing but deformity, but when you examine it by its own the result is quite different.'[31] Archibald Alison is always given the credit for the propagation of these ideas in Britain. But he was not well known south of the Border until he was noticed by Francis Jeffrey in the *Edinburgh Review* of 1811. 'There is no such thing as absolute or intrinsic beauty', Jeffrey concludes; 'it depends altogether

18

on ... associations. ... All tastes [if not all men of taste, are therefore] equally just and correct.' Universal standards of taste had thus no foundation except in 'universal associations'.[32]

The key point here is the abandonment of the idea of objective standards of beauty – absolute values – and in particular the rejection of classical harmonies as the eternal verities of architectural taste. Classicism is no longer the universal style. Architecture is no longer synonymous with classical architecture. What occurred was a kind of aesthetic Reformation, in which private judgement – in this case stylistic multiplicity – triumphed over prescriptive authority. So much so, that the mysteries of classical proportion came popularly to be regarded as a forgotten secret. 'A rule of proportion there certainly is', lamented William Gilpin in 1792, 'but we must inquire after it in vain. The secret is lost. The Ancients had it. They knew well the principles of beauty; and had that unerring rule, which in all things adjusted their taste. ... If we could only discover their principles of proportion.'[33] Even in 1792, that was not entirely true. The Vitruvio-Palladian system of proportional harmony was not quite lost. Architectural skill was still thought to consist in the manipulation of standardised components. But there had been a distinct shift in aesthetic attitudes: from objective to subjective, from the pursuit of harmony to the cult of sensibility, from absolute standards to relative values, from unitary style to plurality of choice, from mimetic to expressive, from classic to eclectic. We call that shift of taste Romanticism.[34]

Alison's personal taste was basically Neo-Classical. But his theories had a far wider application. By giving birth to a kind of stylistic agnosticism, associationist thinking opened up a veritable Pandora's box of stylistic choice. 'The principle [of association]', Coleridge complained, 'is too

4 James Stuart, Temple of Theseus, Hagley Hall, Worcestershire (1758–9). The Arcadian vision.

5 William Wilkins, Grange Park, Hampshire (1805–9; partly dem.).
'There is nothing like it on this side of Arcadia'.

vague for practical guidance – Association in philosophy is like the term stimulus in medicine; explaining everything, it explains nothing; and above all leaves itself unexplained'.[35] Certainly Richard Payne Knight seized upon this vagueness to build up his own theories of eclectic associationism.

It was Payne Knight who produced the definitive statement of associationist thinking:

> As all the pleasures of intellect arise from the association of ideas, the more the materials of association are multiplied, the more will the sphere of those pleasures be enlarged. To a mind richly stored, almost every object of nature or art, that presents itself to the senses, either excites fresh trains and combinations of ideas, or vivifies and strengthens those which existed before: so that recollection enhances enjoyment, and enjoyment heightens recollection ... [For example] a person conversant with the writings of Theocritus and Vergil will relish pastoral scenery more than one unacquainted with such poetry. [And a] spectator [whose] mind [is] enriched with the embellishments of the painter and poet ... [feels] beauties which are not felt by the organic sense of vision, but by the intellect and imagination through that sense.[36]

Hence, most famously, C. R. Cockerell's compounded delight on seeing William Wilkins's recreation of a Grecian temple at Grange Park, Hants

20

(1805–9)[5]: 'Nothing can be finer, more classical or like the finest Poussins . . . . There is nothing like it on this side of Arcadia.'[37]

That viewpoint had been nicely summed up some years before, in 1769, by William Gilpin, in a letter to William Mason. 'I have had a dispute lately', writes Gilpin – with Mr Lock of Norbury Park – 'on an absurd vulgar opinion, which he holds – *that we see with our eyes*: whereas I assert, that our eyes are only mere glass windows; and we see with our imagination.'[38] Not a bad explanation of the physiological process by which the brain makes sense of the images transmitted to it by the eye.[39]

Ruins were the most obvious stimuli. 'Bless'd is the man', mused Payne Knight,

> . . ., who, 'midst his tufted trees,
> Some ruind castle's lofty towers sees.[40]

These 'towers and battlements', noted Sir Joshua Reynolds in 1786, these 'Castles of Barons of ancient Chivalry', bring 'to our remembrance ancient costume and manners', and 'give . . . delight . . . by means of association of ideas'.[41] 'Real ruins', explained Whateley in 1790, produce the best 'effects . . . but [effects] are [also] produced in a certain degree by [ruins] which are fictitious; the impressions are not so strong, but they are exactly similar.'[42] Robert Adam's Hulne Priory (1778) at Alnwick, Northum, for instance; or Miller's Chichele Tower at Wimpole, Cambs (1750; 1768) – both designed in conjunction with 'Capability' Brown.[43]

In 1772 Sir William Chambers noted that the Chinese had thought of the same thing long ago:

> They are fond of introducing [into their gardens] statues, busts, bas-reliefs . . . [for] they are not only ornamental, but . . . by commemorating past events, and celebrated personages, they awaken the mind to pleasing contemplation, hurrying our reflections up into the remotest ages of antiquity . . . their aim is to excite a great variety of passion in the mind of the spectator.[44]

For Chambers, such excitements – what Gilpin and Knight called 'the chain of ideas'[45] – formed the basis of architectural aesthetics. 'Materials in architecture', he wrote in 1759, 'are like words in Phraseology; which singly have little or no power; and may be so arranged as to excite contempt; yet when combined with Art, and expressed with energy, they actuate the mind with unbounded sway.'[46] By 1791 he had managed to link these two arguments – the power of architectural composition and the magic of scenic symbols – into a workmanlike theory of association. The effect of visible objects, he notes, 'is not alone produced by the image on the [eye]; but by a series of reasoning and association of ideas, impressing and guiding the mind in its decision.'[47] Certainly Kew Gardens

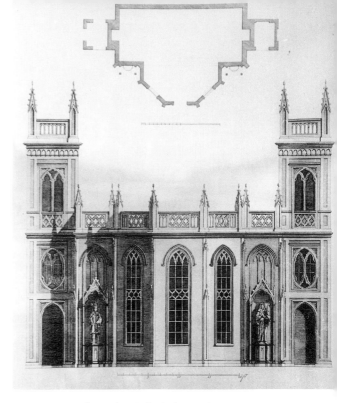

6 Sir William Chambers, The Pagoda, Kew (1761–2). 'The chain of ideas'.

7 J. H. Muntz, The Gothic Cathedral, Kew (1753–9; dem.). 'The aim is to excite a great variety of passion in the spectator'.

became an advertisement for Chambers' theories.[48] Besides his Chinese Pagoda (1761–2)[6], there was a ruined Roman Arch (1759–60), Ionic temples of Victory (1759) and Peace (1763), and Tuscan temples of Aeolus (c.1760; 1845) and Bellona (1760), a Mosque and an Alhambra – all by Chambers – as well as a Gothic Cathedral (1753–9)[7] and Moorish Alhambra (1750; 1758) by J. H. Muntz, a Palladian bridge, and a House of Confucius (designed c.1750 by Goupy or Chambers with furniture by Kent). Queen Charlotte's Cottage (1770; 1805) adds a touch of vernacular rusticity. Kew Gardens had indeed become a nursery of architectural exotics. Picturesque values put a high premium not only on variety, but on novelty and surprise.

So all styles were grist to the associationist mill. But were all styles equally appropriate? And if not, why not? In 1743, Robert Morris attempted a fairly simple system of differentiation. Architecture, he announces, 'is divided into three classes, the Grave, the Jovial, and the Charming' – and the choice should depend on purpose and situation. Thus 'a Champaign open country requires a noble and plain Building .... A situation near the Sea requires ... Rusticity and Lowness.... The Cheerful Vale requires more Decoration and Dress, and if the View be long, or some adjacent River runs near by it, the Ionic Order is the most proper.'[49]

As early as the 1730s and 1740s, at Stowe, Gothic and Grecian styles had been used symbolically. Ancient Virtue (Kent, 1734) is a classical temple: antique ideals expressed in classical symbols. Old English liberties, on the other hand, take on Gothic forms, as in Gibbs's Temple of Liberty (*c.*1740–44). Inside, ceilings were decorated with emblems of the Saxon Heptarchy.[50]

Lord Kames, whose *Elements of Criticism* (1762) developed Hume's 'Association of Ideas', distinguished – rather speciously – between the impact of Greek and Gothic ruins. 'Should a ruin', Kames asks, 'be in the Gothic or Grecian form? In the former, I think; because [a Gothic ruin] exhibits the triumph of time over strength: a melancholy but not unpleasant thought; a Grecian [or Roman] ruin suggests rather the triumph of barbarity over taste: a gloomy and discouraging thought.'[51] But Kames did concede that beauty in architecture was twofold: relative and intrinsic – intrinsic beauty consisting in proportion, harmony, etc.; relative (or extrinsic) beauty consisting in a building's fitness for purpose, contextual relevance, etc. For example, he thought Inverary Castle (1745 onwards)[8] appropriately Gothic because of 'the profuse variety of wild and great objects' in the vicinity. Dr Johnson was more forthright: 'what

8 Roger Morris *et al.*, Inverary Castle, Argyll (1745 onwards). Castle and symbol.

9 Humphry Repton, 'Characters of Houses' (1816). Character modified by ornament.

I admire here', he boomed, 'is the total defiance of expense.'[52] In fact, Kames and Johnson were both right: Inverary is a symbol of wealth and power – a trigger of neo-feudal emotions – but it is also a symptom of habitual stylistic preference, in other words, taste.

But it was Humphry Repton who made stylistic differentiation popular. Repton was not greatly concerned with symbols. He was concerned with pictorial impact, that is, he was concerned to maximise – partly through architecture – the picturesqueness of a given site: to bring out the genius of the place.[53]

In his poem *The Landscape* (1794), Payne Knight had summed up the indissolubility of architecture and landscape:

> ... Mixd and Blended over let it be
> A mere component part of what you see.[54]

In his *Fragments on the Theory and Practice of Landscape Gardening* (1816), Repton set out to explain the mechanics of that fusion. He showed first how Grecian, Gothic or castellated trimming could change the nature of otherwise identical buildings[9]. And then how Grecian and Gothic compositions suited different settings.[55][10] Grecian suited a site which was in Burke's sense Beautiful, that is pastoral or Arcadian.[56] Gothic maximised the pictorial impact of a setting which was already Picturesque. And Gothic could, in turn, be divided into 'castle Gothic' and 'abbey Gothic': 'castle Gothic' for a rocky eminence, 'abbey Gothic' for a

24

GRECIAN   GOTHIC

10 Humphry Repton, 'Grecian' and 'Gothic' (1816). Style suited to setting.

fertile valley.[57] In his *Sketches and Hints on Landscape Gardening* (1795), Repton had already pointed out that irregular Gothic houses looked best surrounded by deciduous trees, classical buildings looked best surrounded by 'spiry-topped' or coniferous trees. Partly that was due to contrast: the horizontal lines of Greek architecture contrasted well with vertical pines and cypresses. Partly, however, he admits the effect is due to association: 'the ideas of Italian paintings [or paintings on Italian themes], where we often see Grecian edifices blended with [pines], firs and cypresses.'[58]

In Repton's writings, the choice of style in landscape or garden buildings is dictated as much by considerations of status, situation or use as by historical associations. He recommended a rustic hut[11] for a primaeval forest;[59] an irregular Gothic house for an irregular landscape, as at Luscombe, Devon (1800–04); a cottage orné, as at Endsleigh, Devon

11 Humphry Repton, 'Rustic' Hut (1816). Refuge and symbol.

12 Humphry Repton, Apsley Lodge, Woburn, Bedfordshire (c. 1805). Archaeological accuracy.

(1800–11), for a small-scale, variegated landscape;[60] or again a seat in the manorial style, as at Stanage Park, Radnorshire (1803–7), for the sort of place where 'the Lord of the Soil' resides among his Tenants.[61]

By means of landscape buildings strategically placed and appropriately styled, Repton turned landscape gardening into a species of furnishing. And it was period furnishing of a fairly precise kind. He dismissed James Wyatt's Sheffield Park, Sussex (c.1779) as a 'heterogenous mixture of Abbey, Castle and Manor House . . . [a] mongrel breed of architecture . . . propagated . . . by buildings of all dimensions from the Palace to the Pigsty.'[62] When he came to design Apsley Lodge, near Woburn, Beds (c.1805)[12], he cited no less than eighteen different precedents to guarantee its archaeological accuracy.[63]

Still, Repton never claimed to be a scholar. He did, however, put himself forward as a theorist. His design for the Royal Pavilion at Brighton gave him the chance to fabricate a whole theory of architectural development.[64] 'We are on the eve', he wrote in 1806, 'of some great future change . . . in gardening and architecture . . . in consequence of our having lately become acquainted with scenery and buildings in the interior provinces of India.' From this would arise 'a new species of architecture more applicable to this country than either Grecian or Gothic.'[65] In other words, Hodges and Daniell were to do for India what Stuart and Revett did for Greece.[66] He begins by allegorising the progress

26

of architecture through the ages[13]: castellated Gothic, ecclesiastical Gothic, mixed Gothic (or Elizabethan), Grecian (or classical) – and then, half hidden by Time – his own Indian style. Just as classical architecture had been introduced by Inigo Jones under royal patronage, so he hoped this new oriental style would benefit from royal favour. The Castle Style, he thought, was now only suitable for prisons, the Abbey Style for colleges. Mixed Gothic was by definition imperfect; pure Grecian posed innumerable problems of adaptation. The 'Modern Style' – diluted Neo-Classicism – lacked character altogether. For Brighton Pavilion, therefore, Repton proposed to transform Henry Holland's demure classical villa into something worthy of England's imperial destiny. We raise the Reptonian flap: and lo and behold, he has invented an Anglo-Indian mode.

So Repton was certainly an eclectic. But he was an eclectic in taste rather than an eclectic in style: he never developed the idea of synthesis. 'To add Grecian to Gothic, or Gothic to Grecian', he wrote, 'is equally absurd.'[67] The result would be a mere *'pasticcio*, or confusion of discordant parts'.[68] He preferred to think of himself as a stylistic utilitarian. When it came to designing conservatories, he found Gothic easily adaptable: 'it is better to apply old expedients to new uses than to invent a new and

13 Humphry Repton, 'Changes in Architecture' (1808). The progress of style.

absurd style of Gothic or Grecian architecture.' At Plas Newydd[14], for instance, he took the idea of a cathedral chapter house, and turned it into a green-house-cum-prospect-pavilion, a charming conceit, especially delicious by moonlight.[69] Conservatories he thought particularly suited the 'flat Gothic arch of Henry VIII', because it admitted more light.[70] In short, adaptation not synthesis is Repton's keynote. 'This', he explained, 'I call *characteristic architecture.*' Too often 'our hospitals resemble palaces, and our theatres appear like warehouses ... every building ought to tell its own tale.'[71]

Repton's ideas can be traced in a whole series of publications on picturesque design, by Plaw, Malton, Elsam, Lugar, Gandy, Papworth, Middleton, Goodwin, and others.[72] In particular, Repton's theories formed the basis of J. C. Loudon's writings. Repton's 'amenity' becomes Loudon's 'function', and both are heavily dependent on Alison's 'association'. The architectural styles in Loudon's *Encyclopaedia* are only minimally concerned with utility. Their expressive role is functional in no more than a symbolic sense. What Loudon called 'the beauty of truth'[73] turned out to be no more than association made popular, Alison suburbanised. Hence his influence. Social and functional propriety finds its expression in a hierarchy of style. The chain of influence, forwards from Blaize Hamlet, nr. Bristol (1811), through Great Tew, Oxon (1819 onwards) – school of Loudon rather than Loudon himself[74] – to Park Village, Regent's Park (1824 etc.)[35], and thence to innumerable suburbs, is clear enough. So is the chain backwards: 'it's a long way from Tew to Tivoli',

14 Humphry Repton, Conservatory, Plas Newydd (1805). Gothic adapted.

15   R. Payne Knight, Downton Castle, Herefordshire (1771–8). 'Gothic without and Grecian within'.

noted Christopher Hussey, but the Italian origins of the Picturesque are unmistakable.[75] Still, Loudon was enough of a radical – in social and aesthetic matters – to talk wistfully of the fading away of style: traditional taste, he believed, would eventually go the way of traditional social attitudes.[76] However, this withering away of the empire of style never actually happens: Loudon's *Encyclopaedia* – with all its multitude of styles – remains a compendium of bourgeois taste.[77]

For an evolving eclecticism of style we must look not to Repton or Loudon but to Richard Payne Knight. 'In the pictures of Claude and Gaspar', he notes, 'we perpetually see a mixture of Grecian and Gothic architecture employed with the happiest effect in the same building, and no critic has yet objected to the incongruity of it.'[78] Such a 'miscellaneous' or 'mixed style', Knight recommends as 'the best style for irregular and picturesque houses'.[79] And he designed his own house, Downton Castle, Herefordshire (1771–8)[15], to be – as he put it – 'Gothic ... without, and Grecian ... within.'[80] The fact that trabeation and arcuation, to say nothing of domestic and military forms, might be 'promiscuously mixed' in the same building, did not worry him. Gothic, he believed, was a corruption of Roman, and anyway there was no such thing as 'pure Gothic'.[81]

Now whether eclecticism – conscious, synthetic eclecticism – can be traced back before Knight to William Kent and Batty Langley, and even before that to Vanbrugh, is a matter for debate.[82] More likely is the assumption that Knight derived his concept of Graeco-Gothic synthesis from one Scots writer, William Duff, and one French writer, the Abbé de Cordemoy.[83] But Duff and Cordemoy dealt in abstractions. Payne

29

16 William Kent, Waynflete's Tower, Esher, Surrey (remodelled 1729–32). Rococo Gothick.

Knight built Downton Castle. In consciously propagating synthesis rather than accumulation, Knight was well ahead of his contemporaries. He certainly anticipated Thomas Hope who – at the Deepdene, Surrey (1818–19; 1823) – managed to mingle Gothic, Greek, Tuscan, Pompeian and Lombardic.[84] J. C. Loudon, writing a generation later than Knight, never went so far. For Loudon multiplicity of style was a function of multiplicity of purpose, not a method of producing novelty through fusion. He did have a rudimentary knowledge of architectural semiotics. He thought that English emigrants to Van Dieman's Land might – in their early days at least – be justified in building houses like church towers, because their 'associations' were 'so characteristic of British scenery and civilisation'.[85] Only when a new, post-colonial culture had developed, would a new, post-colonial style emerge. But Loudon's *Encyclopaedia* is more of a pattern book than a treatise on aesthetics. Payne Knight is the subtler mind. In particular, Knight took one key conceptual step: his synthesis was consciously *modern*. 'The design of almost every age and country', he wrote, 'has a peculiar character ... [every house] should ... maintain the character of a house of the age and country in which it is erected.'[86] That proto-Hegelian notion – what Summerson once called 'the Mischievous Analogy'[87] – had a long life ahead of it.

Let us sum up the argument so far. At the European level, the classical tradition: the notion of a universal system of aesthetic values gradually eroded by its own practitioners – character in Vitruvius, individualism in Alberti, fitness in Perrault, appropriateness in Blondel, symbolism in Ledoux. At the English level, the Picturesque: perception in Locke, emblem and expression in Whateley, association in Alison, eclecticism and modernity in Knight. So the cult of styles can be traced back, effectively, to the early eighteenth century, to that cultural watershed when nature replaced religion – perhaps became religion – as the motive force for creative artists.[88] Nature, often enough, in ideal form. A hundred years later, attitudes had changed. 'A gentleman's park is my aversion', wrote Constable in 1823 – thinking of Fonthill, Wilts. (1796–1812); 'it is not beauty because it is not nature.'[89] But in Augustan England, the Romantic landscape is indeed contained in a gentleman's park, controlled and idealised: in a word, classicised. 'Nature', wrote Chambers, 'is incapable of pleasing without the assistance of art'[90] – in particular, the art of architecture. So historic architectural styles – that is, alternative sets of post-structural conventions – have a key part to play in the reciprocal operation of the Romantic imagination: a process by which art controls nature and nature controls art.[91]

Now we can be more specific, and examine these ideas at work: first in one style, and then in a whole spectrum of styles. Firstly, the Gothic Revival. Gothic emerges as a stylistic term in the sixteenth century, with Vasari; and that emergence confirms the idea of style in architecture.[92] But in England it is not until the early eighteenth century, when Revival can be clearly distinguished from Survival, that Gothic takes its place as simply one option in a range of available modes. Sir Christopher Wren's approach was essentially environmental: Gothic was chosen for Tom Tower, Oxford (1681–2) – as for Westminster Abbey (1698–1722) – to avoid 'a disagreeable mixture'. Hawksmoor, however, at All Souls, Oxford (1715–40), takes a major step towards stylistic autonomy. William Kent goes one stage further: his Rococo syntheses of Gothic and Classic – at Esher (1729–32)[16], Hampton Court (1732) or Rousham (1738–41) – indicate a shift from environmental to associational design. And in the work of Batty Langley, Sanderson Miller and their circle the evolution from environmental to associational thinking is complete. The Rococo rejoiced in severing the link between form and structure, and treated Gothic ornament simply as a species of communication – a kind of visual morse code tapping out the message 'medieval'. By comparison the Picturesque placed less emphasis on ornament and more on pictorial impact. Thanks to the cult of Picturesque attitudes – at Edge Hill, War-wicks (1747–50) for instance – architectural design becomes basically a scenic device: these buildings are pictorially conceived as memories in three dimensions. Miller's Tower at Edge Hill echoes Guy's Tower at Warwick, but there are other echoes too: it was designed to enshrine a statue of the Saxon hero Caractacus on the spot where Charles I raised his standard against the Roundheads, and it was ceremonially opened on the anniversary of Cromwell's death.

Uvedale Price had recommended that an architect should 'accommodate his building to the scenery, not make [the scenery] give way to the building'.[93] And he put his theories into practice when, at Castle House, Aberystwyth (*c.*1795; dem. 1845) he forced Nash to produce a triply octagonal structure designed to take full advantage of the coastal site.[94] Thus the Picturesque completed what the Rococo began, the conjunction of architecture with nature. Picturesque theory subordinated architectural detail, architectural planning, and indeed architecture itself, to scenic considerations. This tendency was accentuated by new techniques of architectural drawing and by new tendencies in architectural criticism: henceforward the architectural perspective takes a prominent place at the Royal Academy. Architects, critics, and the public are all thinking pictorially. The habit of regarding buildings as scenery – as aggregates of separate visual units – encouraged not only irregular skylines and asymmetrical plans, but triangular, hexagonal and octagonal features, eyecatchers and all manner of follies: the polygonal Bird House at Knole, Kent (1761) for example. This Picturesque habit of breaking up architectural composition into a series of scenic tableaux – based on the principle of the mobile spectator – certainly encouraged drawing-board architecture: designing a house from the outside inwards rather than from the inside outwards. It was a process of design ideal for landscape features – Thomas Harrison's Hawkstone Citadel, Shropshire (*c.*1824) for instance: a multi-angular plan recalling several designs in Richard Elsam's *Essay on Rural Architecture* (1803). Here we have the reciprocal Picturesque: buildings designed to be looked *at* as well as looked *from*; scenographic design, based on spectator-mobility and on the multiplication of points of vision.[95]

Clever enough. But it was a dangerous game. And taken in conjunction with the multiplication of stylistic choice, it came near to disintegrating architectural design altogether. As in the Menagerie at Woburn, Beds (*c.*1806), where Repton suggested different styles for each elevation: Classic for the formal approach, Gothic for the informal.[96] Or at Castleward, Co. Down (*c.*1762)[17], a house with separate Palladian and Gothic facades. Or at Castle Goring, Sussex (*c.*1790): Neo-Classical and Castellated; a stylistically schizophrenic house designed by Biagio Rebecca for the eccentric Shelley family. Eccentric or calculated, this pursuit of

17 (a) & (b) Castleward, Co. Down, Ireland (c. 1762). Palladian and Gothic façades.

optical effect lay at the root of Picturesque thinking. Smirke's Lowther Castle, Westmorland (1806–11) was Gothic on one side and Baronial on the other. Wilkins' Senior Combination Room at King's College, Cambridge (1823) has Grecian windows facing one way and Gothic windows facing another. And the greater the range of stylistic choice, the greater the danger that architectural composition would disintegrate into a mosaic of Picturesque devices. That was the nub of Soane's criticism of Smirke's Covent Garden Theatre (1809–10); each facade was independently conceived.[97]

One man whose career encompassed all styles was John Foulston of Plymouth, the leading Regency architect of the West of England. He was a Gothic Revivalist who could rival Wilkins. He was a town planner who could rival Nash, and he was a Neo-Classicist who could occasionally rival Soane. But Foulston will always be remembered for something else.

18 John Foulston, Kerr Street, Devonport, Plymouth (1821–4; partly dem.).
'A series of edifices exhibiting the various features of the architectural world'.

He appears in every textbook as the architect of the extraordinary group of buildings at Kerr St., Devonport, Plymouth (1821–24)[18]. Here no less than five styles are simultaneously represented: a range of terraced houses in Roman Corinthian; a Greek Doric Town Hall and Naval Column; an 'Oriental' or 'Islamic' or 'Mohammedan' Mount Zion Chapel (now demolished); a pair of Greek Ionic houses (now also demolished); and an Egyptian Library (now – appropriately perhaps – an Oddfellows Hall).

What was Foulston trying to do? He called it an 'experimental group', and he justified his actions as follows:

> It occurred to [me] that if a series of edifices, exhibiting the various features of the architectural world, were erected in conjunction, and skilfully grouped, a happy result might be obtained. Under this impression, [I] was induced to try an experiment (not before attempted) for producing a picturesque effect, by combining in one view, the Grecian, Egyptian, and a variety of the Oriental.[98]

Architecture was starting to flex its muscles for the Battle of the Styles. But as yet there is no conflict. There is a choice, but Pugin had yet to give the dilemma a moral dimension. The style of the Commissioners' Churches, for instance, is entirely arbitrary: neither the traditional elasticity of Georgian nor the passionate experimentalism of Victorian church design. It is all symbol and no substance – even the churches of Sir John Soane[19] are stylistically haphazard. In the 1830s and 1840s, the

34

choice of styles tended to settle down on typological grounds: Gothic for churches, Greek for art galleries, Renaissance for banks and insurance offices, Romanesque for gaols, Tudor for schools and almshouses – and any one of these for villas. But the categories are not yet exclusive. Regency architecture, in all its chameleon variety, was an architecture appropriate to the age of Romanticism. Neo-Gothic, Neo-Greek, Neo-Egyptian, Neo-Oriental: styles equally exotic, equally remote in time and place, but not yet equally assimilated or understood. Classical archaeology, for instance, was still far more sophisticated than its medieval or oriental counterparts. But clearly the comparability of styles has become something of an article of faith. As Thomas Hopper put it in 1830: 'it is the business of an architect to understand all styles, and to be prejudiced in favour of none.'[99]

Foulston's successor, George Wightwick, clearly found the experiment irresistible. In 1840 he published an architectural romance entitled *The Palace of Architecture*, in which he portrays just the sort of stylistic fantasy Foulston was dreaming of, a veritable 'epitome of the architectural world'. Wightwick's imaginary palace would have outdone Fonthill in its scale,

19 Sir John Soane, Commissioners' Churches: alternative styles (drawn by J. M. Gandy, c. 1818).

just as it outdid in its variety another Regency fantasy of eclecticism, Charles Kelsall's *Phantasm of a University* (1841).[100] 'My book', Wightwick explains, 'aspires to that station in regard to Architecture which the novels of Scott occupy in relation to History.' The palace itself was Neo-Classical. But its gardens were the *reductio ad absurdum* of Picturesque theory; an anthology of all styles known to man: Indian, Chinese, Egyptian, Greek, Roman, Constantinal (i.e. Lombardic Romanesque), Norman, Decorated Gothic, Old English or Manorial, Tudor Gothic, Turkish, Protestant Baroque, Soanean, Anglo–Greek, and Anglo–Italian. But it was reserved for the entrance gateway[20] to combine all these styles. This fantastic portal, compounded of fragments of all styles, Wightwick explains, 'symbolises MUSEUM. . . . A masonic riddle, teeming with multiplied significancy, and exhibiting a kind of monstrous combination, in which discordant features seek to harmonise themselves with a general outline of forced conformity – the dark rock of India, the granite of Egypt,

20 George Wightwick, *The Palace of Architecture*
(1840). Entrance incorporating all styles.

21 Richard Brown, 'Norman, Tudor, Grecian and Roman' (1841). Four styles in suitable settings.

the marble of Greece and the freestone of Italy and middle Europe, [are] here commingled; each compartment being as distinct in form as in material, and the whole, in its composition, wearing an aspect which, at the same time, challenges admiration and defies criticism.'[101] Indeed it does: the only comparable conflation which comes to mind is Joseph Hansom's design of a mausoleum for the Duke of Sussex (1843), also combining all styles – Gothic buttresses, Egyptian entrance, Roman arches and Grecian mouldings.[102]

Wightwick made no attempt to explain the choice of any particular style; he merely rejoiced in the fact that choice existed. But in the following year, 1841, a book appeared which did attempt such an explanation: Richard Brown's compendious volume, *Domestic Architecture*. Here every conceivable historic style is set out: Cottage Orné, Tudor, Stuart, Florentine, Flemish, Pompeian, Venetian, Swiss, French Chateau, Egyptian, Grecian, Roman, Anglo-Grecian (which is actually Soanic), Anglo-Italian, Persian, Chinese, Burmese, Oriental, Morisco-Gothic, Norman, Lancastrian, Plantagenet, Palladian. . . . And to assist the budding architect or patron, Professor Brown suggests that the choice of each style should be determined by purpose and situation. He illustrates, in one view,[103][21] appropriate landscape settings for at least four styles: Norman, Tudor, Grecian and Roman – that is, rugged mountains

37

22 J.M. Gandy, 'Comparative Architecture'
(1836). A visionary synopsis of style.

for a Norman castle; bosky plantations for a Tudor seat; rolling wood-
lands – with hints of Arcadia – for a Grecian villa; and verdant pasture –
with hints of the campagna – for a Roman (i.e. Palladian) mansion.

Alas, he makes no attempt to explain either the uses or the settings
appropriate, for example, to Burmese, Chinese, Persian, or Morisco-
Gothic. And, of course, there could be no such appropriate setting. The
choice of these bizarre styles had nothing to do with utility, and everything to do with romance. Henry Holland's Dairy at Woburn, Beds (1792)
is Chinese; Cockerell's Dairy at Sezincote, Glos. (1827?) is Moorish.
The choice of style is dictated neither by setting nor by purpose. During
the Regency, English architects were simply indulging their imaginations.
Sezincote (c.1805), was indeed a nabob's retreat, but its 'Indian' style
had no contextual relevance to the Cotswolds.[104] 'In the midst of all
this', noted John Weale in 1844, 'there was but one man, the late Sir
John Soane, who dared to be positively original. All others were mad in
some particular foreign fashion; but he alone was mad in his own way
... there was a method in the old knight's madness.'[105] Indeed there was.
But half the impact of Soane's genius stems from the genius of J.M.
Gandy. And it is Gandy's illustrations to Soane's Royal Academy lectures
which provide historians with their most eloquent commentary on the
roots of Regency taste.[106]

Gandy himself adopted an eclectic viewpoint. Imitation he denounced
as 'unworthy of modern genius'; 'a comprehensive mind', he explains,
'will select from all styles'; we 'moderns [must] prepare a system selected
from all tastes ... [culled from] the beauties of every climate and every

38

age.'[107] Such assumptions readily lent themselves to fantasy, and it is for example, in Gandy's 'Tomb of Merlin' (1815)[108] that we see his dream of 'a new style of architecture' emerging from a fantasised vision of Roslyn Chapel, a dim confusion of late antique and early medieval forms. In the whole spectrum of historic styles, Gandy believed, there must be some unifying bond; some explanation of the elusive link between style and culture. Without it there could be no hope of finding that architectural philosopher's stone: a new style for a new age. Hence his diagrammatic fantasy, 'Comparative Architecture' (1836),[109][22] an attempt to decode the mnemonic power of style by a codification of all styles. Here, in effect, Gandy was attempting to find a future in the past; to trace the mystic symbolism of architectural form back to its organic roots, back to its 'Natural Model' (1838)[23]. Out of what he calls the primeval 'protocol of architecture', that new style would one day emerge, 'a symbolic system ... perfect, durable, and universal.'[110]

23 J. M. Gandy, 'Architecture: its natural model' (1838). The organic root of architecture.

39

24 Sewell's Folly, Battersea Rise (c. 1830; dem). A precursor of Modernism?

Alas, it did not emerge in Gandy's own architecture. Some of his villa designs do indeed possess a prophetic simplicity, and as such they appealed powerfully to the Modernists of the 1930s. But on the whole, Gandy – just as much as any of his generation – was locked into the Picturesque system. Sewell's Folly, Battersea (*c.*1830)[24], was a folly not a prototype.

By 1844, one commentator, John Weale, was able to spot what had happened: Neo-Classicism had fallen victim to the Picturesque. Among all those revivals, Neo-Classicism at least, in its abstract geometry, suggested – negatively speaking – a way out of the historicist jungle. 'A feeling for what was termed "classic simplicity" pervaded every art', writes Weale, 'even our tea-caddies became mere cubes of wood.' Then came the graphic revolution. 'The introduction of our richly illustrated ANNUALS administered more and more to that taste for *picture* which had already existed; and . . . what may be termed the romance of architecture obtained a considerable influence on the public [Salvin's stables and laundry at Mamhead, Devon, 1828–33,[25] are an extreme example][111] . . . architects were now induced to leave the academical formalities of their Greek and Latin Grammars, and to cultivate . . . picturesque effects.' Hence 'the triumph of picture over geometry – the conquest of poetry over mathematics.'[112] He meant, of course, the victory of imagination over reason; the victory of atectonic criteria over structural harmonies. In other words, the triumph of the eye over the mind: the triumph of the Picturesque.

Let us go back for a moment to Edmund Burke. 'No work of art can be great, but as it deceives.'[113] That was Burke's answer to the rationalist credo – beauty is truth, truth beauty – and in a sense all Picturesque art is the art of illusion. Perhaps illusion – or at least artifice – is the basis of all conscious (i.e. post-vernacular) architectural design. Even Laugier – arch-rationalist of the eighteenth century – conceded this point with his doctrine of *apparent* utility.[114] But architecture in the age of Romanticism was peculiarly susceptible to illusory treatment. For if the Romantic aesthetic has any basis, it lies in the cult of subjective criteria. Classicism aspires to the absolute, Romanticism glories in the incidental. Where Classicism is abstract and universal, Romanticism is concrete, particular, personal. Thus the architecture of Romanticism subordinated objective criteria – harmony, balance, proportion, utility: the formal and functional values of classical tradition – to criteria which are primarily subjective: the autocentric criteria of sensation and association. Hence the primacy of pictorial values – composition, silhouette, texture, in other words *appearances* – in early nineteenth-century architectural aesthetics. Hence, indeed, the whole panoply of eclectic historicism.

By the late 1830s, the time was ripe for a return to rationalism – and rationalism did indeed return. But it returned in a rather devious way. It returned in the guise of the arch Victorian romantic: Augustus Welby Northmore Pugin.

25 Anthony Salvin, Mamhead, Devon: stables, laundry and brewhouse (1828–33). 'The triumph of picture over geometry'.

2 Pugin and Ecclesiology

'To *Puginise*: to mix up political and theological speculations with architectural ones' (W.H. Leeds, 1843).

IN THE CELEBRATED FRIEZE on the Albert Memorial, Pugin occupies an outsider's position among the immortals. He seems to be turning his back on Cockerell, Barry, Chambers, Wren, Inigo Jones and the entire classical tradition. True enough: Pugin did reject pagan classicism in favour of Christian Gothic. But he made his name – architecturally speaking – by rejecting something else: the philosophy of the Picturesque. In doing so he destroyed the reputation of one architect so effectively that he had to be omitted from the Albert Memorial's pantheon altogether. That architect was James Wyatt.

The turning point in the transition from Picturesque Gothic to Victorian Gothic occurred dramatically in 1834 with the destruction by fire of the old Houses of Parliament. Wyatt's Gothic refacing of the ancient Palace of Westminster 'had been expected', in Soane's words, 'to produce a burst of Architectural Scenery ... unparalleled in any part of Europe.'[1] Its destruction was, in effect, a bonfire of Picturesque principles. From the ashes of that fire arose, eventually, Pugin's greatest achievement: the new Palace of Westminster. Young Pugin witnessed the inferno with joy:

> It was a glorious sight to see [Wyatt's] composition mullions and cement pinnacles and battlements flying and cracking, while his two-and-sixpenny turrets were smoking like so many manufactory chimneys till the heat shivered them into a thousand pieces. The old [stone] walls stood triumphantly amidst the scene of ruin while [Wyatt's] brick walls, framed sashes, slate roofs, fell faster than a pack of cards.[2]

When Pugin visited Fonthill Abbey, Wilts (1796–1812) in 1833 – eight years after the tower had collapsed[26] – he was equally delighted.[3] Wyatt's evocation of a medieval monastery was indeed the flimsiest of stage sets, and the nemesis which overtook it was not unexpected. Wyatt's cathedral restorations provoked him almost to apoplexy: 'the villain Wyatt'; 'the Destroyer'; 'this monster of architectural depravity';

26 James Wyatt, Fonthill Abbey, Wiltshire (1796–1812; collapsed 1825). 'Entirely misconceived and built in the slightest manner'.

'this pest of cathedral architecture'. Like Horace Walpole's Strawberry Hill (1749 onwards), Wyatt's Gothic simply made Pugin feel 'disgusted'.[4]

Other Regency architects – John Nash or William Porden, for instance – seemed to Pugin almost as depraved as Wyatt: Gwyrch Castle, Denbighshire (1819 onwards), by Busby, Rickman and Hesketh[27], represented all that he despised.

27 C. A. Busby, T. Rickman and L.B. Hesketh, Gwyrch Castle, Denbighshire (1819 onwards). 'The kitchens alone are real; everything else is a deception'.

What could be more absurd than houses built in ... the castellated style? Portcullises which will not lower down ... drawbridges which will not draw up ... turrets so small that the most diminutive sweep could not ascend them! ... guard rooms without either weapons or guards; sally-ports, out of which ... a military man never did go out; donjon keeps which are nothing but drawing rooms, boudoirs, and elegant apartments; watch-towers, where the house-maids sleep, and a bastion where the butler keeps his plate: all is a mere mask, and the whole building an ill-conceived lie .... [As for] the Abbey style ... [it is often] a mere toy ... devoted to luxury. The seeming abbey-gate turns out a modern hall, with liveried footmen in lieu of a conventual porter: the apparent church nave is only a vestibule; the tower a lantern staircase; the transepts are drawing rooms; the cloisters, a furnished passage, the oratory a lady's boudoir; the chapter house a dining room; *the kitchens* alone are real; everything else is a deception.[5]

In other words, Pugin was condemning the interchangeability of ecclesiastical and secular forms; the confusion of decorative and structural elements; and the distortion of scale and purpose inherent in Picturesque Gothic. It was not just a question of inaccurate detail. During the Regency period Carter, Britton and Rickman had done much to establish archaeological canons. It was the composition of buildings in a way which was artificially Picturesque which particularly angered Pugin. Rickman's St John's College, Cambridge (1827–31),[6] for instance, seemed in that

28 Haddon Hall, Derbyshire (12th—17th c.). 'The true Picturesque'.

29 G. L. Taylor, Hadlow Tower, Kent (c. 1840). 'The modern Picturesque'.

respect little better than Wyatt's Fonthill. For Pugin, the *true* Picturesque must express in its silhouette the functional irregularity of its plan.

Compare Haddon Hall, Derbyshire (twelfth to seventeenth century)[28] with Hadlow Tower, Kent (by G. L. Taylor, *c.*1840)[29]. For Pugin the 'modern' Picturesque was a sham: 'when a building is *designed to be* picturesque, by sticking as many ins and outs, ups and downs, about it as possible ... [it is like] an artificial waterfall or made-up rock ... so *unnaturally natural* as to appear ridiculous'. How different were 'the old English catholic mansions'. The old builders made beauties out of necessities. 'Each part ... indicated its particular [purpose]: the turreted gate-house and porter's lodging, the entrance porch, the high-crested roof and louvred hall, with its capacious chimney, the guest chambers, the vast kitchens and offices, all formed distinct and beautiful features, not masked or concealed under one monotonous front, but by their variety in form and outline increasing the effect of the building, and presenting a standard illustration of good old English hospitality.'[7] That was the '*true* Picturesque'.

45

30 A. W. Pugin, Scarisbrick Hall,
Lancashire (1836—47). Structural
timberwork.

31 S. Wyatt and F. Bernasconi, Blithfield Hall,
Staffordshire (c. 1820–2). Unstructural vaulting.

So Picturesque Gothic was unacceptable to Pugin as the style of the nineteenth century. What style did he suggest?

By the end of the 1830s the classical tradition had begun to crumble. For some time it had been undermined by the accelerating forces of Romanticism, and permeated by the relativist philosophy of the Picturesque.

> We are just emerging [wrote Pugin in 1843] from ... the dark ages of architecture .... The breaking up of this wretched state of things has naturally produced a complete revulsion in the whole system of arts, and a Babel of confusion has succeeded to the one bad idea that generally prevailed. Private judgement runs riot; every architect has a theory of his own .... This may, indeed, be appropriately termed the *carnival* of architecture: its professors appear tricked out in the guises of all centuries and all nations; the Turk and the Christian, the Egyptian and the Greek, the Swiss and the Hindoo, march side by side, and mingle together; and some of these gentlemen, not satisfied with perpetrating one character, appear in two or three costumes in the same evening .... Oh! miserable degradation![8]

46

What was the explanation of this confusion? 'The architecture of our times', Pugin explained, 'is not the expression of existing opinions and circumstances, but a confused jumble of styles and symbols borrowed from all nations and all periods.'[9] The reason seemed to him simple: 'Styles are now *adopted* instead of *generated*, and ornament and design *adapted to*, instead of *originated by* the edifices themselves.'[10] 'Vitruvius', says Pugin, 'would spew if he beheld the works of those who glory in calling him master.'[11] Greater learning had merely produced more forms of ugliness. 'Nothing can be more dangerous', he told Lord Shrewsbury, 'than looking at prints of buildings, and trying to imitate bits of them. These architectural books are as bad as the Scriptures in the hands of the Protestants.'[12] Somehow the Renaissance and the Reformation had combined to produce architectural 'inconsistency' and 'miserable confusion'.[13]

For Pugin, the way out of this deplorable state of affairs lay in the adoption of a single style – Gothic – firstly as the symbol of an integrated form of society; secondly as the expression of an integrated system of building. A few contrasts will make the argument clearer.

Look at the ceilings of Pugin's Scarisbrick Hall, Lancs (1836–47)[30] – beamed, painted but above all structural – and compare them with the unstructural – grotesquely unstructural – plaster vaults by Bernasconi at Blithfield Hall, Staffordshire (c. 1820–2)[31]. Scarisbrick[32] – a Catholic manor house – was designed by Pugin to express in its plan the functional

32 A. W. Pugin, Scarisbrick Hall, Lancashire (1836–47). A Catholic manor.

requirements of its purpose, and to express in its structure and silhouette the functional demands of its plan. Wyatt's Wycombe Abbey, Buckinghamshire (*c.*1803–4)[33] is very different: a Georgian box tricked out with sub-Gothic cosmetics. Compare it with Pugin's own house and church at Ramsgate, Kent (1843–52)[34]: a truly Gothic complex of house, out-buildings and church, expressing in the irregular silhouette its variety of purpose, and in the excellence of its materials the integrity of its builders. Remember Pugin's dictum: '[Classical] *buildings* . . . [or classical buildings with Gothic trim] *are designed to suit the elevation* . . . [in truly Gothic buildings] *the elevation* [is] *made subservient to the plan.*'[14]

Pugin saw no inconsistency in using Gothic rather than Renaissance for modern public buildings and secular works. After all, he remarked, 'we are not Italians, we are Englishmen'. 'Our climate', he explained,

33 James Wyatt, Wycombe Abbey, Buckinghamshire (c. 1803–4). Gothic cosmetics.

34 A. W. Pugin, The Grange and St. Augustine's, Ramsgate, Kent (1843–52).
A truly Gothic complex.

'remains of course precisely the same as formerly ... [and] we are governed' – he wrote in 1843 – 'by nearly the same laws and same system of political economy' as in the Middle Ages: church, law, monarchy, parliament, schools and universities were all still essentially medieval. Therefore the Gothic revival was 'warranted by religion, government, climate, and the wants of society. It is the perfect expression of all we should hold sacred, honourable and national, and connected with the holiest and dearest associations.'[15] 'England,' he had to admit, 'is certainly not what it was in 1440'; but – he assured Lord Shrewsbury – 'the thing to be done is to *bring it back to that era*'.[16] And could Gothic really assimilate the functions and materials of the new industrial age? Pugin affected to see no problem. He produced model Gothic designs for shops and railway structures. 'The railways', he explained, 'had they been naturally treated, afforded a fine scope for grand massive architecture. Little more was required than buttresses, weathering and segmental arches [embodying] resistance to *lateral* and *perpendicular* pressure.' Alas, he thought the Great Western Railway's stations were 'mere caricatures of pointed design – mock castellated work, huge tracery, shields without bearings, ugly mouldings, no-meaning projections, and all sorts of unaccountable breaks ... costly, ... offensive, and full of pretension.' As for the famous Euston Arch, Pugin called it a 'Brobdingnagian absurdity'.[17]

49

35 John Nash and James Pennethorne, Park Village, Regent's Park, London (1824 onwards). Regency Picturesque.

36 A. W. Pugin, Priest's House, St John's Hospital, Alton, Staffordshire (c. 1842). Puginian 'reality'.

Pugin may not have reformed railway architecture, but he did revolutionise domestic design. Look at Nash and Pennethorne's Park Village (1824 onwards)[35], just off Regent's Park; and compare it with Pugin's clerical-schoolmaster's house (*c.*1842) at St John's Hospital, Alton, Staffordshire[36]. 'I would sooner jump off the rocks', Pugin later exclaimed, 'than build a *castellated residence for priests.*'[18] Puginian 'reality' has replaced the Regency Picturesque. It was a lesson taken up by Butterfield and Webb in years to come. Alton indeed – Hospital (1839–42) as well as Castle (1840–52)[37] – perfectly embodies Pugin's architectural theories. Despite early misgivings, he came to see it as 'a perfect revival of the true thing.' The empire of a Catholic paternalist – Lord Shrewsbury – seemingly growing out of the very rock; its silhouette the true Picturesque: hospital, school, almshouses, and convent buildings expressing not only their architectural function but their social purpose.[19]

At this point it is perhaps appropriate to recapitulate Pugin's theories of design. 'The two great rules for design', he says, 'are these: 1st, that there should be no features about a building which are not necessary for convenience, construction, or propriety; 2nd, that all ornament should consist of enrichment of the essential construction of the building.'[20] Now these principles were by no means new. They can be traced back to Laugier, and Lodoli, and the Neo-Classical rationalists of the eighteenth century. They can be traced further back to the dawn of the classical tradition: after all, 'convenience, construction and propriety' are not too far away from Wotton's Vitruvian canon – 'commoditie, firmness and delighte'. But Neo-Classical theory had been rationalist rather than functional: Laugier's criterion had been '*apparent* utility'. Pugin took

37 A. W. Pugin, Alton Castle, Staffordshire (1840–52). The empire of a Catholic paternalist.

over Neo-Classical theories of *design* and applied them to Neo-Gothic *construction*. In other words, he functionalised a style which had previously been first decorative (Rococo Gothick) and then scenic (Picturesque Gothic).

Here, then, was a utilitarian philosophy couched in medieval terms. He aimed at what he called 'reality ... in design, material and construction'.[21] 'The fundamental principle of Gothic design,' he announced, is 'the decoration of utility': organic rather than scenic design.[22] 'Decorate your construction', Pugin advises; do not 'construct your decoration.'[23] Of course he is highly selective: he allows spires but not porticoes, crockets but not friezes, labels but not pediments.[24] And at the same time he explains: 'I seek *antiquity* and not *novelty*. I strive to *revive not invent*.'[25] Gothic, he claims, is the only system permissible in a Christian society. And yet again, Gothic is 'not a style but a principle'.[26] 'Is it not wonderful', Cardinal Newman noted, 'that he should so relentlessly and indissolubly unite the principles of his great art with the details.'[27] Anyway, wonderful or not, it was Pugin – muddled and ambiguous – who began the search for an architectural Holy Grail; the search for a universal style, a style combining beauty and utility, past and present. In a powerful memoir J. D. Crace claimed that it was Pugin who defined 'for the first time in the history of Art what are the immutable laws which must govern all constructive design, if it is to appeal successfully to human intelligence. ... The principle of adjusting design to requirement and ornament to construction', Crace concludes, 'seems obvious enough now .... [But it was Pugin] who brought order out of chaos.'[28] Well, perhaps. But he also introduced a crucial element of confusion: he apparently equated function and propriety, utility and beauty. '*Every building that is treated*

38 A. W. Pugin, Mount St Bernard, Leicestershire (1839–44). The monastic community revived.

naturally', he claimed, *'without disguise or concealment, cannot fail to look well.'*[29] There lay at least a few of the seeds of the Modern Movement. There, certainly, lay the seeds of doubt which – as we shall see – tormented so many Victorian architects: the guilt of suppressed functionalism. Ruskin was going to have at least one answer to that: 'the most beautiful things in the world are the most useless.'[30] But Pugin, in effect, created the dilemma of style. For it was Pugin who injected *morality* into architecture. As his *Times* obituary put it, 'It was [Pugin] who first showed us that our architecture offended not only against the laws of beauty, but also against the laws of morality.'[31] Ethical values had now replaced visual and associative values. Henceforth the question to ask of any building was not 'is it beautiful?' but 'is it true?' The dilemma of style was now a moral dilemma.

To sum up, Pugin set out to establish several stylistic truths. Unfortunately these 'laws' were not only unprovable as axioms; they were also intrinsically incompatible. Firstly, he held that each age and nation must have its own particular style: there could be no plurality of styles.[32] Secondly, that Gothic alone was the style indigenous to Northern Europe – especially England; yet at the same time Gothic was peculiarly Catholic, and must therefore hold an eternal stylistic monopoly throughout all the nations of Christendom. Thirdly – and most fatally – he held that the criteria of architectural excellence were independent of style, indeed independent of decoration; but, at the same time, only one stylistic and decorative system was permissible, namely Gothic. In other words, Pugin's theories – persuasive, potent, riddled with contradictions and ambiguities – were the making of the Gothic Revival and its destruction.

The root of these contradictions lay in Pugin's religion. W. H. Leeds scored a bull's eye when he coined the verb 'to *Puginise*: to mix up political and theological speculations with architectural ones'[33] – what philosophers call a category mistake. Or as the semiologists would say, Pugin had confused intrinsic and extrinsic meanings, denotation and connotation, to say nothing of emblem and expression.[34] Perhaps such confusion is inevitable, rooted in the necessary duality of architectural aesthetics: commodity versus delight – the root of the architect's dilemma. But by committing himself to Catholicism, and by then identifying Catholicism with medieval Gothic, Pugin placed his aesthetic theories in a stylistic straitjacket. By giving his theories a metaphysical sanction, he deprived them of purely terrestrial validity. As a result, his immediate impact lay in the field of ecclesiastical rather than secular design. Pugin dreamed of re-creating a world of Gothic, a Catholic world centred on the church: the world of Mount St. Bernard, Leics. (1839–44)[38]. But

39 Sir Charles Barry, St Peter, Brighton, Sussex (1824–8). Ecclesiastical Picturesque.

40 (a) & (b) *facing*. A. W. Pugin, St Giles, Cheadle, Staffordshire (1841–7). Sacramental planning and composition.

the irony of his achievement in this sphere lay in his influence on the *Anglican* church. Pugin was by no means wholly contemptuous of Anglicanism. In fact his ambivalent views on Anglican orders nearly got one of his pamphlets placed on the Index.[35] The Anglican hierarchy proved much more sympathetic to the Gothic Revival than did its Catholic equivalent. For every Catholic church designed by Pugin there must be a thousand Anglican churches throughout the world designed or altered on his 'true principles'. Pugin thus became the godfather of Anglican ecclesiology.[36] Gilbert Scott would not have been afraid to admit that he was Pugin's architectural godson.

In church-building, as in secular building, Pugin reacted against the Picturesque. Barry's St Peter's, Brighton (1824–8)[39] is a key element in the Brighton townscape, correct enough in detail but artificially three-dimensional: the western porch, for instance, is cunningly brought forward between buttresses to create an illusion of depth. Its silhouette is unrelated to its plan. Pugin's St Giles, Cheadle, Staffordshire (1841–7)[40] is 'the true thing': a Catholic church revealing in its every section –

54

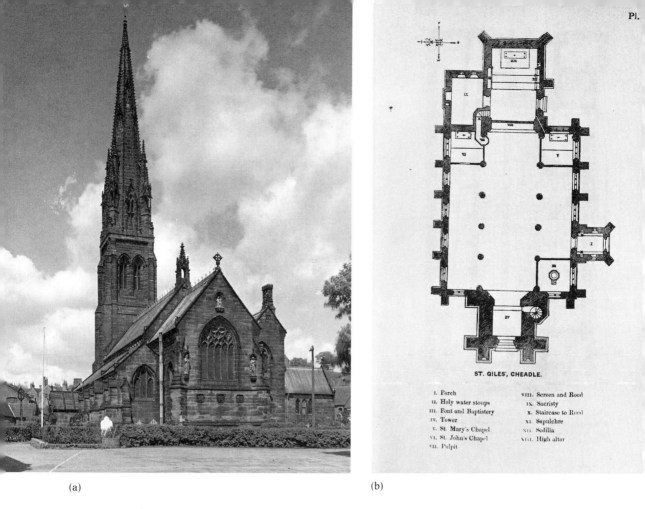

ST. GILES', CHEADLE.

I. Porch	VIII. Screen and Rood
II. Holy water stoups	IX. Sacristy
III. Font and Baptistery	X. Staircase to Rood
IV. Tower	XI. Sepulchre
V. St. Mary's Chapel	XII. Sedilia
VI. St. John's Chapel	XIII. High altar
VII. Pulpit	

(a)   (b)

nave, chancel, aisles, porch, spire, presbytery, convent, school – the functional and symbolic demands of Catholic liturgy and practice. Barry's church is a piece of urban scenery; Pugin's church is a machine for praying in.

Rickman and Pugin make an equally telling comparison. Rickman had gone some way towards systematising Gothic typology. But he progressed very little in the direction of structural authenticity or liturgical planning. His church at Carlisle (1828–30) suggests that he was hardly an archaeologist, and certainly not a liturgiologist. He was, after all, a Quaker. Pugin's chapel at Cotton College, Staffordshire (1840–8) would have been outside his aesthetic and theological parameters.[37] Catholic ecclesiology has replaced the Protestant Picturesque. Rickman's church plans are basically Protestant auditoriums in medieval dress. Pugin's designs – St Giles, Cheadle, for instance[40a,b] – aim at re-creating the sacramental system in three-dimensional form. No wonder the Catholics of Birmingham rejected a Rickmanic chapel and settled for a Puginian cathedral (1839–56). 'The exterior of St Chad's'[41], Pugin explained, 'like the

41 A. W. Pugin, St Chad's Cathedral, Birmingham (1839–56). North German inspiration.

42 A. W. Pugin, St Chad's Cathedral, Birmingham (1839–56). Interior before mutilation.

cathedral at Munich, presents little more than a mass of perforated brick walls and high roofs', but the interior[42] is 'glorious ... purple with stained glass and rich with gilding, with everything, even vestments in character.'[38] Inside and outside, St Chad's reveals not only Pugin's scholarship, but his commitment to sacramental theology. Or it did. The interior was grossly mutilated in the 1960s; and Pugin's screen is now – ironically – preserved in an Anglican church, Holy Trinity, Reading: a piece of ambonoclasm (as Pugin called the destruction of screens) which makes a fitting commentary on his career and influence.

Those towers at Birmingham do have a north German look about them.[39] And Continental inspiration *can* be traced in Pugin's work, especially towards the end.[40] He travelled widely in France, Belgium and Germany. In 1847 he visited north Italy and found it 'a perfect mine of medieval art'.[41] Several of his church interiors were decorated with original medieval fittings imported from Germany or France – the famous Oscott lectern, for instance. And, throughout, Pugin suffered from an over-fondness for *height* – 'internal altitude', as he called it – a Continental attribute which he particularly favoured as a young man: St Alban's, Macclesfield (1839–41), is one example. In an Irish context – as at St Michael's, Gorey, Wexford (1839–42) – he was prepared to countenance Romanesque. And in humble churches he regarded Early English as appropriate: Our Lady and St Wilfrid, Warwick Bridge, Cumb. (1840), for

56

instance. But on the whole – despite an early fondness for Perpendicular – it was English Decorated Gothic which remained his bible: St Thomas of Canterbury, Fulham (1847–8), for example; or Tolbooth Church, Edinburgh (1841–4, designed in conjunction with Gillespie Graham). 'I would not depart from our own peculiar style of English Christian architecture', Pugin wrote in 1841, 'on any account. I once stood on the very edge of a precipice in this respect, from which I was rescued by the advice and arguments of my respected and reverend friend Dr Rock .... Captivated by the beauties of foreign pointed architecture, I was on the very verge of departing from the severity of our English style, and engrafting portions of foreign detail and arrangement. This I feel convinced would have been a failure.'[42]

St Giles, Cheadle (1841–7), shows Pugin at his happiest. He called it 'a perfect example of an English parish church of the time of Edward I', that is, *c.*1300. As always, the plan[40b] and silhouette[40a] are the 'true thing': 'I must have *outline* and breaks', he once remarked, 'or the building will go for nothing.'[43] But it is the richness of detail which astonishes. The porch is almost excessively buttressed. The insignia on the doors are almost too bold. Even so, the exterior is just an *hors d'oeuvre*. The real feast occurs inside[43]. That the articulation is logically

43 A. W. Pugin, St Giles, Cheadle, Staffordshire (1841–7). 'Perfect Cheadle'.

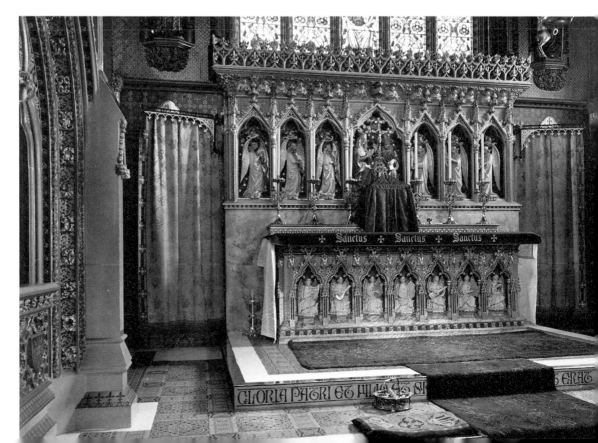

functional goes without saying. It is the kaleidoscope of polychromy which is unusual. Many of the details are Norfolk in origin. Others derive from examples in the midlands and south: the Easter Sepulchre recalls Aylmer de Valence's tomb at Westminster. But, among the fittings, the corona is a fifteenth-century Flemish original. And other details have Continental echoes, notably the missal bindings, modelled on those at Maintz. The painted diapering was apparently an afterthought – Lord Shrewsbury decided to spend even more money, after Pugin had visited Paris and seen Viollet-le-Duc's 'glorious' re-colouring at the Sainte Chapelle.[44] Walls and floors are as rich as Pugin and Minton can make them; the stained glass shows Pugin and Wailes in glorious combination.

Cardinal Newman regarded Pugin as 'a bigot', although 'a genius'.[45] But when he visited the newly-burnished Cheadle in 1846, all his reservations were abandoned. 'The new Cheadle Church … is the most splendid building I ever saw. It is coloured inside every inch in the most sumptuous way – showing how Gothic – in those countries where there is no marble, contrived to make up for the mosaics etc. of the South. The windows are all beautifully stained. The Chapel of the Blessed Sacrament is, on entering, a blaze of light – and I could not help saying to myself "Porta Coeli" …. Already', he adds, 'it has cost £30,000 or £40,000.'[46]

Newman, like Pugin, was of course a convert to Rome. What of those who stayed behind, nursing Puginian principles inside the Anglican fold? Their story is the story of the Ecclesiological Society. The Cambridge Camden Society – known after 1846 as the Ecclesiological Society – was originally based on Trinity College, Cambridge.[47] Its three stalwarts, the Rev John Mason Neale (of *Hymns Ancient and Modern*), the Rev Benjamin Webb and Beresford Hope, M.P., were all Trinity men. Its President, the Ven. Archdeacon Thorp, was a Fellow and Tutor at the same college. In fact the story of the society's foundation has the right undergraduate ring. Apparently Webb and Neale called on their tutor, Thorp, at ten o'clock one night, bearing an elaborate brass rubbing as testimony of intent, and refused to leave until their tutor had agreed to become senior member. Neale was a romantic sacramentalist;[48] Webb was a romantic ritualist;[49] Hope was a romantic Tory.[50] All three were romantic Goths, committed medievalists, enthusiasts for apostolicity and sacramentality. Yet all three managed to avoid the magnetic attraction of Rome.

Unlike the Oxford Movement, the Cambridge Movement concentrated on aesthetics rather than theology, and stayed firmly within the Anglican fold. In Oxford neither Keble, Newman nor Pusey were keen ritualists.[51] Their field of study was not the Middle Ages but the Reformation and Patristic eras. Nor were they particularly interested in architecture.[52]

> I never joined the Camden Movement [Newman later recalled] I never com-
> mitted myself to the Rubric movement ... I did not even join Dr Pusey's
> movement ... [Gothic] was once the perfect expression of the church's ritual
> ... it is not the perfect expression now. [There is more to religion than] the
> ... antiquarianism of Puseyites, poets and dreamers.[53]

So architectural history at Oxford was left largely to historians, like
Freeman, Froude and Parker.[54] They were the key figures in the Oxford
Architectural Society. And this was a much less polemical body than the
Cambridge Camden Society, even though young John Ruskin was a
member.[55] Newman called it 'the only neutral ground in Oxford'.[56]
Perhaps Oxford Movement theology supplied enough polemics for one
university. Anyway, the difference between the two universities was
striking. 'It is clear to me', Neale explained to Webb, 'that the [Oxford]
Tract writers missed one great principle, namely the influence of Aesthetics.'[57] It was as though, in the history of the High Church revival, Oxford
supplied the text and Cambridge the illustrations. Cambridge stepped in
to fill the visual dimension lacking in Oxford theology. In effect, the
Ecclesiological Society adopted Pugin's aesthetics and Pusey's church-
manship: a combination of fourteenth- and fifteenth-century Gothic and
sixteenth- and seventeenth-century theology.[58] The result, in both universities, was anathema to Evangelicals. Aesthetically and theologically,
the Church of England seemed to be returning to Rome. As the Rev
Francis Close complained in a Guy Fawkes sermon at Cheltenham in
1844, 'Romanism is taught *Analytically* at Oxford, [and] ... Artistically
at Cambridge – that is inculcated theoretically, in tracts, at one University,
and ... *sculptured, painted* and *graven* at the other.'[59]

Now ecclesiology means the science of church design, although to
theologians it also means the study of 'the church' as a mystical entity.
But Canon Clarke put it better when he explained that ecclesiology is to
church building as astrology is to astronomy.[60] In other words, it was
not so much the science as the mystique of church design. In the first
place, however, ecclesiologists accepted implicitly Pugin's functional,
anti-Picturesque dogma: 'we are more and more convinced', announced
the *Ecclesiologist* in 1851, 'that the true picturesque follows the sternest
utility.'[61] But in the second place, they sought to embody in structure
and in ornament – through Rubrical Planning – the numinous qualities
of sacramental religion – a limited sacramentality, of course, derived from
seventeenth-century Anglican divines, such as George Herbert and
Lancelot Andrewes. The transformation of Anglican churches which
inevitably followed can be measured, for example, by comparing James

44 James Spiller, St John, Hackney, London (1792–7). Anglican auditorium.

45 R. D. Chantrell, St Peter, Leeds (1837–41). Anglican shrine.

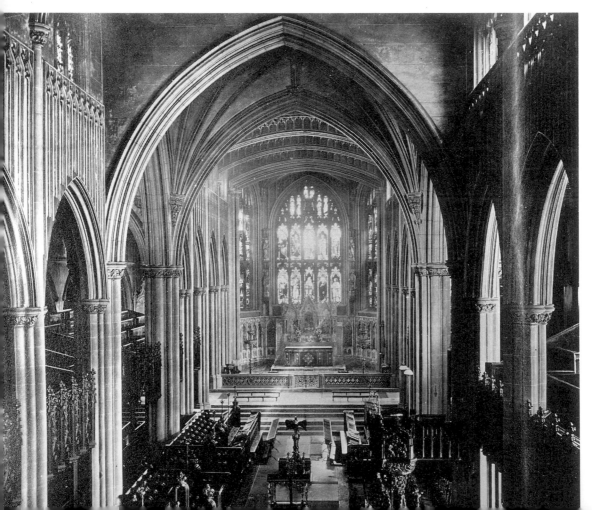

Spiller's St John, Hackney (1792–7)[44] with R. D. Chantrell's St Peter, Leeds (1837–41).[62][45] The auditorium has become the shrine.

What style did the ecclesiologists prescribe? They settled on late thirteenth- and early fourteenth-century Decorated or Middle Pointed: the least adaptable of all Gothic forms, and the most difficult to master in its details. No wonder, in its early stages, ecclesiology was confessedly copyistic. 'It is no sign of weakness', the *Ecclesiologist* announced in its first volume, 'to be content to copy acknowledged perfection.'[63] 'We have not [yet] learned our alphabet', it repeated in 1846; 'and it is absurd to attempt to compose .... All that we can expect to do is to copy carefully in hopes of realising at the last, through numberless copyings, some first principles which we may store up for our children to make use of.'[64] 'The merely imitative position of architecture at present', Freeman explained in the same year, 'is both an undeniable fact, and ... a necessary stage in the revival of a lost art.'[65] The model then, the yardstick of excellence, was later thirteenth- or early fourteenth-century Decorated: Heckington, Lincolnshire,[46] or Hawton, Nottinghamshire; the west front of Peterborough (1220 onwards), or the Angel choir at Lincoln (1256

46 St Andrew, Heckington, Lincolnshire (14th c.). A model for ecclesiologists.

47 St Andrew, White Colne, Essex (1869). A medieval church before and after restoration.

48 Benjamin Ferrey, St Stephen, Rochester Row, London (1847–50). Ecclesiology in London.

onwards).[66] Not too early, not too late, but just right. This, of course, was a prime instance of what Geoffrey Scott later christened the Biological Fallacy: the belief that – as a law of nature – styles are born, grow to maturity, and then decay. Pugin had actually anticipated this belief.[67] But even Pugin was criticised by the ecclesiologists for being too eclectic.[68]

It was perhaps this element of conviction, of certainty, of *authority*, which struck a chord in the hearts of Victorian High Churchmen. They welcomed the Gothic Revival as an authentic expression of sacramentalism: what Coleridge called 'the petrification of our religion'. After the decorative Gothic of Rococo, after the scenic Gothic of the Picturesque, functional Gothic had been rediscovered – liturgically as well as structurally functional. This new discovery – Pugin's discovery – was ruthlessly applied by the ecclesiologists, with results which were sometimes beautiful, but often deplorable. St Andrew, White Colne, Essex[47] – before and after treatment (restored 1869 by C. J. Moxon) – will serve as an example of ecclesiology in action. 'Our object ... all along', admitted the *Ecclesiologist* in its last number in 1868, 'has ... been propagandism ... and ... we have the satisfaction of retiring from the field victors.'[69] By 1854 a quarter of all parish churches had been restored; by 1873 one third.[70] Between 1830 and 1860, fifteen hundred new churches were built in England, as against only two thousand between the Reformation and 1830.[71] As early as 1852 Webb could boast that advice had been sent to 'the Canadas, Bombay, Ceylon, Sierra Leone, Mauritius, the Himalaya, Tasmania, Guiana, Australia and New Zealand, Newfoundland, Egypt and Hongkong.'[72] Fifteen years later the triumph of ecclesiology was incontestable. On a wave of Anglo-Catholic revival, a group of Cambridge undergraduates had succeeded in transforming the appearance of nearly every Anglican church in the world: Fredericton, New Brunswick, has a cathedral modelled on Snettisham, Norfolk;[73] Buckland, Tasmania, has a church modelled on R. C. Carpenter's St John the Baptist, Cookham Dean, Berks (1844).[74] Parish churches all over the world were subject to the same procrustean rules.

During the 1840s 'approved' ecclesiological architects were permitted to graze only within Decorated Gothic boundaries – Benjamin Ferrey, for example, at St Stephen's, Rochester Row (1847–50).[48] Any other form of Gothic was either barbaric, if earlier; or decadent, if later. As for Romanesque, its introduction was denounced as positively 'EVIL': an importation of a 'foreign (we had almost said un-christian) style'.[75] In the 1840s John Mason Neale was particularly vehement that only fourteenth-century *English* Gothic was permissible.[76] Not until the 1850s did Beresford Hope swing the *Ecclesiologist* towards European prototypes.

Meanwhile, Camdenian Gothic became an identifiable style, and in R. C. Carpenter and Henry Woodyer it produced architects worthy of the Puginian mantle: Carpenter, the Anglican Pugin,[77] at St Paul's, Brighton (1846–8) and St Mary Magdalen, Munster Square, London (1849) – where, incidentally, incense was first used in an Anglican context, in 1859.[78] Or Carpenter, in secular vein, at Lancing College (designed 1848; executed 1854–8). Or Woodyer, ingenious and inventive within Decorated limits, at Highnam, Gloucestershire (1848–51)[49], a patriarchal village complex of school, church, lodge and vicarage for the ecclesiological squire, Thomas Gambier Parry.

The anathemas of the ecclesiologists were indeed effective. This 'first age of ecclesiological science' had, in Beresford Hope's words, achieved 'shape, reason and consistency ... unity, form and method.'[79] Or as Pugin put it, a new notice seemed to be permanently pinned in every church porch: 'Beware of the Camden [Society]!'[80] The index of the *Ecclesiologist* vol. iii (1843–4) lists 'Architects Approved': Butterfield, Carpenter, Ferrey; 'Architects Condemned': Barry, Blore, Cottingham. When Gilbert Scott dared to enter – and win – the competition for a *Lutheran* church in Hamburg, his temerity was denounced as sinful.[81] The Rev J. L. Petit was attacked because he dared to suggest that an element of *taste* was involved in church design.[82] 'Church architecture is no longer tentative [or tasteful]', the *Ecclesiologist* announced in 1854; 'It approaches to something of the completeness of an exact science. It is ... a subject not so much of taste as of facts. It has rules, principles, laws ....'[83]

Inevitably the ecclesiologists were attacked from both sides of the theological fence. As Webb complained to Neale, 'we poor aesthetical fellows get kicks from everybody'.[84] On the one hand there were the Evangelicals. 'We want *Protestant* Churches', complained the Rev Francis Close, 'not Papist Mass-Houses!'[85] The Rev P. Maurice, Chaplain of New College, regarded Newman's church at Littlemore with horror, and attacked it in a pamphlet entitled *The Popery of Oxford Confronted, Disavowed and Repudiated* (1837). 'I felt an indescribable horror stealing over me [at Littlemore]', he wrote; 'as I carried my eye towards the eastern wall ... and beheld a plain, naked cross.'[86] It even contained a stone altar – several years before the Camden Society's notorious altar in the Church of the Holy Sepulchre, Cambridge. Of course, after his conversion, Newman was able to repudiate such architectural half-way houses. In *Loss and Gain* (1848) he caricatured Anglican ecclesiology as a sham: candlesticks, but no lighted candles; niches, but no statues; tabernacles, but no consecrated host.[87] To a Catholic Frenchman like

49 Henry Woodyer, Holy Innocents, Highnam, Gloucestershire (1848–51).
Ecclesiology in the Cotswolds.

Montalembert the whole thing was a charade, an 'absurd ... empty pageant'.[88] And Pugin turned the knife in the wound when he told his Anglican followers in 1843: 'it is as utterly impossible to square a Catholic building with the present [Anglican] rites as to mingle oil and water ... *either the* [Book of] *Common Prayer or the ancient models* [of church design]

65

must be abandoned .... It is quite impossible for any man who abides in the Anglican Church, as she is at present constituted, to *build a Catholic church and use it afterwards* .... Copes and two candlesticks are not the test of Catholicism. [In fact] patching up Protestantism with copes and candles, would be no better than whitening a sepulchre.' And he concludes – this is 1843 – with a prophetic warning: 'The *via media* is rapidly narrowing on those who tread that dangerous and deceptive road; it will soon be utterly impracticable.'[89] Newman crossed the Rubicon two years later.

The ecclesiologists' relationship with Pugin was inevitably difficult.[90] In a way he could only be publicly praised after his death.[91] From the start his works were admired, and his precepts followed. In 1844 the society even went to Pugin for the design of its new seal.[92] 1845, however, was the year of Newman's secession: the seal was withdrawn; the ecclesiologists now had to distance themselves, publicly, from Rome. Early in 1846 the *Ecclesiologist* therefore published an article by Beresford Hope attacking Pugin as an architect who dared to work occasionally in inferior styles – Early English or Perpendicular; and an architect who, in any case, had failed to live up to his early promise.[93] More seriously, Neale and Webb criticised Pugin for failing to develop Gothic design into a fully-fledged symbolic system: Pugin's theory of *reality* is 'true as far as it goes', they said, 'but . . . it does not go far enough'. Each item of design – spire, chancel, windows in triplets and pairs, cruciform plans, porch, octagonal font, even bell-ropes and door-knockers – each must symbolise elements of Christianity. In essence, Tractarian art was the art of analogy: the Coleridgean or Wordsworthian view of art as an abstraction from Nature, and Nature as an emanation of the eternal. In other words, the aesthetics of Romanticism.[94] According to this view, Pugin's structural *reality* must become symbolic *sacramentality*, for 'by the outward and visible form is signified something inward and spiritual . . . the material fabric symbolises, embodies, figures, represents, expresses, answers to, some abstract meaning.'[95] Really, Pugin complained, 'they accuse *me of being indifferent to Symbolism in architecture*!!! after all I have written and done this is too bad.'[96]

There was certainly an element of absurdity in the ecclesiologists' position: weather-cocks, they held, symbolised preachers, since the cock proclaims the new dawn and the preacher proclaims the Day of Judgement.[97] As one French critic, Didron, put it: 'symbolism seduces, if indeed it does not blind, the best intellects'.[98] But the point that Neale and Webb were making was valid – although it ultimately rebounded against themselves. Pugin's principles, they explained, 'apply as well to any secular building as to a church: they are true for construction but not adequate in themselves to form a rule for ecclesiastical design.'[99] Quite so: Pugin, for all his religiosity, was propounding an architectural aesthetic. The aesthetics of the ecclesiologists were theologically based.[100] Ecclesiology turned out to be relatively ephemeral. Pugin's principles lived on.

Pugin's vision was astonishing[50]. But his buildings may sometimes disappoint. As Benjamin Webb put it, 'his architectonic science bore no

50 A. W. Pugin, 'The Present Revival of Christian Architecture' (1843).

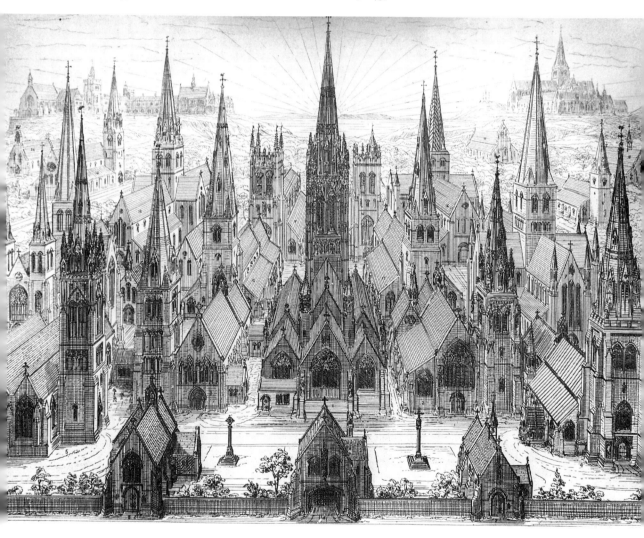

proportion to his constructive skill'.[101] But it would be difficult to over-estimate the influence of Pugin's writings. In a career of little more than twelve effective years – 1836-48 – he transformed architectural thinking. For Benjamin Webb he was 'one of the most remarkable men of his generation ... impetuous, prejudiced, but honest and sincere ... [with] all the eccentricities of real genius.'[102] Purcell called him 'the Gibbon of architecture ... the Newman of art .... His mind seemed to give out light.'[103] As a journalist, as a caricaturist, he was unbeatable. Above all – compared for example with Ruskin – he possessed the blessed gift of brevity. And his message – the moral superiority of the Middle Ages; the aesthetic superiority of Gothic – caught exactly the radical, backward-dreaming, almost chiliastic mood of the 1840s. 'Acknowledged or not acknowledged', announced the *Builder* in 1843, Pugin 'is the virtual Pope' in Gothic.[104] 'That wonderful man', as Burges called him, was the lodestar of a generation of Goths.[105] 'I was awakened from my slumbers', Gilbert Scott recalled, 'by the thunder of Pugin's writings ... his image in my imagination was like my guardian angel, and I often dreamed that I knew him.'[106]

Pugin never fulfilled his ambitions. He never wholly converted the Catholic clergy to Gothic: they retained a fondness for Baroque, and even for Byzantine. Towards the end of his career he was even losing Catholic commissions in the Gothic style to lesser architects like Hadfield and Hansom. 'I have passed my life', he complained in 1849, 'in thinking of fine things, studying fine things, designing fine things, and realising very poor ones.'[107] 'With every building ... I have been compelled to commit suicide.'[108] Only Cheadle[40], [43] and Ramsgate[34] really satisfied him. *'Perfect Cheadle'*, he wrote; 'Cheadle my consolation in all my afflictions.'[109] But he did realise his achievements as a communicator. 'My writings', he told Hardman in 1851, just before his death, 'much more than what I have been able to do, have revolutionised the taste of England. My cause as an architect is run out .... Our [works] are only good when compared with the Beasts, the Brutes who belong to this age, but by the true standard [of the Middle Ages] they make me ill. As we gain knowledge, conviction of failure is inevitable .... I believe we know too much.'[110] That might almost stand as an epitaph on the whole Gothic Revival.

3 Ruskin and Viollet-le-Duc

'Disturbed sleep, dreaming I had introduced myself to M. Viollet-le-Duc, and that he wouldn't have anything to do with me' (Ruskin's diary, 1882).

JOHN RUSKIN and Eugène-Emmanuel Viollet-le-Duc: Italian Gothic *versus* French Gothic; emotion *versus* reason; surface ornament *versus* structural expression. Those are the usual polarities.[1] In fact, in any interpretation of Victorian Gothic, there is plenty of room for both. A number of English Gothic revivalists followed Ruskin towards medieval Italy, in pursuit of a new eclectic style flexible enough to suit the needs of the nineteenth century; others followed Viollet towards medieval France, hoping to find there a fresh hunting-ground for that architectural Holy Grail: a Victorian Style. But these two routes were not mutually exclusive. Medieval Italy and medieval France overlap as sources of High Victorian Gothic. Viollet's emphasis on structure, Ruskin's emphasis on texture; Viollet's emphasis on purpose, Ruskin's emphasis on appearance; Viollet's emphasis on technology, Ruskin's emphasis on morality – all these can be traced, in productive counterpoint, within that evolving synthesis which we call High Victorian Gothic.

Both men had a considerable following. 'No man,' wrote Gilbert Scott in 1857, 'Pugin alone excepted, has so strongly influenced [our architecture, as Ruskin] . . . the effect of his writings has been enormous.'[2] 'We all crib from Viollet-le-Duc', admitted William Burges, 'although not one buyer in ten ever reads the text.'[3] In a way, Victorian architects were able to absorb both Ruskin and Viollet-le-Duc by simply ignoring their most important teachings. Ruskin's economic and social criticism, Viollet's rationalist theories, these might be too difficult to swallow. But details and motifs, Venetian Gothic or Early French, these could be – and were – absorbed. 'Ruskinian Gothic' turns out to be a pretty nebulous concept. Structural polychromy, significant ornament, naturalistic carving, north Italian motifs, horizontal massing – all these might legitimately be described as Ruskinian factors in architectural design. But which, if any, is exclusively associated with Ruskin's writings? The answer seems to be that – like any popular writer – Ruskin told people what they wanted to hear. Towards the end of the 1840s that 'archi-

51 R.C. Carpenter, St Mary Magdalen,
Munster Square, London (1842–52).
A country church in town.

52 William Butterfield, All Saints,
Margaret Street, London (1849–59).
A 'real' town church.

tectural imperator',[4] that 'dictator',[5] that 'autocrat',[6] was buying into a
rising market: the market for north Italian Gothic. Similarly, when in
the later 1850s, the pendulum of taste swung away from Italy to France,
Viollet's great dictionary was there, at just the right moment, index and
reflex of a new aesthetic.

In 1849, the year of Ruskin's *Seven Lamps*, two churches were the talk
of fashionable London: R.C. Carpenter's St Mary Magdalen, Munster
Square (1842–52),[7][51] and William Butterfield's All Saints, Margaret
St (1849–59).[52] Their differences stem less from Ruskinian theory than
from the ecclesiologists' search for a new archetype: no longer a Middle
Pointed country church, on East Anglian lines, but a 'real' town church –
brick-built, polychrome, and Continental in inspiration.[8] Thereafter – in
churches of the 1850s and 1860s – Ruskinian theory and ecclesiological
preference combined to produce forms which we now recognise as
characteristically High Victorian.

Pugin's architectural theory had been based on the Keatsian syllogism:

Beauty is truth, truth beauty.

But which truth? To followers of Pugin in the 1840s, 'truth' meant the
'true Picturesque': aggregated units expressing organic plan. For Ruskin's
followers in the 1850s, 'truth' meant the 'true Sublime': planar shapes,
volumetric composition, geometry, mass, weight.[9] So the material of the
1840s was Kentish rag: rough-hewn, soft-textured. The material of the
1850s was brick: smooth, polychrome, geometrical, shadowless. The
Puginian Picturesque had been replaced by the Ruskinian Sublime.

70

But when All Saints, Margaret St, was eventually finished in 1859, it was already old-fashioned.[10] In their search for a Victorian Style, the young Goths had already moved on, from Anglo-Italian to Early French. From 1854 onwards, Viollet-le-Duc replaced Ruskin as the Gothic Revival's leading pundit. From 1855 onwards, William Burges replaced Butterfield as the movement's rising star. 1854 was the year of the publication of the first volume of Viollet's great dictionary. 1855 was the year of the competition for Lille Cathedral, won by Burges (and Henry Clutton) against international odds.[11] The chief model for the design was the church of Notre Dame at Châlons-sur-Marne. Early French had displaced Italian Gothic. But just as Ruskin's enthusiasm for north Italian prototypes had been preceded by Benjamin Webb, James Wild and T. H. Wyatt,[12] so Viollet's passion for Early French had been anticipated by Lassus and the Didron family.[13] Both Ruskin and Viollet-le-Duc moved with the taste of the time, and not against it.

Ruskin began his rise to influence by benefiting from a reaction against Puginian orthodoxy. By 1849 'the true thing' was no longer enough. Despite all his denials, Ruskin certainly borrowed from Pugin, especially from *True Principles* (1841).[14] But the similarities between the theories of the two men are infinitely less than the differences. Pugin's inspiration was first and foremost English Gothic: he did not visit Italy until 1847.[15] Again, the thrust of Pugin's architectural writings was essentially rationalist; Ruskin's imaginative. Pugin and Ruskin shared two major commitments: in social matters, the idea of the organic community; in architectural matters, the notion of truth to materials. Both regarded decorative deceit as a form of moral delinquency.[16] And both detested the classical tradition,[17] a tradition which continued, of course, despite all their fulminations. But on other issues – notably established religion and structural truth – Pugin and Ruskin were fundamentally at odds. They agreed about the ethical state of builders, but not about the ethics of building.

For both Pugin and Ruskin Gothic was a style of universal applicability.[18] But applicable in which degree? Whereas Pugin had distinguished architecture from building only by ideas of propriety and hierarchy, Ruskin graded them in terms of aesthetic excellence. 'The essential thing in a building', he explained, 'its *First* virtue – is that it be strongly built, and fit for its uses. [But] the noblest thing in a building, and its *highest* virtue, is that it be nobly sculptured or painted.'[19] Do not 'connect the delight which you take in ornament with that which you take in construction or in usefulness. They have no connection, and every effort that you make to reason from one to the other will blunt your sense of beauty ... Remember that the most beautiful things in the world are the most useless; peacocks and lilies for instance.'[20] 'That building', he concedes, 'will generally be noblest, which to an intelligent eye discovers the great secrets of its structure', but 'the architect is not *bound* to exhibit structure'.[21] Nor has he ever done, except selectively. And as for decorating construction, why decorate Gothic spandrels and leave the columns bare? Look at the exterior of S. Zeno Maggiore in Verona[53]: whatever 'a disciple of Mr Pugin might say', Ruskin reminds us, the ornament is simply ornamental. 'I wish you especially to notice [this] because the false theory that ornamentation should be merely decorated structure is so pretty and plausible, that it is likely to take away your attention from the far more important abstract conditions of design.'[22] Or look at the exterior of the Baptistery at Pisa[76]: again the link between ornament and structure is tenuous in the extreme. The fact of the matter is this, he concludes: architectural decoration – like sartorial decoration – can assume any form at all, provided it does not hopelessly compromise 'the notion of use', that is the *idea* of utility.[23]

So for Ruskin, architectural beauty means above all the beauty of decorative expression: texture, symbol, association. He was more interested in polychromy than in vaulting.[24] 'Features necessary to express security to the imagination', he reminds us, 'are often as essential parts of good architecture as those required for security itself.'[25] The fact that expressive ornament occasionally involved architectural deceit – late Gothic roof pendants for instance[26] – was something he preferred to ignore. Ornament *per se* was art; structure *per se* was science. In the first edition of the *Seven Lamps* (1849) he maintained that ornament must be subordinate to structure. In the second edition (1853), that position is reversed.[27] So, despite an early enthusiasm for the Lamp of Truth, Ruskin became an anti-rationalist. Indeed he came to believe that the low state of the arts was all the fault of an excess of reason.[28] Architecture, he concluded, cannot be great if 'it cannot be decorated'.[29] And that decoration must be based on nature, because 'all noble ornamentation is the expression of man's delight in God's work'.[30] That is, nature conventionalised[31] – not nature abstracted, as in Pugin's *Floriated Ornament* (1849). In mere abstraction there can be no perfection.[32] Finally, all decoration reflects the mental and social state of the craftsman.[33] Hence the need for social reform as a condition of architectural reform.

Unlike Pugin, Ruskin was not interested in ecclesiology. He regarded art as an emanation of divinity. But religious symbolism plays no part in his aesthetic. In fact it was Ruskin's Protestant instincts – what the *Ecclesiologist* sadly called his 'monomania ... against Catholicity' – which

53 S. Zeno Maggiore, Verona (12th–14th centuries). 'Whatever a disciple of Mr Pugin might say, the ornament is simply ornamental'.

54 'The Election Car' of J. B. Hoy, M.P. (1830). Classical symbols of authority.

helped to make Gothic palatable to a wider audience.[34] Spurgeon denounced the pointed arch as an invention of the devil. But by the 1860s dissenters of all kinds had joined the Gothic Revival. The Congregational Chapel at Over, near Middlewich, Cheshire (by Douglas, 1864–5) for instance, combines polychrome banding, reminiscent of Catholic North Italy, with prominent busts of Luther and Calvin. Despite Ruskin's obvious religiosity, there is a secularity about his thought which is never found in Pugin. For Pugin, good Catholics made good buildings: hence his emphasis on the church. For Ruskin, good men made good buildings: hence his emphasis on society – a message William Morris was not slow to pick up.

Ruskin's *Nature of Gothic* attempted to explain not the structure of Gothic buildings, but the psychology of Gothic builders. Whewell and Willis had tackled systems of vaulting.[35] Ruskin tackled systems of thought. Of course the essence of Gothic – the 'Gothic spirit' – was impossible to pin down. Ruskin played with ideas of 'savageness', 'changefulness', 'naturalism', etc. None was conclusive. Thanks to what he later called 'my pert little Protestant mind',[36] he was chary of equating Gothicism and Catholicism. That, after all, had been Pugin's mistake. But he did dare to explore the links between mind and art, culture and society: the 'moral imagination' of the artist. In the end, however, he fell back on one all-purpose explanation – the soul of society: the organic community producing organic architecture. Moral states, economic structures, and aesthetic codes were thus all irretrievably mixed up. And perhaps they should be. But on the whole – apart from the 'Gothic will to form' school of Riegl and Worringer – art historians since Ruskin have steered clear of such holistic explanations.[37]

Ruskin was as much a moral censor as an aesthete: good architecture, he believed, is the product of a state of grace; bad architecture betokens original sin.[38] He condemned classicism, therefore, on moral grounds: 'it is the moral nature of it', he wrote, 'which is corrupt.'[39] Its decorative forms – often used politically[54] – had always been symbols of authority and privilege. Similarly it was the social and mental conditions at the root of Victorian architecture which Ruskin identified as the source of its degradation. Building for profit; the status-seeking of the new architectural profession; the division of labour and the fragmentation of design; the competitive ethic; the mechanisation of building; the squalor of industry and the commercialisation of art – these were, in Ruskin's eyes, the basic causes of architectural decadence.[40] 'Good art', he told a Cambridge audience in 1850, 'has only been produced by nations who rejoiced in it; fed themselves with it, as if it were bread; basked in it, as if it were sunshine; shouted at the sight of it; danced with the delight of it: quarrelled for it; fought for it; starved for it; did, in fact, precisely the opposite with it of what we want to do with it – they made it to keep, and we [make it] to sell.'[41] No wonder Tolstoy called Ruskin 'one of those rare men who think with their hearts.'[42]

How then, according to Ruskin, should the Victorians build? His publication of the *Seven Lamps* (1849) and the *Stones of Venice* (1851–3) coincided with several crucial developments in the economics of construction. As if to demonstrate to all art historians the interaction of aesthetic and socio-economic factors, the duties on glass were repealed in 1845;[43] the tax on bricks in 1850;[44] and the window tax in 1851.[45] The scene was set for a High Victorian breakthrough into plate glass and polychromy.[46] At the same time the increasing use of cast and wrought iron threatened to overturn the whole basis of traditional aesthetics. Then there was the climatic factor: Ruskinian polychromy was as much an answer to Dickensian smog as a reaction against Neo-Classical purity.[47] So a new style there had to be. But what form was this new Victorian style to take? 'We know what the Gothic of the Plantagenets was', complained the *Building News* in 1858, 'and the Gothic of the Edwards. [But] what is the Victorian Gothic?'[48]

In 1849, in the *Seven Lamps*, Ruskin argued for the rejection of styles and the pursuit of style. 'We want no new style in architecture ... But

74

we want *some* style.'[49] Once a single style had been universally accepted, its adaptation would eventually produce a new style suitable to a new world. Unfortunately, however, Ruskin recommended not one style but a choice of four: Pisan Romanesque, as in the Baptistery and Cathedral at Pisa; Early Gothic of the western Italian republics, as in the Palazzo Tolomei, Siena; Venetian Gothic – Sta Maria dell' Orto, for example; and early English Decorated, as in the north transept at Lincoln. Of these four, he claimed to favour the last, flavoured perhaps with a touch of French.[50] But in practice his influence was all in favour of the third possibility: Venetian Gothic. In the *Stones of Venice*, Ruskin had compared Italian Gothic and late French Gothic – Verona and Abbéville – to the disadvantage of France. 'The Veronese Gothic', he wrote, 'is strong in its masonry, simple in its mass, but perpetual in its variety. The late French Gothic is weak in masonry, broken in mass, and repeats the same ideas continually. It is very beautiful, but the Italian Gothic is the nobler type.'[51] Alas, as Ruskin might later have admitted, this was a false comparison: he should have compared Italian Gothic with Early French – Siena and Amiens for instance. Had he done so, Early French might well have been the winner.[52] Instead he was publicly committed to north Italian Gothic. And, apart from a brief flirtation with the idea of a totally new style,[53] Italian he remained. In the 1855 edition of *Seven Lamps* he went out of his way to modify this commitment to Venetian Gothic. 'The Gothic of Verona', he wrote – S. Fermo Maggiore, for example – 'is far nobler than that of Venice; and that of Florence nobler than that of Verona. [But] for our own immediate purposes that of Notre-Dame of Paris is the noblest of all.'[54] In 1859 he agreed that Chartres was ten times as fine as St Mark's, Venice.[55] But in vain: Ruskin and Venice were forever linked. Ruskin's name became a sanction for a particular form of eclecticism. The phrase 'Ruskinian Gothic' had entered the English language.

Precisely what that meant was never spelled out by Ruskin. At the close of the *Stones of Venice* (1853), he speculates briefly on the future; a future architecture based on the best of European Gothic, north and south: 'the pure and perfect forms of the Northern Gothic, [worked] out with ... Italian refinement'; that is, 'buildings designed in the forms of English and French thirteenth-century *surface* Gothic ... wrought out with the refinement of Italian art in the details.'[56] A year later appeared the first volume of Viollet-le-Duc's great dictionary: a vote of confidence in the structural rationality of Early French.

One young architect who took up this double challenge was G. F. Bodley. That very year, at St John, France Lynch, Glos (1854–57), he

55 G. F. Bodley, All Saints,
Selsley, Gloucestershire (1862).
Influences from France,
Italy and Austria.

56 E. W. Godwin, Northampton Town Hall
(1861–4). 'Altogether Gothic but utterly
un-Medieval'.

was combining Early French capitals from Laon or Canterbury with
foliage from Venetian models.[57] Four years afterwards, at St Michael's,
Brighton (1858–61), he was combining Early French plate tracery from
Lausanne with Venetian capitals, bases and impost mouldings – borrowed
directly from the *Stones of Venice*.[58] And before long, at Selsley church,
Glos (1862)[55], he was combining simplified plate tracery from Laon
with hints of the interior apse of S. Francesco, Bologna, plus – as a tribute
to his patron Sir Samuel Marling – a mighty echo of the saddleback tower
of Marling in the Tyrol. Soon after that, however, Bodley changed course:
he reversed his allegiance, from Ruskin to Pugin. He moved away from
Viollet-le-Duc; away from both Venetian Gothic and Early French; back
to Pugin's English Decorated. It was a decisive change. Even so, all his
life – when faced with a particularly tricky problem – Bodley used to
mutter: 'I wonder what Ruskin would make of that?'[59]

No doubt E. W. Godwin often muttered the same sort of thing, with
the same sort of ambivalence. When he described his Northampton Town
Hall (1861–4)[56] as based on the principles of the *Stones of Venice*, he
was speaking for a whole generation of Gothic revivalists.[60] But his Town
Hall at Congleton, Cheshire (1864–6) is more French than Italian;[61] and

his Plymouth Town Hall (1870–74) is decidedly Early French. Neither Ruskin nor Viollet could count on total allegiance. What Godwin's generation was trying to do – especially in civic and domestic architecture – was to find a style which was 'altogether Gothic, but utterly un-Medieval'.[62] And in that pursuit architects looked for help to both Ruskin and Viollet-le-Duc.

Few mid-Victorian Gothic buildings were exclusively north Italian. George Somers Clarke's General Credit and Discount Co. (1866–8) at 7, Lothbury, next to the Bank of England, was one;[63] his Merchant Seamen's Orphan Asylum, now Wanstead Hospital (1861)[57] – echoing Venice, Mantua and Bergamo – was another.[64] But Ruskin seems not to have been impressed by Somers Clarke. He was impressed by Benjamin Woodward.

Woodward was a junior partner in a firm of Irish architects known as Deane and Woodward[65] who came to prominence in 1853 with their new Museum (1853–7)[58] – later the Engineering School – at Trinity College, Dublin. His early work – Queen's College, Cork (1847–9); Killarney Asylum (1848–50) – had been Puginian.[66] Continental influence emerges only in 1851 with his competition design for Cork Town

57 G. Somers Clarke, Wanstead Hospital, Essex (1861). Echoes of Venice, Mantua and Bergamo.

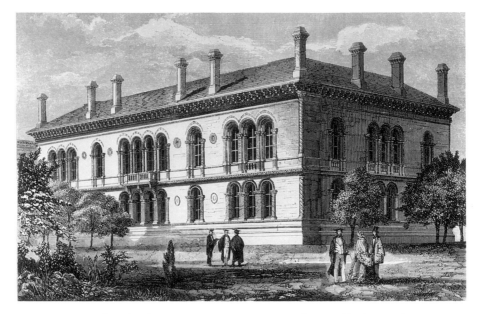

58 Benjamin Woodward and T. N. Deane, Museum, Trinity College, Dublin (1853–7).
'The first realisation' of Ruskin's principles.

Hall.[67] That had been Flemish or 'Belgic' in style. But within a year or
so Woodward's Gothic had become more Italian than Flemish: it had
become Ruskinian. 'Yesterday in Dublin', wrote William Allingham to
Rossetti in 1855, 'I saw but hastily the part-finished building in Trinity
College, which is after Ruskin's own heart. Style early Venetian (I suppose) with numberless capitals delicately carved over with holly leaves,
shamrocks, various flowers, birds and so on … [No doubt] all you
cognoscenti will be rushing over to examine the Stones of Dublin.'[68]
Outside, Venetian Cinque-Cento, Byzantine-Renaissance with touches of
Celtic and French Romanesque; inside, Irish marbles and Continental
motifs: Byzantine-Morisco-Gothic, with occasional touches of Early English. The building was certainly a monument to the new eclecticism. It
was also an eloquent advertisement for Ruskin's theories of design: 'the
first realisation I had the joy to see, of the principles I had … been
endeavouring to teach' – that is, truth to nature, truth to materials,
constructional polychromy, significant ornament, and the creative
autonomy of the craftsman.[69] The Seven Lamps have replaced the True
Principles.

   Then came the University Museum, Oxford (1854–60)[59].[70] Not only
an essay in Ruskinian Gothic, but a full-blown experiment in progressive

design, secular, civic, modern; an attempt to combine historic forms with the materials of the railway age – glass and iron. Its design brought together very different sources: windows from Venice, mouldings from Verona; Byzantine carving and a Netherlandish roofline with echoes of Ypres, or Brussels, or Nuremberg; a quadrangular plan on traditional Oxford collegiate lines; and, finally, an octagonal laboratory whose ancestor – a very long way back – was the monastic kitchen at Glastonbury. Its appearance in Oxford caused an aesthetic *frisson*: the Oxford Architectural Society hailed it as 'the noblest and greatest, the purest and truest secular building of modern times'.[71] Tennyson, however, called it 'perfectly indecent'.[72] And eventually even Ruskin came to see it as a failure.[73]

Besides Woodward, Ruskin had particular faith in one other young architect: Alfred Waterhouse of Manchester. Now it was one of the bases of Ruskin's thinking that there was some mystical link between Renaissance architecture and the capitalist process, between the Reformation and the industrial revolution, between commerce and classicism. So for Ruskin, himself a Protestant and a capitalist, the classical palazzo

59 Benjamin Woodward and T. N. Deane, University Museum, Oxford (1854–60). Ruskinian Gothic.

60 Alfred Waterhouse, Assize Courts, Manchester (1859; dem.). 'New Secular Gothic, partly French, partly Italian, partly English'.

of early Victorian Manchester seemed to epitomise all that was evil in the modern world.[74] When he delivered his first lectures on economic theory – *The Political Economy of Art* (1857) – he chose to deliver them in Manchester, the capital of laissez-faire economics. What he put to his audience of free-trading business men was an alternative ideal: a pre-industrial society, paternally governed, organically structured, communally cooperative – and Gothic. Gothic: the organic style as product and symbol of an organic community; a community not based on equality,[75] but founded on responsibility, and held together by a network of reciprocal duties and obligations. Well, Ruskin did not convert Manchester to Ruskinian economics. But he did convert Manchester to Ruskinian Gothic.

Gothic came to Manchester with the Assize Courts competition of 1859. The obvious models for a large, secular, civic building in the Gothic style were the town halls of Belgium and Holland. So, before starting work, Waterhouse visited town halls at Bruges, Ypres, Ghent, Oudenarde, Brussels, Louvain, Malines, Antwerp and Courtrai. But none of these formed a precise precedent. His composition might stem from the Netherlands, but his design embodied just that combination of northern and southern Gothic which Ruskin had recommended in the *Stones of Venice*:

80

Anglo-French Middle Pointed, with an admixture of Italian Gothic in the details[60].[76] 'The character is . . . Gothic', noted the *Builder*, 'yet neither English, nor . . . Venetian.'[77] The roofline may be Belgian, but the lowest windows have a Tudor feel. The tracery on the first floor is Early English or French Geometrical; the second floor windows are as much north Italian as Early English. And the line of the imposts and string-courses running across the façades supply what Gilbert Scott called the horizontality of Italian Gothic. In other words, Waterhouse's design is eclectic.[78] The *Ecclesiologist* hailed it as an example of the 'New Secular Gothic, partly French, partly Italian, partly English';[79] 'the most important specimen of civic Gothic which the revival has yet produced.'[80]

Ruskin agreed. 'I have had a nice day at Manchester', he told his father in 1863, 'the Assize Courts are much beyond everything yet done in England on my principles. The hall is one of the finest things I have ever seen; even the painted glass is good . . . It is vast and full of sculpture [by Woolner and O'Shea] and very impressive. The workmen were pleased to see me; the clerk of the works, when he was a youth, copied out the whole three volumes of [my] *Stones of Venice*, and traced every illustration.'[81] So Ruskin was well pleased. William Morris, however, did not care for this building. He called it a 'dreary, pretentious heap'.[82]

The details of Waterhouse's greatest work, Manchester Town Hall (1868–76)[61], are Anglo-French thirteenth-century Gothic. But Waterhouse claimed – and rightly – that his style was 'essentially of the nineteenth century.'[83] In effect, he had succeeded in creating a new style by a ruthlessly eclectic process, adapting historic forms to nineteenth-century conditions by ingenious planning, and by bold use of new materials, notably iron, plate glass and terracotta. Waterhouse accepted wholeheartedly Pugin's idea of the 'true Picturesque'. 'The architect', he believed, should 'make his work grow so naturally out of [the site] as to seem and be the inevitable building for the spot.'[84] Hence the fluency of his town hall plan, and hence the drama of its silhouette. At the same time, however, he has managed to divorce Puginian planning from the limitations of Puginian Gothic. He has clearly been reading Viollet-le-Duc.

The cult of Early French by Waterhouse's generation began as a reaction against the excesses of Ruskinian Gothic: its pitiless polychromy, its anti-structural aesthetic. 'No man's works', noted William Burges, 'contain more valuable information than Mr Ruskin's, but they are strong meat, and require to be taken by one who has [already] made up his mind . . . [For] to one in search of a style, and just beginning his architectural life, [Ruskin] is almost destruction.'[85] Street came to agree: 'this

61 Alfred Waterhouse, Town Hall, Manchester, (1868–76). 'Essentially of the 19th century'.

hot taste', he concluded, 'is dangerous.'[86] The new Victorian Style would have to stem from forms which were more 'natural', 'truthful', and 'real': Early French. Now Burges's flight from Italian to French Gothic can be traced very clearly in the development of one design, his scheme for the Crimea Memorial Church in Constantinople.[87] Between 1856 and 1863 his design – alas, unbuilt – became not only smaller and cheaper, it became more French and less Italian; it lost its polychromy and assumed a style which was harder, sterner and self-consciously plainer. His model had changed, from Vercelli to Noyon. Ruskin had been supplemented by Viollet-le-Duc.

Around the time of the 1862 Exhibition, Burges was typical of his generation in believing that Early French – monochrome, primitivistic, muscular, archaic – represented 'the best ... escape from our present difficulties'.[88] In its development lay the road to modernism. Architects, he was delighted to see, were at last moving backwards, from the luxury

82

and decadence of Decorated to the primitive vigour of an earlier phase. 'Our architecture', he wrote, 'seeks [now] to simplify itself by adopting the sterner French types, such as Chartres and Laon.'[89] The square abacus was replacing the round, and decoration tended towards sculpture, as at St Remi, Rheims, rather than foliage, as at Lincoln.[90] If we are looking for the basis of a Victorian Style, Burges claims, 'English thirteenth-century Gothic [as at Lincoln] certainly won't do'. It is Early French (like Laon or Chartres), or Transitional (i.e. between Romanesque and Gothic) which offers the greatest scope for modern adaptation. German Gothic – here Street agreed with Burges – seemed to lack the necessary 'nervous manliness'.[91] Not so Early French. Medieval *English* builders 'delighted in small pretty [churches], with delicate details, which would be out of place in our smoky atmosphere. In *French* art everything is upon a larger scale.'[92] Compare Soissons and Exeter. 'The mouldings in English thirteenth-century work', Burges notes, 'are far more beautiful in their sections than successful in their perspective, looking too much like bundles of reeds separated by hollows.' Whereas 'the French architect of the same period looked more to effect and less to the section, he left more plain surfaces ... thus his mouldings, when he did use them, have a more telling effect.'[93] French Gothic seemed nobler, cheaper to produce and – this is the crux – more characteristic of the modern age. 'The distinguishing characteristics of the Englishman of the nineteenth-century', wrote Burges in 1861, 'are our immense railway and engineering works, our line-of-battle ships, our good and strong machinery ... our free constitution, our unfettered press, and our trial by jury ... [No] style of architecture can be more appropriate to such a people than that which ... is characterised by boldness, breadth, strength, sternness, and virility.'[94]

Apart from the psychological implications of this obsession with strength, it is interesting that Burges equated muscularity with Liberalism. Robert Kerr seems to have had the same idea. He described England as 'the very home of rough and ready muscularity'.[95] And Viollet-le-Duc, whose instincts were secular and republican, admired Laon even more than Beauvais because of its '*democratic*' roughness and plainness.[96] Marx and Engels took a rather different line. In their *Communist Manifesto* (1848) they equated muscularity with reaction: what 'the reactionary forces so greatly admire about the medieval period', they claimed, is its 'brutal expression of strength'.[97] Still, what Burges chiefly had in mind was the adaptability of Early French to nineteenth-century conditions. 'The stern, solemn majesty of Laon', agreed Street, 'is just what we modern men ought to ... impress ourselves with.'[98]

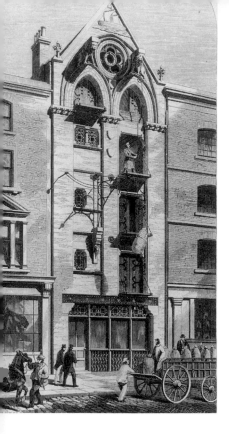

62 William Burges, Skilbeck's Warehouse, London (1865–6; dem.). 'Out of this *may be* developed a good strong 19th-century architecture'.

63 William Burges, Mr McConnochie's House, Park Place, Cardiff (1871–80). Admired by Viollet-le-Duc.

64 Sir William Emerson, Muir College, Allahabad (1872–8). A solution to the dilemma of style?

Burges's Cork Cathedral (1863 onwards), perhaps.[99] There are echoes there of Chartres and Amiens, Laon, Nèsle and Etampes, as well as S. Zeno at Verona, and even Merton College, Oxford – all distilled in pursuit of abstraction and muscularity. But a cathedral is, after all, a cathedral. What about secular buildings? Skilbeck's drysalters' warehouse (1865–6)[62][100] was certainly a bold attempt to Gothicise commerce. E. W. Godwin thought it 'strikingly clever'.[101] But was this the Victorian Style? 'Out of this *may be* developed a good strong nineteenth-century architecture', Godwin concludes, 'but neither Mr Burges nor anyone else has shown us how.'[102] What, then, of Mr McConnochie's house in Cardiff (1871–80)[63]?[103] Viollet-le-Duc singled it out for praise.[104] Early French is here not only domesticated but suburbanised. But was that enough? Burges remained uncertain.[105] On the face of it he appears a belligerently confident designer. And that confidence seems positively manic in his Law Courts competition scheme of 1866: a glorious fantasy on themes from Poitiers, Pierrefonds, Amiens, the Musée de Cluny and the Palazzo Vecchio.[106] Lockwood and Mawson took the style to Bradford.[107] Josiah Conder took it to Japan.[108] R. Selden Wornum took it to Spain.[109] H. H. Richardson developed parts of it in America.[110] And Sir William Emerson – via Burges's Bombay Art School design (1867) – carried it to a memorable conclusion in India: Emerson's Muir College, Allahabad (1872–8)[64] is an eclectic *mélange* of Gothic, Indian, Egyptian and Islamic.[111] But was this a solution to the dilemma of style? As Viollet-le-Duc put it, was 'the nineteenth century condemned to end without ever possessing an architecture of its own? Is it to transmit to posterity nothing but pastiches and hybrids?'[112] Burges was not at all sure. And neither was the man who epitomised the whole cult of Early French: Viollet-le-Duc himself.

Unlike Pugin, Viollet saw Gothic buildings as expressions of an emerging secular, bourgeois society: a view which owes something to Augustin Thierry and Francois Guizot. Unlike Ruskin, he saw Gothic forms as both skeletal and diagrammatic: a view which owes something to Willis and Bartholomew,[113] but more to the rationalist tradition of French classicism.[114] Most of all, unlike those of Pugin and Ruskin, Viollet's theories were stylistically neutral. 'A locomotive ... has style', he explains. 'Some will call it an ugly machine. But why ugly? Does it not exhibit the true expression of the brute energy which it embodies? ... There is no style but that which is appropriate to the object ... A gun has style, but a gun made to resemble a crossbow will have none. Now we architects have for a long time been making guns while endeavouring to give them ... the appearance of crossbows.'[115] 'The engineers who have made locomotives, have not dreamt of copying horse-drawn coaches.'[116] 'Architecture can only equip itself with new forms if it seeks them in the rigorous application of a new structure.'[117] That – for Viollet – was the lesson of the Middle Ages. 'Medieval principles consist precisely in submitting everything – materials, forms, plans and details – to *reasoning* ... [their] architecture and construction cannot be separated ... the architecture is nothing else than a functional form commanded by the construction itself.' Well, it was a short step from functional design to the morality of function. 'Architecture', he concluded, 'is mouldings' – but mouldings as functioning forms; not mouldings – in the Ruskinian sense – as products of pleasure and objects of delight.[118]

Such theories struck few chords in Mid-Victorian England. Viollet's only serious follower among English architects was his translator Benjamin Bucknall, architect of an extraordinary, unfinished essay in Gothic structuralism, Woodchester Park, Glos (*c.*1845–68).[119] England's leading exponent of Early French, William Burges, was no friend of Viollet-le-Duc. Burges regarded Viollet's *Dictionnaire* as quite invaluable.[120] But he was critical of Viollet's *Entretiens*: he thought the woodcuts 'excellent', but the essays 'long-winded' and some of the theories about geometrical composition positively pernicious.[121] He certainly felt very little sympathy with Viollet's fantasies of metallic vaulting.[122] Even so, he was not above cribbing from the Frenchman's archaeology: his Bombay Art School smithy (1867) is based on Viollet's Benedictine kitchen at Marmoutier.[123] Burges's final judgement is characteristically candid: Viollet was a great scholar, an average architect and a disastrous restorationist.[124]

In one respect, however, Burges – like most of his contemporaries – underrated Viollet-le-Duc's importance: he underplayed the Frenchman's pursuit of architectural rationality. By the 1860s, Viollet was convinced that architecture in its traditional form was dying. The historicist phase had produced mere simulacra: 'bodies without souls, the fragments of some departed civilisation, a language incomprehensible even to those who employ it.'[125] Unlike Pugin, Viollet conceived of Gothic as a tectonic system independent of religion. Unlike Ruskin, he envisaged an evolving language of architectural form based on – but ultimately independent of – the structural aesthetics of medieval Gothic. When in this century Pevsner came to trace the origins of the Modern Movement, he too undervalued Viollet-le-Duc. Pevsner's thesis was almost a case of 'Hamlet without the Prince', Summerson remarked, for 'Viollet ... was the alchemist who produced a workable concept of rational architecture out of romantic archaeology.'[126] Well, maybe. But in looking at Viollet's own buildings, one would never guess.

65 E. Viollet-le-Duc, Unexecuted design for an iron-vaulted concert hall (1864).

66 G. E. Street, Cuddesdon College, Oxfordshire (1853–4). Puginian.

As Viollet's career progressed, his theories became increasingly radical, and his buildings increasingly pedestrian. Burges rightly dismissed his gate-lodge at Coucy as 'awful . . . something frightful'.[127] From his famous fantasy of an iron-vaulted concert hall (*c.*1864)[65], to his miniature Custodian's House (1866) in the shadow of Notre Dame – even at Pierrefonds (1858–70) – there is an awkwardness about his buildings which defies admiration. In attempting to translate Gothic into a viable nineteenth-century style he failed, and he admitted his failure.[128] His ideas and his practice moved further and further apart. As a theorist, he entered a world of cosmic geometry.[129] As an architect he ended up – with Paxton of all people – designing the Château de Pregny, near Geneva (1860–3; gallery 1875), in overdressed mixed Renaissance.[130] No wonder English Goths preferred Ruskin. Ruskin himself, however, always suffered from something of an inferiority complex as regards Viollet-le-Duc. The Frenchman might not be much of an artist, but at least he was a scholar. Ruskin could never have written the *Dictionnaire*. 'Were you not glad when that book came out?' Sir Sydney Cockerell asked him in 1888. 'No, I was very jealous', Ruskin replied; 'I ought to have written it myself.' On 18 October 1882, he noted in his diary: 'Disturbed sleep, dreaming I had introduced myself to M. Viollet-le-Duc, and that he wouldn't have anything to do with me.'[131]

Apart from Woodward and Waterhouse, the only architect Ruskin regularly praised was George Edmund Street. Street had no sympathy with Viollet's dreams of novelty; his loyalties were first and foremost to Early French Gothic. He ranked Chartres and Amiens with the Parthenon as 'the noblest and most masculine ... architecture in the world'; in Paris, Notre Dame was 'supreme' and the Sainte Chapelle a 'work of inspired genius'.[132] By comparison north Italian Gothic seemed basically imperfect. It lacked the 'completeness in ... development' of English and French Gothic.[133] It lacked the visible engineering – the buttresses, the multiple vaulting, the petrified science – of north European Gothic.[134] It never entirely shook off the incubus of antique classicism: hence its hybridity in plan and form.[135] It was the product of many nationalities: 'the Italians employed Greeks, Moors, Frenchmen, Germans, Catalonians ...' The result, Street confessed, was 'very eclectic'.[136] On the other hand, it was exactly this synthesis which made it so appealing as a model for the eclecticism of the nineteenth century.[137] And although its work-manship was 'inferior' to the Gothic of France and England, the pro-fessionalism which created it – and its application, to secular, urban domestic and public buildings – made it peculiarly relevant to the prob-lems of Victorian architects.[138] Most of all, 'in ... the introduction of colour in construction ... Italian architecture of the Middle Ages teaches us', Street concluded, 'more than any other architecture since the com-mencement of the world.'[139] Polychromy – whether incrusted in the Venetian manner,[140] or constructional in the manner of Bergamo,[141] Cremona[142] or Como[143] – polychromy was the answer to the inhibiting puritan aesthetic of north European Protestantism.[144] The average Eng-lishman's 'insane hatred of bright colours', he thought, was best cured by a holiday in Italy.[145] And that holiday should have as its climax the wondrous triple church of Assisi.[146]

Italian Gothic, therefore, was not a prototype worthy of precise imi-tation – that privilege was reserved for Early French – but an inspiration and a stimulus, a key ingredient in the creation of a new synthesis. That was Beresford Hope's conclusion when he came to review Street's book on *Brick and Marble in the Middle Ages* (1855). Here, he noted, was 'a contribution to the solution of that great problem – an architecture of the future'.[147] Here was a basis for a new synthesis. A synthesis which, in Street's own words, combined 'the verticality of Pointed with the repose of Classic architecture'.[148] Street's version of that synthesis is seen at its most complex in his greatest building, the Law Courts in London

67 G. E. Street, St James the Less, Westminster, London (1860–61). Ruskinian.

68 G. E. Street, Law Courts, London (1868–82). Eclectic.

(1868–82).[149] Having passed through a first phase (Cuddesdon College, Oxon, 1853–4)[66] – Puginian, English and Picturesque – and a second phase (St James the Less, Thorndyke St, Westminster, 1860–61)[67] – Ruskinian, Italian and Sublime[150] – Street settled in middle age on a personal style which owed something to England and Italy, something to Spain and the Netherlands, but most of all to France.[151] His Law Courts building is the culmination of this eclectic progression: Pevsner calls it English;[152] Hitchcock calls it French;[153] but we might equally call it Italian – especially the Carey St front. For it is all three: English, French and Italian; eclectic and triply so – even if, from a compositional point of view – its parts are greater than their sum. The most striking exterior unit in the design – the Sienese tower on the Carey St front[68] – must seem doubly familiar to Italian eyes. It strongly recalls the tower Street designed for the American Church in Rome (1873–6).[154] Street's polychromy is by no means entirely Ruskinian: he preferred the 'structural colouration' of Pisa or Siena to Venetian marble veneering. And in that respect – in its emphasis on structurally expressive ornament – his whole approach is a fusion of Ruskin and Viollet-le-Duc.[155]

In their different ways, both Woodward and Street were trying to follow Ruskin's advice: to call in the Gothic of southern Europe – its colour, its variety, its fire – to rejuvenate the Gothic of the north. So too

90

was Gilbert Scott. The title page of Scott's *Secular and Domestic Architecture, Present and Future* (1858) sums up this Ruskinian approach: an imaginary town square, where the Doge's Palace of Venice – Ruskin's 'central building of the world'[156] – faces the Cloth Hall at Ypres, north and south in easy fellowship.

Being slightly older than Woodward and Street, Scott began his career very much in the Puginian mould. His Martyrs' Memorial at Oxford (1841–3) is still English in form, modelled on the Eleanor Crosses of the thirteenth century. But by the end of his career, at the Albert Memorial (1863–72) in London – inspired perhaps by Orcagna's shrine at Orsanmichele in Florence – he has fully absorbed the form and spirit of Italian Gothic.[157] Scott always regarded Pugin as 'the great hero'.[158] But as his career advanced he looked more and more beyond England, to Flanders, France, Germany, Italy. Eclecticism became the hallmark of his secular style: Glasgow University (1867–70) and the Albert Institute, Dundee (1865–7)[69], for instance, fuse north and south, Caledonian, Italian

69 Sir Gilbert Scott, Albert Institute, Dundee (1865–7). Franco-Scottish Gothic.

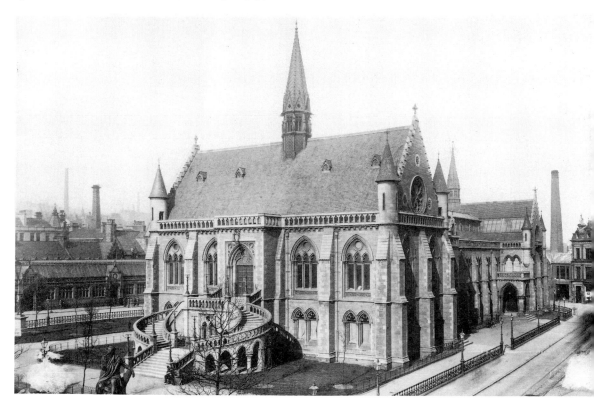

and French elements in happy combination.[159] His eclectic progress really begins with the Whitehall competition scheme of 1856; develops with Kelham Hall, Notts (1858–62)[160] and the Sandbach Institute, Cheshire (1858);[161] continues with Preston Town Hall (1862–7), Leeds Infirmary (1864),[162] Beckett's [National Westminster] Bank, Leeds (1864–6) and Hafodunos, near Llanrwst, North Wales (1861–6); and culminates in St Pancras Station and the Midland Hotel (1865–74)[92].

For Whitehall, Scott told Lord Palmerston he had devised a style which was 'a bona fide revival', with 'an innate elasticity which makes it bend to all requirements';[163] an answer, in fact, to the conundrum he had set himself: 'the construction upon a Gothic basis of a new palatial style.'[164] 'I did not aim at making my style Italian Gothic', he explained; 'my ideas ran much more upon the French [the courtyard, for instance, owes something to Blois], to which for some years I had devoted my chief study. I did, however, aim at gathering a few hints from Italy, such as the pillar mullion, the use of differently coloured materials, and of inlaying. I also aimed at another thing which people consider Italian – I mean a certain squareness and horizontality of outline. This I consider pre-eminently suited to the street front of a public building. I combined

70 F. W. Stevens, Victoria Terminus, Bombay (1878–88). 'An architectural Sodom'?

this, however, with gables, high-pitched roofs, and dormers.'[165] Lord Palmerston, alas, still believed that all true architecture was Palladian. He vetoed Scott's Gothic design *and* an alternative Byzantine version.[166]

At St Pancras, however, Scott got his chance. This time he decided to play down the Italian element. The polychromy is still there. But the skyline is no longer rectangular but syncopated, no longer Italian but Dutch or Flemish; and some of the details are Early English and Early French. The Cloth Hall at Ypres is the origin of the station entrance tower; Oudenarde town hall probably supplied the inspiration for his gabled and pinnacled hotel entrance; the mouldings around the great portals are Early French; the first-floor oriel windows incorporate distant echoes of Bishop Bridport's tomb at Salisbury Cathedral; other windows, just as clearly, are Anglicised Venetian. With a pedigree like that – Pugin, Ruskin and Viollet-le-Duc – no wonder Scott thought his design almost *'too* good for its purpose'.[167]

Such eclecticism was exported all over the world. To America, for example: Harvard Memorial Hall, by Ware and Van Brunt (designed 1867; built 1870–8). In New York there already existed polychromatic churches: a 'Church of the Holy Zebra' (All Souls, by J. W. Mould, 1853–8; dem.) and a 'Church of the Holy Oil-cloth' (Holy Trinity, by L. Eidlitz, 1873–4; dem.). But neither carried quite the *cachet* of Memorial Hall.[168] 'By the mercy of God', noted C. H. Moore of Harvard in 1863, 'Ruskin has been sent to open our eyes and loose the seals of darkness.'[169]

Did the citizens of Bombay feel much the same? Formidable examples of Indo-Venetian-Victorian in the centre of that city still testify to the influence of the *Stones of Venice* under the British Raj: the Public Works Offices (1869–72) by Col H. St Clair Wilkins, RE;[170] Municipal Buildings (1888–93) and Victoria Terminus (1878–88)[70] by F. W. Stevens. By comparison with Victoria Terminus even Scott's St Pancras begins to look anaemic. Scott himself designed Bombay University (1868–77), executed by native workmen under sappers' supervision. Even in its heyday, Bombay must have been a difficult test for taste. In 1931 Robert Byron condemned it as 'an architectural Sodom'. 'The nineteenth century', he wrote, 'devised nothing lower than the municipal buildings of British India. Their ugliness is positive, daemonic.'[171]

What – as Bodley used to say – would Ruskin have made of that? And – closer to home – what did he make of the Cobden Hotel, Birmingham (W. Doubleday, 1883)?[71]

Twenty years after the publication of the *Stones of Venice* Ruskin was still bitterly regretting the popularity of Venetian Gothic. Or rather, Venetian Gothic translated into Victorian terms.[172] Living in suburban

71 W. Doubleday, Cobden Hotel, Birmingham (1883; dem.). 'I wonder what Ruskin would make of that?'

London, near the Crystal Palace, he saw himself surrounded by Anglo-Italian Gothic villas – 'Frankenstein monsters' of indirectly his own making, like 107 Tulse Hill[72], built to designs by Charles Hambridge in 1865. He need not have taken all the blame himself. Viollet-le-Duc must have been indirectly responsible for quite a few Frankenstein Monsters too. But then Viollet hardly had to live with the results. Ruskin felt compelled to flee to the Lake District.[173]

Nevertheless, Ruskinian Gothic had its triumphs, and in ways which Ruskin, no doubt, least expected. In 1860 E. M. Barry designed the definitive Ruskinian school: at St Giles in the Fields, London.[73][174] In 1862 the *Art Journal* hailed the advent of the Ruskinian factory chimney: 'they rise aloft in architectural harmony ... mercantile architecture ... thoroughly decorative ... without being decorated ... [no longer] brick monstrosities ... smoking in absolute ignorance of all decorative construction.'[175] 'Remember', Ruskin wrote, 'that it is the glory of Gothic architecture that it can do *anything*.'[176] That dictum came nearest to fulfilment in the unlikely shape of the High Victorian warehouse and multi-storey office building, and in the employment of multiplied grid façades.

Bristol, Manchester and London were the three urban centres which best exploited this Ruskinian medium in a commercial context. And nowhere more strikingly than Bristol, the city which once vied with Amsterdam as the Venice of the north. 'Bristol Byzantine' was a style

94

72 C. Hambridge, 107 Tulse Hill, London (1865). One of Ruskin's 'Frankenstein Monsters'.

73 E. M. Barry, National School, St Giles in the Fields, London (1860). Ruskinian school-building.

74 A. C. Ponton and W. V. Gough, The Granary, Welsh Back, Bristol (1869–70). 'It is the glory of Gothic that it can do anything'.

75 George Aitchison, 59–61, Mark Lane, London (1864). Ruskinian office-building.

which reached its apogee with one very remarkable warehouse: The Granary, Welsh Back (1869–70)[74].[177] This was designed by a local firm, Ponton and Gough, for local clients, Messrs. Wait and Jones, with distinctly north Italian imagery – 'looking, in some lights', as Sir John Summerson puts it, 'like the palace of an eccentric doge with a prophetic passion for skyscrapers.'[178] Ten stories high; £6000 worth of brick, iron, timber and concrete; mechanically operated, with hydraulic lifts in each corner, feeding sliding containers which disgorged their contents – 12,000 quarters of wheat – through multicoloured portholes: north Italian prototypes have been industrialised, synthesised, abstracted.

Manchester and London never quite matched that. But they still possess a number of effective examples. Business premises like 73–5 Princess St, Manchester (1863), by Clegg and Knowles;[179] factories like Lavers and Barraud's stained glass works in Endell St, London, designed by R. J. Withers in 1859; or offices like several in the City of London: in Throgmorton St, by J. Chatfield Clarke (1869); in Poultry, by J. and J. Belcher

(1870) and R.H. Moore (1869); in Cannon St (1860) by Frederick Jameson. Anglo-Venetian Gothic lent itself admirably to the multiplied grid formation of urban commercial properties. The grid could be chopped into sections, or extended indefinitely, or even wrapped round corners, as at Albert Buildings in Queen Victoria St, London (1871), by F.J. Ward.[180]

It was left to George Aitchison, an enthusiast for Viollet-le-Duc, who as a young man had travelled with Burges in Italy, to carry the flexibility of the new style to its logical conclusion. At 59–61 Mark Lane[75] in the City of London, Aitchison designed a façade in 1864 consisting of three tiers of Byzantine-Gothic arches decorated with bands of inlaid black mastic. Behind, and independent of, the whole façade is an autonomous, fireproof structure of cast iron.[181] Ruskin's theory of the wall-veil – the façade as expressive skin, an idea derived from medieval Italy – had been turned to novel advantage. The future development of the Chicago skyscraper had been foreshadowed, in miniature, in a London City back street. With pardonable exaggeration, the work of Louis Sullivan has been called 'the culmination of Ruskinism'.[182]

By the late 1860s, the influence of neither Ruskin nor Viollet-le-Duc on Victorian architecture was clearly identifiable as such: both had been absorbed into the mainstream of eclectic historicism. The more one looks at the medieval sources of High Victorian Gothic, the more one realises that inspiration is very rarely direct. Compared with Puginian Gothic, compared still more with the precise archaeology of Georgian and Regency Neo-Classicism, High Victorian Gothic is consciously imprecise. That was why Robert Kerr called Ruskin 'the high priest of all latitudinarians'.[183] Ruskin's celebration of Romantic criteria in art – freedom, creativity, originality, subjectivity, imagination – had, paradoxically, released Victorian architecture from the incubus of historical orthodoxy. By comparison, the influence of Viollet-le-Duc was limited: Early French details were simply used in a Ruskinian way. As a prophet of evolutionary technology, Viollet became obsolete even in his own lifetime. But as the ultimate critic of industrial ethics, Ruskin's appeal increases with every passing year. In one respect, however, both men shared the same aim and the same failure: in the eyes of their contemporaries, both tried and failed to identify and propagate a truly nineteenth-century style. Classicism continued, but by the 1860s, it had been deserted by most of the pundits. English Gothic had been tried with Pugin. Italian Gothic had been tried with Ruskin. French Gothic had been tried with Viollet-le-Duc. Gilbert Scott tried all three at the same time. But where was the Victorian Style?

4 The Architect's Dilemma

'The peculiar characteristic of the present day, as compared with all former periods is this – that we are acquainted with the history of art'
(Gilbert Scott, 1857).

ARCHITECTURE IS TWO THINGS: it is service and it is art. Hence the tension between structure and appearance, function and form. Hence too the discord built into that eternal triangle: commodity, firmness and delight. Therein – at all times – lies the architect's dilemma. But during the nineteenth century that dilemma was compounded firstly by changing demands, secondly by advancing technology, and thirdly by the whole phenomenon of historicism: the multiplication of stylistic choice. The result was a crisis of confidence. In religion, literature and philosophy the mid-Victorian period was an age of doubt.[1] So too with architecture: even the greatest Victorian architecture was shot through with uncertainty. That uncertainty was the dilemma of style.

The Victorian obsession with the idea of a new style was itself new. Before the late eighteenth century, architectural style had generally been the accepted language of the age, even if that language itself had been historically based – as with the Renaissance or Palladianism – or subject to personal interpretation, like the Baroque or the Rococo. For the mid-Victorians such easy acceptance was inconceivable. 'Progress' was the air they breathed. Evolutionary thinking had gripped the minds of a generation. The impact of progressive historiography – history as an index of improvement – was inescapable. Romanticism had dissolved the classical tradition into a puzzling plurality of modes. The solution to that puzzle – the achievement of a new stylistic identity – seemed to lie in the paradox of finding a future in the past. But once the habit of looking back, for comparative or inspirational purposes, was established, spontaneous development became impossible. Innocence had been driven out by the possibility of choice. And choice had been complicated by the fragmentation of the productive process.[2] There could be no such thing as a Victorian vernacular.[3] Architecture could no longer evolve naturally because architects were aware of their own evolution. 'The peculiar characteristic of the present day, as compared with all former periods', confessed Gilbert Scott, 'is this – that we are acquainted with the history

98

of art.'[4] Or as Sir Edmund Beckett put it, 'In the days when there was real architecture there was no architectural philosophy.'[5] 'In primitive times', wrote Viollet-le-Duc, 'style imposed itself on the artist; today the artist has to rediscover style.'[6] Mid-Victorian architects faced a challenge unprecedented in scale and scope: new materials, new structural processes, new building-types.... new style?[7] That was the central problem of Victorian architecture.[8]

In 1847, in his influential *History of Christian Art*, Lord Lindsay called for 'a distinctly new style of architecture, expressive of the epoch in human progression of which Great Britain is the representative'. He looked at the Baptistery and Duomo at Pisa[76] – a legendary stylistic breakthrough – and then looked in vain for its nineteenth-century equivalent. Who would be the Victorian equal of that Pisan master, Buscheto the Greek?

76 Baptistery and Duomo, Pisa (11th–14th c). Where was its 19th-century equivalent?

> This ... is the problem – England wants a new Architecture, expressive of the epoch, of her Anglican faith and of the human mind as balanced in her development, as heir of the past and trustee for the future – a modification, it may be, of the Gothic, [but just] ... as the Gothic was a modification of the Lombard, the Lombard of the Byzantine and Roman, the Byzantine and Roman of the Classic Greek, the Greek of the Egyptian. We have a right to expect this from the importance of the epoch, and I see no reason why the Man to create it, the Buscheto of the nineteenth century, may not be among us at this moment, although we know it not.[9]

Lindsay's solution lay in synthesis: a proto-Hegelian dialectic – probably derived from Schiller and the Schlegels via Coleridge – based on what he called Progress by Antagonism.[10] In this case, presumably, a Victorian synthesis of Gothic and Classic.

Dialectical or not, evolution seemed to be the universal key. Everywhere, the logic of discovery, of progress, seemed irresistible. Science and technology, theology and metaphysics, breathed alike the same evolutionary ethos. Only architecture seemed to lag behind, limping along in the cast-off clothes of more creative generations. In 1851 the Royal Academy of Fine Arts in Munich offered a prize for an architectural design in a wholly new style.[11] At Antwerp, in 1861, an international 'artistic congress' was held to debate the great question: 'why our epoch, superior in so many respects to former centuries, has not its own particular form of architecture.'[12] Again and again, in lectures and letters, in books, pamphlets and periodicals, T. L. Donaldson's cry goes up: 'Are we to have an architecture of our period, a distinct, individual, palpable style of the nineteenth-century?'[13] In the 1850s and 1860s Anglo-Italian or Early French, or a mixture of both, had been chosen by the *avant-garde* as a chrysalis from which the butterfly of a new style might emerge. But the confidence of even the fiercest Goths in the validity of eclecticism was never absolute. To them, as to Victorian architects right across the spectrum, the new style still seemed as far away as some 'undiscovered Cape of Good Hope'.[14] 'We are oppressed', Ruskin confessed, 'by the bitter sense of inferiority ... we are walled in by the great buildings of other times, and their fierce reverberation falls upon us without pause, in our feverish and oppressive consciousness of captivity'.[15] 'The last fifty years' – he is speaking at the RIBA in 1865 – 'have produced more brilliant thought, and more subtle reasoning about art than the 5,000 years before them, and what has it all come to?'[16] Even Burges – the most belligerent supporter of Early French – could not escape the disease of his generation: doubt.[17] Gilbert Scott spoke for the middle-of-the-road man when he justified Gothic *faute de mieux*. 'I am no medievalist', he said; 'I do not advocate the styles of the middle ages as such. If we had a distinctive architecture of our own day, worthy of the greatness of the age, I should be content to follow it; but we have not.'[18] From its very first volume in 1843, the *Builder* consistently called for a new style: a style which would emerge 'from the workshop, the mine and the laboratory'. But by 1853 the same journal could see no way out of the 'dungeon' of archaeology.[19]

Despair was deepest among professors of architecture. 'This ... is a most critical period, announced Professor T. L. Donaldson in 1842: 'we are all ... in a state of transition; there is no fixed style now prevalent.... We are wandering in a labyrinth of experiments ... trying by ... amalgamation to form a homogeneous style.'[20] 'It is useless to deny', confessed Professor Sydney Smirke in 1864, 'that aesthetics generally have not kept pace with time.' There was only one hope, he felt: in eclecticism lay 'the best chance of ultimately arriving – it may be after a long purgatorial period of folly and excess – yet ultimately arriving at a sound, consistent and original style, worthy of the genius and civilisation of the nineteenth century.'[21] 'For three hundred years', Professor George Aitchison announced in 1891, 'the profession has been groping in the dark';[22] in fact 'architecture has been [lost] in a wood since the fifteenth century.'[23] Our 'epoch is that of ... science ... architecture is very low down.'[24] In fact, 'we have no architecture of the nineteenth century'.[25] The best 'architects of the day are ... ashamed of [the present] chaos of paraphrases'.[26] 'Like all the world', Aitchison had admitted in 1864, 'I am waiting for the new style which is to come.'[27] It never came, and by 1897 he had to confess: 'I am almost in despair.'[28] Unless we can escape from 'the present jumble of styles', the sheer 'chaos' of copyism, 'the sooner the whole [present] generation [of architects] is swept away ... the better'.[29] 'If architecture cannot progress', he concludes, 'it must be swept into the limbo where heraldry, necromancy, astrology, and perpetual motion now moulder in peace.'[30]

Aitchison was not some obscure, disgruntled architect. He was simultaneously Professor of Architecture at the Royal Academy, President of the RIBA, and Royal Gold Medallist.[31] His despair has to be taken seriously. Its roots lie, superficially, in the battle for status between architects and engineers; more deeply in the changing technology of construction; and, fundamentally, in the twofold nature of architecture itself – architecture as service and architecture as art: function *versus* form. For the Victorian architect, evolution – of function and form – was not a hypothesis but a necessity, not an abstraction but a daily challenge. At the Oxford Museum – scene of the great Apes *versus* Angels debate

77 I. K. Brunel, The Clifton Suspension Bridge, Bristol (1836–64).
'Surely the men who do these things are giants!'

in 1860[32] – Benjamin Woodward faced the challenge of evolutionary thinking more directly than either Huxley or Wilberforce. The 'science of the architect', noted one critic in 1864, 'is continually urging him onward ... his art ... is ever bidding him to look ... back.'[33] Such was the dilemma of style.

The dilemma of style was more fundamental than the Battle of Styles. The Battle of Styles – Gothic *versus* Classic – reached its peak in 1859–60, during the debate on the design of the Foreign Office, Whitehall. In that event the Goths were defeated by Lord Palmerston and the Classical lobby. But at the same time, a much more important debate was taking place: architecture *versus* engineering. In this debate the leading speaker is James Fergusson. He speaks for science, for engineering, for progress. He speaks, in effect, for Isambard Kingdom Brunel.[34]

'Within the last hundred years', announced Fergusson in 1863 – in a review of Samuel Smiles[35] – 'engineers have doubled the mechanical power, and more than doubled the productive resources of mankind.' Linked by steam and telegraph, 'a thousand million ... human beings ... can combine to ... effect any given object; the world looks forward to results ... such as have not yet been dreamt of in our philosophies.' Most wonderful of all is 'the express engine rushing past at a speed of fifty to sixty miles an hour.... Nothing that man has done comes so near the creation of an animal as this ... the great steam-engine factories ... are the glory of the mechanical engineer, and ... among the most remarkable triumphs of mind over matter that the world has yet witnessed.' In the cotton mills of England, thirty million spindles ply; 'fairy fabrics are spun and woven by an iron beast as heavy and as strong as fifty elephants.' At sea paddle steamers give promise of ocean-going vessels almost without 'practical limit'. From the Ganges Canal in India to the Dnieper Viaduct in Russia, communication has been revolutionised. Vast harbours and cyclopean breakwaters create 'calmness and shelter in the midst of tempest'. Lighthouses – 'the most perfect specimens of modern architecture' – 'send their rays through the darkness with ... space-penetrating power'. Viaducts, tunnels and bridges of stupendous size[77] have been achieved, annihilating the Menai Straits or even the Alps. 'If any one had proposed twenty years ago to throw a railway bridge over ... Niagara, he would have been looked on as a madman. Yet this has been accomplished.' In railway stations, too, the engineer has 'conquered space ... there is no practical limit to the extent of our roofs'. As for the electric telegraph, it has made 'London and New York ... within speaking distance' of each other. 'Surely the men who do these things are giants!' All honour, therefore, to 'that noble example of the dominion of man over the earth – the science of Engineering.'[36]

But what of architecture? For Fergusson, real architecture had been undermined in the age of Renaissance, and destroyed in the age of Revival. In the sixteenth century, 'men forsook the principles on which [architecture] had been practised from the beginning of time ... in order to reproduce certain associations with which education had made them familiar.' Thus, 'a Technic art came to be cultivated on principles which belong only to one of the Phonetic class' – that is, architecture, a functional art, had come to be treated as a communicating art like speaking, writing, painting or sculpture. More important, architecture – a co-operative art – had been confused with individual creativity. Hence the continuity of ancient architecture, and the discontinuity – the fashion-show – of modern architecture.[37]

What was the result? Today, he concludes, 'we have no Style of architecture, and of the two absurdities [Greek and Gothic Revivals] the Gothic is perhaps less absurd', being based on models rather nearer to the nineteenth century.[38] There was only one hope: the RIBA 'must write over its doors, "Archaeology is not Architecture".'[39] Alas, 'the building profession is divided against itself.' While engineers challenge the future, architects cower in the past. And who is to blame? 'Architects', Fergusson concedes, 'would delight in the reunion of architecture and engineering' –

78 Adam Anderson, Water
Works, Perth (1832). Engineering
in Classical dress.

79 Pumping Station, Streatham Common,
London (1888). Engineering in Islamic dress.

after all, architects and engineers only broke away from each other at
the end of the eighteenth century.[40] Professional separation dated only
from the 1830s. It was public preference[41] which forced engineers into
fancy dress, producing water works – for example – in Classical, Islamic,
Byzantine or Baronial garb.[78][79][42] It was the public's conception of
status which persuaded the Institution of Civil Engineers to choose a
Classical building by Charles Barry Jnr as its London headquarters.[43] It
was public taste which lured a shipping magnate like Temple into living
in a fairytale retreat at Leyswood, Sussex (1866–73);[44] or an armaments
king like Armstrong into building an Old English fantasy at Cragside,
Northumberland (1869–84).[130] Even the great Brunel collected medieval and renaissance antiquities.[45]

The task, as Fergusson saw it, was therefore twofold. Firstly, persuasion: Fergusson neutralising Ruskin; secondly, example: Stephenson
and Brunel neutralising Burges, Street and Butterfield. The grand strategy
was clear: 'To call architecture back within the domain of logic and
common sense'.[46] Only then will the new style appear. But that new style
will apparently be worth waiting for: 'that style will not only be perfectly

suited to all our wants and desires, but also more beautiful and perfect than any that has ever existed before'.[47]

There is a touching simplicity about Fergusson's faith in technology. But his methodology is at fault: architecture is both Technic and Phonetic. By seemingly separating architecture as service from architecture as art he fell right into the functionalist fallacy. And his optimism does not extend to concrete suggestions about style.[48] In fact his speculations on the future of architecture add up to little more than bombastic hypotheses.[49] For all his brave words about function, Fergusson's commitment to ornament – and historic ornament at that – was just as deep as that of his contemporaries. That certainly is the message of the very few architectural designs which he did himself produce. In 1857, in the Battle of the Styles, he placed himself on the side of the Classicists; and a Classicist, in essence, he remained, albeit an eclectic. Still, to the public at large he was the man who championed the Crystal Palace.

The Crystal Palace was really the climax of a long tradition of conservatory design: the hot-house at Kew Gardens (1844–8) by Turner and Burton being simply the best known example[80]. In 1837 J. C. Loudon had forecast that the coming age of iron would mean an end to all established architectural systems: 'all habitual notions of ... proportion must, of course, be discarded'. Instead of adapting 'the new material to their designs', architects would have to 'adapt their designs to the new

80 Richard Turner and Decimus Burton, Hot House, Kew Gardens (1844–8). New materials, new forms.

81 T. C. Hine, Flintham Hall, Notts. (1853–7). Juxtaposition rather than integration.

material'.[50] On the whole, however, glass and iron remained extraneous to architectural composition: at Flintham Hall, Notts, for instance (1853–7 by T. C. Hine)[81], the conservatory is juxtaposed rather than integrated in the design.[51] Pugin seems to have been as confused as anyone on this issue. For him, architecture and engineering were poles apart. 'No engineer', he wrote, 'ever was a decent architect, and if they attempted Gothic it would be frightful.'[52] Yet when he saw the railway stations on the line from Strasbourg to Mannheim, designed by Friedrich Eisenlohr[82], he told Sir Charles Barry they were 'the best modern architecture' he had ever seen. 'The stations are beautiful', he wrote in 1845, 'all constructive principle. If the roofs had a higher pitch, they would be almost perfect.'[53] Presumably they satisfied Pugin's doctrine of function – just as much as his own masonry designs for railway structures. But Pugin's other doctrines of propriety and hierarchy in building and architecture quite prohibited him from integrating architecture and engineering. And there, in Pugin's confusion, lay the origins of the Victorian dilemma.

Pugin filled the Medieval Court of the Great Exhibition with Gothic exhibits. But when he was introduced to Sir Joseph Paxton and asked what he thought of that knighted gardener's Crystal Palace, he replied: 'Think? Why that you had better keep to building greenhouses, and I will keep to my churches and cathedrals.'[54] In private he talked of that 'glass horror', that 'crystal humbug', that 'glass monster ... as friendly and intimate as Salisbury Plain'.[55]

The Crystal Palace (1851–4)[83] seemed to lie outside the world of architecture, outside even the world of engineering. The criteria by which it might be judged still awaited formulation. In Hitchcock's words, Paxton's scheme 'owed its aesthetic qualities to factors hitherto unrecognised – the repetition of units manufactured in series, the functional lace-like patterns of criss-cross trusses, the transparent definition of space, the total elimination of mass and the sense of tensile, almost live, strength as opposed to the solid and gravitational quality of previous masonry architecture'.[56] The vocabulary of a machine aesthetic had yet to be developed.

When the Crystal Palace was transferred from Hyde Park to Sydenham in 1852, its most significant permanent exhibits were a series of *tableaux*, or period courts, each one encapsulating a phase in architectural history. Fergusson and Layard designed the Nineveh Court. Owen Jones designed the Greek Court, the Roman Court, the Egyptian Court and the Moorish Court or Alhambra[84]. Matthew Digby Wyatt was responsible for Pompeii, Renaissance Italy and Byzantium, as well as for the Medieval

82 F. Eisenlohr, Freiburg Station (1845; dem.). Pugin thought it 'the best modern architecture'.

83 Sir Joseph Paxton, Crystal Palace, Sydenham (1851–4). Criteria for judging it were still unformed.

84 Owen Jones, Moorish Court, Crystal Palace. Replicated archaeology.

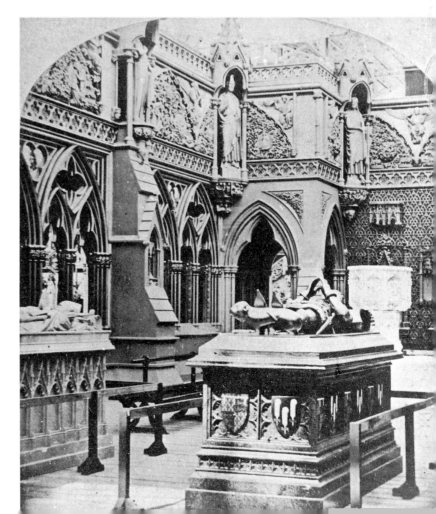

85 M. D. Wyatt, Medieval Court, Crystal Palace. 'Is Architecture behind the Age?'

Court[85] – divided into German, French, Italian, and English sections. English Gothic was represented by facsimiles of a doorway from Tintern Abbey, statues from Westminster and Wells, and cloister arcades from Guisborough Priory.[57] In the eyes of the public Paxton's marvel of pre-fabrication was as nothing to these marvels of replicated archaeology. 'Is Architecture Behind the Age?' asked the *Building Chronicle*. Will 'our greatness and *our* sense of beauty ... be equally acknowledged ... in some future museum'?[58] The question was confusing for pundit and patron alike. In 1855 the Duke of Devonshire, Paxton's principal sponsor, arrived at Lismore Castle in Ireland, and saw for the first time its new-built battlements bristling high above the Blackwater. 'Go, Crystal Palace', he scoffed; 'What are you to this quasi-feudal, ultra-royal fortress?'[59]

One of the few thinkers to grapple with the aesthetic implications of new structural techniques was Edward Lacy Garbett. From eighteenth-century theorists he borrowed the idea of associational aesthetics. From Fergusson he borrowed the idea of phonetic art; from Bartholomew the idea of constructive unity; from Pugin the idea of expressive ornament; from Ruskin the idea of didactic art. And to all these he added ideas of his own: architecture as a polite art (i.e. environmentally conscious); architecture as a learned art (i.e. eclectically evolved); and, above all, architecture as a structural art (i.e. tectonically determined). Garbett's *Rudimentary Treatise on the Principles of Design in Architecture* (1850; revised 1863) divided the whole of recorded architectural history into three phases: 'The DEPRESSILE, the COMPRESSILE, and the TENSILE methods – the *beam*, the *arch*, the *truss*'; of which the two former, he claimed, 'have been made the basis of past systems [Greek and Gothic]: the third is ours ... Let us not mistake what we have to do. It ... has been done only twice before: in the time of Dorus and in the thirteenth century.... Let us not deceive ourselves: a style never grew of itself; it never will. It *must* be sought, and sought the right way.... A new style requires the generalised imitation of nature and of *many* previous styles; and a new system requires, in addition to this, the binding of all together by a new principle of unity, clearly understood, agreed upon, and kept constantly in view.'[60]

Garbett's logic was impeccable. His thinking might have supplied a link between Technic and Phonetic; between rationalists and romantics: between Classical eclectics like Fergusson and Gothic eclectics like Beresford Hope. Indeed Garbett was the ultimate eclectic. To the question, when is eclecticism more than copyism, he answered, in effect, when it is universal: 'every style ... every accessible source of artistic precedent

... from old Egypt or young America, from polished Greece or the savage isles of the south [seas] ... all ground down and assimilated in the powerful transforming gizzard of some great ... nameless artist.'[61] Engineering was only one element in the new synthesis, for to Garbett engineering was simply 'de-decorative or man-beaver architecture'.[62] Ruskin considered Garbett's arguments weighty enough to justify a separate reply as an appendix to the *Stones of Venice*.[63] But we hear little more of Garbett. He ended his days a forgotten guru, writing pamphlets on biblical exegesis.[64]

'Engineering of the highest merit and excellence, but not architecture.'[65] That was the *Ecclesiologist's* view of the Crystal Palace. 'Not architecture but a packing case.'[66] That was Garbett's opinion. And Ruskin did not disagree. In the days of the Oxford Museum he had been willing to give iron a fair chance. By 1880 he had given up hope. 'The ferruginous temper', he noted, 'which I saw rapidly developing itself' thirty years ago, has 'since that day ... changed our Merry England into the Man in the Iron Mask'.[67] Like Pugin, Ruskin was willing to accept iron, but only in disguise: as a cement but not as a support, for binding but not for propping. In one unguarded moment he confessed that 'the time is probably near when a new system of architectural laws will be developed, adapted entirely to metallic construction'.[68] But in general his thinking denied such a possibility. A real architecture of glass and iron, he claimed, was 'eternally impossible'. His reasoning ran as follows. Colour and form were the only 'means of delight in all productions of art.... Form is only expressible in its perfection, on opaque bodies, without lustre.... All noble architecture depends for its majesty upon its form: therefore you can never have any noble architecture in transparent or lustrous glass or enamel. Iron is, however, opaque ... and, therefore, fit to receive noble form' – but only 'as noble as cast or struck architecture can ever be: as noble, therefore, as coins can be, or common cast bronzes, and such other multiplicable things – eternally separated from all good and great things by a gulph which not all the tubular bridges nor engineering of ten thousand nineteenth centuries cast into one great bronze-foreheaded century, will ever overpass one inch of.' Thus to Ruskin the Crystal Palace was not Art – that is, the expression of genius, labour and love. Its value as an emanation of humanity was negligible. Its worth consisted merely in one 'single ... thought' by Paxton – its ridge and furrow glazing – plus 'some very ordinary algebra'.[69]

That had been Pugin's position. 'Mechanical improvements' are very useful things, he wrote, but we must 'not allow *mere mechanism* to usurp the place of art'.[70] For Ruskin too, whole areas of building lay simply outside the realm of architecture. 'There is a general law', he wrote, 'of particular importance to the age in which we live, namely not to decorate things belonging to purposes of active and occupied life.... Wherever you can rest, there decorate; where rest is forbidden, so is beauty: you must not mix ornament with business.'[71] Even Fergusson, who in 1851 had hailed the Crystal Palace as the start of a new era,[72] came very close to agreeing with that. 'Where the engineer leaves off', noted Fergusson, 'the art of architecture begins.'[73] Lutyens himself would have said the same – and did so: 'architecture begins where function ends'.[74]

Fergusson defined architecture as the 'art of ornamental and ornamented construction'.[75] 'A work of art', he claimed, 'is valuable in the direct ratio of the quantity and quality of the thought it contains.'[76] And that thought must be aesthetic rather than mechanical: 'the satisfactory architectural effect of a building is nearly in the reverse ratio to the mechanical cleverness displayed in its construction.'[77] Hence the necessity for architects as well as engineers, 'to elaborate Building ... into Architecture'.[78] Lacking that additional quality, the Crystal Palace cannot really be Architecture at all: it is 'not ornamental to such an extent', says Fergusson, that it is elevated 'into the class of the Fine Arts.'[79] 'Art ... will not be regenerated by buildings so ephemeral as Crystal Palaces, or so prosaic as Manchester warehouses, nor anything so essentially utilitarian as the works of our engineers.'[80] So here again, even in Fergusson, we see Puginian notions of propriety and hierarchy at odds with Puginian rationality: hence the dilemma.

Leo von Klenze took the same restricted view. 'Paxton', he announced in 1854, 'conceived his task like a gardener.'[81] Viollet-le-Duc thought much the same.[82] So did César Daly.[83] 'Architecture', it was claimed in 1879, 'is educated engineering.'[84] That was the nub of the matter. A kind of professional apartheid set up social and linguistic barriers which were then piled high with cultural luggage. As the Victorian architect grew in status – further away from the builder, the surveyor, the engineer – the problem of style became increasingly intractable. At the end of the century, the *Building News* counted the cost: 'the separation of these functions' – professionalising the separation of reason and imagination – 'has been the means of covering our land with abortions and monstrosities.' In engineering, 'the iron fiend has triumphed; practical utility of unmitigated crudeness and barbarity has been asserted.' In architecture, 'ornamented construction' is the order of the day, 'worse, if possible, than "constructed ornament".'[85] If only both engineers and architects had acknowledged their interdependence: after all, 'engineering is construction; architecture is grace'.[86] To the church architect, and the 'Art

Architect' in particular, most engineering was simply 'uncivil'.[87] And innovations of the Crystal Palace kind were simply 'inventions'.

Such thinking certainly carried the day in the 1850s and 1860s. When J. B. Waring attempted to form what he called 'a style of my own', he did it by synthesising historic styles, rather than by integrating architecture and engineering. His *Designs for Civic Architecture* (1850) go some way towards creating fresh combinations of new materials and historic forms.[88] But his scheme for the reconstruction of Burlington House, Piccadilly, as a National Institute of Art and Science, was an indigestible conflation of Classic, Saracenic, Byzantine, Italian and Gothic.[86][89] T. Mellard Reade's eclectic *Suggestions for the Formation of a New Style of Architecture especially adapted to Civic Purposes* (1862) was no more successful.[90] Nor were John Cotton's *Suggestions in Architectural Design: prefaced with Thoughts on Architectural Progress* (1896): they began at

86 J. B. Waring, Burlington House, Piccadilly (1850; unexecuted). A design in 'a style of my own'.

the wrong end of the conundrum, toying with new details instead of formulating new links between form and structure.[91] Those who campaigned for a wholly new 'Metallurgic Architecture', like William Vose Pickett in England or Jean-Baptiste Jobard in France, were dismissed as eccentrics.[92] Outsiders like the inventor W. Bridges Adams might applaud Pickett's plan for an iron and glass Regent Street Quadrant, or a prefabricated, exportable Regent's Park Colosseum;[93] but the architectural profession was implacable. T. L. Donaldson made sure that Pickett's ideas were never seriously considered by the RIBA.[94] 'I do not believe', Street announced flatly in 1852, that such systems 'constitute architecture at all.'[95] L. A. Boileau's 'synthetic' churches of stone and iron aroused only vicious hostility among English and French critics.[87][96] Paxton remained the only major prophet of what Fergusson called 'Ferro-Vitreous Art'. The others remained fantasists.

The architectural establishment was embarrassed by the whole subject. At Paddington Station (1853–4) the mastermind is Brunel; Owen Jones and Digby Wyatt are reduced to the level of interior decorators.[97] Digby Wyatt's metalwork there was certainly original in form, but at least one critic noticed that it was 'designed on the principle of avoiding recourse to precedent' not on the principle of exploiting 'the peculiarities' of the material.[98] Gilbert Scott admitted that metallic construction opened out 'a perfectly new field for architectural development'.[99] But it was not a field which he ploughed with either consistency or conviction. At Brighton, his Brill's Baths building boasted an iron-framed Gothic dome.[100] His staircase in St Pancras Hotel[88] incorporates exposed cast iron beams with flamboyant confidence. And along the platforms of St Pancras Station he forces Gothic arcades to mingle with the ribs of Barlow's gigantic train shed on terms of heroic equality. But, in general, Scott played safe. His decorated iron girders at Kelham Hall, Notts (1858–62), scarcely go beyond the principle of Butterfield's Gothicised iron beams in the presbytery (1850) at All Saints, Margaret St. And his secret use of iron in the Albert Memorial (1863–72) aroused accusations not only of illogicality but of immorality.[101]

There was one way out of the dilemma. But Victorian architects were not yet ready to take it – or rather they were not yet ready to admit that they had already taken it. Namely to treat decoration as symbol rather than expression; to abandon the attempt to integrate structure and ornament; to treat ornament as all classical architects had treated it ever

88 Sir Gilbert Scott, Staircase, Midland Hotel, St Pancras (1865–74).
'A new field for architectural development'?

89 Thomas Telford, Conway Suspension Bridge
(1821–6). A bridge in the spirit of a castle.

since the Renaissance, simply as a visual language, with its own canons
of coherence, based on the aesthetics of association. Above all, to remember that architecture is not simply a mechanical contrivance but an essay
in the art of communication, a complex web of memories and messages.
That was what Telford had realised at Conway in 1821–6, when he
created a suspension bridge in the spirit of a castle[89]. That was what
Pennethorne did at the Public Record Office, London (1851–66)[90].
Pennethorne's fireproof cast iron structure is as rationalist as its modern
neighbours. But its Gothic skin consists of ornament by *association*: after
all, it houses a great collection of medieval manuscripts. Pennethorne's
symbolism is extrinsic rather than intrinsic. It scarcely develops structural
metaphor. But thinking along these lines might well have solved the
dilemma a hundred years sooner. The intellectual ingredients were there,
for example, in Semper's theory of sartorial form: human costumes,
Semper explained, 'clothe the naked form with elucidating symbolism'.[102]
Alas, the Victorians were not yet ready for semiotics: the science of signs
and symbols. If they had been, they might have been able to bridge
Fergusson's artificial gap between Technic and Phonetic.[103]

Some philosophers tell us that semiology is a spurious system because it cannot be universalised without becoming meaningless. But in a limited way it can help us to understand architecture, and it might have helped the Victorians to understand their predicament. One or two architects were beginning to fight their way through by means of 'the transmission theory of style': that is, Semper's theory of an evolutionary process in which functional elements – as in Greek architecture – survive as symbols.[104] The trouble was that Pugin had muddied the waters for them by confusing function and propriety. Take the famous contrast of Cubitt's

90 Sir James Pennethorne, Public Record Office, London (1851–66). Fireproof structure; ornament by association.

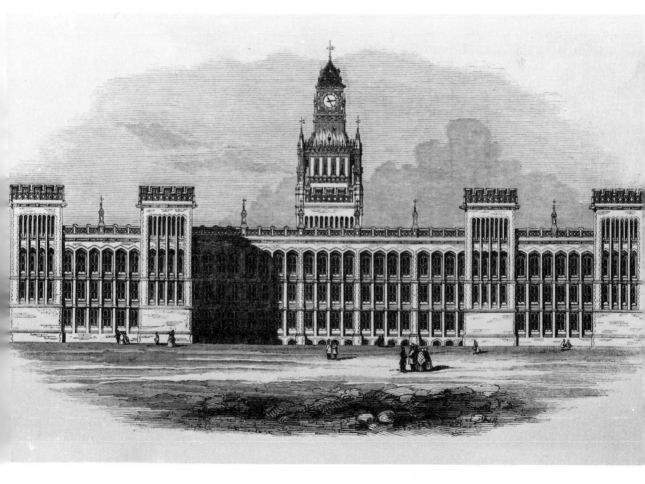

91 (a) & (b) Lewis Cubitt, King's Cross Station, London (1851–2).
'A railway station in working dress'.

King's Cross (1851–2)[91] and Scott's St Pancras (1865–74)[92] – a
debatable contrast, of course, because we are comparing a station with
a hotel. Still, a useful comparison. Both conceal their structure. Both
make use of structural metaphors, though the metaphors at St Pancras
have become a little mixed. But their language of metaphor – of concealment – is different: Cubitt's Neo-Classicism – French, in the manner
of Durand, with Italianate touches derived from Parker's *Villa Rustica*

92 Sir Gilbert Scott, St Pancras Station and Midland Hotel (1865–74). 'A business man's hotel'.

(1832–41) and Loudon's *Encyclopaedia* (1832) – makes a nice pretence of function, according to Laugier's doctrine of 'apparent utility'. Its façade is a simulacrum of utility. It announces: 'I am a railway station in working dress'. That is one sort of propriety. By comparison, Scott's Neo-Gothicism stakes all on another sort of propriety – an image of luxury, prestige and cosmopolitan sophistication: it announces, 'I am an international business man's hotel'. But Scott – and still more his critics, then and since – suffered agonies of doubt, over the sins of suppressed functionalism. In fact, Scott's generation – victims of the Puginian dilemma – were trying to square the circle: to find a new style in the past, *and* to equate function and propriety. No wonder they thought they failed.

Such major attempts as there were, to integrate new materials and old forms, proved mostly disappointing. Of course the Oxford Museum[93] became a legend: an attempt by 'an architect of genius – who died while his genius was unripe – [at] devising "an iron style".'[105] In 1855 it had been hailed as 'an experiment ... of the greatest importance to architecture'; an attempt 'to try how Gothic art could deal with those railway materials, iron and glass'.[106] Alas, most commentators agreed that the result was a disappointing pastiche, this time in metal rather than stone. The *Building News* was correct in its prediction that Skidmore's roof would 'not convert the world to a belief in the universal applicability of Crystal Palace architecture Gothicised.'[107] 'We consider the principle of [Skidmore's iron roofing] to be erroneous', the *Ecclesiologist* concluded in 1861. After all, this is merely a stone-vaulting system in iron. 'The shafts, arches and ribs all follow the type of a stone construction. The effect is fairy-like, we admit; and some of the perspectives are exceedingly novel and striking. But the doubt recurs whether after all this is a proper metallic construction.... The domical treatment of [Sydney Smirke's] magnificent round reading room of the British Museum (1851–7) is far more satisfactory.... [Besides at Oxford] the iron roof and the ... sides of the quadrangle ... are not blended together, but are planned in crude juxtaposition.... The problem has been beyond the powers of ... Messrs Deane and Woodward, who have been entrusted with the perilous honour of developing the unknown capacities of a new style'.[108]

It had also been beyond the capacities of the ecclesiologists themselves: their prototype Iron Church, designed in 1855 by Slater and Carpenter, suffered from much the same defects.[109] It was 'an attempt', they admitted, 'to show how a churchlike building may be constructed in iron.'[110] It was 'a stone church built in iron', rather 'than a design built on purely metallic principles'. Once again, Puginian propriety had overcome Puginian rationality. The result certainly was not beautiful. W. Vose Pickett was damning: 'there could scarcely be, in the whole range of construction', he says, 'anything so repulsive as the exterior of this church.'[111] It appealed neither to the eye nor to the intellect. Contemporary railway structures – Brunel's Royal Albert Bridge at Saltash, Cornwall (1857–9), for example – at least appealed to the intellect. But they made little appeal to the eye. That indeed was the problem: sheer utility *may* be beautiful; but its beauty is contingent, not necessary. The Modern Movement has taught us that lesson. And the lesson was already there for those who cared to read their Ruskin: 'All architecture proposes an effect on the human mind, not merely a service to the human frame'.[112] Unfortunately for architecture, since Ruskin's time the utilitarians have

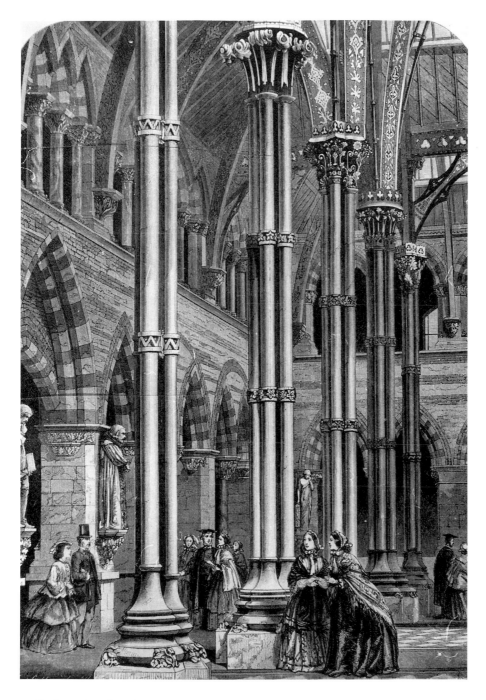

93 Benjamin Woodward and Skidmore of Coventry, University Museum, Oxford. (1854–60). 'An iron style'?

94 Sir J. Fowler, Sir B. Baker *et al.*, The Forth Bridge, nr Edinburgh (1882–90). Functional demands balanced by aesthetic choice.

had the best of the argument. Beresford Hope, for example, admitted that a new style based on Paxton's Crystal Palace was simply beyond his understanding: 'As to the Crystal Cathedral, I must humbly say that I cannot grasp so novel an idea'.[113] Gottfried Semper was stating no more than the truth when he remarked that in many cases, 'faced with such a material [as iron], a stylist's mind ceases to function'.[114] When steel replaced iron during the 1880s the architect's dilemma was merely reinforced.

95 Sir Horace Jones and Sir John Wolfe Barry, Tower Bridge, London (1886–94). Function overwhelmed by associations.

96 H. Heathcote Statham,
Tower Bridge improved (1897).

SKETCH·FOR·TOWER·BRIDGE·SHOWING·
SUSPENSION·CHAINS·CARRIED·BY·THE·
MASONRY··THE·INNER·GIRDER·OF·HIGH·
LEVEL·BRIDGE·SHOWN·VISIBLY·AS·THE·
CARRIER·OF·THE·TENSION·CHAIN ::

For most Victorian architects, a structure without decorative expression was no more beautiful than a skeleton without flesh and blood. But the logic of that viewpoint beckoned enticingly towards the absurd: away from the Forth Bridge, towards Tower Bridge.[115] Now the Forth Bridge (Sir J. Fowler *et al*: 1882–90)[94] has often been seen as a paradigm of utilitarian design. In fact only its upper arcades owe their shape to functional demands; the shape of the lower arcades reflects aesthetic choice. But in the case of Tower Bridge (Sir Horace Jones and Sir John Wolfe Barry, 1886–94)[95], that element of aesthetic choice has indeed run riot. The balance between tectonic and atectonic factors has been upset. Associational criteria – reverberations of the adjacent Tower of London – have completely overwhelmed the still small voice of function.[116] Statham, editor of the *Builder*, called it 'a gigantic and tawdry sham'. Not only was the steel structure concealed by the masonry towers, but these were in turn made to support – quite fictionally – the massive suspension chains of the bridge. 'Either the bridge should have been built frankly as a steel bridge', Statham explained, 'or the masonry towers should have been genuine monumental structures carrying the high level bridge and the suspension chains.' So he produced a design of his own[96] which attempted to square the circle. The ends of the high-level girders are carried through the masonry towers, and then visibly attached to the suspension chains: honesty plus monumentality.[117]

123

Few Victorian architects were as ingenious, or as persistent. Most lost what little faith they had in the new materials. Some, like Aitchison, continued to chew at the problem.[118] Most threw in their hands. Owen Jones, for instance. As a radical young architect, imbued with the scientific materialism of Saint-Simon and Fourier, Auguste Comte and César Daly, he too had called in 1835 for a new style. 'Mammon is the god', he announced; 'Industry and Commerce are [now] the high priests'; works worthy of the new age can only stem 'from the triumvirate [of] Science, Commerce and Industry'.[119] In middle age, as 'Alhambra Jones', he certainly dreamed of vast Paxtonian structures like the Great Northern Palace at Muswell Hill (1859) or the exhibition building at St Cloud in Paris (c.1860).[120] One of his commercial arcades even managed to force the new technology into the trilobe roof-shape of S. Zeno, Verona. But he ended as an interior decorator at the Charing Cross Hotel, working for plutocrats like Alfred Morrison of Fonthill. By 1864 he looked about him and saw only 'confusion' and 'disorder': 'no doubt', he concluded lamely, 'the future will produce a better style.'[121] His unexecuted scheme of 1865 for the Midland Hotel at St Pancras[97] – Second Empire Classicism overwhelmed by Barlow's colossal train-shed – sums up the unequal struggle between architecture and engineering in the mid-Victorian period.[122] No wonder he suffered from what *The Architect* called 'the self-doubting of a fastidious intelligence'.[123]

After 1855, and still more after 1870, building regulations in London actively discouraged the use of exposed-iron construction. Fire hazards, and the dangers of oxidisation and fragmentation, inhibited easy acceptance of the new material. By the 1870s not only had the search for an iron architecture been abandoned, a series of spectacular failures – at the Surrey Music Hall, for example – had gone some way towards discrediting iron construction altogether. Steel was by then the material of the future.[124] G. E. Street dismissed the search for a new, metallic architecture as 'a wild goose chase'. If people really wanted to see logical and characteristic examples of metallic design, he claimed, they had only to visit a few of the public lavatories of London – like the cast iron *pissoir* behind the Law Courts, probably designed by Matthew Digby Wyatt.[125] In 1853 he had justified the use of Gothic on technological grounds: the pointed arch had superseded the lintel. 'That architecture', he claimed, 'cannot be the best which is content to forego the use of the greatest mechanical advantages and inventions.'[126] Fair enough, but what about iron? Street believed it was better for an architect to stick to 'the materials which God had given him – brick, stone and wood'. 'The field of discovery in architecture', he believed, 'is exhausted. It is undeniable, as Ruskin tells

97 Owen Jones, Unexecuted scheme for St Pancras (1865).
'No doubt the future will produce a better style'.

us, that no principle of construction has been discovered for centuries ...
[in fact] Gothic architects have left nothing to be found out worth
finding.'[127] He had no time for iron construction: 'I do not believe that it
is architecture at all. It is simply engineering.' And 'ugliness' was 'the
very essence of engineers' structures'.[128]

For Street, 'iron architecture' was a contradiction in terms. He regarded
the use of hidden metallic construction as 'hateful' because it falsified the
evidence of the eye. An architect's 'great object', he believed, 'was to
show construction, and not to conceal it.' Now concealed construction
was certainly a denial of Puginian theory: a new structural system would
ultimately mean a new aesthetic system. Iron architecture would, one
day, simply mean iron used architecturally. In theory, Street was all in
favour of adapting 'our architecture to every want of this nineteenth and
most exigent of centuries.'[129] He was all for originality: 'Oh ... for the
days when men shall have cast off their dependence on other men's
works.'[130] He even used exposed ironwork himself in the great library at
Dunecht, Aberdeenshire (1867–81).[131] But he felt there was something
almost sinful about an architect employing iron girders. 'Whenever he
had introduced them', he confessed, 'he felt conscious of having done
something which he ought not to have done.' Meanwhile, 'designs in
iron' – like the iron-fronted houses in New York – made him 'ashamed
for the future'. In effect, he had really refused to think about the subject:
so much so that he quaintly assumed that Barlow's great train shed at
St Pancras sported a pointed profile on associational grounds.[132]

William White felt much the same: iron was suitable only for the baser
sorts of building, the lower ranges of the architectural hierarchy: large-

scale, utilitarian structures – factories or bridges, for instance. 'Where was the massiveness so essential to architecture – the bulk – above everything else, the shadow? How could there be architecture without shadow?'[133] 'Ferrotecture' and architecture were fundamentally different systems: 'ironwork must always be rigid, cramped and attenuated in its proportions, and, from its nature as a metal, was unfit for domestic uses ... the massiveness, the bulk, the play of light and shade, the superposition, which were essential features of architecture, could only be given to iron construction by destroying its leading characteristics. Indeed, were iron generally used for buildings, architecture would be extinguished.'[134] Iron may well be the key to the future, White concludes; but 'so far as I am concerned, it may predominate in Utopia!'[135]

Such attitudes as these help to explain the apparently destructive atavism of the mid-Victorian architectural profession. We need not be too surprised at their intellectual blinkers. Like representational painters after the invention of photography, they could hardly be expected to jettison the accumulated wisdom of several thousand years in return for a few crumbs of experimental science. Victorian architects clung to pre-industrial aesthetics in a mid-industrial world, just as today perhaps we cling to Christian ethics in a post-Christian society. They turned their backs on the implications of contemporary technology, and sought salvation in an eclecticism of the past. But that decision was only the start of their problems, for – as Beresford Hope put it – what were they to eclect?[136]

That was the headache – what Sir Ernst Gombrich has christened 'the neuralgic point' of nineteenth-century aesthetics.[137] That headache lingered on for a generation, from the 1840s to the 1860s. Then, in the 1870s, architects began to think that they had found a cure: they simply pretended the headache wasn't there. Well, it didn't work. By the 1880s it was clear that the search for a new style was never going to succeed. Now that is not at all the same thing as saying that Victorian architecture was itself a failure. Far from it. But Victorian architects had failed, on their own terms, in the object they set themselves. But the object they set themselves was, in a sense, unnecessary. They set out to establish a style of architecture characteristic of, and suitable to, the needs, values, materials and ethos of their own age. Looking at their work today, that is precisely what we see. As Sir Arthur Elton observed, in one particular instance, 'the style of Butterfield was the nineteenth-century style'.[138] Victorian architects found a Victorian architecture all right. But it was not the architecture they were looking for. They found it in spite of themselves. What they found was a method rather than a style, an attitude of mind rather than a structural system: the historicist approach; the matrix for a multitude of styles. Robert Kerr called it the '*Omnium Gatherum Victorianum*.'[139][98]

As a young man, in 1850, Kerr had tried his hand at novelty: he exhibited a design for a public building composed of colonnades linked by single sheets of plate glass.[140] But by the end of his life he had emerged as the most vocal exponent of latitudinarianism. In that latitudinarian approach – the acceptance of plurality of style; a tendency Kerr identified in Ruskin – lay the only valid escape from Pugin's procrustean logic. For eclecticism is the vernacular of sophisticates, and plurality is the price of freedom. Walter Pater sensed this in 1874. 'The nineteenth century too', he wrote, 'will be found to have had its style, justified by necessity ... an intellectually rich age such as ours [is] necessarily an eclectic one.'[141] Back in 1859 the American architect Henry Van Brunt had called for 'a representative architecture', representative of an age of iron, an age of machines, an age of collectivism – of 'aggregates rather than individualities'.[142] But by 1886 he too had settled for the 'chaos' of libertarian aesthetics: in the 'inchoate, nebulous mass' of late nineteenth-century design, posterity will discern 'not a style ... but ... a sort of architectural

98 H. W. Brewer, Fifty Years of Victorian Architecture (1843–93). 'The Omnium Gatherum Victorianum'.

constellation . . . [a] reflection of the spirit of the times in which we live.'[143] Robert Kerr got it right in the end: late Victorian England – capitalist, imperialistic, liberal – found its ultimate aesthetic expression in the architecture of *laissez-faire*. And that process – architectural free trade – found its ideal medium in the architectural competition.[144]

Of course it was heady stuff, and some architects lost their balance. Faced with a veritable cornucopia of seductive precedents, Fergusson had called for abstinence and a steady nerve: 'the great want now', he wrote, 'is self control'.[145] But instead of self-control, the journals of the 1880s and 1890s positively pullulate with the indulgent aestheticism of Queen Anne and her uglier sisters.[146]

At his death in 1886, the *Builder* – loyal for nearly half a century – called Fergusson the Vitruvius of the modern world.[147] But he too had clearly failed to solve the artistic conundrum of the nineteenth century. In the end he shrugged off responsibility altogether; he felt it was up to the great British public to go back to the Renaissance and bring forth truth, to square the aesthetic circle by finding the future in the past.[148] But the public showed little sign of dissatisfaction. In fact its capacity to digest historical motifs seemed insatiable. In 1880–1, for instance, four bizarrely related structures were rising simultaneously in Oxford: a rustic cricket pavilion (T. G. Jackson), an Old English boat-club (J. Oldrid Scott), a Jacobean barge (J. Oldrid Scott) and a castellated mess-room for military cadets (Ingress Bell).[149] Associationist thinking had become generalised as a collective state of mind. Morris turned to revolution: in social revolution he saw the only hope of 'a new and living style'.[150] That was his solution to the stylistic conundrum: Pugin's dream secularised, Ruskin's dream politicised. The stylistic debate had indeed broken down in confusion. 'It is impossible', noted one journal in 1880, 'that human nature can go on much longer producing the vulgar crudities which are at present the rage. Such is the strain upon English taste, just now, that as the Americans say, something is bound to burst. It must either be our insanity or our – sanity.'[151] Burst it did, of course, during the next two generations: first under the impact of *Beaux Arts* classicism, and then at the frontal assault of the Modern Movement. Meanwhile, however, the Goths were in retreat, the Classicists untrained. In civic and commercial buildings at least, the 1880s were a low point in English architectural history.[152]

Fergusson, more than anyone, illustrates the collapse of progressive thinking in the 1880s. For years he damned both Greek and Gothic revivals with equal ferocity. But when forced to predict the style of the future, he had to come out of the cosmos and confess his own humanity:

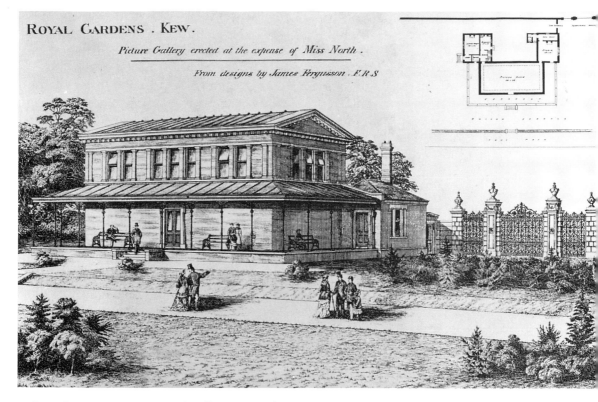

99 James Fergusson, Marianne North Gallery, Kew Gardens (1881).
'The Vitruvius of the modern world'.

'The answer is simple', he admits, 'I do not know.'[153] E. W. Pugin scored
a bullseye when he challenged the great panjandrum to design something
himself.[154] Faced with the necessity of choice, Fergusson plumped for
'that combination of classicality and common sense known as Italian'.[155]
When pressed, he would also admit the current validity of Romanesque
or Rundbogenstil. What style, then, did he choose for the Marianne North
Gallery in Kew Gardens, built to his own designs in 1882?[156][99] Stripped
classicism, in the broadest sense, seems to have been his aim. Its adaptation of Grecian lighting may have been ingenious. But aesthetically the
result is scarcely impressive. Fergusson was no wiser than the Goths,
certainly no wiser than the supporters of Queen Anne.

In fact the conjunction in Kew Gardens, of Fergusson's sub-Italianate
gallery (1881) and Nesfield's Dutch lodge (1866), is more eloquent than
any speech could be, of all the ambitions and uncertainties of the 1860s
and 1870s. Fergusson, the greatest Victorian critic of historicism, was

himself limited and conditioned by the omnipresent historicism of his own age.[157] Back in 1849, when criticising the Greek Revival architecture of Smirke's British Museum, he had suggested instead a system of construction based on standardised industrial units, as in Marshall's Flax Mill, Leeds. Alas, he played down the fact that Marshall's Mill was dressed up as an Egyptian Temple, since its business was Egyptian cotton.[158] And as for his own designs, his schemes for the Foreign and India Offices in Whitehall (1857)[100] suggest an equally associational approach: a gargantuan Renaissance palazzo, festooned with memories of India and Rome.[159]

In 1862 Fergusson actually proposed Wollaton Hall, Notts (1580: Robert Smythson) as a model for nineteenth-century secular design: with a little purification, he thought, it 'would be good for today'.[160] Paxton presumably thought the same when (with G. H. Stokes) – piling eclecticism on eclecticism – he modelled the Rothschild seat of Mentmore, Bucks (1852–4) on that same Elizabethan prodigy-palace. The point is that Fergusson, as much as Paxton, suffered from what William Morris called 'that special gift of the nineteenth century – the gift of the historical sense'. This sense Morris believed – quite correctly – grew out of a reaction against industrialism. It was 'a kind of compensation for the ugliness

100 James Fergusson, Unexecuted design for the Foreign and India Offices, Whitehall, London (1857). Whistling in the dark?

which surrounds our lives at present.'[161] As such, it proved to be both the salvation and the curse of nineteenth-century art and architecture, the creative dynamic behind so much beauty and so much ugliness.

The burden – and the challenge – of the past hovered like an incubus over all Victorian thinking. 'When I look at this age', wrote Nietzsche, 'with the eyes of a distant future, I find nothing so remarkable in the man of the present day as his peculiar virtue and sickness called "the historical sense".'[162] To describe this, Lord Acton noted in 1895, 'the depressing names historicism and historical-mindedness have been devised'.[163] In origin, this historical sense was a product of the Romantic rebellion against classical ideals: a cult of the remote, the particular, the personal, the subjective.[164] Hence the medley of styles, and the architect's first dilemma: the dilemma of choice. But in its fuller development, this acute awareness of history clashed with the results of evolutionary thinking. Because evolutionary thinking seemed to dictate the use not of historic style but of contemporary style, the burden of the past became a springboard for a 'flight into the future.'[165] Hence the architect's second dilemma: the dilemma of contemporaneity. 'The great generalisation of Darwin', noted the editor of the *Builder* in 1887, 'one of the greatest generalisations ever made by one mind, has permeated all contemporary thought.' But Victorian 'Science has known what she wanted, [Victorian] Art has not'.[166] Everywhere, teleology seemed the key to existence. The new biblical criticism of Strauss and Feuerbach, the new science of Darwin and Huxley, filtered Divinity itself through the eye of history. 'If only the Geologists would let me alone, I could do very well', Ruskin complained; 'but those dreadful hammers! I hear the clink of them at the end of every cadence of the Bible verses.'[167] Both aesthetic uncertainty and metaphysical doubt – historicism in art and relativism in religion – sprang ultimately from the same source: what Troelstsch called 'the historicising of our entire knowing and experiencing of the spiritual world, which took place in the course of the nineteenth century.'[168] As C. R. Cockerell put it: 'we are identified with time; we ourselves become a part of history.'[169] History, in Olsen's graphic phrase, became 'the opium of the aesthetes'.[170]

Tennyson, after all, had faced a similar problem:

> Why take the style of those heroic times?
> For nature brings not back the mastodon
>   ... and why should any man
> Remodel models? ...
>   ... a truth
> Looks freshest in the fashion of the day.[171]

The Idylls of the King: 'I should be crazed to attempt such a thing', Tennyson told his American publisher in 1858, 'in the heart of the nineteenth century.'[172] But attempt it he did, and he got round the problem by putting the whole epic, metaphorically speaking, into quotation marks.[173] No one would deny his success. Malory's fifteenth-century *Morte d'Arthur* was to Tennyson what Wilars de Honecort's thirteenth-century notebook was to Burges.

Or was it? And could it ever be? Architecture, after all, is not like poetry; it is service as well as art. And in the nineteenth century that eternal dilemma was doubly acute, thanks to the problem of stylistic multiplicity, *and* thanks to the problem of stylistic modernity. All through Victorian architectural theory, the guilt of suppressed functionalism keeps bubbling to the surface. Science seemed to be progressing, art retrogressing. In 1881 one journal looked at Professor Huxley's teleological explanation of the crayfish, and despaired at the irrelevance of historicism: 'our building and our architecture parted company centuries ago.'[174] Now this division had been concealed by custom, by the omnipresence of symbolic – or semiotic – systems of design. That is why we have to seek out the keys to Victorian architectural thinking within an artificial, socially-sanctioned system of visual values. For architecture is the most social of the arts: it is function, symbol, status and science, as well as a mere matter of aesthetics.[175] And in the Victorian period, architect and patron alike were prisoners of two pervasive socio-aesthetic categories: propriety and association.[176] Associational thinking – that is, architecture as embodied memory – and the idea of architectural propriety – that is, style as an expression of status as well as of purpose – supplied both explanation and justification of the whole panoply of historical forms. At the same time, Pugin's other legacy – the mythology of function – acted as counterpoint and critique to the very bases of historicist thinking. Hence the dilemma of style.

Here then, lay the roots of that art-historical paradox, the paradox of creative eclecticism: Gombrich's 'neuralgic point of nineteenth century aesthetics'.[177] Perplexed by change, tortured by doubt, Victorian architects tended to shout to keep their spirits up. Whistling in the dark, perhaps. But what a glorious tune! A tune, moreover, which we might usefully learn to whistle as we stumble from the certainties of the Modern Movement into the uncertainties of Post-Modern architecture.

5 Modern Gothic

'We were all intensely Gothic – and intensely wrong'
(Richard Norman Shaw, 1902).

IN 1913 A YOUNG ARCHITECT called Harry Goodhart-Rendel attended a house party in the west of England. He left behind him in the visitors' book a sketch of a house called 'Rockets'.[1] 'Rockets' was Victorian; Victorian Gothic; High Victorian Gothic. In Victorian slang, it had 'GO'. And in 1913 its style was regarded as a very bad joke. A generation later, in 1949, Goodhart-Rendel delivered a lecture at the RIBA which tried to explain that style – Modern Gothic – to the modern architectural establishment. The lecture was called 'Rogue Architects of the Victorian Era'.[2] Its heroes were a group of stylistic eccentrics, architectural rogue-elephants, most famously William Butterfield, E. B. Lamb, S. S. Teulon, F. T. Pilkington, E. Bassett Keeling and Thomas ('Victorian') Harris. What these six architects had in common was what musicians call 'attack': a commitment to originality at all costs; and a rogue-elephant energy which smashed through the barriers of historicism. Their style was 'Modern Gothic', an eclectic cocktail based on the harshest, most primitive components of Anglo–Venetian and Early French. It was an attempt to combine medievalism and modernity, traditional forms and new materials, pointed arches and plate glass. And it was popular. Rogue architecture became the demotic Gothic of the 1860s.[3]

The origins of Rogue architecture are to be found in Ruskinian Gothic and in Early French, in the controlled muscularity of Burges and Street.[4] Street's pulpit, at Denstone, Staffs (1860–62)[101], sums up that phase in the evolution of the Gothic Revival. Neither Burges nor Street could ever be a Rogue: Street had too great a sense of responsibility, and Burges too great a sense of humour. But between them they created an aesthetic climate in which Rogue architects could flourish.

Rogue architecture was an attempt to construct a brand new style out of the pulverised fragments of the Gothic Revival. As such, it was doomed to reflect the egos of its practitioners. Burges called it 'the Original and Ugly School'.[5] Samuel Sanders Teulon, the archetypal Rogue, was an architect of undoubted talent.[6] But at Bestwood Lodge, Notts (1862–4),

101 G.E. Street, Pulpit, All Saints, Denstone, Staffordshire (1860–62). Controlled muscularity.

102 S.S. Teulon, Elvetham Hall, Hampshire (1859–62). 'The Original and Ugly School'.

the silhouette is asymmetrical to the point of frenzy; the detail crude almost to the point of brutality. And at Elvetham, Hants (1859–62)[102], his frenetic pursuit of originality in pattern and colour comes near to destroying unity and coherence of design altogether.[7] But there is no doubt about his ability. At St Stephen, Rosslyn Hill, Hampstead (1869–71), he exploits geometrical shapes and polychrome patterns with colossal power. Continental Gothic – Italian and French – has been purged of precise archaeology and bludgeoned into service as a vehicle for vigour and abstraction.[8] As T.F. Bumpus put it, with masterly understatement, such designs are 'original, but in some points rather deficient in reserve'.[9]

E.B. Lamb, our next Rogue, belonged to an earlier generation.[10] His sins, if we count his originalities as sins, stemmed from excessive pursuit of the Picturesque rather than from over-indulgence in the Sublime.[11] As a young man, his design for the new Houses of Parliament showed him anxious to include 'as much originality' as possible: 'precedents drawn from ancient buildings should be considered merely as the foundation of a new style'.[12] At present, he complained in 1846, 'copying is the alpha and omega' of architecture; 'a perfectly new style' may be 'next to impossible', but by means of a 'continuation' of Gothic, 'we may ultimately arrive at a national style of art, blending all the known forms with modern improvements and comforts, on the soundest principles of philosophy'.[13] 'Sound philosophy' is not quite the impression created by

Eye Town Hall, Suffolk (1857)[103]: a conflation of Baroque composition and East Anglian vernacular detail.[14] Two years later, Lamb entered the Whitehall Battle of the Styles on the side of the Classicists, or rather as a supporter of T. L. Donaldson and the anti-Goths. In a paper headed 'Aphorisms' he attempted to persuade Lord Palmerston of the virtues of eclecticism:

> Architecture is a progressive art, and there is no instance on record, in Ancient times, of a retrogression, or a reproduction of the works of preceding periods … Convenience, scientific construction and durable materials should be considered before style or ornament…. Style is the mere vehicle by which architectural beauty is obtained; but is not necessarily beautiful in itself: it is the proper application of style which constitutes aesthetic beauty.[15]

Palmerston remained unconvinced: he preferred Palladian. So Whitehall was spared a monumental version of Nun Appleton Hall, Yorks (*c.*1864; dem.).[16]

Lamb's most characteristic churches – Gospel Oak in London (1866)[104],[17] for example – are really a series of Gothic assembly halls,

103 E. B. Lamb, Eye Town Hall, Suffolk (1857). 'Sound philosophy'?

104 E. B. Lamb, St Martin, Gospel Oak, London (1866). Idiosyncratic detail, Broad Church planning.

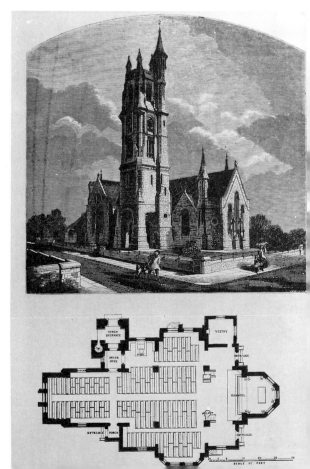

105 F. T. Pilkington, Barclay Church, Edinburgh (1862–4).
'Ugliness is not strength'.

106 E. Bassett Keeling, St George,
Campden Hill, London (1864).
Rogue Gothic.

centrally planned on Broad Church lines, Picturesque in silhouette and
weirdly idiosyncratic in detail. Sometimes the complexity of the detail –
as at Englefield Green, Surrey (1859)[18] – destroys the broader impact of
their design. Lamb's ecclesiastical interiors, in particular, add up to a
nightmare of notched and chamfered timber. Commenting on Brompton
Hospital chapel (1849–50; altered), the *Ecclesiologist* noted: 'the roof is
decidedly astonishing ... Such a chaos of carpentry so near our heads
we have seldom seen. . . . Those who can swallow this chapel can swallow
anything ... May the attendance [of the hospital's patients] ... not prove
fatal to any of them.'[19] Not surprisingly, E. B. Lamb never won the
ecclesiologists' approval.[20]

By comparison with F. T. Pilkington, however, Lamb seems positively
tame. Pilkington was an eclectic first and a Goth second. In his early
years in Edinburgh, he built himself a house – 38, Dick Place (1864) –
which combines scenographic planning with vaguely Romanesque
exterior details and explosive Rococo interior plasterwork.[21] Craigend
(1867–9), also in Edinburgh, combines Scots Baronial, Early French and
rogue-Ruskinian Gothic in an equally cavalier way. In his later period
in London, he designed the gargantuan Army and Navy Hotel, Victoria
St (1882; dem.): its grotesque classical forms and 'Brobdingnagian proportions ... pushed audacity of treatment to the extremest point'.[22]
Pilkington's churches – Kelso (1863–6), for instance, or Barclay
Church, Edinburgh (1862–4)[105] – undoubtedly contain explosive
merit. But it seems that he began by seeking severity, and ended up with
an affectation of barbarism. Micklethwaite's criticism of 1873 comes very
near to the truth:

136

The common symptoms [of GO] in our churches are harshness, even to brutality of general design, with studied ugliness and systematic exaggeration and distortion of details, stumpy banded pillars, stilted arches, a profusion of coarse carving, notches, zigzags, curves ... and long wiry crockets bursting out of unexpected places ... like hatpegs. ... GO is in fact architectural rant, and may be defined as the perpetual forcing into notice of the personality of the architect ... 'See', he says in his work, 'what a clever fellow I am'.[23]

Burges put it more simply: 'Ugliness is not strength.'[24]

Burges was even ruder about our next Rogue, Enoch Bassett Keeling.[25] Keeling was a Wesleyan architect from Co. Durham who came south, bringing muscularity to the metropolis. His Music Hall in the Strand was the talking point of 1864: 'Acrobatic Gothic', in the jargon of the day. Anglo-Venetian and Early French were his starting points. But excess seems to have become his basic principle, and vulgarity – in colour, material and form – his besetting vice. The Strand Music Hall was attacked by Seddon, Burges, Christian, Scott – indeed by the whole Gothic establishment – for its 'eclecticism ... eccentricity ... vulgarity ... and ... coarse hugeness'.[26] The Rogues were giving Modern Gothic a bad name.

Bassett Keeling defended himself with appropriate vigour. 'I may have been eccentric', he wrote, 'but no one can accuse me of plagiarism. I claim to have produced an eclectic design, but it is eclecticism and not patchwork. I have taken Continental Gothic as my basis ... [I have not aimed at] tenderness and delicacy ... What I have wished to secure is general picturesqueness, and in detail piquancy and crispness.'[27] Pevsner simply calls Keeling's church on Campden Hill, London (1864)[106] 'atrocious'.[28] But there is no point in looking for classical virtues – balance, harmony or taste – in Bassett Keeling. There is no point even in looking for Puginian delicacy. By 1864 Pugin's decoration of the Houses of Parliament seemed 'effeminate in its detail to the last degree'.[29] High Victorian Goths preferred weight and power, geometry, abstraction; in other words – in the language of the day – they preferred masculinity.

Whatever its implications in terms of psychology,[30] in terms of design, masculinity meant abstraction. As Owen Jones put it, 'the basis of all form is geometry'.[31] It was above all through geometry – two-dimensional or three-dimensional – that architects hoped to break open the prison of historic form. As with Neo-Classicism in the eighteenth century; as with Modernism in the twentieth century, geometrical abstraction was regarded as the open sesame to a new style, a new visual vocabulary which would sweep away all the archaic stereotypes of traditional forms. Some called their new medium the Vigorous Style. Others called it the

107 Thomas Harris, Design for a terrace, Harrow, Middlesex (1860). 'In the Victorian Style'.

Shadowless Style.[32] Whatever they called it, far, far off, the Modern Goths of the 1860s seemed to sense the Holy Grail of a new style beckoning dimly on the horizon. Alas, it remained dim.

No one sought more desperately to achieve this Victorian style than our next Rogue, Thomas Harris – 'Victorian' Harris as he became known. Harris was remembered by Harry Batsford as 'a huge shaggy man with a big sombrero hat, rather scraggy beard and tremendous hooked nose, with a deep booming voice, [who] could explode in a rather terrifying way ... laughed sardonically and made weird puns.'[33] We need 'an indigenous style of our own', explained Harris, for this 'age of new creations ... Steam power and electric communications [are] entirely new revolutionary influences. So must it be in Architecture.'[34] His design for a terrace at Harrow 'in the Victorian style' (1860)[107][35] sums up many of the pretensions of popular Gothic in the 1860s. Fortunately, perhaps, it was never built. Burges put it succinctly: 'some modern buildings look as if they had been shaken around in a hat.'[36]

'Victorian' Harris was not the first to call for a Victorian style. But he did call loudest. He demanded a universal style which would 'realise the spirit of our own time ... [A] style ... embodying the spirit of the good of every age, and springing out of ourselves ... an honest, independent,

138

simple expression of the true God-fearing English character.'[37] Take away the 'cant', snorted the *Ecclesiologist*, and he is merely calling for the same thing as 'nearly all architecturalists have learned to desire, viz. a characteristic development of the national Pointed, so as to meet all the wants of the age, and to assimilate all the new processes and materials which are now available.'[38] It was the architect's dilemma all over again.

Harris's early theories were perhaps a young man's vanity. Several of his early designs, like his polychrome chemist's shop at 26, South Audley St, Mayfair (1858; dem. 1892), are odd rather than original.[39] But by all accounts his commercial interiors were most ingenious,[40] and his warehouse in Lisson Grove, London (1874)[108] did approach novelty – at least a novelty by negation: it clothed its cast iron and timber frame with minimal brick detailing.[41] As so often in the Victorian period, Puginian 'propriety' permitted such reticence only in the lower orders of design. As he grew older, however, Harris abandoned his 'new style phantasy' and returned to conventional eclecticism: his half-timbered house at Milner Field, Yorks (1873) for Sir Titus Salt, is a characteristic example.[42] At the Philadelphia Exhibition of 1876, his designs are still shuffling the historicist pack, and with no more talent than many of his contemporaries.[43] Towards the end of his life, in a more carefully considered book – *Three Periods of English Architecture* (1894) – he came to the same lame conclusion as most of his generation: a new style

108 Thomas Harris, Warehouse, Lisson Grove, London (1874; dem.). Novelty by negation.

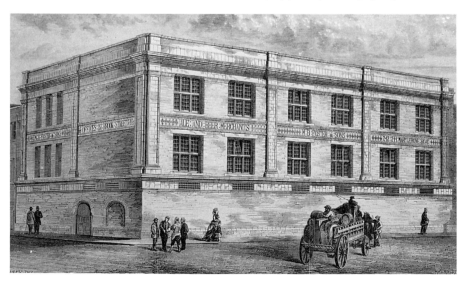

will emerge one day, born of new structural processes, notably iron.[44] Meanwhile – and this could almost be the epitaph on a whole epoch – he requotes George Aitchison's dictum of 1864: 'let us dare to think for ourselves, even if our efforts are unsuccessful; let our works be uglier than they are, only let them be original.'[45] In short, the doctrine of creative error. As Nietzsche put it, 'blessed are those who have taste, even although it be bad taste.'[46]

That quotation from Nietzsche was used to good effect by Kenneth Clark when he came to discuss Butterfield and the High Victorians. And in this century Butterfield more than any other Victorian has become the whipping boy for the sins of a whole architectural generation. Goodhart-Rendel gave him a prominent position in his Rogues' Gallery. He was certainly a Modern Goth: he showed – at Rugby School (1867–84) for instance [109] – that Gothic was 'a living language, having words for rackets-court, operating theatre, and latrine'.[47] But Butterfield was never the leader of a school. His dogmatic muscularity, his syncopated polychromy, his capacity for endless geometrical invention – all this is entirely his own.[48] In that sense he counts as a fully qualified Rogue. But in recent years we have got to know rather more about Butterfield.[49] A whole bundle of myths has had to be discarded. In the first place, his sources of inspiration were as much English as Italian. Of course there is polychromy at Verona or Pavia. But there is medieval polychromy as well at King's Lynn or Higham Ferrers. And all his life he retained a fondness for Georgian sash windows. So out goes Butterfield the disciple of Ruskin.[50] Out too goes Butterfield the colour-blind, fanatical, proto-Brutalist rogue-elephant, catering for the depraved taste of an emerging middle class. In comes Butterfield the churchman – contemporaries called him 'the Fra Angelico of nineteenth-century architecture';[51] Butterfield the scholar, Butterfield the artist, Butterfield the protégé of Tory landowners, Butterfield the master of texture and silhouette; above all, Butterfield the genius of polyphonal colour and abstract geometrical shapes. Butterfield's personal style, as at St Augustine, Queen's Gate (1865–71) – a mixture of German, English, French and Italian[52] – was the result neither of ignorance nor of malice. He was simply playing the eclectic game, and playing it to please himself. The result was Modern Gothic: 'a tentative solution', as Benjamin Webb put it – thinking of All Saints, Margaret St – 'of the problem [of] what the architecture of the future [is] to be'.[53]

The revaluation of Butterfield has involved a revaluation of the terminology of appreciation – in particular, a revaluation of the word 'Ugly'. It has lately become fashionable to deny the existence of ugliness in

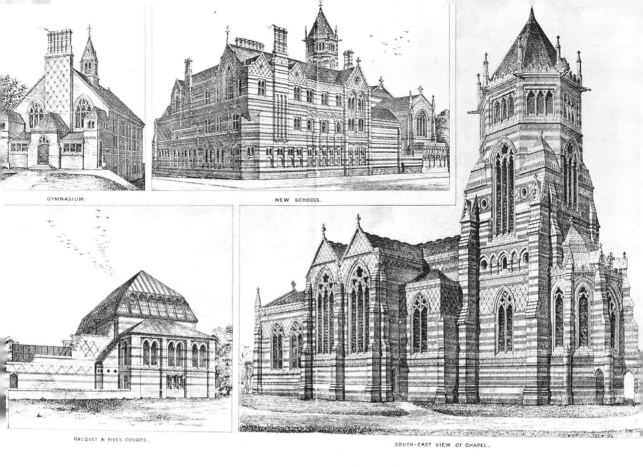

GYMNASIUM.

NEW SCHOOLS.

RACQUET & FIVES COURTS.

SOUTH-EAST VIEW OF CHAPEL.

109 William Butterfield, Rugby School (1867–84). Modern Gothic for all purposes.

Butterfield's work. But if by ugliness we understand a willingness to shock rather than a desire to please; an anti-classical fondness for contrasting forms and colours, 'volumetric violence',[54] planar conflict, broken lines, exaggerations and awkward juxtapositions; obsession with honesty, primitivism and vigour, in other words a combination of Puginian Reality and High Victorian 'GO' – Romantic aesthetics carried to excess – then we are fully in agreement with Butterfield's contemporaries.[55] E. A. Freeman complained of the 'hideous nakedness' of the transept at St Matthias, Stoke Newington (1849–53).[56] The *Ecclesiologist* recognised in All Saints, Margaret St a 'deliberate preference for ugliness',[57] as in the stridency and angularity of many Pre-Raphaelite pictures.[58] Ugliness in that sense does not represent a deficiency of genius, still less a barrier to appreciation: we are merely encountering the visual vocabulary of High Victorian aesthetics; an aesthetic deriving from Romantic notions of association, and thus fundamentally subjective. 'We are living', Butterfield told the Warden of Keble in 1873, 'in an age most terribly subjective and sensational.'[59] Butterfield himself was not at all

141

happy about it. He tried continuously to combine the inevitably subjective impulses of design with the objective realities of building: architecture as service as well as architecture as art.

In 1857, Coventry Patmore noticed a congruity of approach between Butterfield and Rossetti. 'Rossetti . . . is, among painters', he wrote, 'what Mr Butterfield is among architects – that is to say, about the most startlingly original living.'[60] But by 1859 Benjamin Webb was already worried by Millais's 'unhealthy love for the ugly'.[61] And in 1864 James Thorne found St Alban's Holborn 'unnecessarily ugly'.[62] In the 1870s the Aesthetes would swing still further away from 'ugliness': their fatal fondness for prettiness would grow out of a natural reaction to the 1860s' cult of abstraction and strength.[63] Thus Ruskinian Sublimity gave way to a revival of the Picturesque. Masculinity replaced femininity. But the style first identified by Charles Handley-Read as High Victorian Geometrical found no abler exponent than William Butterfield.

Butterfield's modernity, his uncompromising idiosyncrasy, certainly worried his contemporaries. E. A. Freeman called Balliol chapel (1856–7) an 'injury' to all Trinity men, especially 'to me'.[64] 'Keble College', wrote J. D. Sedding in 1885, 'can never look mellow. No one supposes that it ever will look less startling and raw than its talented author took pains to make it. Mellowness is a quality it ever must lack. Nature – who is a soft-hearted creature – will try her best to throw her charitable cloak over its crude walls; but Keble will be a nature-puzzling, time-defying object till the crack of doom, and will stare with its peculiar nineteenth-century stare straight into the eyes of eternity.'[65]

What we admire about Butterfield today is precisely that idiosyncrasy, that capacity for abstraction and synthesis: that talent for taking the Gothic, reducing its forms to their primary components, and then combining them with new materials like machine-made brick, engine-polished marble, and plate glass – as at Milton Ernest, Bedfordshire (1856)[110].[66] How much of the spirit of Modern Gothic is contained in that name: Milton Ernest. How much of the spirit of Butterfield. Butterfield's architecture, however, also contains the germs of a style that will eventually replace the Gothic Revival as a leader of fashion: Queen Anne. Those sash windows, those ribbed brick chimneys, those sawn-off gables, those vestigially structural Gothic arches – young Philip Webb has noted them well.

One likely candidate is missing from Goodhart-Rendel's Rogues' Gallery: Alfred Waterhouse, the most prolific exponent of Modern Gothic. He is not missing because his designs lacked vigour and GO. He is missing because, as a leader of the profession, he could hardly be classified as a

110 William Butterfield, Milton Ernest Hall, Bedfordshire (1856).
Puginian 'reality', High Victorian 'GO'.

rogue elephant. But in some ways Waterhouse is best understood as the ultimate Modern Goth. When another architect told him that Gothic architecture had been utterly ransacked and exhausted, he replied: 'I feel that having ransacked the world for Gothic detail, and studied Gothic under every form, that is just the time to go on in it, and not to give it up.'[67] In fact, Waterhouse carried Ruskin's latitudinarian approach to an anti-Ruskinian conclusion. In his later years he became largely indifferent to style – that is, indifferent to the choice of style. At Gonville and Caius College, Cambridge (1869–70)[68] – poised between Classic and Gothic – he managed to combine memories of at least two Loire chateaux – Chenonceaux and Blois – in a way which is still fundamentally medieval in composition. As Lethaby put it, he was 'an able planner and organiser ... an able constructor ... an intelligent eclectic ... a semi-modern.'[69]

The rhythms and proportions of Waterhouse's later buildings reflect their hidden metallic structure. His yardstick is the rolled iron beam, not the masonry vault. Hence his rejection of Puginian – and ultimately Ruskinian – Gothic in favour of a flexible eclecticism based on iron structures and terracotta facings. Thus his Natural History Museum,

143

111 Alfred Waterhouse, Natural History Museum, London (1873–81). Gothic, Baroque, Romanesque and Modern.

South Kensington (1873–81)[111] combines interiors which are Gothic in detail and Baroque in disposition, with an exterior based on Romanesque motifs from Bamberg, Andernach, Le Puy, Normandy, Worms and Regensburg.[70] At the same time its proportions stem from its steel-framed structure, and its profiles are the product of its terracotta finish. Waterhouse, therefore – architect to the Prudential Assurance Co. – is the link between High Victorian GO and later Victorian Free Style. It would be foolish to pretend that his buildings are easy to swallow. J. F. Bentley once remarked that comparing Waterhouse with Street was like comparing paste with diamonds.[71] Pevsner finds his 'harsh, logical mind ... a psychological puzzle'.[72] Sometimes he can be positively repulsive – but he is never negatively repulsive. His punch and vigour are more suitable to large-scale civic structures than to domestic work. 'Mr Waterhouse's Gothic style', noted the *Builder* in 1874 'is certainly his own.' He has combined 'Medieval and Modern ... to an extent that has not been achieved elsewhere.' There is something about it which is 'cold and deficient in feeling'. Still 'Mr Waterhouse [has] settled his path in architectural design (a great thing to say for an architect in these days) and we have little doubt that the buildings he will leave in this style will

144

always command approval and commendation, even when they fail to arouse enthusiasm.'[73] And so they do.

But not all Modern Goths were as sophisticated as Butterfield or as ingenious as Waterhouse. To be successful, Modern Gothic required skill and restraint. In the mid-Victorian period it slipped easily into polychromania and 'wild excess'.[74] Gilbert Scott readily admitted that his own technique could be dangerous when diluted. Just 'as we were generating a secular style peculiarly suited to our wants', he complained in the later 1860s, it fell into the hands of 'an ignorant and untutored rabble'.[75] 'Ruskinism, such as would make Ruskin's very hair stand on end [as in the Memorial Hall, Manchester, 1864–6, by Thomas Worthington];[76] Butterfieldism, gone mad with its endless stripings of red and black bricks [as with houses in Banbury, Oxfordshire, 1866, by W. Wilkinson[112] – remember Street's warning: 'this hot taste is dangerous']; architecture so French that a Frenchman would not know it,

112 W. Wilkinson, Houses, Banbury, Oxfordshire (1866). 'This hot taste is dangerous'.

145

113 R.L. Roumieu, Vinegar Warehouses, Eastcheap, London (1868). 'An incredible worship of the Ugly'.

out-Heroding Herod himself [St Mary Magdalene, Tavistock, for instance, by Henry Clutton, 1865]; Byzantine in all its forms [except] those used by the Byzantines [Dublin University chaplaincy, for example, by Hungerford Pollen, 1855–6];[77] mixtures of all or some of these; 'original' styles founded upon knowledge of old styles, or upon ignorance of them ... violent strainings after something very strange, and great successes in producing something very weak; attempts at beauty resulting in ugliness, and attempts at ugliness attended with unhoped-for success [the Vinegar Warehouses, perhaps, at 33–35 Eastcheap, London, 1868,[113] by R.L.

Roumieu – one of Goodhart-Rendel's minor Rogues]. 'All these', says Scott, 'have given a wild absurdity to much of the architecture of the [1860s], which one cannot but deplore: but at the same time it must be allowed that much of the best, the most nervous, and the most original results of the revival, have been arrived at within the same period.'[78] It was indeed a precarious balance, poised between originality and absurdity.

In the language of the day, architects were walking a tightrope between 'reality' and 'ugliness'. William Morris, for instance, came to see the mid-Victorian decades as a time when 'hope was strong', after 'the feeble twaddle and dilettantism of the later Georges'; a time of 'experimental designing – good, very good experiments some of them.' But by the 1870s, he realised that experimentation had produced in lesser hands a popular Victorian style – almost an eclectic vernacular – which was 'no longer passively but actively ugly, since it has added to the dreary utilitarianism of the days of Dr Johnson a vulgarity which is the special invention of the Victorian.... The ordinary builder is covering England with abortions which make us regret the brick box and slate lid of fifty years ago.'[79]

In 1874 'Jock' Stevenson saw no point in mincing words:

> [The Gothic Revivalists] urged that ... [Gothic] become again, as it had once been [our] vernacular architecture ... [Their] wish has been granted. The nineteenth century has expressed itself in Gothic; and, in gin-palaces, rows of houses built to sell, semi-detached villas, chapels and churches, Gothic, which of old was simple and unpretentious, by means of its boasted freedom from restraint has lent itself with fatal facility to the expression of loudness, vulgarity, obtrusiveness, and sensationalism more objectionable far than the dreariest Classic of Gower St. or Wimpole St. *That* may be very dull prose; the other is screeching sensational poetry or *Daily Telegraphese*.[80]

Of course, that was unfair. Stevenson was talking of GO rather than Gothic. But the excesses of Rogue architecture – at least in less able hands – constituted a formidable warning against novelty for novelty's sake.[81] In its High Victorian phase the Gothic Revival was really making impossible demands – on the abilities of its practitioners, *and* on the credulity and tolerance of the public. As Robert Kerr put it in 1864, its claim 'to universal dominion for Medievalism ... [was] arrogant and transcendental'; and its products evinced 'an incredible worship of what can only be fitly called the Ugly ... to set up Ugliness for an idol [is a mark of] intellectual despair.'[82] The Rogues had tried to break out of the historicist prison with a desperate mixture of novelty and archaeology. The public was outraged and the profession despaired. 'Crude Art of all

114 Basil Champneys, John Rylands'
Library, Manchester (1890–1905).
Arts and Crafts Gothic.

115 G. F. Bodley, All Saints, Cambridge (1863–
8). 'English architecture ought to be English'.

kinds is very much in fashion just now', noted *The Architect* in 1871.
'The learned professors of the twentieth century [will conclude with]
astonishment [that this is] the first time in the history of Art [when]
crudity has been directly and laboriously sought out for ... its own ...
sake ... Never before ... has refinement been positively discountenanced
as imbecility. [All the arts are suffering from this] self-denial of taste, [this
cult of] severity ... archaism and ... asceticism. [Such a] preference for
the Crude [is understandable as a reaction against Regency taste, a revolt
against Picturesque composition and] the principle of the fictitious ...
But ... how far is it to go?'[83]

Well, of course there was a reaction, the reaction known as the Queen
Anne Revival. The public turned away from Gothic. How did the Goths
themselves react? After years of optimism,[84] Benjamin Webb simply
lapsed into silence. Burges, Street and Butterfield were all too set in their
respective ways to change their styles in the 1870s.[85] But other Goths
were more flexible: they abandoned muscularity and settled for sensibility;
they rediscovered the flexibility of late Gothic; they returned to the
fifteenth and sixteenth centuries.[86] By 1876 Perpendicular was back on
fashionable drawing boards for the first time since the 1830s. 'Shall we',

148

asked the *Building News*, 'see another Gothic Revival?'[87] J. P. Seddon and
J. D. Sedding firmly answered 'Yes'.[88]

This new phase of the Gothic Revival – climax or dying fall, according
to taste – was dominated by the practice and principles of the Arts and
Crafts Movement: most persuasively in E. S. Prior's Roker church, Co.
Durham (1906–7),[89] for instance; or in Randall Wells's Kempley church,
Glos (1903).[90] Late medieval English prototypes were synthesised,
abstracted, harmonised with modern materials, and fused with ingenuity
and passion. But the Gothic Revival was no longer at the centre of the
architectural stage. It had been pushed to one side by a wider eclecticism;
it had been marginalised by changing social priorities; by the shifting
imperatives of economics and technology. It would certainly be foolish
to underestimate Arts and Crafts Gothic: Basil Champneys' Rylands'
Library, Manchester (1890–1905)[114], for example. Its flexibility was
admirable; its detail was often exquisite; its adaptability incontestable.[91]
And in its final phase – where Arts and Crafts Gothic shaded into Sedding
and Wilson's *art nouveau* – it achieved rare flashes of real brilliance.[92]
But had architecture been left behind for stage design and interior decoration? To any Goth worth his salt it must have seemed a poor substitute
for the stern geometry of Early French.[93]

The contrast between the Gothic of the 1850s and the Gothic of the
1880s is indeed striking. How did this reversal of taste come about?

Even at the height of the Early French fashion, there had been those
who continued to believe that 'English architecture ought to be English'.[94]
And in 1863 the *Ecclesiologist* had hailed Bodley's All Saints, Cambridge,
as a welcome portent: a swing back to Puginian purity.[95] Bodley had
once been among the leading exponents of High Victorian muscularity:
Franco-Italian at St Michael's, Brighton (1858–61); Early French at
Selsley, Glos (1862).[55] He seemed to be in the vanguard of those in
pursuit of a new style; those who hoped to break through the barriers of
history by a process of eclecticism and geometrical abstraction. Then
suddenly he changed his approach. Bodley's change of style at Cambridge,
in 1863–8,[115] from Early French to English Decorated, had been made
at the request of the incumbent and the university – Dr Whewell in
particular. Bodley agreed to the change with 'great regret': so much for
the legend that at Cambridge he eagerly pioneered the shift from High
Victorian to late Victorian Gothic.[96] Still, Cambridge was the heartland
of ecclesiology. The swing back to English Gothic was rather more obvious
there than it could ever be in what were actually Bodley's first willing
experiments in reviving native forms: St Salvador's, Dundee (1865–70)
and St John's, Tue Brook, Liverpool (1868–70). Anyway, Bodley had now

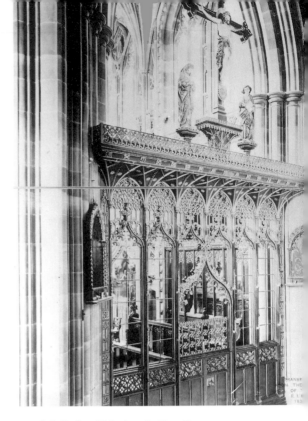

116 G.F. Bodley, St Augustine, Pendlebury, Lancashire (1870–4). Influences from Albi and Toulouse.

117 G.F. Bodley, Holy Angels, Hoar Cross, Staffordshire (1871–6; 1891–1900). Pugin redivivus.

moved into Decorated; he had yet to mingle Decorated and Perpendicular. That occurred at Pendlebury, Lancashire (1870–4)[116] and at Hoar Cross, Staffs (1871–6 and 1891–1900).[117]

Both Pendlebury and Hoar Cross are joint works, by Bodley and his partner Thomas Garner. Though their details are stylistically linked – English fourteenth-century tracery, for example – their composition could hardly be more different. Hoar Cross traces its distinctive tower to the fifteenth-century church of Ilminster in Somerset. Pendlebury, on the other hand, owes the formation of its West front to St Sernin at Toulouse, and its broad-based, internally buttressed plan to Albi Cathedral. Albi had been noticed by the *Ecclesiologist* in 1846 as affording 'hints for the future development of Christian architecture'. Despite its 'gigantic spirit', however, its 'anomalous' style seemed 'hardly ... safe ... as a model' back in 1846.[97] Thirty years later its time had come: in plan, if not in detail, Albi – with passage-aisles and built-in buttresses – became perhaps the most influential source for late-Victorian Gothic churches.

At Hoar Cross Bodley chose that mixture of Decorated and Perpendicular motifs characteristic of English architecture at the time of the

Black Death in 1349. He believed the catastrophe of the plague had interrupted the 'Golden Age of English Architecture'; he hoped to take up the threads again, continuing its development towards perfection.

> Internally [Edward Warren wrote of Hoar Cross in 1910] it is the fervid, almost passionate realisation of an ideal. Seen ... in the deepening twilight of a clear Autumn evening, when the details of the interior are softening into gloom, and the chancel, with its stately altar, its sumptuous hangings and its gleam of gold, is dimly visible beyond the screen, while the rich tones of its painted windows make a soft resplendent glow, it gives an indescribable impression of medieval glamour, of poetry and mystery; a visionary rehabilitation of the ancient glories of the Church.[98]

Well, perhaps. And yet there is something about Hoar Cross – and still more about Bodley's church at Clumber, Notts (1886) – which arouses intellectual unease. Can it really have been right to revive Pugin forty years on? Might not the whole operation be described as a triumph of misdirected learning? That was the *Builder*'s opinion when Bodley exhibited his design at the Royal Academy in 1890.[99] When the American architect Ralph Adams Cram visited Hoar Cross in 1899, he thought it 'crystalline in [its] delicate perfection ... [But perhaps] inevitably .... there is something of self-consciousness [about it], of the striving for perfection; but', he adds, 'attribute no blame for this to the architects. The cause lies in the spirit of the epoch, and no man shall escape it.'[100]

The shift back to Perpendicular certainly shocked some of the older ecclesiologists. In the 1840s Webb and Neale had regarded Perpendicular as symbolising 'worldly pomp instead of the Catholic Faith'. 'It is a style', they announced, 'which we trust will never be revived, and which it is much to be wished had never been invented.'[101] To Scott it represented 'corruption and decay'.[102] To Ruskin it was 'weak, dangerous [and] disagreeable'.[103] Now, in 1872–3, G. G. Scott Jnr proclaimed it the climax of Gothic Art.[104] At Cattistock in Dorset, for example, in 1874, he quite eclipsed his father's Second Pointed church with a Perpendicular tower modelled on nearby Charminster. And during the next two decades, young Scott, Bodley, Seddon, Sedding, Bentley, Jackson and Caröe, proceeded to demonstrate the apparently infinite flexibility of Perpendicular forms. Sometimes the beauty they achieved was – to use Comper's distinction – a kind of beauty by exclusion: historicism pure and simple. Goodhart-Rendel called Bentley's Holy Rood, Watford (1887) simply 'perfection ... the most lovely church the nineteenth century gave to England'.[105] More often it was beauty by inclusion: eclecticism running free. Anglo-Jackson's Gothic – his High Street front at Brasenose College,

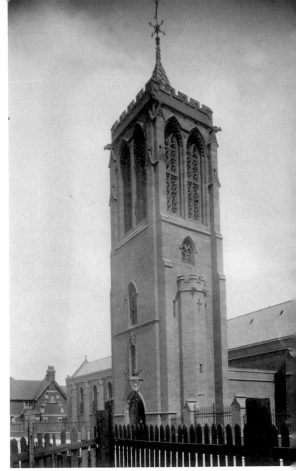

118 T. G. Jackson, Brasenose College,
Oxford (1886–1909). Gothic Survival
revived.

119 G. F. Bodley, St Chad, Burton-on-Trent,
Staffordshire (1903–10). 'The wages of good
taste is death'.

Oxford (1886–1909)[118] – for instance, was so late in style that it even absorbed Elizabethan and Jacobean, becoming in effect Gothic Survival revived. The Victorian Gothic Revival had come full circle: from pre-Puginian Perpendicular right round – via Anglo-Venetian and Early French – to Bodleian Perpendicular. Perhaps there was little left to choose. As Summerson once remarked, 'the naughtiness of enjoying "late" works was, perhaps, one of the few pleasures left to the jaded sensibilities of the 'eighties.'[106]

It was Bodley more than anyone who brought about this change. It was Bodley who first re-embarked on Late Flowing Decorated; Bodley who first deviated into Perpendicular; Bodley who first revived the use of painted mural decoration – in the Puginian manner – after a decade of structural polychromy. And in the field of stained glass, it was Bodley who led the shift from Pre-Raphaelite to Arts and Crafts Gothic: from

Powell and Ford Madox Brown at Scarborough, Yorks (*c.* 1861–72),[107] to Kempe and Burlison and Grylls at Hoar Cross.[108] To deny Bodley's achievement merely because he worked in an increasingly traditional style would be foolish. As Goodhart-Rendel put it, 'no historian, prophet or teacher can prove that because a work of art is anomalous in point of style it need fail in the essentials of beauty'.[109] But it has to be admitted that Bodley solved the dilemma of style simply by ignoring it.

'I need not discuss the *style* in which our churches should be built', Bodley wrote in 1881. 'This is an age of Science, not of Art, and it is not ripe for any *new* style . . . Style is, after all, only a language. New things may be said in an old tongue; and one need not invent a new language to write a new book.'[110] True enough. But by 1881 the linguistic analogy was beginning to wear a little thin: even a rationalist like Viollet-le-Duc had only managed to produce – in Summerson's words – 'a sort of esperanto'.[111]

In his early days, Bodley had seemed close to breakthrough. At Eccleston in Cheshire (1899), however – with all the resources of the Grosvenors at his command – he seems not only to have lost his stylistic nerve, but even to have given up trying. 'True refinement', he came to believe, 'denotes restrained power.'[112] But restraint and refinement are not quite the same thing. As late as 1903, at St Chad, Burton-on-Trent (1903–10; completed by Cecil Hare)[119], Bodley was still combining the Pendlebury arcades and the Hoar Cross tower in increasingly feeble attempts to be 'refined'. Goodhart-Rendel was damning: 'I have never seen good taste more ghastly! Bodley's obsession with being a gentleman seems to have quenched all his early promise in the end. And this church, as far as I am concerned, is the end.'[113] Even Sir Ninian Comper, who inherited and developed Bodley's cult of 'sweetness', once confessed that 'there is [in Bodley's later work] a trace of slight preciousness, an affinity perhaps with Pater, or [an over] delicate expression of the aesthetic side of William Morris, and . . . the Pre-Raphaelites.'[114]

Something of the same came to be true of J. L. Pearson.[115] In the 1840s he had been conventionally Puginian: his demolished church in Bessborough Gardens, London (1849–52) might have been mistaken for one by Benjamin Ferrey. In the 1850s and 1860s he becomes appropriately High Victorian: in fact it would be hard to think of a more dogmatically High Victorian design than his house at Quar Wood in Gloucestershire (1858–61); or of a church more characteristic of its generation than Freeland in Oxfordshire (1869–71). At Scorborough (1857–9) and Appleton le Moors (1863–5), both in Yorkshire, Puginian scholarship is reinforced by High Victorian vigour; and at St Peter,

120 J. L. Pearson, Reredos, St Peter, Vauxhall, London (1862–4). High Victorian geometry.

121 J. L. Pearson, St Augustine, Kilburn, London (1870–80). Influences from Caen, Albi, Salisbury and Fountains.

Vauxhall (1862–4)[120], the need for economy produced a church with ornament more dogmatically geometrical than almost any of its generation. At St Augustine, Kilburn (1870–80)[121], Pearson achieved his masterpiece: outside, St Etienne at Caen; inside, Albi with touches of Salisbury and Fountains. Here High Victorian muscularity is mitigated by late Victorian sensitivity, and the whole structure is an eloquent testimony to Pearson's essentially architectonic talent. Finally, at Truro (1880–1910)[122] he combines motifs from Whitby, Durham, Lincoln, Westminster, Jumièges and Caen in a composition of extraordinary elegance and grace. But in 1882 the *Builder* was severe:

> Pearson at his best ... [he is] the most complete master of reproduced Gothic architecture since the death of Scott ... [but there is] not a new thought in the design; it is simply a Medieval cathedral over again ... a mere resuscitation of the architecture of the past.[116]

That is not quite fair. Pearson's handling of interior space, for instance, is masterly and original. But the criticism is substantially true. Undiluted historicism, taste and refinement, have replaced the thrust of Modern Gothic.

154

Bodley liked to define architecture as 'the refinement of building'.[117] Some said he confused refinement and religion. As Canon Clarke put it, 'Bodley brought Gothic to a state of refinement which it had probably never reached before (certainly never in the Middle Ages!). Whether Gothic ought to be refined is a different question.'[118] Goodhart-Rendel had no doubts about the matter: 'all that [Pearson, Bodley and Temple Moore] could teach ... their disciples', he concluded, 'was good taste, and the history of art has shown ... that ... the wages of good taste is death.'[119]

That is a hard saying, and yet it keeps coming to mind when one looks at the work of Bodley's architectural offspring. The line of descent is clear enough. Bodley begat G. G. Scott Jnr, and G. G. Scott Jnr, begat Temple Moore. Sir Ninian Comper[120] was a pupil of Bodley and Garner; and Walter Tapper[121] was an assistant to the same firm. Bodley, who did not die until 1907,[122] had in effect re-founded the Gothic Revival. To devotees of this last phase, Temple Moore's work still exerts a powerful attraction. There can be no denying his technical skill: in a full-scale country-house church like Sledmere, Yorkshire (1897–8); or in a rustic chapel like

122 J. L. Pearson, Truro Cathedral (1880–1910). 'Will 19th-century Gothic do?'

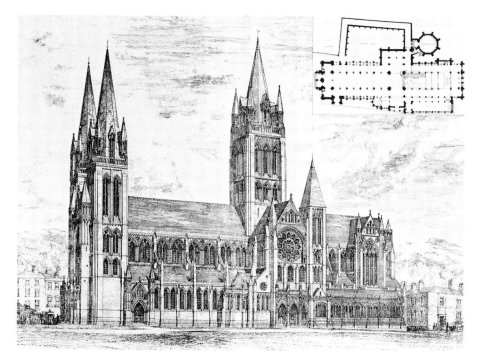

Rievaulx (1906), nestling near the shadow of the ruined abbey. And yet something is missing. The quality is at best autumnal. Christopher Hussey called Sledmere 'a perfect Perpendicular church, but not a twentieth-century one'.[123] Goodhart-Rendel considered Pusey House, Oxford (1911–14) a superlative specimen of 'Gothic design', but stylistically 'unreal': 'inferior intrinsically to the elastic, dynamic Gothicism of Keble and Balliol.'[124]

Temple Moore's finest church, St Wilfrid's, Harrogate (1905–14; 1935), is certainly a *tour de force*. But in 1928 Beresford Pite summed up the feeling of unease which must come over anyone who declines to suspend his critical faculties altogether:

> The work of Temple Moore [he told the R.I.B.A.] is rather distressing to some of us, because we cannot imagine what is to come after. [In his work the Gothic Revival seemed to have] reverted ... from an eclecticism which was an effort to make the style universal and applicable to all purposes, including the sash windows of the Law Courts and St Pancras ... to a purely medieval point of view. Instead of making a move into a new world, such as Butterfield, Waterhouse and Sir Gilbert Scott had anticipated, the ideal of the Gothic Revival retreated back five centuries into the Middle Ages, and became content with the perfection of the late fourteenth century as an ideal for our own times. That this [phase of the revival] has extraordinary power [Pite concludes] is mainly due to the work of G. G. Scott Jnr. The whole of the school of Bodley followed in his train, and it seems to me that Temple Moore's work is the last example of that phase.... The great wheel of the Gothic Revival [has] turned full-circle, and stopped.[125]

That was 1928. But in a way the most dramatic triumphs of the Gothic Revival were still to come: Lancing College Chapel (1868–1978)[123] and Liverpool Cathedral (1906–79)[124]. Here surely the Gothic Revival at last fulfilled its founders' dreams. Or did it?

Lancing is a monument to one man's vision, that of Nathaniel Woodard.[126] A succession of architects – R. C. Carpenter, William Slater, R. H. Carpenter, Stephen Dykes-Bower – have contributed to a complex of buildings which certainly comes nearer to Pugin's dream than any building Pugin ever built. The style is French: thirteenth-century details and fifteenth-century proportions. Its authenticity is not in question: the problem is its credibility. As Goodhart-Rendel remarked in another context, modernists may prove to their own satisfaction that this church *ought* not to be beautiful. 'But to deny its beauty they will have to shut their eyes.'[127] And there lies the nub of the problem: architectural aesthetics must be based not only on the eye, but also on the understanding. Once it was enough to dismiss Lancing Chapel as an irrelevance,

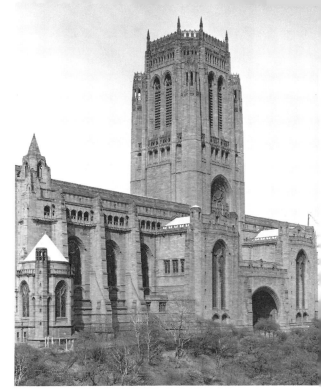

123 R. C. Carpenter, *et al.*, Lancing College Chapel, Sussex (1868–1978). Climax or dying fall?

124 Sir Giles Gilbert Scott, Liverpool Cathedral (1906–79). 'The death of the Gothic Revival'?

a hangover from the nineteenth century. That was to confuse – in Geoffrey Scott's phrase – the criteria of evolution with the criteria of aesthetic judgement. But there *is* a problem here, which will not go away. Presumably, the Lancing argument would run along the lines that Christianity is timeless, and therefore 'modernity' and 'relevance' are an illusion. But 'timeless' is exactly what Lancing is *not*: it is an evocation of *Medieval* Faith. It does not really address itself to the question: how can the beauties and principles of Gothic be translated into a different technology, a reformed religion and an alien world? How can the Gothic Revival be made both intellectually and visually acceptable? At Lancing such dilemmas are simply ignored. At Liverpool they are confronted if not head on, then at least obliquely.

In 1903 the competition for Liverpool's Anglican Cathedral was won by Giles Gilbert Scott – Great Scott's grandson – at the age of twenty-one. Work began in 1906, partly under Bodley's direction. Over a period of three-quarters of a century – the twentieth century – the style of decoration changed from English to Spanish, and from archaeological to abstract: from Neo-Gothic to Neon-Gothic. The Lady Chapel (1906–10) was built under Bodley's influence. Then comes the influence of Spain:

157

the under-tower has been traced to the 'new' cathedral of Plasencia; the reredos to the *retablo* of St Nicholas, Burgos, or to the gateway of the College of St Gregorio at Valladolid.[128] Later fittings, such as the font canopy, show Scott's genius floating free of medieval prototypes. After Bodley's death in 1909, Scott redesigned the plan, making it spatially electrifying, but liturgically irrelevant. The skyline he revised again and again, in 1909–10 and in 1924–42. Like Sir Christopher Wren at St Paul's, he refined and re-refined that silhouette, without slipping into the trap of what Bodley called 'refinement'.

Writing in 1942, Summerson described Liverpool Cathedral – which he knew closely as a young man – as 'a meteor from the eclipsed firmament of Gothic revivalism'. 'To appraise the extraordinary qualities of this building', he noted, 'will never be easy, and is today impossible. There is, perhaps, no building in the world which reflects, on a comparable scale, the changing mentality of a generation focused at the drawing-board of one man.'[129] Goodhart-Rendel was less evasive. To him Scott's tower marks 'the death of the Gothic Revival'.

> It is a scenic prodigy [he writes] displaying the great imaginative power of its designer, and producing upon spectators an emotional effect of extraordinary intensity. It stands aloof from architectural reality, having neither the functional nor the constructional inevitability of the ancient buildings whence its forms are ultimately derived – it is either a great engine of emotion or it is nothing. Those susceptible to its spell need not, should not, disenchant themselves by any attempted exercise of criticism. It has not the guarantee of permanent enjoyability that more rational architecture may hope to possess … [Its] permanence … [is] as a memorial of the lofty aim of countless able artists who [during the course of the Gothic Revival] in three generations, spent their efforts in the service of Romance … [Its] tremendous tower … [marks] the … last resting-place … of romantic architecture.[130]

Still, a cathedral is a cathedral. By that date the dilemma of style was essentially a secular dilemma. The great church-building movement had peaked long before, in the early 1870s.[131] Gothic churches continued to be built right through the 1920s and the 1930s. Cachemaille-Day's St Saviour, Eltham (1932–3), for instance, managed to develop the Albi prototype in a way which was wonderfully spare and economical.[132] Shearman's St Silas, Kentish Town (1912), which Goodhart-Rendel curiously described as 'over-sexed', managed to anticipate the qualities of Dutch expressionism years before Berlage. At St Andrew, Felixstowe (1930), Raymond Erith translated Perret's Notre Dame, Le Raincy, into East Anglian Tudor.[133] And in Charterhouse Chapel (1922) and St Andrew, Luton (1931)[125], Giles Gilbert Scott seemingly achieved the impossible: that very combination of modern technology – i.e. reinforced concrete – and historic associations, for which generations of Gothic revivalists had searched in vain.[134] But by that date architects did not want to know. The Modern Movement had taken command.

At the end of the nineteenth century, all that lay in the future. In the 1880s and 1890s, it seemed that the Goths had ransacked the Middle Ages and failed to find the Holy Grail. Their debate on 'the point of departure' had never been satisfactorily resolved: did you start 'developing' where Gothic culminated, in the fourteenth century, or where it stopped, in the sixteenth century? Or did you go back to where it all started in the twelfth and thirteenth centuries? All three methods had been tried. But the Victorian Style – that elusive vernacular – apparently refused to emerge. Henry Wilson went on experimenting, at Welbeck Abbey (1891–6), for instance.[135] But he knew he was whistling in the dark: even in Holy Trinity, Sloane St (1888–90). J. D. Sedding, he wrote, 'has shown us the promised land', though 'we shall never see this; we shall die in the wilderness.'[136] He meant a wilderness of pastiche: Romaine Walker's Stanhope House, Park Lane, London (1899–1901) perhaps. Most of the Goths simply gave up searching. They settled back into the arms of Queen Anne. The horns of the dilemma were becoming rather too uncomfortable.

The central irony of the Gothic Revival – at least since Pugin – lay in the fact that its principles could only be realised by abandoning its details: to succeed, the movement had first to wither away. Philip Webb was the only Goth who managed to make himself stylistically invisible. That turned out to be not the least of his legacies to the next, eclectic generation. Meanwhile Victorian Gothic – the dream of a universal style, medieval yet modern – was all but over. Ruskin, of course, had given up

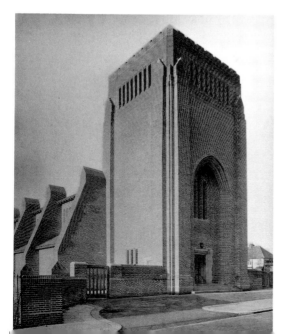

125 Sir Giles Gilbert Scott, St Andrew, Luton, Bedfordshire (1931). Modern techniques and historic associations.

159

hope long before.[137] So had William Morris. Even the best Victorian Gothic buildings, Morris admitted in 1884, were 'exotics': 'though they were built in this century they are not of it'. The disjunction between style and society, art and economy, craft and technology, was just too great.[138] In the same year, J. P. Seddon, once the most optimistic of Goths, admitted that the Gothic Revival had been 'an absolute failure': Pugin, Morris, Ruskin and all the Goths – even 'the incomparable William Burges' – had all failed, not in regard to 'true principles', but 'in their endeavours to revive old form for its own sake'.[139] In other words, the Puginian dilemma – principle or prototype – had never been resolved. By 1887 it was openly admitted that 'revived Medieval architecture ... has not been a success as a modern style'.[140] Even Burges's 'variety and originality' was seen to be 'the variety and originality of a thirteenth-century architect, not of a nineteenth-century one'.[141] Pugin's aesthetics, Ruskin's ethics, Morris's politics, these of course lived on. So did Gothic as one ingredient in an ever-evolving eclecticism. But by the end of Victoria's reign the Gothic Revival as a unitary stylistic movement was moribund.

In 1902 Norman Shaw made no bones about it. 'The Gothic Revival', he wrote, 'is dead ... From 1851 until recently we were all intensely Gothic – and intensely wrong. We were trying to revive a style which ... is totally unsuited to modern requirements.'[142] Lethaby agreed. 'The Gothic Revival', he noted in 1917, 'still lingers on as antiquarianism'; it is 'not quite vanished into the limbo of things forgotten'; but as a movement it is 'dead and buried beneath the ponderous sepulchre of Street's Law Courts'.[143] By 1921 even a posthumous Goth like Giles Gilbert Scott was admitting that in the secular or civic field, at least, Gothic was indeed finished: the spatial requirements of modern buildings ruled out an arcuated system and demanded some form of trabeation.[144] And by 1935 Goodhart-Rendel – the man who resuscitated the Rogues – had to confess that 'even the best Gothic detail nowadays has to be used ... as it were in inverted commas. It has ceased to have any constructional significance for us, and has become a stage property of religion.'[145] Worse still, it has begun 'to play to the gallery'.[146]

The failure of the Gothic Revival was heroic. As *The Globe* put it as early as 1874, 'there was something great about the Gothic Revival.'[147] Despite all their misgivings, the best of the Modern Goths eventually found what they were looking for: a style both old and new. But it could never be the universal style of which they dreamed. So architects in search of a style for their own age gave up Gothic, and turned instead to a broader base. They turned to Progressive Eclecticism.

160

6 Progressive Eclecticism

'Eclecticism! Eclecticism! What horrors have been perpetrated in thy euphonious name' (J. P. Seddon, 1872).

MORE THAN FIFTY YEARS AGO Henry-Russell Hitchcock set out an explanation of nineteenth-century architecture in terms of eclectic progression: from accumulation to synthesis, from Eclecticism of Taste to Eclecticism of Style.[1] Eclecticism was certainly a continuous theme in nearly all architectural thinking – Gothic or Classic – between the rise of the Picturesque and the genesis of the Modern Movement. It seemed to offer – then as now – a way out of the dilemma of style. It seemed to supply a solution to the perennial conundrum: the search for a new style; an alliance between history and progress; a reconciliation of art and industry, architecture and engineering; a mystical union of form and structure, beauty and truth. So in the mid-Victorian period, one catchphrase was on every critic's lips: Progressive Eclecticism. It was a slogan popularised in 1858 by Beresford Hope.

Alexander James Beresford Beresford Hope was the son of Thomas Hope, Neo-Classical Hope of Deepdene. He was President of the RIBA, proprietor of the *Saturday Review*, and for many years President of the Ecclesiological Society. He was rich, he was learned, he was religious, and he was more than a little absurd.[2] Absurd or not, his influence on architecture was considerable: Robert Kerr ranked him with Fergusson, Ruskin and Pugin.[3] But as a politician, as a writer, as a churchman, as a leader of taste, he ended his career in the wilderness.[4] Towards the end of his life he was even unable to see that his own theory of Progressive Eclecticism had in fact been vindicated by time: it emerged, full-blown, as the architecture of Free Classicism.

In several ways – socially, intellectually, financially, politically – Beresford Hope was the leader of the Victorian Gothic Revival. He supported it for half a century, 'by voice, pen and purse'.[5] In the heyday of ecclesiology he was a 'potentate' of taste, whose disapproval could break an architect.[6] He was Butterfield's patron at St Augustine's, Canterbury and at All Saints, Margaret St; he was Scott's advocate in the battle for the Foreign Office; he was Burges's champion in the Law Courts competition.

Even when the Gothic Revival began to wane, he remained in church-building matters an adherent of 'creative restoration': so much so that he denounced the SPAB's manifesto of 'anti-scrape' as 'a Gospel of Death'.[7] Yet although he was 'a Gothicist to his heart's core', he was a Goth with more than a sneaking respect for classicism. 'I am a Goth', he once admitted ' – more than that, a Northern Goth, but I am anxious to beautify the Northern Gothic with the best points of other styles, namely Italian Gothic and Italian Italian' – that is, he was willing to fuse Italian Gothic with Italian Renaissance. Indeed he found Gothic principles – in skyline, composition and planning – in Venice and in Amsterdam alike; in seventeenth-century Paris and in fifteenth-century Bruges. Almost everywhere, in fact, except in Palladianism and Neo-Classicism.[8]

Whereas James Fergusson gloried in the elemental properties of engineering, Hope believed in the synthesising potential of architecture. He knew that any new style must have its basis in previous styles.[9] Fergusson believed that a new style would one day simply replace all its predecessors. Hope realised that such a cultural cataclysm was unlikely to happen again. Total styles were the product of primitive civilisations. By the nineteenth century, a 'counteracting influence' had emerged: 'the creation thanks to modern civilisation, [thanks] to printing, engraving, increased locomotion and so on, of the feeling of *association*, that is, of archaeology made popular.'[10] Hence 'the Babel of schools'. Hence the search for 'a real style': 'the aim ... of all philosophic writers on architecture in modern days.'[11]

For Beresford Hope there was only one way out of the dilemma: 'Liberal' or 'Progressive Eclecticism'. That is 'the very key-stone of our system'. What we hope to develop is a 'type of art ... which, though called medieval, is still modern and progressive.'[12] In its origins the new style will be universal, but in its formulation it will be English: 'this style, while boldly eclectic in its detail must, in its main principles, vividly embody the historical characteristics of England, for whose material uses it will come into being.'[13] Patriotism, evolutionist thinking, cultural imperialism: all these will have their part to play. 'In the style of the future ... very much will be borrowed from Gothic ... [But] it will incorporate the beauties and conveniences of all other styles ... it will be as massive as Egyptian, ... as light as Saracenic, ... and ... proportioned like a Grecian temple. But that Gothic [i.e. a synthesis of Northern and Southern Gothic][14] *must* be the main ingredient appears to us demonstrable from the fact that Gothic was the universal emanation of the mind of Christian Europe, or at least of its active portion, in the days when that polity which is now overspreading the world was cradled. It was European – it was Christian – it was conclimatic with the chief regions of organised civil polity. With such an origin, we believe that it must prove itself a germinating power in the germination of Europe, in both hemispheres, just as the [Saxon] Witenagemot has been the seed from which have sprung the Parliaments of Belgium, Holland, and Sardinia, Legislatures (such as they are) in Spain and Greece, the Congress of the United States, and the Colonial Assemblies of the Cape, Australia, and Jamaica.'[15]

'The only style of common-sense architecture for the future of England', Beresford Hope concludes, 'must [therefore] be Gothic architecture, cultivated in the spirit of progression founded upon eclecticism. But here', he admits, 'our difficulties only begin ... [for] what are we to eclect?'[16]

In the 1830s and early 1840s, Hope explains, we chose English Gothic as 'our point of departure', 'the starting point for that which was then our only dream, the development and perfecting of our English Gothic.' In the battle between 1st, 2nd and 3rd Pointed, victory went to 2nd – Decorated – 'the golden mean of English Gothic'. 'It certainly flattered our insular pride. We were the best men in the world – nobody was like us – nothing [was] like our style.'[17] In the 1850s the basis of the revival broadened: Italian, French and even German Gothic were all absorbed. Speaking at Oxford as early as 1846, Hope had called for the broadest of all possible bases: 'we must be as familiar with San Clemente, Santa Sophia, and the church of the Holy Sepulchre, as with Heslington and York Minster ... We should remember that Great Britain reigns over the torrid and the hyperborean zone, that she will soon have to rear temples of the True Faith in Benares and Labrador, Newfoundland and Cathay.'[18] Ten years later he was still seeking a foundation, 'more broad and comprehensive ... To be truly eclectic, we must be universally eclectic – we must eclect from everything which has been eclected; and we must assimilate and fuse everything that we eclect, for without such fusion the process remains after all only one of distributive collection ... Ours is only an eclecticism of the past.... I imagine there will be an eclecticism of the future.'[19] The new style will draw upon 'resources unknown to the fourteenth century. There will be the knowledge of all the architecture of all the ages and countries, out of which to absorb a variety of materials, every day augmented to an extent almost bewildering; and there will be processes, gigantic as steam power, or minute as photography, to abridge labour or to facilitate invention.'[20] New materials, both decorative and structural, 'must in time revolutionise all architecture; but I believe it will be a peaceful ... revolution [supplementing] ... the good tradition of the old time.'[21]

And where will all this stop? 'I will stop', Hope concludes sagely 'where common sense tells me to stop. When I can no longer assimilate I will cease to absorb.'[22] Meanwhile, 'absorption is the thing to be aimed at'; for absorption is 'conducive to invention.'[23] Let the message go forth: 'progress through eclecticism.'[24]

Of course, eclecticism was a risky business. Rogue architects occasionally overstepped the mark.[25] Still, Beresford Hope remained optimistic, at least through the 1860s. At the very least, he thought, 'our architects have begun to think', and to think 'in an empiric spirit'. At present there may be confusion. The state of English architecture may even be 'chaotic'. But remember: *splendide errare*.[26] Creative eclecticism necessarily involves creative error. 'There may be here and there exuberance, if not extravagance; but this is only the natural recoil from the *malebolge* of stock-brick and cement in which we have so long been wandering.'[27] Polychromy, for instance: 'if you go into this style at all, you should do so boldly.' The aim must be an evolving synthesis: mere multiplicity is not enough – 'the choice of styles is Babel'.[28] 'A real style' will only emerge if its base becomes 'conservative . . . not destructive, retrospective no less than prospective, national rather than cosmopolitan, and yet encircling its native tradition by the imported and assimilated contributions of other lands.'[29]

In his belief in Progressive Eclecticism Beresford Hope spoke for the bulk of his architectural generation in England. J. Sulman defined it as 'not . . . the haphazard jumbling of incongruous fragments but a judicious combination and modification of forms.'[30] 'This judicious, and indeed inevitable eclecticism', wrote Benjamin Webb, 'is the distinguishing glory of our English architects. Nothing of the sort has yet been seen in France or Germany.'[31]

Eclecticism as a philosophical doctrine had first emerged in France, in the 1830s, with the writings of Victor Cousin; and the notion of architectural history as a *progrès continuel* had been formulated in the writings of Léonce Reynaud and Hippolyte Fortoul around 1840.[32] But most French architects generally resisted its aesthetic implications. They still maintained Quatremère de Quincy's idea of progression by reduction: from historical model to historical type.[33] César Daly only accepted the idea of eclecticism as a transitional phase on the road to a new style. 'In the architecture of the future', he announced in 1853, 'we shall have arches, vaults, beams, pillars and columns, as in ancient architecture, but we shall also have an aesthetic principle which will bear the same relationship to past principles as a locomotive bears to a stage-coach.'[34] Forty years later, when he received the RIBA Gold Medal, he was still

126 Capt. Francis Fowke, Exhibition Buildings (1862; dem.). 'Neither Grecian nor Gothic, but thoroughly nineteenth century'.

waiting.[35] Viollet-le-Duc was even less sure. By reforming education – by integrating architecture and engineering – he hoped to stimulate the emergence of a modern architecture, a synthesis of novelty and tradition. But in his *Entretiens* of 1863, he warned that a new style could only be based on a new constructive system; without that, eclecticism – on the nosegay principle – would merely produce a 'macaronic style'.[36] In 1856 Lassus denounced eclecticism as the 'plague of art . . . the common enemy . . . the scourge of our epoch'.[37]

In England such views found little support. In the *Builder*, George Godwin consistently supported eclecticism not as an end in itself, but as a means, 'an instrument of transition'.[38] 'Englishmen', agreed the *Building News* in 1858, 'are the most eclectic of the human race.'[39] Over the years any number of critics toyed with eclecticism as an answer to the problems posed by evolutionary thinking and technological change: Goths like Gilbert Scott;[40] rationalists like James Fergusson;[41] syncretists like H. N. Humphreys,[42] Samuel Huggins,[43] James Boule[44] and James Knowles;[45] pessimist Classicists like T. L. Donaldson;[46] pessimist Goths like J. T. Emmett;[47] eternal optimists like Robert Kerr.[48] And their ultimate, collective, aesthetic goal was still that same eclectic goal set out by Beresford Hope's father – Thomas Hope of Deepdene – in 1835: 'an architecture . . . at once elegant, appropriate, and original . . . "Our Own".'[49]

Beresford Hope's trumpet call to eclecticism, *The Common Sense of Art*, appeared in 1858. In that year two experimentally eclectic combinations of new materials and historic forms could be compared: Benjamin Woodward's Oxford Museum and Sydney Smirke's Round Reading Room at the British Museum. The first was Gothic, the second Classic. Beresford Hope began by preferring Woodward,[50] and ended up preferring Sydney Smirke.[51] Four years later current design was put under a microscope at the Exhibition of 1862. What was the result? The Exhibition building[126] had been designed by Capt Francis Fowke, an engineer not an architect, and a rather different sort of eclectic. Fergusson welcomed

127 David Bryce, Fettes College, Edinburgh (1864–9). Historicism in labour.

Fowke's characteristic *mélange*: 'neither Grecian nor Gothic, but thoroughly nineteenth-century.'[52] But for Beresford Hope the building was an 'architectural fiasco': its walls displayed 'that particular combination of Venetian and emasculated Byzantine which might be termed the Cosmopolitan-Governmental architecture of this century';[53] its brick-based glass domes – 'dish-covers' . . . 'cucumber-frames' – were 'the basest and most purposeless crystallo-chalybeate bubbles which earth has yet egurgitated.'[54]

Clearly Beresford Hope found engineers' eclecticism too difficult to swallow. Still, he believed that in 1862, from many different routes, 'a new style' seemed to be germinating, 'derived from, but not servilely following, existing systems.' Lined up that year, facing each other 'like rival armies', the British exhibition of architectural drawings emphasised that the mid-Victorian age was indeed 'an epoch of vast material and intellectual activity in the pursuit of architecture'. There they were, 'the Gothic on one side, the classical and the renaissance on the other, but peacefully commingled in the . . . galleries . . . devoted to the Scotchmen.' Scots Baronial:[55] here indeed was eclecticism with a vengeance. Bryce's Fettes College, Edinburgh (1864–9)[127], for instance: here the Hôtel de Ville at Compiègne and the Loire chateaux of Blois and Chenonceaux, mingled with echoes of the Hôtel de Cluny, Fyvie Castle, Roslyn

166

Chapel and Canongate Tolbooth.[56] Here was historicism in labour: 'the eager, sometimes exuberant, oftener healthy, search for originality'; the battle of ideas from which, one day, one style would come.

The Wedgwood Memorial Institute (1863–9)[128], at Burslem, Staffordshire, perhaps. Resplendent in polychrome brick and terracotta; pullulating with sculpture by Rudyard Kipling's father, it seemed to Beresford Hope to embody Progressive Eclecticism in the heart of industrial England.[57] Such was the hope of English architecture. 'We have everything the thirteenth and fourteenth centuries could give us', he explained in 1863, 'together with all that is our own, and all that the invention of printing and the spread of literature have opened up. Art is in a transitional state; the minds of men are in a transitional state ... Empires are crashing, new worlds are forming ... And in the midst of all this zeal and turmoil, there is the grand figure of Christian, progressive, European, and especially English art, rising higher and higher from the dark and surging waters of the ocean.'[58] 'Whatever beauty any other style possesses, that beauty we embrace; and we hope, or dream ... that in some later day the hidden link that joins it to the seemingly rival

128 R. Edgar and J. Lockwood Kipling, Wedgwood Memorial Institute, Burslem, Staffordshire (1863–9). Progressive Eclecticism.

developments may be discovered. Art we believe is one, only man has not yet mastered the secret of its unity.'[59]

By the mid-1860s Beresford Hope was claiming to see, all over London, the permeation of classicism by Gothic principles. Classicism, in a variety of Renaissance forms, was still a valid option for civic and commercial structures. But ever since the 1830s its supporters had been on the defensive. In 1864 Hope looked at the Grosvenor Hotel (by J. Knowles, 1860–1)[60] and he looked at the Langham Hotel (by J. Giles and J. Murray, 1864–6)[129][61], and he came to the conclusion that the Classicists were in retreat.[62] In pursuit of a transitional style, half Gothic, half Classic, they had apparently abandoned the Antique and the Renaissance for the mongrel classicism of the Loire. The Goths seemed to have triumphed. But by the end of the 1860s, Hope's optimism had evaporated. Instead of absorbing the classical tradition, the Gothic Revival was itself absorbed. And the culprit was Queen Anne. Eclectic classicism replaced eclectic Gothic. How did this come about?

The first renegade Goth to go over to Queen Anne was the Rev J. L. Petit. In 1841 he had sensed the inadequacy of revived Gothic, but he had been willing to wait a generation.[63] By 1856 he was running out of patience, crossing swords with Gilbert Scott.[64] And in a famous lecture of 1861, he publicly called in the Georgian tradition to redress the

129 J. Giles and J. Murray, Langham Hotel, London (1864–6). Half Gothic, half Classic.

130 R. Norman Shaw, Cragside, Northumberland (1869–84). The return of the Picturesque.

imbalance of Victorian eclecticism.[65] But it was in Street's office, in the early 1860s, that the anti-Gothic rebellion germinated: Norman Shaw and Philip Webb turned against their master, and swung English architecture away from Gothic towards Queen Anne. In doing so they set in motion a shift of taste which – within a generation – brought English architecture back to the Renaissance.

First came Old English, a revived form of rustic, home counties vernacular, complete with tile-hanging, hipped gables, casement windows, half-timbering, ribbed brick chimneys, and pargetting. Eden Nesfield and Norman Shaw were the leading figures, renegades both of them from Early French. As early as 1850 George Devey had designed half-timbered cottages, at Penshurst, Kent – taking the Picturesque manner of Humphry Repton more seriously. Butterfield too had occasionally employed false half-timbering. But if any one man invented the 'Old English' style, it was probably Nesfield: Stowford Cottages (1864–5) at Crewe Hall, Cheshire, are an early example.[66] Nesfield was a protean gentleman-genius; Shaw, to adopt J. M. Barrie's phrase, was 'a Scotsman on the make', but the most talented Scots architect since Robert Adam. At Cragside, Northumberland (1869–84)[130],[67] for Lord Armstrong the armaments king, he created an extraordinary synthesis of Gothic and Tudor, and Midlands vernacular half-timbering, handled with almost Wagnerian panache. All the rationalism of progressive Gothic has been abandoned: that half-timbering is merely decorative and evocative. The Picturesque has returned, as though Pugin had never lived and never written. As a style it was dangerously infectious, almost a romantic contagion, spreading via Douglas of Chester and Ould of Liverpool to the lower depths of Stockbrokers' Tudor.

Then came Queen Anne, a flexible urban argot, sash-windowed, brick-ribbed, based on late seventeenth-century vernacular classicism, Dutch, French, Flemish, German and English – all seasoned with a dash of Japanese. Nesfield and Shaw were again the leaders, but backed up this time by a group of rebels from Gilbert Scott's office: G. F. Bodley, J. J. ('Jock') Stevenson, E. R. Robson, G. G. Scott Jnr, Basil Champneys and T. G. ('Anglo') Jackson. Bodley's vicarage at Scarborough (1866–8), for instance, transferred to the Yorkshire seaside the suave urbanity of Queen Anne's Gate, London.[68] And Norman Shaw's Lowther Lodge, Kensington (1876)[131] showed just how far the new idiom could be stretched in pursuit of an urban Picturesque. The Gothic Revival had been secularised

131 R. Norman Shaw, Lowther Lodge, Kensington (1876). The urban Picturesque.

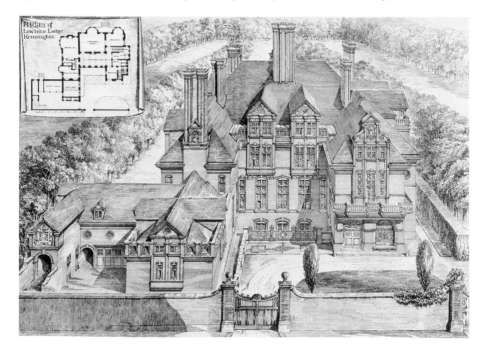

132 Philip Webb, 91–101 Worship Street, London (1862–3). 'The fuse that exploded Victorian Gothic'.

by Scott and Waterhouse. Now Scott's pupils, like Street's pupils, took the logical next step and abandoned the pointed arch.

Hovering in the background, godfather to this new eclecticism, was Morris's own architect, Philip Webb: in Goodhart-Rendel's words, 'the ... man who laid the fuse that exploded Victorian Gothic.'[69] His style – as at 1 Palace Gate, Kensington (1868), or at 91–101 Worship St (1862–3)[132], in London's East End – mingles Gothic and Classic, medieval and Georgian, in a way which defies easy analysis. At the time, the government architect, Pennethorne, who had to vet the Kensington designs, vetoed the Palace Gate house as 'commonplace' and 'perfectly hideous'. He called in Salvin and T. H. Wyatt as referees. They explained they were 'unable to discover what actual style or period of architecture' had been used as a model. That, replied Webb, 'I take to be a sincere compliment.'[70] One might be tempted to agree with Norman Shaw, who described Webb as 'a very able man indeed, but with a strong liking for the ugly'.[71] He certainly loved what he called 'the strength of ... [the]

133 Philip Webb, Red House, Bexleyheath, Kent (1860). Built for William Morris.

134 William Butterfield, Sheen Parsonage, Staffordshire (1852).
Built for the editor of *The Ecclesiologist*.

135 Philip Webb, Clouds, East Knoyle, Wiltshire (1881–7; dem.). Eclectic and progressive.

barbaric'.[72] But Webb would have translated 'ugliness' as 'reality': Pugin-ian or Pre-Raphaelite reality. As Lethaby put it, 'Webb in building, like Browning in poetry and Madox Brown in painting, was first of all a realist; but then he sought for the romantic and the poetic in the real.'[73] Anyway, the ancestry of Webb's eclecticism is fairly clear. Butterfield had been there first, and Pugin had anticipated Butterfield.

Look first at Webb's most famous early work: Red House, Bexleyheath (1860)[133], built for William Morris.[74] Then look back at one or two of Butterfield's rectories: Sheen, Staffs (1852)[134], for instance, built for the editor of the *Ecclesiologist*, Benjamin Webb. And finally, look further back via Butterfield's estate cottages[75] to Pugin's priest's house at Alton (c.1842)[36]. The evolution is clear enough. But there was to be a second phase in Webb's career. Having drawn inspiration from one tradition, he went on to assimilate another: the artisan classicism of the early eight-eenth century. The result was eclectic, and progressive too. Clouds, East Knoyle, Wilts (1881–7)[135] is as much Classic as Gothic.[76] Webb's artistry has fused Renaissance harmony with Gothic freedom. Alas, he lived to see the Renaissance take its revenge.

In a way, Queen Anne was an evolving answer to the Gothic Revival's search for an eclectic vernacular. But that hardly made it more popular with orthodox Goths like Gilbert Scott. Still, it did catch the new mood of the 1870s. Away with Puginian morality, away with religiosity; down with rationality; down with muscularity. Up with comfort, up with fun.

173

Back to the philosophy of Picturesque Gothic without the inconvenience of Gothic forms. From Red House, Bexleyheath (1860) to the Red House, Bayswater (1871); from Kew Gardens (1866)[77] to Kensington Palace Gardens; from the City to the Thames Embankment; from School Board domestic[78] to Pont Street Dutch, the bricky tide swept on: Queen Anne and Old English in harness. By 1868 Philip Webb's London houses had established Queen Anne as a fashionable fact. Thackeray was doing for the new style what Byron had done for the Greek Revival and Sir Walter Scott for Gothic.[79] The world of Samuel Sanders Teulon was giving way to the world of Oscar Wilde.

Now Wilde belonged to a younger generation than Teulon: he was still at Oxford when Teulon was making muscular Gothic popular. By 1870 the scene has changed: stove-pipe hats and buttoned boots have been replaced by cloaks and buckled shoes, silk stockings and knee breeches.[80] Art for art's sake[81] has arrived – that is art and architecture divorced from morality, divorced from all Puginian and Ruskinian sanctions. An art no longer solely medieval, an architecture no longer solely Gothic. The old dogmas have collapsed under a hail of epigrams. There is a new scepticism abroad, a new relativism. Oscar has style – none more so – but he does not believe in any single style, still less in the creation of a new Victorian style, buttressed by morality. Pater has taught him the autonomy of art, the comparability of styles. Decadence has replaced vigour. The Aesthetes have dethroned the Goths. And Norman Shaw is just the man to turn their taste into popular form.

First the furniture, then the plaster, then the wrought iron, then the woodwork, and finally the exterior fabric of Queen Anne houses themselves was packaged and sold to the suburban bourgeoisie. Church Row, Hampstead; Queen's Square and Queen Anne's Gate, with their warm red bricks, their rectangular sash windows, their thick glazing-bars, their shell-headed doorways – these became domestic models of convenience and propriety, synthesised with Old English and François Premier. In Bedford Park (1876 onwards)[136] – the aesthetes' garden suburb – the new fashion reached its apogee. High Victorian Gothic had been inspired by a vision of the Middle Ages, Christian and Feudal. By the 1870s such Puginian mythology was wearing thin. The denizens of Bedford Park gave Christianity a humanistic twist; they preferred aestheticism to asceticism. They preferred softer, more feminine decorations to what Warington Taylor considered those 'painful, geometrical, harsh forms' of Modern Gothic.[82] Above all, they cultivated domesticity.[83]

Domesticity was not what the old-school Goths were looking for. J. P.

136 R. Norman Shaw *et al.*, Bedford Park, London (1876 onwards). The aesthetes' garden suburb.

Seddon and J. D. Sedding dismissed the new mode as 'gibberish' and 'garbage', the prostitution of art by a band of aesthetic Adullamites; a 'mongrel', 'licentious' style; 'barbaric ... baby talk'.[84] Burges called Queen Anne 'an illiterate negro language'. 'I have been brought up', he announced in 1876, 'in the thirteenth-century belief, and in that belief I intend to die.'[85]

Seddon, Sedding and Burges were almost the last to speak out boldly against the new cult. By 1875 most Gothic Revivalists seemed to have lost their nerve. Norman Shaw, Bodley, Nesfield, Webb, Stevenson, G. G. Scott Jnr, R. W. Edis, T. G. Jackson, Basil Champneys – even, it was whispered, Butterfield and Rossetti: they had all deserted the Gothic camp, either to Old English or to Queen Anne.[86] By 1877 even E. W. Godwin – Burges's staunchest ally in the 1860s – had gone over to the enemy, in Bedford Park itself.[87] Classicism however debased, however Flemish and Frenchified, was back in vogue – for the first time since the 1840s.[88]

The names given to the new fashion reflected the confusion of its origins. 'Dutch William', 'Low Dutch', 'Early Georgian',[89] 'Free Classic',[90] 'Mystic', 'Neo-Classic',[91] 'Re-Classic',[92] 'Stuart',[93] 'Re-Renaissance'[94] – these were by no means the only labels suggested. In fact the popular use of the title 'Queen Anne' probably derived from one of Morris's wall-

175

papers – 'Queen Anne' – first used at 26 Queen's Square, Bloomsbury, in 1865. Still, whatever its title – some just called it the 'Bastard Style' – there was no mistaking the new mood: a return, devious and tentative, but a return none the less, to the long-neglected fount of classicism: a renaissance of the Renaissance. One symptom of this aesthetic counter-revolution was a new sympathy for the work of Christopher Wren.[95] Another was Walter Pater's *Studies in the History of the Renaissance*. 'These remarkable Studies', noted the *Saturday Review* in 1873, 'are among the signs of the times. Since the days of the purists, when Mr Ruskin denounced the Renaissance as hollow and unholy, a singular change has come over the younger generation ... Poetry, painting and criticism alike [Rossetti, Swinburne, Burne-Jones ...] all tell of a modern renaissance of the old Renaissance.'[96] The Hellenes had temporarily overcome the Hebrews.

To a certain extent the Queen Anne movement embodied a truce between two warring traditions, a compromise between Gothic and Classic.[97] Hence the interest in Early Renaissance, in François Premier:[98] Chambord as well as the Dutch House at Kew. J. J. Stevenson sensed a close parallel between the transitional sixteenth century and the transitional nineteenth century.[99] E. R. Robson claimed that he was simply trying to create 'a good modern style'.[100] It was medieval in planning and composition; it was classical in the language of its forms. Above all, it was Picturesque. One critic called the new style 'pittoresco-classical'.[101] It was this fusion of competing traditions – 'Free Gothic' as much as 'Free Classic' – which reconciled even William Morris.[102] 'Free Classic', it was noted, was an omnivorous combination of 'High Dutch and Late Georgian'.[103] In fact, it was vague enough to include almost anything of the sixteenth, seventeenth or eighteenth centuries.[104] And the additional cult of Japan – by breaking away from conventional Western prototypes altogether – re-emphasised the movement's freedom from traditional restraints.[105] Pragmatism seemed to have triumphed over dogma: the Georgian vernacular of Church Row, Hampstead, could be combined – without any sense of incongruity – with the fantastic gables of Amsterdam. The result was Dutch, French, English and Japanese:

> A patchwork of Japan,
> And queer bits of Queen Anne
> All mixed upon the plan
> Of as you like, or as you can.[106]

Even a classicist like Robert Kerr, who rejoiced in the displacement of Gothic, called it the 'bric-a-brac style'.[107] And in its full-blown phases –

137 Sir Ernest George, 39–43, Harrington Gardens, London (1880–84). Dutch or double Dutch?

in Tite Street, in Queen's Gate, in Cadogan Square, in Mount Street or Pont Street the bric-a-brac is very miscellaneous indeed. Exothenic (or scenic) architecture had replaced esothenic (or organic) design. The atectonic elements in Renaissance aesthetics had been compounded by a recrudescence of the Picturesque. With the Renaissance, noted J. P. Seddon in 1874, 'architecture became *architecturesque*, that is it looked like architecture but was not ... How we are to come out of the slough of architectural impurity we are [now] in with clean hands I cannot see; there is not a feature of Classic architecture not daily murdered before our eyes by those who pretend to reverence it ... What we want is a return to pure common-sense architecture. Never mind its name.'[108]

The ubiquity of Sir Ernest George and his sketchbook school – from Harrington Gardens, London[109] (1880–84)[137] to the Ossington Coffee Palace, Newark, Notts (1882) – was indeed an index of the omnipresence of the Picturesque. Progressive Eclecticism had lost its sense of direction in a sargasso sea of ornament and scenic device. 'Will a time come', asked the *Builder* in 1897, 'when there shall be no more old things left

138 G. F. Bodley and T. Garner, School Board Offices, Embankment, London (1872–9, 1886, 1891; dem.). Franco-Dutch Queen Anne.

unsketched? Not yet perhaps ...'[110] Muthesius noted that Sir Ernest George 'has done little to further the development of modern ideas', adding with masterly understatement, 'such was probably not his intention.'[111]

On the face of it, it seems odd that those solemn burghers of seventeenth-century Holland should have inspired the architectural environment of Wilde and Whistler. How strange that the world of Jan Vermeer and Peter de Hooch should reappear, transmogrified in the purlieus of Kensington. And yet not so strange. Delft and Amsterdam – bourgeois, capitalistic, individualistic, Protestant – were spiritually far closer to Victorian London than the Puginian or Ruskinian dream of the Catholic Middle Ages. What was strange, even disturbing, was the freedom with which Dutch prototypes were reinterpreted. Ernest George's Albemarle Hotel (1887–9), on the corner of Albemarle St and Piccadilly, owes as much to the Loire as it does to the Amstel.[112] Bodley's School Board Offices on the Embankment (1872–9; 1886; 1891; dem)[138][113] were a

178

mixture of the Butter Market at Haarlem and the Hotel d'Ecoville, Caen. Try comparing Amsterdam and South Kensington: the Heerengracht and Harrington Gardens; the Keizersgracht and Cadogan Square. Cynics were hinting that Dutch was becoming double Dutch.

Queen Anne, in all its multifarious forms, meant the final end of Puginian discipline: decoration no longer expressed structure; it was simply *decoration*. The puritan focus of Puginian theory – the attempt to equate function and propriety – sometimes an ideal, more often a fiction – had finally been abandoned in favour of the aesthetics of hedonism. For structural expression read self-expression. The attempt – by Pugin and Ruskin – to control eclectic historicism by means of morality – had been abandoned. Norman Shaw's half-timbering, Nesfield's roundels, Bodley's Franco-Flemish gables, Ernest George's terra-cotta: art for art's sake meant ornament for ornament's sake. Norman Shaw recognised the problem. 'Old work', he confessed to Sedding in 1882, 'is *real* ... ours is not real, but only like real.'[114] The Queen Anne revival prided itself on only one Gothic legacy, its *truthful* planning. But the principle of absolute truth in architecture as Jock Stevenson pointed out in 1875, was a pernicious illusion – just how pernicious, of course, the Modern Movement eventually demonstrated. Meanwhile, it was gradually realised that revealed construction was no more *natural* than revealed anatomy. Nature sensibly preferred to conceal the organs of human bodies under a protective, and rather more attractive, skin.[115] Puginian truth, Puginian reality, had been replaced – sometimes sensibly, sometimes foolishly – by the aesthetics of aestheticism.[116]

In architecture, if not in the decorative arts, the 1870s and 1880s were years of lowering sights and loosening tensions. It took a strong man to discern – in Shaftesbury Avenue, in Charing Cross Road or in Northumberland Avenue – the germs of a new style.[117] There was, in fact, a widespread sense of despair. 'Eclecticism! Eclecticism!' wailed J. P. Seddon, 'what horrors have been perpetrated in thy euphonious name'.[118] Like the collapse of the Modern Movement a hundred years later, the collapse of the Gothic Revival had left behind it a vacuum of principle.

'These are critical times for us', J. P. Seddon warned the Architectural Association in 1884. 'A strange calm has come. There is a sense of impending change. This is a time of felt uncertainty, of stranded purposes, of searchings of heart.' The architect – 'a blind man leading the blind' – had apparently been ousted by his own assistants, the interior decorator and the structural engineer. One day, he hopes, 'the disorder of modern architecture' will be replaced by the 'vernacular that is to be.' Meanwhile, what is 'your eclecticism'? What is it but 'a very Pandemonium of tit-bit

types'? 'Never since the world began has so much architectural knowledge' been accumulated. And the result has been chaotic: 'all the sad,
bad and mad architecture' of the 'last thirty-five years'.[119]

J. D. Sedding was even gloomier. 'What we call Victorian architecture',
he told the Architectural Association in 1883, 'is nothing in fact but a
retrospective art, an art of plagiarism and odds and ends ... [It] reminds
me of an embalmed corpse in a ball dress. It is historic art made histrionic
... We have no living art [of] ... our own. [Our] failings ... are ... heart-
breaking.'[120] 'Our architecture ... is composed of what naturalists call
"illegitimate crosses" (and mules have no progeny) ...' For architects,
'looking back' has been 'as unfortunate [as it was for] Lot's wife!'[121] And
nothing much could be done about it: 'It took a God', he concluded, 'to
bring order out of chaos.'[122]

Seddon and Sedding might be written off as disillusioned Goths. But
Norman Shaw, riding the crest of the new eclectic wave, was equally
confused. Early on in his career he had lost his faith in Gothic, at least
for secular and domestic work:

> The style dug up might just as well have been Chinese or Egyptian [he told
> J. D. Sedding in 1882] and we have struggled on with that style ... between
> forty and fifty years now ... but that it is in any sense whatever a living art,
> I cannot see ... all the *best* of it is 'purely imitative' ... Is it possible that this
> can be *great* art? I fear not ... [And as for] our vernacular, [it] is not within
> the pale of art at all. I have never seen any rendering of plate glass and
> Portland cement that one could call art ... You say, 'I wish Bodley wouldn't
> copy ...' [But] we are all in the same boat, except Butterfield, who is in a boat
> of his own all by himself. It is bad enough to be in such a doleful plight ...
> but I for one don't want to live and die in a fool's paradise ... my half-timbered
> work and tall chimneys ... [are not] in any way my own ... but ... simply
> indifferent copies of old work.

'The trouble is', he admitted to his wife soon afterwards, 'I enjoy looking
back more than looking forward.'[123] He clearly enjoyed restoring Ightham
Mote in the early 1870s – complete with half-timbered dog-kennel – just
as Cubitt enjoyed fabricating a half-timbered miniature manor-house,
now in the park at Woburn Abbey, for the Paris Exhibition of 1878.

Broadly speaking, 'the Battle of the Styles' – Gothic versus Classic –
was a characteristic of the 1850s; the Battle for a Style – the pursuit of
novelty at all costs – was a phenomenon of the 1860s. After 1870 a
whole generation of architects gave up battling. They lost their faith in
Gothic; they lost their taste for GO. They settled for Queen Anne – 'that
vexatious disturber of the Gothic movement', as Gilbert Scott called
it[124] – an architecture without rules, without illusions. The heroic age of

Victorian architecture was over. Or rather the battlefield had moved across the Atlantic, to the new world of H. H. Richardson. 'Amateurs and architects', announced the *Building News* in 1887, 'have talked themselves dumb.'[125] The search for a Victorian style, Gothic in inspiration, and eclectic in form, had apparently been abandoned. When in 1888 William Simpson asked his audience at the Society of Arts: 'What Style of Architecture Should We Follow?' he offered – and received – no answer.[126] In place of the single, evolving style of Modern Gothic, Queen Anne announced the validity of many styles. The idea of a total style had been replaced – as in the Regency – by the concept of plurality of style: Gothic for churches, Renaissance for town halls and banks, Queen Anne for schools and houses.[127] The battle had been suspended. In a sense, chaos had simply become respectable.[128] 'What the next half-century may produce', wondered Ewan Christian in 1884, 'God only knows.'[129]

The break with the Gothic Revival had done nothing to resolve the dilemma of style. The 1880s – just as much as the 1870s, or the 1860s, or the 1850s – remained trapped in the aesthetics of transition. In 1884 George Godwin, retiring editor of the *Builder*, and his successor H. Heathcote Statham, both agreed that what they were witnessing was the collapse of style, that is style defined as 'a general, pervading homogeneity of idea';[130] 'those qualities of logical and harmonious treatment of every portion of a design in reference to a leading idea.'[131] In 1885 Statham summed up the architectural state of play as follows: 'vacillation ... indecision of purpose, [and] abnormal worship of precedent.'[132] 'There are many of us', noted the President of the Architectural Association in 1876, 'who have quite given up in despair all real artistic interest in our work. The rapid changes of fashion seem to have fairly dazed [us. In effect "there's nothing new, and there's nothing true", and it doesn't matter.'[133]

It still mattered to Beresford Hope. In his inaugural address in 1865, as President of the RIBA, he argued that one solution might be the professional integration of architecture and engineering: 'The Institute ought to be the central regulating Areopagus of Architecture – of architecture as a science, and architecture as an art.'[134] A year later, in his second presidential address, he called – 'in the name of progress and eclecticism' – for the application of modern techniques and materials to Gothic Revival design.[135] And the year after that, in a farewell speech, he again speculated on the progress of architecture, looking back to his father's time, and forward – presumably – to an eclectic future.[136] But time was running out for the Gothic Revival and Beresford Hope refused to concede to Queen Anne the eclectic freedom he willingly granted to

139 G. Truefitt, Brooks's Bank, Manchester (1867–70; partly dem.). Eclecticism with a Gothic base.

140 R. Norman Shaw, Alliance Assurance Office, St James's St, London (1881–3). 'The germ of an original style'.

Gothic. In that respect, Hope – a Gothic eclectic – was far less flexible than a Classic eclectic like Robert Kerr.[137] What he objected to in Queen Anne was not its eclecticism – Dutch, French, Flemish, German, English, Japanese – but the fact that its matrix was Classical, not Gothic. He would have preferred a synthesis like Waterhouse's Clydesdale Bank, Lombard St, London (1866; dem), or Truefitt's Brooks's Bank, Manchester (1867–70; partly dem),[138][139] in which the basis of the mixture was primarily Gothic. Queen Anne, he felt, was different: its synthetic properties were not 'organic' but 'artificial'.[139]

At his death in 1887, the editor of the *Builder* commented on the fact that Hope's plea for Progressive Eclecticism, delivered so optimistically in 1858, had borne some very curious fruit: 'eclecticism has run wild since then'.[140] Wild or not, had it produced a Victorian style?

When Hope's RIBA obituary came to be delivered, his obituarist simply set out the question – 'whether we have really evolved a Victorian style', and urged the audience to look about them.[141] The audience, apparently, were not disposed to look: they heard the speech with 'manifest impatience'.[142] But in that very year, 1887, Basil Champneys produced a Jubilee assessment of 'The Architecture of Queen Victoria's Reign', and came to the conclusion that eclecticism had indeed triumphed, but in 'free classic' form. He instanced three recent buildings: Norman Shaw's Alliance Assurance Office (1881–3)[140] on the corner of Pall Mall and St James's; Bodley and Garner's School Board Offices (1872–9, 1886,

182

1891; dem)[138] on the Embankment;[143] and T.G. Jackson's Examination Schools at Oxford (1876–82; 1887).[144][141]

In all three Champneys identified a union of Gothic and Classic – Classic forms and Gothic principles – 'the germ of an original and harmonious style in the future'.[145] In a way that had been the essence of Queen Anne: by reviving hybrid formulae – François Premier, Flemish or Jacobean – it signalled an escape from stylistic deadlock, a truce in the battle of style. Even so, Champneys was far from optimistic. 'We who have fallen upon these chaotic times', he wrote in the year of Victoria's first Jubilee, 'have no style ready to hand, no tradition to help us, few or no educated workmen to come to our aid. The choice of style is necessarily an arbitrary one. Having no property of our own, we are thrown for charity upon the entire past ... [Architects are like] a pack of hounds who have lost the scent!' There was only one sign of hope: an eclectic synthesis of Gothic and Classic.[146] All around him he saw 'chaos': 'ninetenths of the buildings of the nineteenth century' belong to only one school – the 'school of anarchy'. Even the leaders of the profession were divided: 'when the teachers disagree, it is hard for the pupil to be wise'. Only in ecclesiastical architecture, he believed, was there much sign of

141 T.G. Jackson, Examination Schools, Oxford (1876–82; 1887).
Classic forms and Gothic principles.

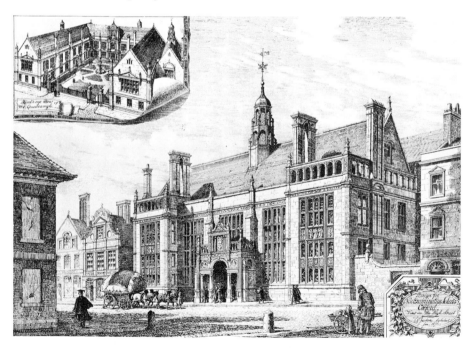

controlled evolution. Civil, public, and even domestic architecture were all in a state of impenetrable confusion. 'The future', he concluded, 'is and long will be dark.'[147]

In one thing the editors of the *Builder* and the *Building News* were agreed: synthesis was the only way out of the dilemma. In a sense, all architects were now eclectics.[148] In pursuit of synthesis, the Goths were trying to build domes: T. G. Jackson, for instance, at Giggleswick School, Yorks (1897–1901)[142]; and the Classicists were trying to build steeples: E. M. Barry, for example, at Halifax Town Hall (1859–62)[143] – crossing and re-crossing the stylistic binary line. E. W. Mountford certainly believed in the magic properties of eclecticism. 'Architecture may be in a bad way', he noted in 1893, 'but it is better than it was.'[149] 'What is wanted [now] is something characteristic of nineteenth-century life and requirements; we do not want people in the year 3000 to look back and be unable to determine whether buildings were erected in the nineteenth, the thirteenth or the first century.'[150]

So how did Mountford propose to satisfy Macaulay's New Zealander? His Sheffield Town Hall (1890–7) was neatly summed up by one critic as 'Classic detail in a Gothic manner'.[151] The architect himself described

142 T. G. Jackson, Giggleswick School Chapel, Yorkshire (1897–1901). Synthesis: a Gothic dome.

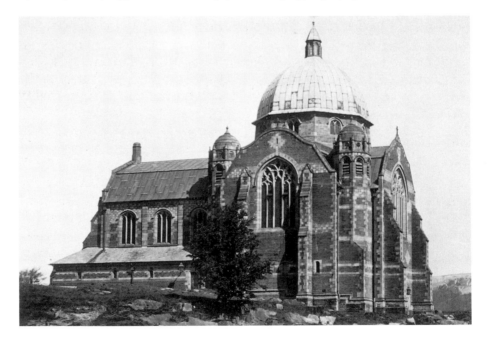

143 E. M. Barry, Halifax Town Hall (1859–62). Synthesis: a Renaissance steeple.

144 Alfred Waterhouse, National Liberal Club, Whitehall Place, London (1885–7). Liberal eclecticism.

it as 'Modern Renaissance': 'as far as possible it is English in character and detail. So far as I know the design is as original as may be in the nineteenth century – that is to say, no existing building has been consciously copied either in whole or in part, excepting of course, in the matter of detail of doors, windows, etc.'[152] In other words, its originality lay in its eclecticism.

Alfred Waterhouse would have understood. His National Liberal Club, Whitehall (1885–7)[144], may not have been national, but it was certainly liberal. Here was a building which was Renaissance, Romanesque, Venetian and French. Its style was eclectic, and its clients were progressive. 'Its style', remarked the *Builder*, 'could not be described in a word', unless that word was Liberal: 'the Liberal party is a heterogeneous jumble of discordant elements, and ... in scattering varied and inconsequential details over his work, Mr Waterhouse has exactly hit off the idiosyncrasies of his clients.'[153] Alas, few architects could match Waterhouse's capacity for integration. His National Liberal Club brilliantly transformed the skyline of Whitehall. But its principles of composition were dangerously diffuse. When James Hay submitted a design for Liverpool Cathedral

185

(1886)[154][145] complete with Gothic towers, a Roman dome and Grecian porticoes, he was merely reducing to the level of caricature a system of composition which it was only too easy to abuse. 'A new style!' cried *The Globe* despairingly in 1870; 'A new style! My kingdom for a new style!' Nonsense, snorted J. P. Seddon, we are already suffering from a surfeit of novelty.[155]

Bric-a-Brac Renaissance – Claridges (1894–8) or Harrods (1894–1912)[146], both by C. W. Stephens – peaked out in the 1890s. Halsey Ricardo called it 'Advertisement Architecture': an expression of the competitive ethic, of *laissez-faire* capitalism.[156] Such things, noted the *Building News*, 'are the mental refuse with which the modern man surrounds himself . . . just as smoke and dust and dirt are the material refuse.'[157] Fitzroy Doll's Russell Hotel (1898) and Imperial Hotel, both in Russell Square (1905–12; dem)[147], had at least the merit of fantasy. But Col

145 J. Hay, Design for Liverpool Cathedral (1886). 'My kingdom for a new style!'

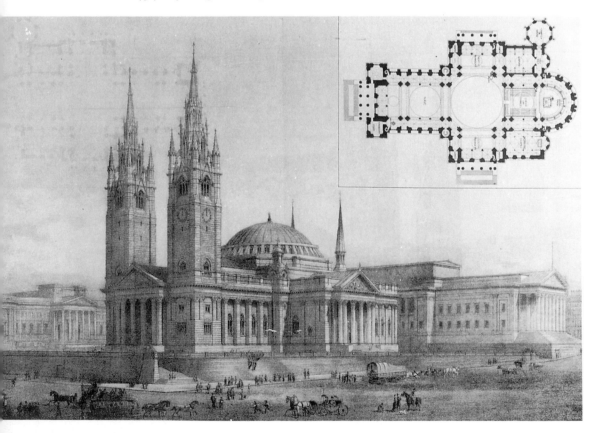

146 C. W. Stephens, Harrods, Knightsbridge, London (1894–1912). 'Advertisement Architecture'.

147 C. Fitzroy Doll, Imperial Hotel, Russell Square, London (1905–12; dem.). Eclectic fantasy.

148 J. Dunn, Surrey House, Surrey St, Strand, London (c.1895; dem.). 'Oh for a tax on ornament!'

Edis's Great Central Hotel, Marylebone (1897–9), shows the style at its feeblest. Scruton – Victor Scruton of Birmingham – called it the 'Hybrid or Pick-and-Choose Style': 'this fact I assert boldly ... that [in] the architecture of the present day, there is a torpor, a disease, and a death, greater than have existed in any nation worthy of the name, Pagan or otherwise, at any time on the face of the globe.'[158]

By the end of the 1890s such Picturesque conflations – shotgun marriages of Gothic and Classic, François Premier or Queen Anne – had come to be regarded as fundamentally misconceived. When the Aesthetes triumphed in the 1870s they had performed a valuable service in blowing apart the mid-Victorian confusion of ethics and aesthetics. But when aestheticism was magnified and distorted during the 1880s and 1890s by a renaissance of the Picturesque, the results – in strictly architectural terms – were certainly worrying.[159] And when these results were diluted, popularised, suburbanised, the effect could be catastrophic. Multiplied knowledge had merely multiplied styles, and in the hands of the 'business' architect', the *laissez-faire* principles of Progressive Eclecticism

188

became simply an excuse for ostentation and commercialism.[160] The streets off the Strand – Arundel St, Norfolk St, Surrey St[148] – noted one American critic, 'suggest ... pieces of pastry or the toy houses of children'.[161] The reign of terracotta, the 'scarlet fever', had left its mark in innumerable incrustations from Cadogan Square to Wimpole St, from Wigmore St to Queen Anne's Gate.[162] 'The demon of prosperity', noted one critic in 1896, has brought about 'the degradation of architecture.'[163]

Opportunities for architects seemed limitless. After all, England was the richest country in the world. In 1883 alone it was estimated that £35,000,000 had been spent on building. And with what result? 'We see nothing', noted one commentator, 'but confusion and divergence of aim.'[164] César Daly expected nothing else: a fragmented society, he believed, meant a fragmented style.[165] The whole Queen Anne revival, T. G. Jackson pointed out in 1885, had begun – with Philip Webb – as a rebellion against pretension, and ended as pretension personified: 'whole fronts are over-loaded with carved brickwork or terracotta, broken pediments, pilasters, consoles and balusters, in vulgar profusion.'[166] Archer and Green's Hyde Park Hotel (Hyde Park Mansions, 1888) perhaps. 'Oh', prayed G. F. Terry in 1889, 'Oh, for a tax on ornament!'[167] Mr Gladstone agreed. 'There is [one] circumstance in architecture', he announced in 1896, 'which terrifies me, and that is ... redundant ornamentation. There are a great many new buildings in London ... [in which] the architect had either a horror or a dread of leaving bare a single square foot of wall, as if [doing so] were something indecent.'[168] 'In walks about London', complained the President of the RIBA, 'one longs to apply the scalping-knife in stripping off meretricious ornament ... [Such] archi tectural quackery ... [is simply indulging] the false and meretricious taste of a luxurious age.'[169] From the Strand to Eastcheap, announced the *Building News*, from Oxford St to Bombay, the architectural 'ranter' is abroad; the modern architect is 'pandering to a taste which he knows to be bad'.[170]

In the end there were two ways out of the quagmire into which Progressive Eclecticism had sunk: architects had either to abandon polite architecture altogether, in search of an Arts and Crafts vernacular; or else they had to go the whole hog, surrender their Puginian and Ruskinian ideals, and return to the classical tradition – as prophesied by Professor Kerr.[171] There was a third way – to discard completely the whole apparatus of historic forms – but that way was reserved for the Modern Movement. In practice, at the end of the nineteenth century there were only two alternatives: back to Chipping Campden or forward to the École des Beaux Arts – Walter Crane or Reginald Blomfield.

Crane's dream was indeed a Socialist Utopia: communal architecture around a communal maypole.[172] According to this view, Egyptian architecture had been priest's architecture; Assyrian architecture the architecture of Kings; Greek architecture was sculptor's architecture; Roman architecture belonged to the engineers; Renaissance architecture was the architecture of scholars; and Victorian architecture was the architecture of capitalism. In its place – in the tradition of Pugin, Ruskin and Morris – Crane continued to argue for the architecture of humanity.[173] Alas, such dreams worked better in Chipping Campden. In London, architects looked about them and despaired. 'It is a melancholy fact', remarked T. G. Jackson in 1888, 'that at no period in the world's history has so much architecture been produced that is either positively bad or else absolutely uninteresting.'[174] To an architect like Blomfield the solution seemed crystal clear: 'the co-operative art of the Middle Ages is no longer possible, some-one must take the lead. A strong individual intelligence is needed to restore order in this chaos of eclecticism.'[175] 'We are offered too wide a choice', only a single style – true classicism – offers a way out of this 'chaos of the nineteenth century'.[176] Away with Ruskin.[177] Back to order, back to discipline, back to proportion; back to the architect as coordinating genius. Back to the Renaissance.

In the meantime, most late Victorian architects put their trust in synthesis. Synthesis was a theme which had been taken up in the 1880s by several critics. Here – in the work of Norman Shaw and Ernest George, T. G. Jackson, Aston Webb and T. E. Colcutt – here was 'a Transitional style', 'Victorian' and 'Modern'.[178] Its nomenclature might be confused. Some of its detail might qualify only too well for the label 'Bric-a-Brac'. And, in any case, there was too much of it. But here, in an eclectic fusion of both major Western traditions, seemed to lie a way out of the dilemma of style. From Lower Chelsea to Upper Chelsea, from Tite St to Pont St, from Cadogan Square to Mount St – eclecticism grew more eclectic, Free Classicism still more free: from Queen Anne to Mixed Renaissance; from Shaw and Godwin to George and Peto. And as Anglo-Jackson – rich but still comparatively chaste – gave way to T. E. Colcutt, eclecticism became overripe to the point of disintegration.

Colcutt's Savoy Hotel (1887–96; 1905; 1910) is certainly free – very free – French Renaissance.[179] Some of his street façades – the City Bank on Ludgate Hill (1890–91), for example – are almost parodies of Norman Shaw. One shop he designed in Fleet Street (1875)[149] combined a vaguely Queen Anne façade with emblems which were partly Japanese and partly Trojan.[180] But Colcutt had at least shown the courage to apply the principles of Progressive Eclecticism – and the theories of Picturesque

149 T. E. Colcutt, 109 Fleet St, London (1875; dem.). Queen Anne, Japanese, Trojan.

150 T. E. Colcutt, Imperial Institute, Kensington (1887–93; largely dem.). 'Essentially Victorian and truly modern'.

composition – to the complexities of public building. His town hall at Wakefield, Yorks (1877–80) is indeed a synthesis: there are hints of Flanders, and Venice, and East Anglia too; the detail may be Renaissance, but the massing and grouping is still vestigially Gothic.[181]

Colcutt's reputation – and, for that matter, the reputation of Progressive Eclecticism – is likely to stand or fall with the Imperial Institute, South Kensington (1887–93; largely dem.)[150].[182] At the time a few critics found the accumulation of motifs too much to swallow. Most, however, were more than satisfied. Here, right at the end of Victoria's reign, was a massive architectural statement – Gothic, Queen Anne, François Premier, Quattrocento, Spanish Renaissance – which seemed to sum up all the optimism – and all the uncertainty – of late Victorian eclecticism. 'The style', wrote one commentator in 1893–4 – with no sense of irony – 'is indescribable ... [This] ... is a building which is essentially Victorian . . . and . . . truly modern.'[183] The editor of the *Building News* put it this way: when people 'ask, "What style is this?" [they] think it strange that they do not get an answer; for it has not yet dawned on the British public that styles have no names till they are dead.' And that – an acceptance of the contemporaneity of all styles – was, as Paul Waterhouse remarked, 'the germ of a very great truth'.[184]

So Progressive Eclecticism began with Beresford Hope and ended with T. E. Colcutt. Hope never found quite what he was looking for. In fact he regarded the whole Queen Anne phenomenon as a reversal of all his aims: an eclecticism which was not progressive but chaotically atavistic.[185] And perhaps he was right. Nevertheless he was nearer to the Holy Grail than he realised. Eclecticism was indeed the Victorian Style, Robert Kerr's 'omnium gatherum Victorianum'.[186] And Beresford Hope had at least identified its secret: he had sensed in all architecture that ambivalence – that multivalence – which is inseparable from sophisticated design. 'Architecture is the calling which, next to that of poet, dives deepest back into the young world's gulf of ages. As it moves on it spins out as part of itself that golden chain of association which ties together the ancient and the new, the foreign and the home-born, the beautiful and the useful.'[187] In a nutshell: Progressive Eclecticism. Beresford Hope's motto might well turn out to be a useful slogan for the new eclectics of today. Meanwhile, back to the Renaissance.

7 From Neo-Classicism to Imperial Baroque

'Palladio is the game, it is so big.... the way Wren handled it was
marvellous....   It is a big game, a high game'
(Sir Edwin Lutyens, 1903).

BETWEEN THE DECLINE OF PALLADIANISM and the rise of the Modern Movement, classical architecture in England went through at least eight phases: Roman, Greek, Graeco-Roman, Italianate, Baroque, Mannerist, Beaux Arts and Neo-Georgian. The first three – Roman, Greek and Graeco-Roman – are late Georgian and Regency; the fourth – Italianate – is early and mid-Victorian; and the last four – Baroque, Mannerist, Beaux Arts and Neo-Georgian – are late Victorian and Edwardian. These phases run parallel to the various stages of the Gothic Revival. Broadly speaking, we call the first three Neo-Classical, and the other five Neo-Renaissance.

Neo-Classical architecture[1] – the Radcliffe Observatory, Oxford (by Keene and Wyatt, 1772–94)[151] for example – can be identified as the conjunction of three factors: first, archaeological inspiration, that is the use of Greek and Roman models free from Renaissance 'corruption'; second, rationalism in design – the distribution of antique elements according to theories of 'apparent' utility; and third, a new kind of composition – the rejection of Baroque or Palladian integration in favour of disparate, geometrical shapes. The first of these factors (archaeology) was Anglo-French in origin: the rediscovery of ancient Greece; the second (rationalism) was Franco-Italian: the theories of Cordemoy, Lodoli and Laugier; and the third (geometry) was common to most parts of Western Europe during the later eighteenth and early nineteenth centuries. If any one of these factors has to be chosen as crucial, it must be Neo-Classical theory: Cordemoy, 'the father of Neo-Classical theory'; Lodoli, the Venetian monk, 'the Socrates of architecture'; and Laugier, the French Jesuit whose influence revolutionised architectural thinking – the man who broke up the Baroque.

Now these three criteria – archaeology, rationalism, geometry – are true for Europe in general. For England we must add a fourth factor: the Picturesque. Picturesque theory links all three main phases of Neo-Classical architecture in England. First, Roman and 'Etruscan', that is Adam, Leverton, Wyatt, Tatham. Second, Greek and Hellenistic, that is,

151 Henry Keene and James Wyatt, Radcliffe Observatory, Oxford (1772–94). Archaeology, rationalism, geometry.

152 Sir Robert Smirke, British Museum, London (1823–47). Climax of the Greek Revival.

Stuart, Dance, Smirke, Wilkins. And thirdly, Graeco-Roman, that is Cockerell, Elmes, Basevi. Neo-Classical architecture in Scotland shows a similar progression, but usually a generation or so later, from Adam, through Burn, Hamilton and Playfair, to Simpson, Sellars, Thompson and Bryce.

The Greek Revival – like Neo-Classicism itself – was the product of both classical and romantic impulses.[2] In fact the Neo-Classical equation had two parts: classical or rationalist theory and romantic or associative archaeology. Each pulled in different directions. As the Neo-Classical movement in architecture progressed, the classical or rationalist element was submerged by the romantic or associative element: the symbolic became more important than the tectonic. Novel geometrical forms – and novel structural techniques – were submerged by the popularity of historical detail.

Regency architects, Sir Robert Smirke for example, saw the danger of this: he dismissed it as architectural transvestism.[3] Instead he pinned his faith on geometry and abstraction. But neither he nor any of his contemporaries was able to resist the acceleration of Romanticism. His own British Museum (1823–47)[152] is structurally dependent on cast iron and concrete, but its entrance front is the most gargantuan instance of stylophily in Britain.[4] Instead of following the logic of Neo-Classicism towards the goal of abstract modernity – Regency architects like Soane thought of 'modern' as a kind of abstracted Neo-Classicism, and perhaps they were right – architects fell back on the comforting thought that attempts to discover a wholly new style were no more likely to succeed than attempts to discover a fourth primary colour. So they gave up.

In a way this was the result of a basic flaw in Neo-Classical theory. Laugier's doctrine of 'apparent utility' was rationalist rather than functionalist. Neo-Classicism was an architecture of appearance, appreciated by the eye rather than by the understanding. Now, at its highest level, architecture depends on a twofold aesthetic: an appreciation of appearances, *and* an understanding of structure and organisation. Great architects – that is, artists planning and thinking structurally, in three dimensions – have always managed to maintain some sort of equilibrium between surface and substance, form and function, architecture as art and architecture as service. But Neo-Classical aesthetics produced a method of design aptly described by Sir John Summerson as 'subjunctive': architecture 'as if' – that is, a surface system of ornament designed *as if* it were a functional system of construction. And as the nineteenth century progressed, this disparity between structure and decoration, fact and fiction, became more and more pronounced.

Lodoli's thought had anticipated this problem: if the material changes, he believed, so also must the system of expressive ornament.[5] In the early nineteenth century Nash and Smirke were already experimenting with cast iron beams as a skeleton clothed in Classical forms. And Cockerell was well aware of the consequent dilemmas of design. But neither Nash, Smirke nor Cockerell could bring themselves to abandon an architectural vocabulary geared first to wooden and then to masonry construction – nor, for that matter, could any other Neo-Classicist. For Neo-Classical architecture was doubly subjunctive: a system prehistorically designed for timber forms had been anciently translated into masonry conventions; and these masonry conventions had been consciously revived to clothe in associational garb a structural system based on iron and concrete. Nash, of course, did not care. Smirke buried his doubts beneath the burden of his own success. And Cockerell allowed the romantic elements in his own nature to overrule the classical. So the gap between form and function began to widen. Popularity eventually killed the Greek Revival by making motif more important than mass. The archaeological element in the equation became more important than the experimental. But at the last moment, the movement was rescued by its greatest exponent: 'Greek' Thomson.

Alexander Thomson was a self-taught Greek. He had no formal academic training, and never visited the Aegean. He spent all his life in Glasgow, and rarely travelled south. His inspiration came not from Greece but from the Greek Revival itself: the work of Thomas Hamilton, Harvey Lonsdale Elmes, W. H. Playfair, and – almost certainly – K. F. Schinkel and Leo von Klenze. But by taking the Greek Revival as his starting point, adding touches of Tuscan, Egyptian, Assyrian and Indian, then pulverising each ingredient, Thomson came up with what he was looking for: a new style. 'The promoters of the Greek Revival', he believed, 'failed, not because of the scantiness of the material but because they could not see through the material into the laws upon which architecture rested. They failed to master the style, and so became its slave.'[6] So his work had to be more Thomsonian than Greek. 'How is it', he asked in 1871 – as so many had done before – 'that there is no modern style of architecture? ... every past period of civilisation had its architecture growing out of it as by a natural process ... How is it then, that there is no modern style?'[7] The solution to what he calls this 'obnoxious question' of style must, he believed, lie in the re-discovery of fundamental architectural laws: secrets, known to the Greeks, but lost since then under a mass of 'accumulated ... traditions'.[8] 'The best way for us to imitate the Greeks', he concludes, 'is rather to follow their example than [to] copy their

153 Alexander Thomson, 'Holmwood', Cathcart, Glasgow (1856–8). 'Modern Greek'.

work.'[9] In effect, he set out to build 'not as the Greeks built, but as they would have built had they lived now'.

The results were certainly revolutionary. His Picturesque villas – notably Holmwood, Netherlee Rd., Cathcart (1856–8)[153] – seem to anticipate the young Frank Lloyd Wright. His domestic terraces – Moray Place (1859) for example – solve the conundrum which puzzled Nash by combining logical planning with Grecian detail and abstract geometrical forms. His commercial designs – Buck's Head Building (c.1863) for instance – incorporate vertical metal stanchions and horizontal glazing bands in a way that seems almost to prophesy the early Chicago School. As for his three great churches – at Caledonia Rd (1856–7); St Vincent St (1857–9) and Queen's Park (1867–9) – each betrays a rare genius for composition and abstraction, plus an extraordinary command of the eclectic process.[10] William Burges – hardly the classicists' friend – called Thomson's work 'Greek Architecture, but the best modern Greek architecture it has been my lot to see.'[11]

Egyptian Halls (1871–3)[154] sums up Thomson's genius very well. In effect he seized upon the trabeated unit of the Grecian mode as a formula capable of indefinite expansion in an age of iron and glass. But by spurning all use of the arch, he chose to fight his architectural battles with one hand tied behind his back. Like Pugin in reverse, his religious convictions – he was a staunch Presbyterian – cut him off from whole sectors of architectural experience. His very conception of architecture

197

was a limited one. 'Architectural design', he explained in 1874, 'consists in moulding and adapting forms and lines into harmonious proportions and combinations, by the exercise of the aesthetic faculty.'[12]

Limited yes: narrow no. Within the parameters of his chosen medium, 'Greek' Thomson was unbeatable. He knew the power of line, mass and gravitational expression. He understood, above all, the communicating role of metaphor. Hence his long-term significance for Post-Modernists. Hence too his insignificance in terms of immediate influence. Even in Scotland, where the classical tradition was still a living force, Thomson's genius for turning antique prototypes into structural metaphors bore no immediate fruit. Further south he was respected, and ignored. By the time of his death, in 1875, the bulk of the profession was more interested in eclecticism than in abstraction. The destabilising influence of the Picturesque had once again done its work.

In England, as opposed to Scotland, the Greek Revival lost its hold on fashionable taste during the 1830s. Neo-Classical gave way to Neo-Renaissance. A visitor to London in 1851 – a visitor in search of Architecture – would have gone not to the Crystal Palace, nor even to All Saints, Margaret St, but to Pall Mall, the street of palazzos. For in 1851 –

154 Alexander Thomson, Egyptian Halls, Glasgow (1871–3).
'As the Greeks would have built had they lived now'.

155 Sir Charles Barry, Travellers Club, Pall
Mall, London (1829–32). Florentine
Renaissance.

156 Sir Charles Barry, Reform Club,
Pall Mall, London (1837–41). Roman
Renaissance.

to the man in the street – Architecture still meant Classical architecture.
Despite Pugin, despite the ecclesiologists, young architects still cut their
teeth on the orders, and old architects – the architects in charge of the
RIBA – still believed in the prestige of Greece and Rome, in the magic of
the Antique and the Renaissance.

Strolling down Pall Mall, from the Trafalgar Square end, our visitor
would be in no doubt as to the way English secular architecture had
developed during the previous twenty years. First Robert Smirke's Union
Club and Royal College of Physicians (1822–7; now Canada House):[13] an
essay in cool, understated, geometry; a dialogue of chastened archaeology
and intersecting planes. Then Decimus Burton's Athenaeum (1827–
30),[14] mitigating Grecian severity with Roman orders and shallow
rustication. After that, Sir Charles Barry's Travellers' Club (1829–
32)[15],[155] announcing the new Italianate fashion: calmly Raphaelesque
at the front in the manner of Florence's Pandolfini Palace; mildly Venetian
at the rear. And after that, the same architect's Reform Club (1837–
41),[16][156] a dramatised adaptation of no less than three Roman
palazzos: the Farnese, the Cancellaria and the Massimi. A veritable 'King
of Clubs', the Reform marked the high point of Italianate or Renaissance
Revival. It also marked the triumph of the Whigs. Not to be outdone, the

199

157 Sydney Smirke, Carlton Club, Pall Mall, London (1854–6; dem.). Venetian Renaissance.

Tories replied with Sydney Smirke's Carlton Club (1854–6; dem.),[17][157] exchanging Barry's sombre Roman cinquecento for the opulence and colour of sixteenth-century Venice. On the other side of the street our strolling spectator could hardly have missed an even lusher specimen of Venetian classicism – stemming directly from the Carlton – Parnell and Smith's Army and Navy Club (1848–51; dem. 1963):[18][158] – its upper floor borrowed from Sansovino's Library of St Mark; the lower from Sansovino's Palazzo Cornaro. Here the triumph of Italy over Greece was complete. At the Carlton Sydney Smirke took up the theme of Sansovino's

158 C. O. Parnell and A. Smith, Army and Navy Club, Pall Mall, London (1848–51; dem.). Sansovino doubled.

great library, then polychromatised that Venetian precedent in pursuit of even greater richness. The layout of the rooms around a central *cortile* echoed that of the Reform. But in density of decoration it quite eclipsed its rival. The florid cornice and figured spandrels, boldly sculptured in high relief, struck the keynote for a whole range of civic and commercial architecture throughout the 1850s and 1860s.[19] And its use – apparently for the first time in London - of polished columns in pink and green granite, set a precedent which proved only too popular. Finally, close to St James's Palace, our visitor would have been just in time to see the scaffolded exterior of Bridgewater House (1845–54). Rich, almost too rich. Safe in the hands of a master. But here Barry's palazzo style has almost reached the stage of overripeness; deliquescence cannot be far away. 'Anglo-Italian', was how Barry himself described it. But the architect's son noted: 'a very good mansion ... [though] ... far from ... pure'.[20]

Purity – that is reverence for a single prototype – went out with the Regency. Even the prince of Neo-Classicists, C. R. Cockerell, diluted Greek with Roman and Renaissance, and came up with Graeco-Roman. His Ashmolean Museum, Oxford (1841–5),[159] has often been described as in itself a liberal education. That trick of breaking through the cornice has both Roman and Baroque precedents. The formal vocabulary – rustication, columns on piers, sculptured panels, moulded bands – is indeed Renaissance. But the architect mixes familiar prototypes with new archaeological discoveries. The bracketed cornice is straight out of Vignola, but the Greek Ionic order is his own rare discovery from Bassae.

159 C. R. Cockerell, Ashmolean Museum, Oxford (1841–5). Graeco-Roman.

160 Thomas Cubitt, Osborne House, Isle of Wight (1845–53). Seaside Italianate.

In theory, Cockerell was all for novelty – and for new materials – provided they could be controlled by 'taste'. In old age he was not without hope that 'the year 1900' would produce an 'architecture ... which never before was dreamt of, characterising the century in a manner worthy of its extraordinary progress in civilisation'.[21] But in practice he stuck to his precedents. And in a sense the Cockerellian formula – as employed by Basevi, or Elmes, or Donaldson, or Tite – needed no further evolution. Graeco-Roman – in Liverpool, in Cambridge, in London, in Huddersfield – supplied a monumental language perfectly attuned to the civic sensibilities of mid-Victorian England.

But by the 1860s classicism was in retreat. 'The old pedantic, if not idolatrous, worship of the "Five Orders"', announced the *Saturday Review* in 1857, 'is a thing gone by with the Corn Laws and the Rotten Boroughs.'[22] It might be tempting to say that the classical tradition went underground, like Gothic Survival during the English Renaissance. Tempting, but wrong. For at the heart of the mid-Victorian architectural establishment – the RIBA itself – classicism was well entrenched. And well argued too: by Sir William Tite, by Professor T. L. Donaldson, by Professor Robert Kerr. As long as Tite, Donaldson and Kerr lived – and they lived until 1873, 1885 and 1904 respectively – the cause of classicism was unlikely to go unnoticed. Of course, Kerr belonged to a younger generation than Tite and Donaldson: he was an eclectic, not a Neo-Classicist. But he remained convinced that 'the Modern European Style' must be some form of classicism: 'the style of the nineteenth century'.[23] Even in the 1860s, classicism was still the style of government, still the basis of architectural training, still the style of innumerable residential and commercial developments. The Gothic Revival had little or no impact on the City of London. And the architecture of nonconformist churches remained predominantly classical until well into the mid-Victorian period.[24] North of the border of course, architects of the stature of Burn, Bryce and Rhind maintained the prestige of the Renaissance tradition undiminished. But down south, by the end of the 1850s, classicism was no longer *chic*, no longer taken seriously by the pundits. It was no longer in the forefront of architectural debate. More important, it was stylistically static.

At Osborne, on the Isle of Wight (1845–53)[25][160] Cubitt built a royal retreat, but a retreat which was simply a palatial version of a mansion in Knightsbridge[161] or even Ladbroke Grove. Banks and Barry's extension at Burlington House, Piccadilly (1872), is a rather more sophisticated performance, but it is a repeat performance, mechanically played. 'The façade', noted Goodhart-Rendel, 'displays the last stale remains of the neo-Italianism that had been normal twenty years before; it has radical

161 Thomas Cubitt, Albert Gate, London (1845). Knightsbridge Italianate.

faults and superficial virtues, and need offend nobody who does not examine it closely.'[26] Classicism continued, but it did not break new ground. Sir James Pennethorne had trained in the office of John Nash, and his Duchy of Cornwall building (1854) is really Nash in Renaissance mood. T. L. Donaldson considered Thomas Bellamy's Law Fire Insurance Office at 114 Chancery Lane (1858–9 and 1874–6)[27] to be worthy of Palladio; in fact it was worthy of Sir Charles Barry. Vulliamy's Dorchester House (1848–63) – modelled on Peruzzi's Farnesina in Rome – would have been even finer had it been designed by Barry, and finer still if it had been designed by Peruzzi. The National Provincial Bank at 15, Bishopsgate (1863–5) – by Barry's assistant John Gibson – conjured up a vision of Soane's Bank of England as it might have been – had it been designed by C. R. Cockerell. And at Todmorden Town Hall, Yorks (1860–75), Gibson actually succeeded – though of course on a smaller scale – in emulating Elmes and Cockerell's masterpiece, St George's Hall, Liverpool (1840–54). There is nothing small scale about Leeds Town Hall (1853–8).[28][162] Here Cuthbert Brodrick borrowed from French and English traditions: Brogniart's Paris Bourse and St George's Hall, Liverpool; there is even a touch of Vanbrugh's Castle Howard. It has progeny among town halls all over the world.[29] But, as a style, its suitability for municipal pomp ruled it out for almost any other form of building.

In a less monumental way, classicism maintained a level of dignified competence in mid-Victorian speculative building. Gilbert Scott once called Barry's Italianate style 'Classic architecture Vernacularised'.[30] That description might, rather more appropriately, have been applied to the work of builder-developers like Thomas Cubitt. From Belgravia to Pimlico the descent is steep. Back in the 1830s the classical tradition had already dwindled into a predictable vernacular – what Disraeli called 'your Gloucester Places, and Baker Streets, and Harley Streets, and Wimpole Streets, and all those dull, flat, spiritless streets.'[31] The process continued into the next generation. In Ladbroke Grove and Notting Hill, in Bayswater, Paddington and Belsize Park, the 1850s and 1860s produced miles of Italianate stucco façades, but – stylistically speaking – few new ideas. In terms of square yards of building, in terms of cubic content, Italianate has perhaps the strongest claim of all to be considered *the* Victorian style. But it was a style which had gone down market. As an architectural ideology it seemed a spent force. No wonder, during the 1870s, fashionable London went over, lock, stock and barrel, to Franco-Dutch Queen Anne. According to J. P. Seddon, the bricky prototypes of Belgium and Holland inspired about one quarter of all designs produced in England in the 1880s.[32] In choosing this new medium, architects

162 Cuthbert Brodrick, Leeds Town Hall (1853–8). Municipal pomp.

abandoned the discipline of both major traditions: Gothic and Classic. In effect, they surrendered to the Picturesque in urban form.

By the 1880s, there were calls for a return to order. The classical grammar had to be learnt all over again, and by a new generation. A whole string of books on the Renaissance were published in one year alone: 1883.[33] And at the Royal Academy, R. Phéné Spiers was already leading budding designers in the direction of Parisian *Beaux Arts*. But the classical tradition – that is classicism as a disciplinary code rather than a medley of antique forms – was temporarily in eclipse. 'A generation [had] arisen' recalled Beresford Pite years later, 'untrained in the orders and systems of proportion.' One day, perhaps, 'in an eclectic hour', that 'bygone Greek music' would be played again, easing new melodies 'from its long-forgotten scores'.[34] One day, perhaps. But not yet. For the permissiveness of Queen Anne had done its work. What the young professionals wanted now was not proportion and harmony, the eternal verities of design, but novelty, variety, flexibility, freedom. 'Palladio, Vignola, Chambers', proclaimed *The Architect*, 'are as dead as Batty Langley.' And as for Vitruvius, all those editions were so much 'waste paper ... What Englishmen want nowadays, vulgar and sordid as it may be in the eyes of the transcendental, is something that will work into good commonplace English design, without making the head ache or the heart either.'[35]

Well, Englishmen had their reward in 1884. That was the year of the competition for the new Admiralty and War Office buildings in Whitehall. It was the grandest architectural competition since the Law Courts: a new headquarters for the greatest army and navy in the world. What was the result? One hundred and twenty-eight entries; only one of them Gothic. The winners were an unknown firm from Halifax, Messrs. Leeming and Leeming.[163][36] The chorus of disapproval was deafening.[37] The designs were modified, but if anything only for the worse.[38] Beresford Hope called them 'vulgar, commonplace [and] overloaded with ornament'.[39] William H. White compared their details to 'the coarse travesties of a music hall'.[40] Sir William Harcourt – Gladstone's Chancellor of the Exchequer – was appalled at this 'bastard, provincial, Town Hall style'.[41]

163 J.L. Leeming and J. Leeming, Winning design, Admiralty and War Office, London (1884). Influences from 17th c. France.

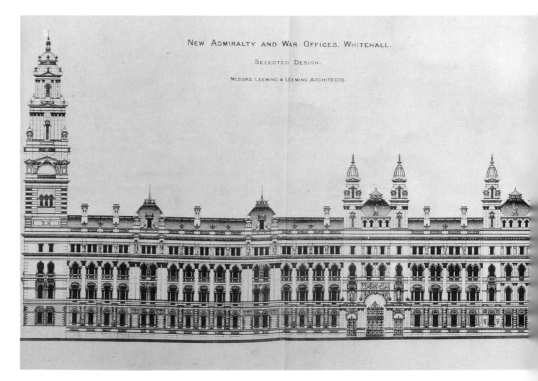

164 Sir Gilbert Scott, Foreign Office, Whitehall, London (1868–73).
Influences from 16th c. Italy.

Lawrence Harvey – hoping for a little Beaux Arts planning – took one
look at the models and exclaimed: 'Behold a pig with one ear!'[42]

The contrast between Gilbert Scott's Foreign Office (1868–73)[164],
and Leeming and Leeming's Admiralty is indeed instructive. A quarter
of a century of 'development' had merely overloaded the vocabulary of
the Renaissance by piling seventeenth-century France on to sixteenth-
century Italy, and then fragmenting the result in pursuit of the Picturesque.[43] When, in the 1890s, Spiers and Middleton started to produce
primers of classical grammar, they had a ready market.[44] In Scotland, of
course, the classical tradition had never died. And it turned out to be
Scottish architects – notably Norman Shaw, John Brydon, William Young
and J. J. Burnet – who brought it south again.

It was Norman Shaw, as much as anyone, who steered English architecture back in the direction of the Renaissance. Having switched horses
once – from Gothic to Queen Anne – he had no compunction in switching
once again: from Queen Anne to Baroque. At New Scotland Yard (1887–

165 R. Norman Shaw, New Scotland Yard, London (1887–90). Franco-Flemish Baronial.

166 R. Norman Shaw, Alliance Assurance Office, St James's St, London (1901–5). Classicism re-instated.

90)[165] he is still in the Netherlands: Beresford Pite thought it conjured up 'a Dutch cheese warehouse from the banks of the Dort'.[45] In fact Shaw's prototype stemmed not from the Dort but from the Loire or the Meuse: the Château of Azay-le-Rideau, or the Mont de Piété at Liège.[46] Anyway, the result was Franco-Flemish Renaissance with more than a touch of Scots Baronial. At Bryanston, Dorset (1889–94) the mood is still eclectic, but eclectic classicism. In Clive Aslet's words, 'an essence of Mme de Pompadour's château at Ménars, a sprinkling of Vaux-le-Vicomte, a solid helping of Coleshill, and garnishings of Stoke Edith and Cobham Hall.'[47] At Chesters in Northumberland (1889–91) – while extending a Georgian house – Shaw threw off eclecticism and turned decisively to Italy, to Borromini or da Cortona. By the end of his career he had, in effect, re-instated the classical tradition. Compare his first Alliance Assurance Office (1881–3)[140] on the corner of Pall Mall and St James's St, with his second building (1901–5)[166] for the same firm, looking down the length of Pall Mall. The first had demonstrated the plausibility of Anglo-Dutch Renaissance in an urban context. The second announced his complete conversion to what Lutyens later called the 'High Game' of classicism.

208

Still, if any one man was responsible for the revival of English Baroque, it was J. M. Brydon.[48] In a series of important lectures and articles, he called for the revival of classical discipline – in composition and detail – as the only way out of 'the architectural chaos' of the late Victorian period.[49] His Chelsea Town Hall (1885–7)[167] was hailed as 'a thoroughly English rendering of the Renaissance, or "Free Classic".'[50] Brydon looked at the classicism of the age of Wren and saw it – despite its French flavour – as quintessentially English: 'a living, working, architectural reality . . . a great mine of artistic wealth open to all . . . to apply to the necessities of our day.'[51] He looked at the world of Inigo Jones and the Palladians and found it not only English but potentially Imperial and Modern: 'who can say that it may not lead to what must be the desire of us all, namely . . . a truly English twentieth-century progressive architecture?'[52]

Back in the 1850s Wren had already been revived, at John Shaw's Wellington College, Berkshire (1856–9).[53] But on that occasion Hampton Court had been heavily diluted by the influence of the New Louvre (L. T. E. Visconti and H. M. Lefuel, 1852–7).[54] Again, in the early 1870s, at Kinmel Park, Denbighshire (c. 1871–4), Nesfield had diluted Wren with copious draughts of Mansart and more than a tincture of Japanese.[55]

167 J. M. Brydon, Chelsea Town Hall, London (1885–7). 'Free Classic'.

Brydon wanted something less eclectic. He found it in English Palladian-ism.[56] And after years of the urban Picturesque, young architects fell upon the purer, more orderly prototypes which Brydon offered them, as 'manna sent from Heaven'.[57] After all, Palladian detail had been 'so much acclimatised [in the eighteenth century] as to seem almost indi-genous'.[58] Here was a basis not only for a nineteenth, but even for a twentieth-century style.[59]

Sometimes it worked. Brydon's additions to the architectural scenery of Bath[60] were algebraically summed up by J. P. Seddon[61] as

$$\frac{Bathstone^2 + Palladio^2}{Modern\ Ideas.}$$

In fact there was more to it than that. His Bath Guildhall incorporates echoes of the towers of Wren's St Paul's. His Pump Room concert chamber evokes the dome of St Stephen's Walbrook. The ceiling of his Council Chamber owes most of its detail to Robert Adam. But its exterior sculpture owes more to Arts and Crafts than to Baroque. Eclectic classicism like this was a recipe for evolution. Commitment to a single prototype was not. Brydon's unexecuted design for the West Ham Technical Institute and Public Library (1896)[62] – a diluted version of Gibbs's Radcliffe Camera, Oxford – was surely a stylistic *cul de sac*.

But it is by his great government buildings on the corner of Parliament Square and Whitehall that Brydon will always be judged. Here, at the heart of Empire, he fulfilled his ambition to re-create the English Baroque. Or did he?

Those Government Offices (1898–1912)[63][168] are not quite as Eng-lish as they seem. Apart from a few touches of Gibbs, the prototypes are Chambers's Somerset House, Wren's St Paul's and Webb's Whitehall Palace. But Chambers had in turn borrowed from Gabriel and Antoine, Wren from Perrault and Mansart, and Webb from Vignola's Villa Farnese at Caprarola. In Brydon's great circular courtyard[64] we are surrounded by echoes not only of seventeenth-century and eighteenth-century England but of sixteenth-century Italy and seventeenth-century France. So Brydon aims high: he consciously challenges comparison with the greatest masters of European classicism. By such standards, inevitably, he falls short – even if we blame civil servants and politicians for omitting two of the towers, and even if we blame his successor – Henry Tanner – for much of the detailing.[65] In the final analysis, Brydon – like Chambers before him – was an assimilator rather than a creator. 'Had he been as competent as Sir William Chambers', Goodhart-Rendel noted acidly, 'he would have built as Chambers built, without any variation ... [indeed]

he thought much more highly of Chambers than Chambers would have thought of him.'[66]

Brydon died in 1901, too soon to see the fulfilment of his Whitehall programme. Happily that programme had already been amply consolidated by yet another Scot, William Young.[67] In his early years, Young confessed – like Brydon – to being 'a Gothicist of the deepest dye ... [a Goth] of the Burges school'.[68] Like most of that generation, however, he lost his Gothic commitment round about 1870. 'There are merits in every style', he eventually concluded; 'each one has ... its fit and proper place.'[69] 'The great art of architecture ... is neither Classic, nor Gothic, nor good Queen Anne, but all of these, and much more.'[70] So by the end of the 1890s Young was a pluralist. But for civic buildings, he had come to see that Architecture meant Classicism, and preferably Baroque.

Young's list of patrons included the Earl of Wemyss: the marble staircase at Gosford House, East Lothian (1883–91);[71] and the Earl of Iveagh:

168 J. M. Brydon, Government Offices, Whitehall, London (1898–1912). Echoes of 16th c. Italy, 17th c. France and 17th and 18th c. England.

169 William Young, Municipal Chambers, Glasgow (1882–90). Roman Renaissance.

the Arab Hall at Elvedon, Suffolk (1899–1903).[72] But it was public buildings rather than country houses that made his reputation. Up in Glasgow, his monumental Municipal Chambers (1882–90)[169] gave him international status,[73] and this was confirmed by his appointment in 1898 as architect of the War Office in Whitehall (1899–1906)[170].[74] In Glasgow the order had been Roman: the temple of Jupiter Stator; the composition Renaissance, from Sanmichele and Sansovino.[75] In

170 William Young, War Office, Whitehall, London (1899–1906). Palladian, Baroque, Mannerist.

171 Sir A. Brumwell Thomas, City Hall, Belfast (1897–1906). Memories of St Paul's and Greenwich.

Whitehall, the great staircase[76] is Palladian – as at Glasgow and Gosford. The exterior is less Palladian than Italian Mannerist and Anglo-French Baroque: those clever corner towers are closer to Wren than to Inigo Jones.[77] But there is another element as well: the sculpture by John Drury betrays the influence of the Arts and Crafts Movement.

Young died in 1900, and the commission had to be completed by his son. But here in Whitehall – best of all, in serried silhouette, as seen from St James's Park – Young's War Office takes its place with Inigo Jones's Banqueting House, William Kent's Horse Guards, Henry Holland's Melbourne House and Gilbert Scott's Foreign Office – Palladian, Neo-Palladian, Neo-Classical, Victorian Renaissance and Edwardian Baroque, side by side: the English tradition of monumental classicism.

In the late Victorian and Edwardian period, that tradition was based predominantly on English prototypes. There are exceptions. For their Institute of Chartered Accountants (1889–93), Belcher and Pite looked to Italy, to Genoa and to Borromini.[78] In his famously unbuilt design for the South Kensington Museum (1891), Belcher had looked to Renaissance Spain, to the Palace at Granada.[79] But most of the sources were closer to home. Wren, Vanbrugh and Hawksmoor – St Paul's, Greenwich, Hampton Court, Kensington – these were the principal quarries. When Ernest George wanted a model for the British Pavilion at the 1904 St Louis Exhibition, he went straight to the Orangery at Kensington.[80] When John Murray wanted a striking motif for his Crown Estate building in Whitehall (1906–10),[81] he went straight to Hampton Court. For Belfast City Hall (1897–1906)[171], Sir A. Brumwell Thomas borrowed directly from Wren: the towers of St Paul's and the domes of Greenwich Hospital.

213

172 Sir Aston Webb, Victoria and Albert Museum, London (1891–1909). Edwardian eclecticism.

At Stockport Town Hall (1904–8) Thomas chose Wren again for the tower, and Hawksmoor for the twin porticoes: piling Pelion upon Ossa in pursuit of the Classical sublime. At Woolwich Town Hall (1903–6) it was Wren once more, with perhaps a hint of Borromini's Sta Agnese in Rome. In C. J. Skipper's Norwich Union Building (1903–5) there is as much of Vanbrugh as of Palladio. And in Arnold Thornley's Mersey Docks building, Pier Head, Liverpool (1903–7) it is Hawksmoor and Wren again: Hawksmoor's aedicules and Wren's rotunda. Similarly Colchester Town Hall (1897–1902): here Belcher and Joass borrowed Hawksmoor's aedicules from the King William Block at Greenwich, and Wren's steeple from Christ Church, Newgate St.[82]

In building up an identifiable architectural image – the English Baroque tradition – a limited range of proto-images was clearly desirable. But once the style had been well established, then the best prizes went to the man who could handle it with greatest freedom: Sir Aston Webb. As a young man, Webb had been a Free Classicist.[83] By middle age he was an Establishment chameleon. His Victoria Law Courts, Birmingham (1887–91) were François Premier – a mixture of Blois and Azay-le-Rideau – but with touches of Tudorbethan and Plateresque.[84] His Imperial College, Kensington (1900–1906) looks to seventeenth-century France; his Christ's Hospital School, Horsham (1893–1902) to Elizabethan England. His Birmingham University (1900–9) mingles Byzantine and François Premier with an idiosyncratic version of the Palazzo Vecchio tower. His Royal Naval College, Dartmouth (1900–3) is Chelsea Hospital gone Mannerist. And as for his Victoria and Albert Museum (1891–1909)[172], it was identified at the time as Burgundian Renaissance with

214

Hispanic touches.[85] Later commentators have also spotted the Certosa at Pavia peeping out from between clumps of François Premier. 'Improvisation', notes Summerson, 'is certainly the word. Aston Webb here is like some talented organist moving from theme to theme and occasionally exploding into what, at least for the moment, seems to be the lost chord.'[86]

Appropriately, Imperial Baroque came of age with the National Monument to Queen Victoria. Five architects were invited to compete. Rowand Anderson offered Flemish Renaissance;[87] Ernest George, Italian Renaissance;[88] Thomas Drew, French Neo-Classic;[89] T. G. Jackson, Italian Baroque;[90] and the winner, Aston Webb, something with a hint of all of these. Thomas Brock was chosen sculptor for the memorial itself. Aston Webb's winning scheme boasted curved colonnades, echoing the Hemicycle at Nancy or perhaps St Peter's Square in Rome. His treatment of the Mall was an obvious reference to the Champs Elysées.[91] Not everybody approved. John Burns MP disliked the whole idea of 'Haussmanising our parks . . . the only result [would be] to make London a second-rate Berlin, a fourth-rate Paris, or a fifth-rate Vienna'.[92] But the Picturesque was now in eclipse. Axial planning was all the rage.[93] Webb was forced to modify his design, but in so doing he improved on his original programme. Admiralty Arch (1906–11)[173] turned out to be the grandest of second thoughts. By a brilliant piece of stage design, his doubly concave façades

173 Sir Aston Webb, Admiralty Arch, London (1906–11). Mannerist Beaux Arts.

create an illusion of axial symmetry, not only linking the Mall with Charing Cross, but – in visual and symbolic terms – Buckingham Palace with Trafalgar Square. Beaux Arts planning and Mannerist composition have combined to create a fitting climax to Edwardian London.[94] There are echoes here of J. H. Mansart's Versailles, but their handling owes more to sixteenth-century Italy. By comparison, Webb's Buckingham Palace façade (1912–13) is no more than conventionally Beaux Arts.[95] In Admiralty Arch the world's greatest navy redeemed the failure of Leeming and Leeming's Admiralty Buildings.[96][163]

Edwardian Classicism was a protean style. Sometimes Flemish Baroque: Rickards' Deptford Town Hall (1900–3). Sometimes Mannerist: Holden's BMA Building, Strand (later Rhodesia/Zimbabwe House, 1907–8). Sometimes Wrenaissance: Arnold Mitchell's University College School, Hampstead (1906–7). Sometimes Parisian Beaux Arts: Mewès and Davis's RAC Club, Pall Mall (1908–11). Sometimes American Beaux Arts: Selfridges in Oxford St (1906–28),[174] by Burnet, Atkinson, Burnham and Swales. Sometimes stripped Neo-Classical: J. J. Burnet's Kodak Building, Kingsway (1911). Sometimes Neo-Grec: Beresford Pite's Assurance Office, Euston Square (1906–12).[97] Sometimes Neo-Regency: Adshead and Ramsay's Duchy of Cornwall Estate, Kennington (1909). But whatever the formal variation, its basis was the reticulated façade, the trabeated structure, the axial plan. Churches and colleges might still be Gothic, or Byzantine. But domestic and civic architecture, on the

174 Burnet, Atkinson, Burnham and Swales, Selfridges, Oxford St, London (1906–28). American Beaux Arts.

175 E. W. Mountford, The Old
Bailey, London (1900–6). 'Truly
characteristic of the period'.

176 John Belcher, Ashton Memorial, Lancaster
(1907–9). Imperial Baroque.

whole, had returned to its classical roots. Classicism – 'the most permanent element in civilised architecture'[98] – was once again, in Bulwer
Lytton's phrase, 'the handwriting of our race.' Even Mackmurdo's cold
storage warehouse in Smithfield (1900) adopted the style of Wren.
Vincent Harris's generating station (c.1906) at Islington paraphrased in
stock brick George Dance's Newgate Gaol. And in Duke St, Mayfair, in
1904–5, with memorable panache, C. Stanley Peach – humanising the
imperatives of technology with the help of C. H. Reilly – designed an
electric transformer station in the guise of an 'Italian Garden'.[99]

Goodhart-Rendel thought most of it rather vulgar. Mountford's Old
Bailey (1900–6)[175] particularly offended him. Its slick Baroque – a
coarser version of James Gandon's work in Dublin – seemed to sum up
only too well the age which produced it. 'Truly characteristic of the
period', he noted, 'its wealth, its insufficient scholarship, its professional
competence, its fundamental insensitiveness.'[100] He was even more cut-
ting about Norman Shaw's Piccadilly Hotel (1905–8): 'not even [Shaw's]
gusto and bravura can obscure the fact that he was playing a new game
of which he was too old to learn the rules, and playing it in a boisterous
and extremely dangerous way.'[101] Well, the pendulum of taste is a
tolerant instrument. Even Lanchester and Rickards' Central Hall,
Westminster (1905–12)[102] – supposedly in a style appropriate to the
spirit of John Wesley[103] – now has its passionate admirers. So too does
Belcher's Ashton Memorial (1907–9)[176] – a Lancastrian Taj Mahal –
paid for by the linoleum King, Lord Ashton, as a monument to his
wife.[104]

177 John Belcher and J. J. Joass,
Mappin House, Oxford St, London
(1906–8). From Baroque to
Mannerism.

178 Edwin Cooper, Port of London Authority
Building, London (1912–22). 'The end of an
era'.

Of course Edwardian Baroque was not all atavistic hyperbole. Walter
Cave's Burberry Shop in London's Haymarket (1912) manages to be
elegant, stylish and contemporary.[105] But there is a problem here, and
the Edwardians themselves were well aware of it. The Queen Anne
Revival had accepted ornament for its own sake. Edwardian Baroque
went one stage further: thanks to the invention of reinforced concrete
and the steel frame – the Ritz Hotel (1906–9 by Mewès and Davis) was
the first major steel frame in London[106] – whole façades could now be
frankly accepted as ornamental. In this way, new technology could be
humanised by absorption into the classical tradition; even in Oxford St
(Atkinson's old Waring and Gillow building, 1901–5). And the method
was simply the oldest trick in the Renaissance book: the separation of
constructional technique and architectural form. A hundred years before,
the Neo-Classicists had tried to square this particular circle by means of
Laugier's doctrine of *apparent* utility. The Gothic revivalists thought they
had solved the problem by taking over the rationalist tradition and
dressing it up in medieval form. The Edwardians made no such effort.
Their separation of function and form – architecture as service and

218

architecture as art – could best be defended – conceptually speaking – by revelling in its tectonic disjunction: by producing acrobatic designs which gloried in the autonomy of decoration. In other words, by combining – just as the Renaissance itself had done – Baroque and Mannerism.

Beresford Pite led the way here, closely followed by J. J. Joass and Charles Holden.[107] Pite had been interested in Michelangelo for years. Joass took over from Belcher and led Edwardian Classicism into exciting new forms: elegantly in Mappin House (158 Oxford St, 1906–8)[177]; anarchically in the Royal Insurance Building (1907–9) on the corner of St James's St and Piccadilly. Steel and glass have here been used to stretch classical forms to their very limit, turning tradition inside out in pursuit of novelty and abstraction.[108]

But few architects had the skill – or nerve – of J. J. Joass. Instead Edwardian Baroque went out with appropriate pomp in the work of Edwin Cooper. His Port of London Authority Building (1912–22)[109][178] in the shadow of the Tower of London, rises up – all pilasters and Portland stone – like some distant echo of the Victor Emmanuel Monument in Rome. This building, noted C. H. Reilly in 1924, marks 'the end of an era'.[110] Looking at Cooper's St Marylebone Town Hall (1911–18), at least one critic could not help wondering 'whether all these colossal columns, domes, towers, groups of sculpture and other imposing features are [really] the only natural and inevitable expression of the necessities of the case'.[111]

But the story was not quite over. Modern Gothic – the dream of unitary, organic evolution – was finished. Classicism had been revived, purified, internationalised and frozen. The whole idea of an architectural vernacular had turned out to be a contradiction in terms. The search for a new style had failed. The search for a universal style had failed. Architects were left with plurality and eclecticism.[112] But there was still plenty of opportunity for style: style as tectonic preference, style as personality, style as a visual flavour, style as the working out of an idea, style as excellence of form. In its perfection, as Alberti pointed out, style – regardless of specific form – aspires to that harmony from which nothing can be subtracted, and to which nothing can be added, without destroying its very essence. For architects, that must always remain the ultimate goal. In 1897, H. Heathcote Statham, for many years editor of the *Builder*, put it like this: 'Architectural design is a kind of symbolism ... [and] in a double sense. In a prosaic sense it may symbolise merely the interior arrangement of the building. But in a more poetic sense it may symbolise moods of feeling or association – power, gloom, gaiety, grace, playfulness.' From this doubly symbolic process, he hopes, may emerge 'life and poetry

... in modern architecture'.[113] Well, emerge it did, in the architecture of Sir Edwin Lutyens.

Lutyens's progress from romanticism to classicism, from Picturesque composition to elemental abstraction, is almost a paradigm of Victorian and Edwardian architectural history – as it might have been. At Munstead Wood, Surrey (1893–7),[114] he had combined the free-planning of Norman Shaw; the sweeping gables and serried mullions of Voysey; the scrupulous craftsmanship of Philip Webb; the landscape magic of Gertrude Jekyll; plus his own instinct for locality, his genius for the *genius loci*. Gradually, however, the classical spirit overcame his youthful enthusiasm for the Picturesque. Classicism encroaches stealthily on the interior of Fulbrook, Surrey (1897), and on the exterior of Tigbourne Court, Surrey (1897).[115] Deanery Garden, Sonning (1899),[116] for Edward Hudson, proprietor of *Country Life*, achieves a marvellous balance between classical and romantic. Marshcourt, Hants (1901–4),[117] is a Tudor house with Caroline interiors; Little Thakeham, Essex (1902)[118] is Elizabethan without, Mannerist within. It is only with the *Country Life* building (1904)[119] in Covent Garden, that Lutyens crosses the stylistic rubicon, and goes for full-blown Wrenaissance. 'Palladio is the game', he told Herbert Baker in 1903; 'it is so big ... the way Wren handled it was marvellous ... It is a big game, a high game.'[120] It was a game he first played with all the stops out at Heathcote (1905–6).[121][179]

At Heathcote, in the suburbs of Ilkley, the high game of Inigo Jones and Christopher Wren returned to Yorkshire, the county of Burlington and Kent. 'I have been scolded', he complained to Baker in 1911, 'for not being Yorkshire in Yorkshire' – for not adopting some form of vernacular revival. Such an approach, 'a window for this, a door for that etc. – a pot-pourri of Yorkeological details ... is futile, absolutely unconvincing ... Would Wren (had he gone to Australia) have burnt his knowledge and experience to produce a lame marsupial style, thought to reflect the character of her aborigines? He would surely have done his best.'[122] At Heathcote Lutyens consciously called in a universal classicism to discipline the local Picturesque: Sanmichele, Palladio and Vignola; Wren, Vanbrugh and Hawksmoor; James Paine and Carr of York; early sixteenth-century Verona in early twentieth-century Ilkley. 'This house', he explained to Baker, 'was for a very rich man who could not spend money: until he met me! in an ultra suburban locality over which villas of dreadful kind and many colours wantonly distribute themselves. The ground was four-square and compact, standing high with large pieces of moor-clad mountain tops about the horizon. The material was York stone, a stone without a soul, as sober as a teetotaller. I wanted something

179 Sir Edwin Lutyens, Heathcote, Ilkley, Yorkshire (1905–6). 'Palladio is the game'.

persistent, dominating, with horizontal lines to stratify the diarrheotic conditions produced by the miscellaneous villadom: in fact an architectural bismuth ... To get domination I had to get a scale greater than the height of my rooms allowed, so unconsciously the Sanmichele invention repeated itself. That time-worn Doric order – a lovely thing – I had the cheek to adopt ... You can't copy it. To be right you have to take it and design it ... It means hard thought all through – if it is laboured it fails.'[123]

Gledstone Hall, Yorks (1922–6),[124] and Middleton Park, Oxon (1938 onwards),[125] mark the culmination of Lutyens's classicism in a country house context. The precision of design at Gledstone extends even to the battering of the walls: antique entasis domesticated. At Middleton, completed by Robert Lutyens, the style is now more French than English, but the old Lutyens games are still being played: rusticated doorways, for instance. Pevsner disapproved: 'as pure design', notes the *Buildings of England*, 'much of it is first class.'[126] In the eyes of the Modern Movement, there was more to architecture than 'pure design': a virtuoso performance in spatial ingenuity and classical abstraction was not enough.[127]

But the classical tradition itself was never enough for Lutyens. The 'High Game' aspired to totality. Grey Walls, East Lothian (1900–1)[128] – a simple house poised on a plan of complex geometry – had been an ingenious abstraction from both English and Scottish Georgian vernacular. Castle Drogo, Devon (1910–30),[129][180] is both abstraction and synthesis. The owner of the house – Julius Drewe, a millionaire grocer – dreamt of a castle worthy of his thirteenth-century ancestor, Drogo de Teigne. 'God keep the Feudal', wrote Lutyens in 1910, 'and preserve all that is best in it.'[130] Lutyens made it feudal, and more: Norman Shaw's house at Flete, Devon (1878–83)[131] geometricised and distilled, a reductive fusion of Gothic and Classic which is indeed unique. Outside: mullions and battlements honed smooth and sharp, a granite silhouette of almost aerodynamic contour. Inside: vaulted kitchens worthy of Diocletian, coffered staircases sublime as Piranesi, and domed corridors which would not disgrace New Delhi.

It was, of course, in New Delhi that Lutyens's High Game was played out to a triumphant conclusion. Since 1450 BC there had been fifteen cities of Delhi. New Delhi – Imperial Delhi – was to be greater than any of these: a mighty symbol of the greatest empire since ancient Rome.

But what style was the new city to take? King George V favoured native forms, Mughal for preference. So did pro-Indian pundits and scholars like E. B. Havell. But the bulk of English architectural opinion was in no doubt that some form of classicism was essential.[132] To Arts and Crafts architects like Voysey, however, such arguments were aesthetic 'claptrap'. And to Indian Nationalists the imposition of any European style was nothing less than an insult. Some form of compromise between East and West was therefore inevitable.[133] Lutyens himself had a profound contempt for native Indian architecture, whether Mughal or Hindu. Equally deplorable, he believed, was the hybrid Eurasian style – 'half-caste architecture' – of the eighteenth- and nineteenth-century colonial buildings in Bombay or Madras. Still worse the prefabricated, Jacobethan absurdities of Simla. Something subtler was needed, something nobler, something worthy of George V's conception of the 'union and fusion' of Indo-European culture. Lutyens found it in an architectural synthesis of his own invention: an Anglo-Indian classicism which drew inspiration from European and Indian traditions without copying either. This was not an occasion for 'fancy dress', he explained: he set out to 'build as an Englishman dressed for the climate', conscious only that his tailor hailed from the Punjab rather than from Savile Row.

The result was eclectic certainly: there are *chujjas*, and *chattris*, and elephant caryatids; the capital of the Delhi order is Lutyens's own invention; but the great dome and its geometric palisade stem from a Buddhist tomb, the Great Stupa at Sanchi. Outside there are echoes of Ajunta and Fatehpur-Sikri, and native traditions of gardening. Inside, the Durbar

180 Sir Edwin Lutyens, Castle
Drogo, Devon (1910–30).
A fusion of Gothic and Classic.

181 Sir Edwin Lutyens, Viceroy's House, New Delhi
(1912–31). 'Hurrah for despotism!'

Hall borrows from the Pantheon and Santa Sophia; the State Library
from St Stephen's, Walbrook. But this is eclecticism purged and
abstracted, purified by the architect's passion for reductive geometry.

'I wonder what you will do', Herbert Baker asked Lutyens; 'whether
you will drop the language [of] the classical tradition and just go for
surfaces – sun and shadow. It must not be Indian, nor English, nor
Roman, but it must be Imperial. In two thousand years there must be
an Imperial Lutyens tradition in Indian architecture ... Hurrah for
despotism!'[134]

Well, Imperial New Delhi certainly was a gigantic echo of Greenwich
on the banks of the River Jumna. Its completion was a joint achievement,
Baker and Lutyens combined. But the two men approached their task in
different ways. Baker was an eclectic, Lutyens a synthesist. Baker's
Secretariat domes are Greenwich gone native. The dome of the Viceroy's
House (1912–31)[181] is a distillation of East and West.[135] 'In all great
styles', Lutyens told Lord Hardinge in 1913, 'you will find the constructional purpose is clearly defined.'[136] So structural lucidity lay at
the root of his conception of classicism. But that was only part of it.
'Architecture more than any other art', he pointed out, 'represents the
intellectual progress of those that are in authority.'[137] So for Lutyens
architecture is both tectonic and symbolic, but its symbolism lies not in
its detail but in its translation into visual terms of the very idea of order.
'This dome', wrote Robert Byron, 'is an offence against democracy.'[138]

Goodhart-Rendel once remarked of Lutyens: 'whatever he did as an
artist he seemed to do rightly. Whether it was the right thing to do is a

different question altogether.'[139] At the last moment he had rescued Imperial Baroque, just as 'Greek' Thomson had rescued the Greek Revival. Both managed, miraculously, to balance symbolic and tectonic, romantic and classic. But that mysterious pendulum of the spirit – which in despair we call taste – was about to swing away again: from ideal to real, from universality to particularity, from absolute to relative values, from hierarchy to democracy, from the age of the Viceroys to the age of the common man – in other words, from classicism to romanticism. Long before Lutyens's death, the ground had already shifted. Taste, and economics, and technology too, were already struggling to give birth to a new aesthetic. In such an age of change, noted Christopher Hussey, 'the artist who founds his work upon ... an eternal ideal, to which the needs of humanity ... take second place ... is courting trouble. It is a question of sanctions. The classical Orders, like those societies that have successfully employed them in their buildings, connote the authority of an autocrat ... In proportion as that authority is reduced or diffused, the sanctions demanded by the classic canon are weakened, until, in a society based upon the greatest good of the greatest number, they become unworkable. The architect under such circumstances is bound to adopt the alternative aesthetic founded on function and [on] practical and social relationships: a romantic empiricism for which no aesthetic canon comparable to classical logic has, so far, been evolved.'[140] Hussey's words – written more than a generation ago – have turned out to be prophetic.

8 From Modern to Post-Modern

'Less is More' (Mies van der Rohe, c.1923).
'Less is a Bore' (Robert Venturi, 1966).

WHEN THE YOUNG JOHN BETJEMAN arrived at Magdalen College, Oxford, in 1925, he was faced with an examination paper which contained the following question: 'Can "skyscrapers" or railway stations be made beautiful? If so, how?'[1] Just how the future Poet Laureate managed to satisfy the examiners on that occasion remains uncertain. But there were two possible answers to the question. Either we build industrial structures in such a way that they fit into received categories of beauty, or else we refashion those categories so that *they* fit the railway station and the factory. Broadly speaking, the first answer – making utilitarian structures fit traditional aesthetics – was tried by the Victorians and Edwardians. The second – tailoring our criteria of beauty to suit the imperatives of technology – was the solution set out by the Modern Movement. Propriety and association were the watchwords of the first method; structural objectivity was the yardstick of the second.

To put it another way, either beauty lies in the building itself or it resides in the eye of the beholder: that is, beauty is either absolute or relative, intrinsic or extrinsic. The associational thinkers of the eighteenth century had argued for extrinsic beauty, so on the whole had Pugin and Ruskin. That was the romantic tradition. For the first time since the disintegration of Palladianism, the Modern Movement put the case for intrinsic beauty. In that respect it marked a return to classicism: a return to objective criteria, in this case the authority of function. Buildings were now to speak for themselves, as structures, without the intervention of imagery, or metaphor, symbol or memory. Architecture as service was to replace architecture as art.

The story of how this came about is the story of the Modern Movement. And that story, long ago, achieved the potency of myth. When Sir Nikolaus Pevsner's *Pioneers of the Modern Movement, from William Morris to Gropius* appeared in 1936, it crystallised that mythology: the Modern Movement as an inevitably evolving aesthetic, first English, then German – from Arts and Crafts to Bauhaus – from the ethics of the Gothic

225

Revival to the aesthetics of the International Style. Alas, on closer inspection, the pedigree of Modernism – like most family trees – turns out to be largely based on wishful thinking.

Even before the First World War, Philip Webb's houses had become symbols of modernity. 'Every brick of [Red House]'[133], wrote Laurence Weaver in 1910, 'is a word in the history of modern architecture.'[2] 'If ever', he added in 1922, 'there is evolved an architecture of reason, a sort of roc's egg required for the perfection of the Palace of Art, it would at least for houses in England, be very much like Philip Webb's domestic work.'[3] Those careful words of qualification, however, are all important: the future of modern architecture turned out not to depend on country houses, still less on English country houses. The Modern Movement – its functionalist ethic, its machine aesthetic – was born in industrial Germany, not in the English home counties, still less in the Cotswolds. And its greatest prophet turned out to be a Frenchman, born in Switzerland.

The Arts and Crafts Movement involved an attitude, not a style.[4] It was anti-academic, anti-professional, anti-Aesthetic,[5] anti-chic. Its basis was the cult of the vernacular, the art of craft. It was Gothic vernacular with Sedding, Temple Moore, Nicholson[6] and Comper. It was Georgian vernacular with Ernest Newton and Mervyn Macartney. It was Cotswold vernacular with Guy Dawber and the Barnsleys. It was Byzantine vernacular with Pite, Wilson and Bentley.[7] It was eclectic vernacular with

182 Leonard Stokes, Minterne House, Dorset (1903–7). Free Style Arts and Crafts.

Voysey and Lethaby. It was Picturesque vernacular with Lutyens.[8] And sometimes it was all of these: Leonard Stokes's Minterne House, Minterne Magna, Dorset (1903–7)[9][182] combines Perpendicular Gothic, English Baroque and West Country vernacular in a way which is perhaps best described as Free Style.[10] But the Arts and Crafts men were not searching for a personal style. Harrison Townshend's art nouveau[11] could never be the basis of a movement. Philip Webb had pointed the way by synthesising a spectrum of styles: Old English, Georgian, Gothic, Renaissance. Such easy fusion – as at Standen, Sussex (1891–4)[12] – was hard to analyse, harder still to follow. Whatever it was, it was not High Art.[13] In attempting to recapture that elusive, organic vernacular, the Arts and Crafts men were attempting to fulfil Morris's prophecy that any 'new and genuine architecture' must spring not from 'experiments in conscious style' but from 'necessary unpretentious buildings'.[14] 'The Gothic dream was virtually over by the 1880s', noted Muthesius.[15] But the aesthetics of Gothicism lived on: organic planning, structural truth, free craftsmanship, sound building, fitness for purpose. Ultimately, however, this generation was more interested in craft than in art. One of Baillie Scott's favourite sayings was 'when in doubt, whitewash'.[16]

By concentrating on domestic architecture – and domestic rural architecture at that – many Edwardian architects were able to duck the question of style altogether.[17] The 'conflict of truth with accustomed beauty', noted Weaver in 1919, 'does not arise in domestic building. The difference in cost between brick and timber on the one side and reinforced concrete on the other ... is not enough to weigh with the owner. In industrial buildings it is otherwise.' Provided we stick to domestic design, he concluded, an adaptation of almost any traditional style is justifiable. 'The question for the client is [simply this]: what manner best expresses his pleasure in the art of architecture.'[18] Such attempts to separate aesthetics and economics could not be sustained indefinitely. Sooner or later a bridge would have to be built between the two sets of parameters. And the bridging mechanism would be the machine.

For Ruskin, great art had been the product of high moral intention. Machines had no conscience, no soul. Hence the intrinsically inartistic nature of machine production. William Morris felt much the same. C. R. Ashbee, however, set out not to ignore the machine but to tame it.[19] Both Morris and Ashbee aimed at social harmony by means of creative craftsmanship. But to Morris's craft aesthetic Ashbee added a machine aesthetic based ultimately on the nobility of collective labour. 'What I seek to show', he explained, 'is that this Arts and Crafts movement, which began with the earnestness of the Pre-Raphaelite painters, the prophetic enthusiasm of Ruskin and the titanic energy of Morris, is not what the public has thought it to be, or is seeking to make it: a nursery for luxuries, a hothouse for the production of mere trivialities and useless things for the rich. It is a movement for the stamping out of such things by sound production on the one hand and the inevitable regulation of machine production and cheap labour on the other.'[20] Even so, the anti-industrial ethos of the Arts and Crafts Movement was too powerful: the Guild of Handicraft gravitated inevitably from town to country. Ashbee may have built, and built urbanely, in Cheyne Walk (nos. 38–9: 1898–9) [183], but his heart was surely in the Cotswolds. When in 1902 he led his little band of workmen from the East End of London to Chipping Campden in Gloucestershire, he set the seal on that rejection of the industrial world which was the strength and weakness of the whole Arts and Crafts Movement.[21]

1902 was the year the Guild of Handicraft decorated the chapel at Madresfield Court, Worcs: an exquisite performance. But, in the context of architectural progression, might it not be described as a performance of exquisite irrelevance?[22] 1902 was also the year when Ernest Gimson migrated to Sapperton in Gloucestershire with Sydney and Ernest Barnsley. Their work at Sapperton – Beechanger (S. Barnsley, 1902), or Upper Dorvill House (E. Barnsley, 1902), for instance – is almost indistinguishable from Cotswolds vernacular.[23] In a sense, it *is* Cotswolds vernacular. But could it ever be more than a bucolic blind-alley?

183 C. R. Ashbee, 38–9, Cheyne Walk, London (1898–9). Urban Arts and Crafts.

184 C. R. Mackintosh, School of Art, Glasgow (1896–9; 1907–9). Classic, Gothic, Vernacular and Modern.

185 Ernest Barnsley, Rodmarton Manor, Gloucestershire (1909 onwards).
Graveyard of the Arts and Crafts.

The Arts and Crafts spirit was anti-industrial, anti-urban. Philip Webb
never built a major civic structure. He designed Red House for Topsy and
Janey, not a factory for Morris and Co. When Lethaby dreamed of a city,
it was an organic city, free from the axial planning and well-drilled
ornament of Parisian *beaux arts*.[24] Occasionally Arts and Crafts architects
executed minor urban commissions, and successfully too: Mackmurdo at
25 Cadogan Gardens (1899); Voysey in Hans Road, Knightsbridge
(1891); Smith and Brewer with the Passmore Edwards Settlement,
Bloomsbury (1895). But when they were faced with sizeable public
buildings, they discovered there was really no substitute for classical
organisation. The greatest English Arts and Crafts architects – Lethaby
and Stokes – recognised that: Lethaby in his Eagle Insurance Office,
Birmingham (with J. L. Ball, 1899–1902); Stokes in his Gerard St Telephone Exchange, Soho (1904; dem. 1930). Further north, the Scottish
vernacular tradition, mixing Classic and Gothic forms, supplied Mackintosh with a matrix of similar regularity. In fact it was Mackintosh's
special genius for balancing Classic order and Gothic freedom within a
visual framework of abstract modernity which made his Glasgow School
of Art (1896–9; 1907–9)[184] such a triumph.[25] Few architects could
sustain such a delicate balance. Lesser men slipped into compositional
chaos. In London, Charles Canning Winmill was involved in a whole
series of public buildings sponsored by the LCC architect's department.
The Euston Rd Fire Station (1901–2) has been hailed as his 'masterpiece'.
Certainly its pragmatism – in planning, composition and detail – is
courageous. But its wayward romanticism, its dogmatic informality, has
been its undoing.[26]

The Barnsleys' Cotswold cottages – like Gimson's cottages in Charn-
wood Forest[27] – are part paradigm, part caricature. They have the eternal
relevance – and immediate irrelevance – of Laugier's Primitive Hut.[28] As
a fashion, rustic vernacular died with the Great War. Its grave is marked
by a sumptuous anachronism: Rodmarton Manor, Glos,[185] built at

229

huge expense from 1909 onwards by Ernest Barnsley for the Biddulphs. 'I've seen no modern work to equal it', noted Ashbee in 1914; it is 'the English Arts and Crafts movement at its best.'[29] Maybe, but it was also the English Arts and Crafts Movement *in extremis*.[30] And in his heart of hearts, Ashbee knew it. 'We have made of a great social movement', he admitted, 'a narrow and tiresome little aristocracy, working with great skill for the very rich.'[31] It was only too easy to slide from rustic vernacular to Edwardian Tudorbethan: what Laurence Weaver called 'the Middle Ages tempered by bath taps'.[32]

It was against such things – the 'make-believe … broken-down picturesque'[33] – that Lethaby rebelled. But it was a rebellion already anticipated by Muthesius. In *Das Englische Haus* (1904–5), Muthesius looked forward to the birth of a new aesthetic based unequivocally on function: 'an entirely new type of beauty', he called it, 'that of a spiritualised practical intention'. 'There are signs of this', he adds, 'in those parts of the house that have to do with hygiene.'[34] Well, there was something in that. Edwardian bathrooms did occasionally turn out to be precursors of modernism. But what Goodhart-Rendel called this 'Lethabitic' doctrine was – in its 'insistence on moral values … [its] distaste for aesthetic values' – 'essentially Protestant, essentially negative; unlikely to gain many adherents except at moments of surfeit and disgust.'[35] The Edwardian age was one of those moments. 'The grave', announced young Charles Holden in 1905, 'yawns for architects' architecture.'[36] Meanwhile, utility and beauty remained uneasy bedfellows.

The Voysey house – Moorcrag (1898)[186] or Broadleys (1898), for instance, both on the verge of Windermere – slated, gabled, rough-cast,

186 C. F. A. Voysey, Moorcrag, Windermere (1898). 'We cannot be too simple'.

187 B. Parker, R. Unwin *et al.*, Letchworth Garden City, Hertfordshire (1904 onwards).
Planning and the Picturesque.

buttressed, multi-mullioned; low-keyed, low-coloured, low-roofed, low-ceilinged, comparatively low-priced – is a statement both radical and reactionary.[37] It *is* a protest against historicism: 'we cannot', Voysey used to say, 'be too simple.'[38] Even so, it is far closer to the world of Sedding and Devey than it is to Le Corbusier. Its aesthetic is rooted in the Picturesque rather than in any theory of functional abstraction. What Lutyens admired, for example, was 'the absence of accepted forms . . . the long, sloping, slate-clad roofs, the white walls, clear and clean . . . [the] old world made new.'[39] Maybe: but Voysey's world remained the old world, not the new. In fact, there is no mistaking a Voysey house. As you approach it, sweeping gables reach out to greet you; as you enter the hall, you crack your head on a beam. To adapt Muthesius's dictum on Arts and Crafts furniture, it looks backwards rather than forwards: 'it would be an anachronism to call it modern, it is reactionary.'[40]

The Arts and Crafts house – child of the Gothic Revival, unwilling ancestor of the Modern Movement – summed up an eternal ambivalence in English aesthetics: puritan instincts and romantic yearnings. 'The English house', Muthesius concluded, 'lies long and low, a shelter and a refuge rather than an essay in pomp and architectonic virtuosity; it lies hidden somewhere in the green countryside . . . a witness to the sound instincts of a people, which, for all its wealth and advanced civilisation, has retained a remarkably strong feeling for nature.'[41] What Lutyens's followers did for the stockbroker, Voysey's followers did for the bank clerk. What Bedford Park (1876 onwards) had done for the middle class, Port Sunlight (1888 onwards) and Bournville (1879 onwards) did for the workers.[42] And what LCC housing[43] did for central London, Hampstead Garden Suburb (1907 onwards) and Letchworth Garden City (1904 onwards)[187] attempted to do for outer London and the suburbs. The garden suburb, indeed, is itself a microcosm of that state of mind: a coalition of romantic sensibility and puritan-progressive values.

231

This romantic puritanism – realistic rather than idealistic, what Muthesius called the Germanic view of art as opposed to the Italian – is summed up in the work of W. R. Lethaby.[44] In his early years, as an Arts and Crafts architect and theorist, Lethaby aimed firstly to develop the vernacular truths rediscovered by the Gothic Revival; secondly to reinterpret traditional forms in terms of new materials, especially concrete; and thirdly to raise utility to the level of poetry through the language of symbolic form.[45] The result was Brockhampton church, Herefordshire (1901–2)[188] and the Eagle Insurance Building, Birmingham (1900).

Lethaby's credo – architecture as a cooperative enterprise; architecture as growth rather than creation; architecture as life; architecture, above all, as the poetry of building – stemmed from a long romantic tradition: Hugo,[46] Thoreau,[47] Ruskin,[48] Morris.[49] An organic community producing organic art. According to this view, architectural theories – archaeological or functional – were irrelevant. The answer lay neither in traditional styles nor in new materials. It lay in society itself. 'The question of materials', Lethaby explained, 'is only an economic one. The mistake lies in the endeavour to design style. Style is only a way of doing things ... There are only two purposes for a building, service and delight.'[50] And when society is in a state of health, both factors – service and delight – will be found in a state of equipoise.

That might be a comforting philosophy for dreamers. But in worldly terms it might aptly be described as a recipe for doing nothing. The contrary viewpoint, the eclectic viewpoint, the Beaux Arts viewpoint, the viewpoint of turn-of-the-century architects right across the board – from Heathcote Statham to Beresford Pite and Bulkeley Creswell – was the professional, pragmatic view: architecture is a presentational not a representational art,[51] an artificial creation, not an emanation of nature;[52] it depends not on building technique but on the use of those techniques for architectural effect; and as the architectural process becomes more complex it inevitably involves a division of labour, a fragmentation of creative effort. So too does engineering. There was no going back: there could never be a Victorian vernacular; modern architectural style involved intellectual choice. Knowledge – associations – had supplemented instinct. According to this 'progressive' view Ruskin's rhetoric was an irrelevance; Morris's utopian socialism 'a gospel of negation and despair';[53] and Lethaby's ambivalence a recipe for inaction.

Lethaby's attitude to the machine was indeed ambivalent. And that ambivalence explains the reluctance – nay outright hostility – with which the Modern Movement was greeted in England, even by those later canonised as its 'Pioneers'. In 1895 Lethaby flatly denied the possibility

188 W. R. Lethaby, All Saints, Brockhampton, Herefordshire (1901–2) The poetry of building.

of creating true architecture by mechanical means.[54] He was all for letting material control form: 'we must absolutely root out, and tread under foot', he announced in 1896, 'the ingrained idea that there are standard art shapes ... that is simply art-cant.... I do not see the use of trying to 'design' anything.... We must try to substitute an ordinary, rational way of common-sense building for the prevailing chaos of architectural design.'[55] He acknowledged construction as central to all architectural development: 'We shall never see the problems of structure simply and whole while we see them through the refractive media of styles.'[56] 'A work of art is a well-made thing, that is all.'[57] But – and here Lethaby's doubts begin – can utility ever be the same as beauty? He suggests, as his easiest example, a violin. That indeed represents vernacular form carried to the point of poetry. As his next example, he suggests an aeroplane. Well, that *might* indeed be beautiful – though the aeroplane of 1918 looks today more an object of curiosity than an aesthetic ideal. Then he suggests a revolver: function made beautiful by purpose? The problem is getting trickier.[58] Then he suggests, as his last example, a plum pudding.[59] Now to confuse gastronomy and aesthetics is indeed a first-class category mistake, and Lethaby should have known better. His own instincts were certainly on the side of architectural plum puddings – that is, vernacular buildings. 'All these modern activities frighten me', he admits in 1918, 'and I would rather be dealing with rubble and thatch than with concrete and steel.' There was no avoiding these new materials. He made use of them himself – suitably disguised – at Brockhampton. Their ugliness, he convinced himself, was not intrinsic but extrinsic: the product of the society which gave them birth. A mean

233

building is merely the product of a mean society. 'The age of iron and concrete', he announced, 'has come; let us face it like men.'[60] 'There is nothing necessarily evil in modern materials or requirements. . . . It is the spirit that matters – concrete, rolled steel, cast-iron, stock-brick, deal-timber are all good in their own way.'[61] Metallic construction, provided it was 'exquisitely neat and precise', could be as handsome as a Swiss watch. Even concrete: it opened up endless possibilities for new forms of beauty, massy, smooth-shaped, 'sound as a china vase' and pierced with prismatic lights.[62] If aesthetics depend on custom, he concludes, then let us develop new customs.

In effect, Lethaby had found his way, painfully, reluctantly, to an acceptance of the machine aesthetic: efficiency as beauty; even the over-head gantries – 'iron giraffes' – at Clapham Junction.[63] That was 1918. Gradually, however, his doubts were beginning to grow. He continued to believe in good building as 'the universal style'.[64] The future, he felt sure, lay in the qualities exhibited in 'railway viaducts, brick kilns, pottery ovens and factory chimneys'. In fact, 'factory chimneys', he noted in 1918, 'are the greatest architectural work of today.'[65] Yet machine-made art remained for Lethaby, almost as much as it did for Ruskin or Morris, *secondary* art. 'Although a machine-made thing can never be a work of art in the proper-sense', he wrote in 1913, 'there is no reason why it should not be good in a secondary order – shapely, smooth, well-fitting, useful' – in fact like a machine itself. 'Machine work should show quite bravely that it is the child of the machine; it is the pretence and subterfuge of most machine-made things which makes them disgusting.'[66]

That became the basis of Lethaby's creed. 'High utility and liberal convenience', he wrote in 1920, 'are enough for architecture . . . Consider any of the great forms of life activity - seamanship, farming, house-keeping – can anyone say where utility ends and style, order, cleanness, precision begin?'[67] Well, perhaps. But by blurring that distinction – the distinction between ends and means – Lethaby certainly contributed to the eclipse of the Arts and Crafts and the rise of the Modern Movement.

In fact Lethaby's approach to design was as confused as Ruskin's. In 1889 he rejected the whole notion of 'conscious' design, and yet he implicitly recognised its inevitability. He never really fell for the myth-ology of utility: 'How can we . . . *plan* according to utility?', he asks. 'Is a vista a convenience?' And he liked to quote Coleridge: 'you must have a lantern in your hand to give light, otherwise all the materials in the world are useless, for you cannot find them, and if you could, you could not arrange them.' It was that sense of arrangement – that 'principle of selection', that 'expression of our instinct for order and beauty . . . the . . .

234

common instinct for its enjoyment', which we call 'art' or 'style' – it is this alone which, expressed in building, is Architecture.... 'All the rest, materials, construction, or archaeology ... is [but] preliminary study.'[68]

True. But by 1918, 'design' had become metamorphosed in his thinking into an agent of evolution: ' "design" is a matter of progressive experiment, the working out of a principle[69] by means of adaptation, selection, variation.'[70] That, however, did not exclude 'decoration' in the strict sense: 'Whoever has seen living decoration – I remember Whistler's wonderful Peacock Room – will understand', he concluded, 'that we must have wall painting.'[71] It was all a question of propriety. 'Functional fitness is the most necessary criterion of beauty. By this rule, as Plato said, a dung-cart is beautiful. It is so in its due level, but the higher the status the greater the beauty. Thus the athlete is more beautiful than the toad.'[72] All very true. But at the last hurdle Lethaby stumbles; beauty in building, he still believes in 1918, 'should be unconscious, like the charm of children'.[73]

Lethaby's cult of simplicity had its merits. 'There is ... a brown-bread and dewy morning ideal of beauty', he wrote, 'and a late champagne-supper ideal.'[74] Indeed there is. The Arts and Crafts men preferred brown bread. But Edwardian England preferred champagne. No wonder English architecture woke up with a hangover and turned instead to a diet of Vichy water labelled 'modernism'.

By 1929 Lethaby was beginning to see the future – in the shape, for example, of Peter Behrens's 'New Ways', Northampton (1926)[189]: the first Modern Movement house in England.[75] And he did not particularly

189 Peter Behrens, 'New Ways', Northampton (1926). First Modern Movement house in England.

235

like what he saw. To his embarrassment, he now found himself hailed as a modernist pioneer. He no longer regarded Clapham Junction as an object of admiration. Instead he called for 'an art of pure scientific structure', not necessarily based on steel, glass and concrete. 'Such a sense of pure construction', he explained, 'would be an anchorage against [the danger of choosing] "Modernism" *as a style* instead of seeking the truly modern.' Much modernism, he now admitted, 'is only an inverted archaeology. It is whim, not reason: "design", not building . . . reasonable building is not necessarily a series of boxes or a structure of steel. The most scientific and sensible building for given conditions might still be in brick and thatch.' In other words, the Windsor Chair might be more truly functional than Rietveld's Armchair of 1917. 'This modernism', he concludes, ' "Ye olde modernist style" . . . is [now] regarded as a style, whereas being truly modern would be simply [being] right and reasonable.'[76] He still finds some pleasure in industrial structures. 'A brick railway viaduct near Surbiton', he noted in 1929, 'always gives me pleasure, and an iron station shelter at Wimbledon is rational and tidy.'[77] The trouble was that engineering techniques were beginning to be used as stylistic tricks, substitutes for creative thought. Tricks of style were simply tricks of style, whatever the language. Instead of 'reality' in building, he lamented in 1930, we have 'the Architecture of Finance, and [the architecture of] Advertisement', a cross between Babel and Belshazzar's Feast.[78] In other words, modernism as capitalism: the Protestant, anti-Ruskinian ethic in three-dimensional form.[79] 'I greatly fear', he concluded – prophetically – that 'a modernist fashion will be imported as a style and not arrive as a natural growth from our own sound building customs. "Modernism" as an inverted archaeology is quite a different thing from experimenting for ourselves and being modern.'[80]

That was almost Lethaby's last message. 'It is the disappearance of poetry from our buildings', he laments, 'that has frightened me. [Poetry in architecture] can only come, as in our ships and airplanes, through a sterner realism, which will eliminate whim, pretence and make-believe.'[81] He might as well have attempted to eliminate original sin. And his rage was indeed hopeless. He regarded most nineteenth-century engineering – railway architecture especially – as 'all of one slatternly Gradgrinding type [in short] profitmongering.' Only a fusion of the best of architecture and the best of engineering held out any hope for the future. 'Beware', he concludes, 'of a style *called* Modernism.'[82] That *was* Lethaby's last word: he died a few months later, in July 1931.

By that date the International Style had at last crossed the Channel. In the eighteenth century, with Neo-Classicism and the Picturesque, we

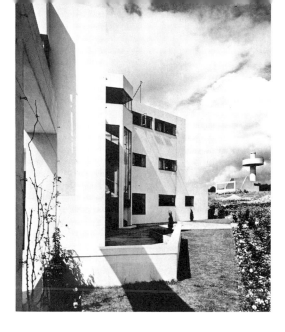

190 Amyas Connell, 'High and Over', Amersham (1929). 'Unalloyed by sentimental clap-trap'.

led; in the nineteenth century with the Gothic Revival, Queen Anne and the Arts and Crafts, we led again; in the twentieth century with the Modern Movement, we followed – reluctantly. Frederick Etchells translated Le Corbusier in 1927, and designed England's first modern office building – Crawford's in Holborn – in the same year. Amyas Connell designed England's first Corbusian house – High and Over, at Amersham, in 1929[190], for Bernard Ashmole, Director of the British School at Rome. And Colin Lucas designed the first monolithic concrete house in 1930: Noah's House, Bourne End, Bucks. Such buildings – like Mendelsohn and Chermayeff's Bexhill Pavilion (1934–6) – introduced England to a veritable new world of design. They must have seemed a revelation: as strange and exotic as artefacts from another planet. 'Here', at High and Over, wrote the young Christopher Hussey, 'is an architecture pure and unalloyed by sentimental reminiscences or clap-trap. One goes away exhilarated as by a fresh and fertile mind or by the consummate simplicity of a Greek vase.'[83] One evening in the late 1920s, young Maxwell Fry gazed at new Devonshire House in Piccadilly (Carrere, Hastings and Reilly, 1927), rising in all its pride of rustication and *amorini*. The game, he realised, was 'played out'. 'In a gesture of moral revulsion', he threw away all his Beaux Arts drawings – learned at the feet of C. H. Reilly in Liverpool – and turned instead to the design of concrete-trussed, working-class flats.[84]

Apart from Fry and T. S. Tait, nearly all the early leaders of the Modern Movement in England had roots abroad. Wells Coates was born in Tokyo and trained in Canada. Raymond McGrath, Amyas Connell and Basil Ward were Australasians. Serge Chermayeff was born in the Caucasus

191 Sir Owen Williams, Pioneer Health Centre, Peckham, London (1935).
Engineering aesthetic, Socialist programme.

and trained in Argentina. Bertold Lubetkin was also a Caucasian who
had practised in Paris. Ove Arup arrived here from Denmark. And Erich
Mendelsohn, Walter Gropius, Arthur Korn, Marcel Breuer, Laszló
Moholy-Nagy and Naum Gabo were all emigrés, in the last instance,
from Germany. Rejected in Germany, the country of its birth; spurned in
Russia, the country of its adoption, the Modern Movement was reduced
to waging aesthetic war in the liberal democracies of the West. In England
it became identified with socialism; in America, eventually, it became a
vehicle for international capitalism. Strictly speaking, in the 1930s, there
was no English Modern School, merely a random group of modernists.[85]
Not until after the Second World War did there emerge a native-bred
generation able to stake its claim to leadership of the new orthodoxy.

What held this pre-war group together was firstly an aesthetic vocabulary, and secondly a social creed: that is an engineering aesthetic and a
socialist programme. A world of aerodromes and grain silos seemed
appropriately reflected in, for example, the Peckham Health Centre (by
Owen Williams, 1935)[191]. The new vocabulary was based, primarily,
on rejection: rejection of stylistic formulae; rejection of adventitious
ornament. 'Although it is difficult for man to learn', wrote Viollet-le-Duc,
'it is much more difficult for him to forget.'[86] Well, the modernists of the
1930s tried very hard. In fact they achieved a kind of collective amnesia.[87]
All the old formal stereotypes had to go. And much of the old mumbo
jumbo was well lost: compare Peter Jones Department Store before[192]
and after[193] the arrival of the Modern Movement. In place of stale
formulae, the gospel of 'function' offered the magic of a *tabula rasa*.

That gospel, however, was rooted in mythology. Le Corbusier[88] may
have announced: 'the styles are a lie ... the house is a machine for living
in ... the plan is the generator.' He may have proclaimed the machine
aesthetic, the primacy of geometry and mass, the harmony of functional
form. But he also drew elementary distinctions between engineering and

238

192 and 193 Peter Jones, Chelsea, London. Back, and new front
by W. Crabtree and F. Singer (1936).

architecture; between function and beauty. Hence his suspicion of the Bauhaus. 'Architecture', he stated firmly, 'goes beyond utilitarian needs.... The purpose of construction is to *make things hold together*; of architecture to *move us*.... Obviously, if the roof were to fall in, if the central heating did not work, if the walls cracked, the joys of architecture would be greatly diminished.... but ... boudoirs, WCs, radiators, ferro-concrete, vaults or pointed arches.... This is construction, this is not architecture. Architecture only exists where there is poetic emotion.' Alas, like Ruskin and Viollet-le-Duc before him, Le Corbusier was honoured in England chiefly by those who misunderstood him. He remained a prisoner of that misunderstanding: his legacy was vulgar functionalism. Despite his protests – he once called functionalism that 'frightful word'[89] – the legend 'utility = beauty' became the Corbusian albatross. That was partly because of the impact of his secondary message: 'architecture or revolution'.

> We must create the mass-production spirit.
> The spirit of constructing mass-production houses.
> The spirit of living in mass-production houses.
> The spirit of conceiving mass-production houses.

By tying architecture to society, style to technology and planning to economics, Le Corbusier set up an architectural dialectic which seemed to suppress aesthetics in favour of politics. 'Building is at the root of social unrest today', he wrote, 'this ... is *the* problem of our epoch. Modern life demands ... a new kind of plan ... if existing property arrangements were changed ... it would be possible to build ... and we should avoid Revolution.' In the new 'City of Towers' – *La Ville radieuse* (1935) – the architect would be King. All those 'wretched' pitched roofs would be swept away, along with those casual 'cafés and places for recreation ... that fungus which eats up the pavements of Paris.' On the fourteenth floor, you will have 'absolute calm and the purest air'.

There it is: the utopianism, the dogma, the totalitarian mind. After all, as he openly admits, 'Art is in its essence arrogant'. The new architecture was to be a compound of Arts and Crafts ethics (Lethabitic truth), Corbusian aesthetics (spatial manipulation through geometrical form) and Bauhaus technology (mass-production of standardised components). Henceforward 'delight' was to consist solely in the conjunction of 'commodity' and 'firmness'.[90] 'Fitness' itself was to be the sole guarantee of beauty. Indeed fitness was now held to be invariably beautiful, given 'the right state of mind'.[91] And how was that state of mind to be achieved? Gropius's Bauhaus programme aimed at total art, 'complete building'; objective form achieved by the integration of art and craft – monumental, decorative, fine and applied.[92] True Bauhaus spirits like Moholy-Nagy believed passionately that mechanisation was the key – but mechanisation in what they called a 'techno-biological' context.[93] 'Building', wrote Hannes Meyer in 1928, 'is a biological process ... not an aesthetic process ... architecture which produces effects introduced by the artist has no right to exist ... the architect [must become] a specialist in organisation ... [because] building is only organisation; social, technical, economic, mental.'[94] In other words – as Ruskin and Morris had already discovered – aesthetic questions ultimately involved political answers. And one 'question', as Christian Barman explained in 1933, was 'on everybody's lips ...: Can human society assimilate the machine?'[95]

No one swallowed Corbusier's rhetoric more willingly than Wells Coates. With his Hollywood good looks and playboy image, Coates was a freewheeling design-technologist; a romantic artist in love with the idea of the 'Maison Minimum': industrialised, rationalised, *rationed*. Therein lay a contradiction: libertarian instincts versus collectivist aesthetics. But Coates remained unworried. The engineer-architect – a sort of Platonic Guardian, probably living in Hampstead; perhaps even in Lawn Road flats – would deal with all such problems. 'We don't want', he noted in his diary, 'engineer and architect combining in plans ... but the architect-engineer, or rather the engineer-architect; and I pin my faith in Sir Owen Williams.' 'Architects', he added, 'are mostly finished.'[96] Well, the English tradition of industrial architecture could certainly be drawn into the argument – and has been – as a series of proto-Modern precedents: from Ironbridge, Shropshire (1777)[97] to H. B. Creswell's Engineering Works, Queensferry, Flintshire (1901–5).[98] But it took the theology of Modernism to elevate utility into myth. In Sir Owen Williams – at the Boots Factory, Nottingham (1930–6); at Wembley Pool (1934)[194] with its canti-

194 Sir Owen Williams, Wembley Pool, London (1934). 'The poetry of fact'.

195 Wells Coates, Lawn Rd. Flats, Hampstead (1933). 'Architecture has to serve the purpose of the people as well as the purposes of beauty'.

levered concrete vault; or at Dollis Hill Synagogue (1937) with its pre-stressed concrete roof – modern architects found an engineer who was even more modern than they: a master of Le Corbusier's 'poetry of fact'.

It was said that Voysey preferred to wear suits without lapels: that was the puritan aesthetic of the Arts and Crafts.[99] But Wells Coates designed his own radio with a transparent glass front: that was the faith of a romantic functionalist. 'The past', he used to say, 'is not always behind us, but more often in front, blocking the way.'[100] Coates was, in fact, a self-taught industrial designer of ingenuity and talent: the D-shaped handle became his trade-mark. Perhaps he was a better designer than he was an architect: the new BBC studios in Portland Place showed him at his best. Indeed, he regarded architecture as simply a compound of industrial processes. In that he was not alone. His flats in Lawn Rd, Hampstead (1933)[195] and Palace Gate, Kensington (1938) became 'ideograms for a whole generation of English architects.'[101] And Coates, more than anyone, was the spirit behind the MARS Group – that 'precious cell of intense and angry young men'[102] – a spirit as dogmatic, as exclusive, as salvationist, as that of the Cambridge Camden Society. Once again, only one style was permissible: once it had been Decorated Gothic; now it was International Modern. Taste was, once again, an irrelevance. 'Architecture', announced Joseph Emberton, 'is not a matter of aesthetics. It is a matter of reason.'[103] 'As creative artists', wrote Wells Coates, 'we

242

are concerned with a future which must be *planned*. . . . As architects of
a new order, we should be concerned with an architectural solution of
social and economic problems.'[104] 'Architecture has to serve the purpose
of the people as well as the purposes of beauty.'[105]

By comparison with High and Over, Lawn Road was indeed revolutionary. High and Over's Cubism is only skin deep: Connell managed
to squeeze the functions of the house into an abstract, symmetrical form.
But in Lawn Road Coates ruthlessly made the exterior express the interior
planning, and the planning express the purpose: Pugin's 'True Picturesque' translated into the industrialised idiom of the International
Style, with monolithic reinforced concrete replacing the pointed arch as
the basic yardstick of design. The *Architectural Review* hailed its 'exter-
nalised' plan in the name of logic and truth: each flat was 'a miracle of
multum in parva compactness'. This was minimal living. Refugees like
Marcel Breuer, Moholy-Nagy and Gropius happily took up residence. So
did Agatha Christie and Mrs Henry Moore. Philip Harben and Raymond
Postgate looked after the supply of food and wine. But the public at large
never took to it.[106] As Paul Klee lamented on another occasion, 'the
people are not with us'.[107]

'What is the *essential intention* in Architecture?', asked Coates. 'Reduced
to its simplest elements it is the provision of *ordered shelter* and an *aspect
of significance* in the arrangement of buildings and the forms of nature in
which they are placed.'[108] *Reduced to its simplest elements:* the world would
not remain satisfied for long with architecture reduced to its simplest
elements. Perhaps the nub of the problem was simply semantic confusion.
'In the English language', Mies van der Rohe once explained, 'you call
everything structure. In Europe we don't. We call a shack a shack and
not a structure. By structure we mean a philosophical idea. The structure
is the whole, from top to bottom, to the last detail – with the same ideas.
That is what we call structure.'[109] And that – we might add – is what
the English properly call architecture. Pevsner admitted the same thing
in 1942, with his famous distinction between Lincoln Cathedral and a
bicycle shed.[110] In fact Geoffrey Scott – echoing Ruskin – had got it right
in 1914: 'Architecture studies not structure in itself but the effect of
structure on the human spirit.'[111]

As regards ornament, Corbusier's followers fell into much the same
trap as Lethaby, Adolf Loos[112] and even Frank Lloyd Wright. 'Beauty',
Lethaby had argued, 'may be ornamental, but it is possible that ornamentation, which arises in such arts as tattooing, belongs to the infancy
of the world, and it may well be that it will disappear from our architecture
as it has from our machinery.'[113] Now the mistake here was to confuse

243

196 Bertold Lubetkin, Finsbury Health Centre, London (1935–8). 'The admiration of aesthetically beautiful things is characteristic of the *bourgeois* aesthetic'.

ornament with surface decoration. Ornamental form can be three-dimensional as well as two-dimensional; structural as well as superficial; and both aspects – compositional or linear – express the same aesthetic impulse, the same instinct for play through form which lies at the root of all artistic creation. Aesthetic impulses will always express themselves in some way or other, and – systematised, socialised – they end up first as style, than as taste.

Architecture without design – in effect, style-less style – is a contradiction in terms.[114] Style in architecture is indeed a way of building codified as image. But its basis is a complex dialectic between function and form, construction and ornament, necessity and instinct, new technology and half-remembered shapes. And, as Hope Bagenal pointed out in 1937, every age 'will die for its shapes.'[115] In abolishing 'the styles', modernists attempted to abolish 'style'. They might as well have tried to abolish fingerprints or reverse the force of gravity. Herbert Spencer's play impulse;[116] Ruskin's ornament as pleasure/decoration as homage – call it what we will – aesthetic preference will out.[117] The modernist dream of objective form – that is form determined solely by function – was always a myth, a mental construct: like Laugier's Primitive Hut.[118] Alas, the modernists ended up by believing their own mythology. They came to believe that Modernism was not another style: it was the final chapter, the Holy Grail.

244

Le Corbusier's ambition was not just to build, but to build 'for the good of humanity'.[119] 'Architects', announced Chermayeff in 1935, 'can no longer concern themselves with construction in a separate professional compartment. They must participate in the reconstruction of society.'[120] Lubetkin – a self-proclaimed Communist – was more specific: he wanted 'not simply to build architecturally, but to build socialistically as well'.[121] His Finsbury Health Centre (1935–8)[196] became the key image of socialist architecture in the England of the 1930s.[122] A building, he believed, should be judged in only one way. 'Is this building, or is it not, a contribution to modern architecture, and through it to social progress?'[123] And modern architecture, he concluded, should not be afraid of any resultant ugliness. 'The admiration', he wrote, 'of aesthetically beautiful things is characteristic of the *bourgeois* aesthetic.'[124] His aim was to reflect 'the struggles of the progressive forces in society'.[125] In this way, social criteria replaced aesthetic criteria. Of course Lubetkin's approach was not exactly new. Durand had said much the same thing at the end of the eighteenth century;[126] Viollet-le-Duc in the mid-nineteenth century.[127] But neither had been in a position to turn theory into practice. Both assumed a historical language of form, one Classic, the other Gothic. Now – in the twentieth century – practice was at last to catch up with theory.

At first, working with the Tecton partnership, Lubetkin experimented on animals: in the Gorilla House (1932) and Penguin Pool (1934) at London Zoo. Then – with Arup responsible for the engineering – he was able to put his ideas into practice on humans: in Highpoint I (1934–5)[197].[128] A symbol of the North London intelligentsia – praised by Le

197 Lubetkin and Tecton, Highpoint I, Hampstead (1934–5). Admired by Le Corbusier.

198 Lubetkin and Tecton, Highpoint II, Hampstead (1936–8). A signpost marked 'Post-Modernism'.

Corbusier himself – this, the first of England's high-rise blocks, was a manifesto in reinforced concrete construction: a fusion of form and structure supposedly based on an equation of economics and use. Of course, its aesthetic subjectivity was obscured by its apparent rationality. And that inevitable subjectivity was openly revealed in Highpoint II (1936–8)[198].[129] The *avant garde* felt betrayed. 'Something has changed', noted Anthony Cox in 1938; 'one has the feeling that a *form* has been imposed on the rooms (which is an altogether different thing from giving the *room* form). It is as if, during the three years that separate the [two] buildings, rigid conclusions have been reached as to what is formally necessary in architecture .... The intellectual approach which has produced ... modern architecture is fundamentally a functionalist approach .... [But in Highpoint II] formal values [have been set] above use-values ... [this] marks the re-emergence of the *idea* as the motive force [in architectural design].'[130] In other words, Modern Architecture had been revealed as a *style*. And that revelation was displayed for all to see in Lubetkin's caryatid porch. As the *Architectural Review* noted, Highpoint II is 'a more deliberate architectural composition'.[131] Indeed it is. The fiction of functional objectivity – anonymous design[132] – has been abandoned. Neither Highpoint I nor Highpoint II was ever intrinsically functional. Highpoint I was an abstract statement; Highpoint II a coded message. That caryatid turned out to be a long-distance signpost marked 'Post-Modernism'.

The constructional logic of Modernism was indeed largely mythical: after all, reinforced concrete concealed its reinforcement. The aim was abstraction rather than structural truth. Its forms were the result not of

246

necessity but of choice. And Oliver Hill, for example, demonstrated –
ambidextrously – that Modernism (Joldwynds, Surrey, 1933) could be
employed, as a style, just as easily as Neo-Georgian (40, Chelsea Square,
1930). The subjunctive functionalism of the Modern Movement had
fallen into the same trap as the subjunctive rationality of Neo-Classicism.
'It may as well be candidly admitted', noted P. Morton Shand in 1930,
'that we erect mechanist buildings, not because we must but because we
like them ... The present age finds the shape of steamers, aircraft, cooking
ovens, turbines, transmission poles and silos so infinitely more beautiful
than traditional art forms.'[133] And if people did not like those shapes?
We shall 'address ourselves only to those capable of understanding us',
announced Maxwell Fry, and we shall 'let the rest go hang.'[134]

In Evelyn Waugh's *Decline and Fall* (1928), Margot Beste-Chetwynde
invites Prof Otto Friedrich Silenus to rebuild King's Thursday as 'something clean and square'. 'The problem of architecture, as I see it', explains
Silenus, 'is the problem of all art – the elimination of the human element
from the consideration of form. The only perfect building must be the
factory, because that is built for machines, not for men.'[135] Such a
mechanistic view of architecture – not so very far from Gropius's ideal:
maximising economy by economising form – was of course at odds with
the nominally humanistic aims of the leading modernists. 'We were
concerned', Maxwell Fry later recalled, 'not with architecture alone,
but with society ... we were filled with a fervour as moral as it was
aesthetic.'[136]

So was architecture – Lorne and Tait's middle class housing in St
John's Wood (1933); or Fry, Atkinson, Wornum and James's working
class housing in Ladbroke Grove (1936)[199] – a social instrument or
simply a mechanist abstraction? In effect, it was both: architecture was to

199 Fry, Atkinson, Wornum and James, Kensal House, Ladbroke Grove, London (1936).
'A fervour as moral as it was aesthetic'.

be mechanised as a means of socialising society. And by thus politicising architecture the modernists fell straight into the Gothic Revivalists' trap. Some modern architecture, Goodhart-Rendel told his students in 1937, is 'not intended to suit people's habits but to change them. To use art in such a way is ridiculous; you are using art when . . . you should properly use dynamite.' This is really 'a very lamentable recrudescence of the worst of the early Victorian fallacies, the fallacy that art is useful when it is used as an instrument of moral good.'[137]

To cover their tracks, a few English modernists maintained that they were merely picking up the Georgian tradition of rational design at the point where it was 'submerged' in an 'orgy of eclecticism'.[138] That was surely wishful thinking. Such an ancestry – from J. M. Gandy's villas to Maxwell Fry's Sun House, Hampstead (1935) – ignored the very basis of Modernist belief: that a new architecture had been created – in Germany, France, Austria, Scandinavia – which turned its back on the entire visual code of traditional forms. In its place it set up a new code altogether: the machine aesthetic.

That aesthetic turned out to be largely fictional: as arbitrary as the Classicism it replaced. Whatever the programme; whatever the requirements – car park or offices; whatever the context – urban or suburban – somehow all these early modern buildings seemed to look alike.[139] The choice of forms was as conscious, as arbitrary, as limiting – ultimately as formalistic – as the choice of any traditional style. Just as the later nineteenth century had found a style – Progressive Eclecticism – without noticing it, so the early twentieth century found 'a style called modern' while refusing to acknowledge its existence. Those early modernists were only nominally empiricists: they were more concerned with formal abstraction than with functional form. They were cubists not pragmatists; aesthetes rather than craftsmen. Instead of developing Continental models in a truly functional way – adapting Le Corbusier, for instance, to a different climate and a different social context – they attempted to impose on English building the visual apparatus of Continental Modernism: flat roofs, picture windows, open balconies, white-washed walls – minus mouldings, of course – all composed in rectilinear shapes. The irony of it was that they thought they were escaping from style when in fact they were demonstrating just how stylistically dogmatic Modernism could be. And their narrow formal vocabulary – their image of modernity – was rendered doubly procrustean by their commitment to a vision of society which was ordered, planned, controlled, and new.

'As architects of the ultimate human and material scenes of the new order', announced Wells Coates in 1934, 'we are not so much concerned with the formal elements of style as with an *architectural* solution of the social and economic problems of today.'[140] Alas, 'socialism and internationalism'[141] could never in themselves guarantee architectural excellence. That balance between tectonic and atectonic criteria which must always lie at the heart of good architecture had once again been upset. 'We will have simplicity', Mies is said to have remarked, 'no matter how much it costs'.[142] In the hands of his followers, the cost turned out to be high. By suppressing ornament, by ignoring context, by eliminating association, by surrendering metaphor and symbol, architecture lost more than half its power of speech. Without detail, even the language of proportion was lost. 'M. Le Corbusier's city', noted A. Trystan Edwards – prophetically – in 1929, 'is a dead city, and it represents nothing more or less than architectural nihilism.'[143]

Not surprisingly, there was opposition: from the Classical establishment as well as from the Arts and Crafts Movement. Lutyens called it, 'the new nude style, grammarless and cheaply adjectived'.[144] In the first place, the new functionalism was not especially functional.[145] The ergonomics of the upright chair, for example, peaked around 1835 rather than 1935. The flat roof did have one advantage: it need never inhibit the plan. But – leaving aside its negative contribution to semiotics – its weatherproofing was often inadequate, its insulation deficient.[146] Highpoint I leaked even more badly than Lawn Road. In both, the metal-framed windows became corroded. At 66, Frognal, Hampstead, the windows have also had to be replaced. In Palace Gate, Kensington, Coates (and Denys Lasdun) decided it was wiser to cover the concrete walls with artificial stone slabs, and to supplement the metal windows with teak. At Highpoint II even Lubetkin decided to cover his concrete frame with panels of glazed tiles. Of course, the battlements of Castle Drogo leaked as well: but Lutyens never set out to create a paradigm of function.

Then there were the intellectual objections. And in the long run these were more important. By confusing structural logic and aesthetic psychology, the Modernist came near to rendering his building semiotically dumb. Reginald Blomfield – a last-ditch defender of Classicism[147] – took pleasure in pointing out the Modernists' ontological deficiencies. In particular, he demonstrated that the equation on which the Modern Movement apparently rested – 'function = beauty' – was simply a *non-sequitur*. Big Bertha – the great German field gun of the First World War – was undoubtedly efficient, and undeniably ugly.[148] Ruskin had spotted this long before: beauty is independent of utility.[149] So had Muthesius. 'Usefulness', he pointed out, 'has basically nothing to do with beauty. Beauty is a problem of form, and nothing else; usefulness is the plain fulfilment of purpose.'[150] In other words, beauty is only a contingent, not a necessary function of utility. That, in the end, was Pevsner's view.[151] Even Herbert Read – *the* guru of English inter-war Modernism – had to agree. 'That functional efficiency and beauty do often coincide may be admitted', he wrote in 1934. 'The mistake is to assume that the functional efficiency is the cause of the beauty; *because* functional, *therefore* beautiful. That is not the true logic of the case.'[152] Functionalism, therefore, was a myth: sometimes therapeutic, more often pernicious.

No. 66, Frognal (Connell, Ward and Lucas, 1938)[200] was a particular insult to Blomfield: he lived just across the road. He thought it a paradigm of 'bolshevik' design. In fact its internal planning is largely conventional, and its servicing is scarcely socialistic. But, in one respect, his criticism rang true. 'I think', he wrote in 1933, 'the new architecture will go the way of other fashions. What is good in it will be absorbed, and the rest of it relegated to the dustbin.' 'Functionalism has gone too far', he explained, 'in that it has misconceived the purposes of architecture .... [Indeed it] is ramming its head against deep-seated instincts which

200 Connell, Ward and Lucas, 66 Frognal, Hampstead (1938). 'Functionalism has gone too far'.

will beat it in the end.'[153] Blomfield turned out to be right. Is our appreciation of St Paul's Cathedral diminished when we discover the falsity of its dome?[154] Has our admiration for the Pantheon, Rome, been impaired by its various changes of function? Surely not. We judge with our eyes first, and our understanding second. After all, if function were the sole criterion, the only perfect building would be an asylum for the blind. Blomfield knew about design:[155] it was his visual sense which turned England's electricity pylons into objects of more than simple utility. But, like Pugin, he tended to confuse beauty and propriety. Both men were so carried away by the associations of architecture that they limited architectural excellence to a single architectural style: in Pugin's case Gothic, in Blomfield's Classic. In other words – like most anti-modernists of the 1930s – Blomfield confused order with the Orders. Indeed he confused two meanings of the word style: style as a formal tradition, and style as excellence of form.

But Modernism itself never shook off the old bogey of association. Houses were now supposed to look like machines,[156] just as Regency dairies were sometimes supposed to look like miniature cathedrals. 'Art Nonsense', Summerson noted in 1935, was being replaced by 'Machine Nonsense'.[157] Designing houses to look like motor-cars; and offices – or car parks – to look like ocean-going liners, was – as Blomfield pointed out – to confuse statics and dynamics.[158] By mixing up ethics and aesthetics, technology and civics, Modernism ran into just the same sort of confusion as Victorian Gothic. And like the Gothic Revival, the Modern Movement eventually dwindled into a fashion. It became modernistic.

England, of course, had been the first industrialised society. But from the start, our mechanical ingenuity had been at odds with our feeling for nature and our instinct for freedom and privacy. So the cult of the machine aesthetic arose not in England but among our European competitors: Austria, Italy, Germany, France, Scandinavia. It was the writing of Loos, Marinetti, Sant' Elia, Moholy-Nagy, Le Corbusier, Oud and Gropius that first spelled out the magic of the machine, the vision of a mechanical universe in which the architect was God. Houses were to be no longer temples, no longer cottages, but simply mechanistic devices. Far from ridding themselves of all imagery, however, architects were merely replacing one set of images with another: the imagery of the machine. That was hardly surprising. After all, architectural style is really no more than a structural system codified in imagistic form. Hence the emergence of an international *Style*. Hitchcock and Johnson spotted that in 1932.[159] The old devil of subjectivity proved difficult to exorcise. To borrow Lionel Brett's notation, the images kept getting in the way of the parameters. And once the Modern *Movement* had been recognised as the International *Style*, the way was clear for the next phase of its development: Modern became modernistic.

When Modern went modernistic it became respectable, as in Grey Wornum's Scandinavian Modern RIBA headquarters (1932–4). It even achieved levels of greatness denied to purist Modernity: Berlage had already demonstrated the compatibility of function and ornamental line (Holland House, Bury St, London, 1914); Holden now demonstrated the compatibility of function and ornamental form (Arnos Grove Station, 1932–3).[160] The style even became popular: the Hoover Factory (Wallis, Gilbert & Partners, 1932–5)[201], for instance; or the Odeon cinemas.[161] The basis of modernistic design was not function but fashion; not ergonomics but stylistics. To purists it was a fake – 'white man's jazz', Myerscough Walker once called it.[162] But, in a sense, it merely accepted the reality of Modernism: the International Style was indeed a style, potentially as coherent and expressive as any other.[163] Even machines require symbolic form if they are to be visually intelligible. In a steam engine, power is *visibly* present; in an electric turbine *invisibly*. So an image of power has to be created: as in Giles Gilbert Scott's power stations at Battersea (1929; 1931–5)[202][164] and Bankside (1955). Again, a motor car has to be decorated with 'streamlining' – the imagery of speed – to communicate its one essential attribute: celerity. So also with modern architecture: its structures, its purposes, baffle comprehension. Therefore its ornament must explain: statics made visible, function in semiotic form.[165] Such proto-post-modernist ideas were unacceptable in Hampstead. But they went down well in Park Lane. In 1929 Sir Owen Williams was commissioned to design a new hotel on the site of Dorchester House. He proposed a concrete-buttressed structure not unlike

201 Wallis, Gilbert and Partners, The Hoover
Factory, Western Avenue, London (1932–5).
'White man's jazz'?

202 Allott, Halliday, Agate and Scott, Battersea Power Station (1929; 1931–5). Modern goes modernistic.

203 H. S. Goodhart-Rendel, Hay's Wharf, London (1930–32). 'Treated as a style and not as a religion, modernism has great capabilities'.

his Wembley Pool. The outcry was deafening. Williams refused to compromise. Curtis Green was appointed in his place; he adjusted the plan and clothed the exterior in smoother, streamlined shapes: fit for 'the shining ones who dwell, safe in the Dorchester Hotel'.[166] 'The new architecture', wrote Frank Pick in 1935, 'is passing from a negative to a positive phase, seeking to speak not only through what it omits or discards, but much more through what it conceives and invents. Individual imagination and fancy will more and more take possession of the technical resources of the new architecture, of its spatial harmonies, of its functional qualities, and will use them as the ... frame-work of a new beauty .... If the architect has in the reaction [to historicism] swung too far over towards the engineer he will, in the counter-reaction, swing back again towards the artist.'[167]

Among those in the vanguard of this counter-attack against 'the functionalist bogey' were Oliver Hill and Elizabeth Scott.[168] But their intellectual leader was H. S. Goodhart-Rendel, architect of Hay's Wharf, London (1931–3).[203] As President of the AA in 1924–6 – in a world of Chelsea Arts Balls and champagne – he had been able to play the iconoclast,[169] damning Regent Street and praising the Kodak Building in Kingsway. But by the date of his second tenure of office – as Director,

1936–8 – Modernism in England had changed from a cult to a political programme, and Goodhart-Rendel – bravely waving the banner of artistic autonomy – was forced into resignation.[170]

Another who queried the obsession with utility was Kenneth Clark. He quickly spotted the semiotic limitations of an architectural language which was so self-consciously negative. 'I cannot believe', he concluded in 1934, 'that the human spirit will for long be content [with] such a starvation diet.'[171] Well, Clark lived to see ornament re-born. And the reaction would have come much sooner but for the aesthetic starvation of World War II and the Age of Austerity which succeeded it.

In 1943 the RIBA held an exhibition at the National Gallery entitled 'Rebuilding Britain'. It was opened by Sir William Beveridge, arbiter of the Welfare State. He called it 'a declaration of war on Squalor'. It was not a declaration of war on ugliness.

> Perhaps [this] Exhibition [Kenneth Clark explained] will seem to some visitors to be more concerned with architecture as a social necessity than with architecture as an art. That is true ... Great buildings must express a belief – a conviction so widely held as to be unconscious. The architecture of the Middle Ages expressed belief in God, the architecture of the Renaissance in the god-like qualities of man's intelligence. These beliefs are no longer strong enough to produce great architecture. But we all share one belief which earlier ages lacked: that everyone has a right to a certain standard of life; that no one need be cold, hungry, dirty or diseased through sheer want. In the past these things were thought of as inevitable. *We* believe that the machine, which so disastrously increased them a century ago, can be used to abolish them today. .... Architecture is a social art .... That is why this Exhibition does not deal with façades, elevations and styles, but with the pre-requisites of architecture: needs, plans, materials. I am sure that this is the right approach, but there is a danger in it – materialism. We may become so involved in questions of hot water and sewage disposal that we forget how much people's spirits depend on questions of space, proportion, light – even texture. And we overlook the vital principle of waste – what Ruskin ... called the lamp of sacrifice. The imagination requires that certain things should exist for their own sakes – not because they do us any demonstrable good. Such were the towers and pinnacles of the Middle Ages, the volutes and sculptural pediments of the seventeenth century; but these things cannot simply be stuck on to buildings; they must grow out of them. They must express a need for play which bursts through the wall, or a sense of glory which shoots into the air and defies the laws of gravity. Perhaps it will be a long time before our buildings blossom in this way; but during the present winter of our architecture, let us not try to raise hot house flowers; let us rather devote ourselves to winter pursuits, to hedging and ditching, to clearing and drawing.[172]

254

204 LCC, Alton West Estate, Roehampton (1954–8). Corbusian housing.

In other words, first things first. Drains before beauty.

In the years after 1946, the priorities were clear: public sector housing; offices for nationalised industries and welfare services; schools, hospitals, universities. And council flats: the LCC's Roehampton Estate (1952–5; 1954–8)[204]; Lasdun's cluster blocks in Bethnal Green (1952). It was Lethaby, of course, who had first propounded the doctrine of architecture as public service.

> In the reconstruction period before us [he wrote in 1918: it could easily have been 1946] we have to recognise that architects constitute the faculty for order in city life. As doctors have charge of health, and ... teachers ... of education ... so we are the ministers of the national service of Architecture. It is a public art – the Housing service. Nothing is much nearer to human need than this, and a shelter-builder is something altogether nobler than a style-monger ... architecture is service and not snobbery .... The architect ... must not think of originality, nor of style, nor of design, he must think of service.... The architectural interest of the present time is bound up with the bettering of civilisation, its great mission is to make cities fit for healthy and happy people.... Architecture is a mode of civic virtue ... For far too long we have [been] ... servants of the rich .... We must find another centre in the service of cities and the State. What we want is a new political economy of architecture .... a Ministry of Reconstruction .... Architects, first of all, and over all, are town builders, not epicures of shapes.[173]

205 Festival of Britain, South Bank, London (1951). Picturesque Modern.

In short: a shift of emphasis, from aesthetics to social policy. Hampstead had taken over from Chelsea. 'What has set architecture on a new path', wrote Maxwell Fry in 1945, 'is no less than a return to this country, via the Continent, of the original moral impetus William Morris gave it at the dawn of the century; the accent upon morality being ... the quality which, above all others, distinguishes modern architecture, and at this moment joins it with so much else that is good in the world; with poetry, painting, social science, and whatever we have of a true religion.'[174]

During World War II, plans for reconstructing England's shattered cities became one of the chief ingredients in the maintenance of national morale.[175] That morale was buoyed up by a sense of community, of common purpose, of coordinated priorities, of social – and socialist – planning. All these factors coalesced in the vision of a New Britain, a New Architecture, a New Morality.[176] When Clement Attlee addressed the students of the AA in 1949, he urged them to seek in their buildings the 'soul' of 'modern' England.[177] Duncan Sandys, Minister of Works in 1945, put it this way: 'we desire as much as anyone to maintain diversity of design and scope for ... individual talents. But first things must come first. The houses must go up, and nothing must stand in their way.'[178] Planning was now more important than design.

The 1951 Festival of Britain[205] turned out to be an interruption: a brief interlude in this serious business of social reconstruction. 'Here in London', wrote Lionel Brett, we see 'the long-awaited opening of the flower of modern architecture.' Here is 'engineering touched with magic'. These buildings 'foreshadow the public architecture of the fifties'.[179] It did not turn out quite that way. Coventry Cathedral (Basil Spence, 1951–62) became the apotheosis of the Festival Style. But the long-term legacy of 1951 turned out to be not stylistic but ideological: the 'classless style' of the New Towns.[180] 'Architecture', Le Corbusier once announced, 'is the spirit of truth.'[181] It was now, it seemed, to be the spirit of economy – and the spirit of the Welfare State. The Festival, confessed Misha Black years later, 'released a flood of the worst kind of bastardised modern architecture.'[182] That is, architecture which was firstly cheap, and only secondly Modern. The language of Sullivan, Otto Wagner, Wright and Behrens was to be blunted – in Goodhart-Rendel's words – into forms as crude and unsubtle as Basic English.[183] In America, Kahn and Johnson were already moving into post-Miesian virtuosity. In England, crude functionalism became the credo of the public sector architect. The proletarianisation of architecture was about to be tested, and tested on a large scale.

Since the Middle Ages, there have been three great phases of building in England: the classicism of the Enlightenment; the eclecticism of the Industrial Revolution; and the Modernism of the Welfare State.[184] The Hertfordshire Schools, the New Towns, the LCC Housing Programme – Corbusier in Roehampton (1952–5; 1954–8)[185] – public works had now replaced private dwellings as the flagships of the Modern Movement. The captain of the flagship – *in absentia* – was undoubtedly Le Corbusier. The crew were those rebellious AA students who had forced Goodhart-Rendel into resignation in 1938.[186] But the first and second mates were Alison and Peter Smithson.

The New Brutalism[187] emerged in the early 1950s as the Modernism of the Young Turks in the LCC architect's department: a reaction to

206 Joseph Emberton, Yacht Club, Burnham-on-Crouch, Essex (1931). Heroic Modern: Warehouse Aesthetic I.

the Scandinavian revisionism of their superiors; an escape from the Picturesque Modern of 1951. Brutalism – the Warehouse Aesthetic – set out to continue the pure dogma of Modernism: from Joseph Emberton's Yacht Club at Burnham (1931)[188][206] to the Old Vic workshop (by Lyons, Israel and Ellis, 1958) on the South Bank. 'The Heroic Period of Modern Architecture', the Smithsons believed, 'is the rock on which we stand.'[189] In Reyner Banham's words, they were 'not offering a style but a set of moral responsibilities': a three-dimensional morality as a-formal as *musique concrète*.[190] And there was something else in the air as well. The publication of Le Corbusier's *Modulor* coincided with that of Wittkower's *Architectural Principles of the Age of Humanism* (1949). All of a sudden, architects were hell-bent on the pursuit of modular relations and mystic harmonies.[191] Mies van der Rohe was even credited with a reverence for the Golden Section.

The Smithsons claimed that their Hunstanton School (1949–54)[207] owed as much to Mies as to Le Corbusier, and as much to Japan as to Mies. They summed it up as 'poetry without rhetoric'. 'The invention', they explained in 1973, 'of the formal means whereby, without display or rhetoric, we sense ... the ... presence of the mechanisms supporting and servicing our buildings, is the very heart of present day architecture.'[192] Well, maybe. But there is a problem of sensibility here. For the Smithsons, the brutality of New Brutalism consisted in its directness, not in its inhumanity. In their own GLC Housing Estate at Robin Hood Gardens, Poplar (1972) they claimed to see – with Corbusian vision – not faceless bureaucracy but 'the new softly smiling face of our discipline'.[193] The machine aesthetic humanised. Alas, the tenants disagreed.

258

207 Alison and Peter Smithson, Hunstanton School, Norfolk (1949 54). New Brutalism; Warehouse Aesthetic II.

208 LCC, Hayward Gallery, South Bank, London (1965–8). 'Who would guess that these gloomy bunkers were built to celebrate the pleasures of the senses?'

And nobody asked the children of Hunstanton. In fact the Smithsons had been rumbled even as Hunstanton approached completion. Because 'this building', noted the *Architect's Journal*, 'seems often to ignore the children for whom it is built, it is hard to define it as *architecture* at all. It is a formalist structure which will please only architects, and a small coterie concerned more with satisfying their personal design sense than with achieving a humanist, functional, architecture.'[194] Within a few years, Hunstanton School was notorious: 'functionally inadequate, technically naïve, noisy, cold and dirty.'[195] Only its reputation as a milestone – or millstone – of Modernism has preserved it from demolition.[196]

'Brutalism', announced the Smithsons, 'tries to face up to a mass-production society.'[197] Well, the South Bank – once the home of Picturesque Modernism in 1951 – became the *reductio ad absurdum* of Brutalist theory: the functionalist fallacy writ large. 'Who would guess', notes Lionel Esher sadly, 'that those gloomy bunkers were built to celebrate the pleasures of the senses? ... [The] LCC designers [of the Hayward Gallery complex] (1965–8)[208] have remained sensibly anonymous.'[198] Back in 1930, Howard Robertson – looking at 'High and Over' – had recognised that the traditional game was up. 'The blow is falling', he wrote, 'prepare to meet the shock!'[199] New Brutalism was the delayed impact of that collision.

It all stemmed from a tragic mistake: a misunderstanding of the nature of Modernism. As a young man Peter Smithson had certainly been aware

259

of the errors of vulgar functionalism. 'In the 1930s', he wrote in 1956, 'through some phenomenon that is too complicated to understand properly, something called functionalism superseded all the separate and distinct flavours of the heroic period [of modern architecture]. By functionalism was meant the abolition of ornament and the abandoning of pitched roofs and the Orders. The stylistic void thus created was somehow to be filled by function and sociology. In this way a rejection of style (and with it ... the [very] concept of architecture) ... came to represent Modern Architecture to a generation who never really knew what the original excitement was all about.'[200] By 1967 he was aware that the Modern Movement had created 'inhuman conditions of a more subtle order than the slums'.[201] But just as the Gothic Revivalists had talked function and built history, so the New Brutalists talked humanity and built barbarism. Would that Gropius's partial recantation had been listened to. 'Rationalisation', admitted the arch-modernist in 1951, 'which many people imagine to be the cardinal principle of present design, is really only its purifying agency. The satisfaction of the human psyche is just as important as the fulfilment of material requirements.'[202]

1946–56 had been a honeymoon decade for Modern Architecture in England. Then followed two decades – 1956–76 – of 'boom' on borrowed money: Modernism minus its morality. There was too much building and too little architecture. Too much process and not enough style. Between them, property developers and official architects – Col R. Seifert at one extreme, Sir Denys Lasdun at the other – seemed to be creating an architectural wilderness: an admass society housed in mass concrete. Seifert's skills were those of an architectural pragmatist.[203] Lasdun did have an aesthetic credo: architecture as a 'metaphor for landscape'. And his Royal College of Physicians, Regent's Park (1960–64)[209] is a virtuoso

209 Sir Denys Lasdun, Royal College of
Physicians, Regent's Park, London (1960–64).
Volumetric abstraction.

210 J. L. Womersley, Park Hill – Hyde Park,
Sheffield (1958 onwards). The Martian Utopia.

performance in volumetric abstraction. But the public at large never
shared his preference for an urban landscape of shuttered concrete.[204] The
gulf between architect and public seemed to be becoming unbridgeable.[205]

Sheffield is a notorious example. The fortress-like Park Hill and Hyde
Park developments[210], built under the direction of the city architect,
J. L. Womerslcy, from 1958 onwards: street decks, pedestrian promen-
ades, piazzas, bridges – all skied high above the old city in a giant,

261

Brutalist crescendo. At the time Reyner Banham thought it represented 'a moral crusade'. Its ideal, he explained, is 'the English conception of social justice, as expressed through the English system of local government .... The conscience of the world's architecture has been permanently enriched by the Brutalist ethic.'[206] Indeed he goes on to say that 'Brutalism ... was ... the first consequential British contribution to the living body of architecture since the collapse of the "English Free Building" of Voysey and Lethaby around 1910.'[207] In fact it was not all English. Park Hill, admitted Maxwell Fry, was conceived not so much by its own architects (J. L. Womersley, J. Lyon and I. Smith), as 'by Gropius and Le Corbusier, and the Mars Group, and by Ruskin and Morris, and by Blake' – by everyone, in fact, who ever dreamt of building a New Jerusalem in England: 'this, my friends, is civilisation agitating the entropic mass to achieve identity ... a new conception of life in the heart of industrial England ... measured in terms of human value ... but drawn out of the sinews of industry.'[208]

That was 1959. Fifteen years later it was beginning to look decidedly shabby. Park Hill, noted Pevsner, 'has been hailed universally in the technical press as ... visually as well as socially satisfactory ... No English city except London can show so impressive an architectural record.' That is, he adds, as regards 'planning ... elevationally there is less to single out'. Even socially he had reservations: 'there can be no doubt that such a scheme of closely-set high blocks of flats will be a slum in half a century or less .... It may, however' – he adds optimistically – 'be a cosy slum.'[209] So much for the Martian Utopia.

More than anything, it was the traffic engineering of the 1960s – Spaghetti Junction, Birmingham, most famously – which turned a whole generation into conservationists. By the end of the 1970s, there were about three hundred thousand active members of conservation societies in England, not to mention one million members of the National Trust. The past seemed suddenly rather more attractive than the future. Liverpool was devastated. Birmingham became a wilderness of motorways. T. Dan Smith and John Poulson set out to make Newcastle 'the Brazilia of the North'. It turned out to be more like the Stalingrad of the South. Long before the collapse of Ronan Point – a system-built tower block in Canning Town, Newham – on 16 May 1968, the worm had turned. Blocks of high-rise council flats were not only inefficient, they were hugely unpopular. The 'Piggeries' at Everton, Easterhouse in Glasgow, East Stratford in London ... system-building had merely produced systematic slums.[210] Faceless monsters like Possilpark Flats, Glasgow, trapped council tenants in a nightmare world of anonymity, alienation, vandalism and decay. Architects responded with still more visionary schemes: Archigram promised yet more of the same, and bigger.[211] Soon rumours of leaking and instability were greeted with grim satisfaction.[212] News of demolition aroused a mixture of outrage and jubilation.[213] Then, after 1973, the economy entered a downward spiral that was to outlast the decade. The Modern Movement in England – already a long time in dying – was now well and truly buried.

Modernism had been based on a return to classical, that is objective, criteria: it posed as the architecture of reason and function. Such criteria, however, were uneasily harnessed to a set of romantic attitudes centred on a utopian belief in perfectibility through planning: a bureaucratic paternalism which predictably clashed with the individualistic instincts of the man in the street. Those instincts eventually found expression in Post-Modernism: identity in an age of anonymity; plurality after years of prescriptive authority; populism after decades of paternalism; an architecture of symbol and metaphor, of colour and form, after two generations of functional mythology. The pendulum of taste had swung back to romantic subjectivity. In England it was given a considerable push by an odd alliance of the new right and the old left. The new right condemned the modern architecture of welfare; the old left condemned the modern architecture of capitalism. Cambridge aesthetics and Marxist economics combined to destroy what was left of the Modernist ethic.

Back in 1951, the Festival of Britain's 'Live Architecture' show in London's East End had contained one joke exhibit – 'Gremlin Grange' – a caricature of a suburban semi, in by-pass Tudor style.[214] Less than a generation later, 'Gremlin Grange' had made a come-back: in fact it had never really lost its popularity in the suburbs. And its return to favour highlighted a return to all the old stylistic dilemmas which had plagued the nineteenth century. In the late eighteenth century it had been the collapse of Palladianism which created the dilemma of style. In the late twentieth century it is the collapse of Modernism which has resuscitated that dilemma.

In England the Modern Movement came late and left early. England has no building by Le Corbusier. No building by Aalto or Frank Lloyd Wright. No building by Mies van der Rohe: the Mansion House Square inquiry of 1984 – Peter Palumbo's plan to build a Miesian tower-block at the very 'hub of Empire' – marked the final defeat of Modernism by the conservationists.[215] Ironically, almost the only prominent building associated with the name of Gropius is the old Playboy Club in Park Lane. In the field of private housing, Modernism in England has never had more than a tenuous foothold. In the corporate sector, even the pressure

263

211 David Roberts, Sacher Building, Longwall St, Oxford (1961–2). Blinded by non-visual dogma.

of international finance was slow to impose an international style. Not until the 1950s did Modernism take control by capturing both the media-intelligentsia and the staff of central and local government agencies. The early 1960s marked the highwater mark of Modernism in England. By the end of the 1970s, Post-Modernism had been born.

When Robert Venturi's *Complexity and Contradiction* first appeared in 1966 – it had been written in 1962 – it seemed a daring counterblast to the Puritan fundamentalism of Modernist theology. In a memorable phrase – 'Less is a bore' – Venturi reversed Mies's negative dictum ('less is more'), and set in motion what turned out to be a tidal wave of post-functional theory: structurally ambiguous, visually multivalent; calling in Lutyens and Borromini to redress the dominance of Mies and the minimalists. As with Corbusier, so with Venturi, England was slow to react: the first English edition of *Complexity and Contradiction* did not appear until 1977. By then Post-Modernism had already made considerable headway in undermining Modernist morale. Then came the symbolists and semiologists.[216]

'I will give you the soul of technocracy': that had been the promise built into the Seagram Building in New York (1956–8).[217] The post-Miesian generation wanted more: they turned again to ornament, to symbol, to emotion, harnessing the resources of technology to an anti-technological conclusion. Such a reversal of taste was fairly predictable. In fact César Daly had predicted it long before: first an alliance of architecture and reason, in the late nineteenth and early twentieth century; then an 'alliance of architecture and sentiment' in the later twentieth century.[218] In other words, first Modernism, then Post-Modernism.

The Modern Movement in England failed, not because it lost its nerve,[219] but because it lost its eyesight. Only an architect blinded by non-visual dogma could commit an atrocity like the Sacher Building in Longwall St, Oxford (David Roberts: 1961-2)[211]. A building, after all, has to be seen as well as used. But what sealed the fate of Modernism as a fashion was not the sneers of the aesthetes, but the discontent of the common man. The inhabitants of all those tower blocks, the clerks in their offices, the housewives in their supermarkets – they were the ones who finally rebelled. The slump of the later 1970s blew the whistle just in time. A break in redevelopment at last gave planners time to think. What emerged at the start of the 1980s was a new contextualist consensus based on the aesthetics of conservation: old places, old buildings, old styles, old values. Just as the Victorians fled to the past to escape from the ugliness of industry, so the Post-Modern generation called in the fading beauty of the old world to redress the squalor of the new.

Post-Modernism is a generic term, legitimised by Arnold Toynbee in 1956.[220] Architecturally, it has come to mean 'post Modern Movement'. It has little to do with traditional Neo-Georgian, as practised by Francis Johnson, Raymond Erith or Quinlan Terry.[221] It is far wider in scope than mere Post-Modern Classicism.[222] And – despite persuasive claims for Classicism's integrating, mythopaeic power[223] – it is far more serviceable too. Its basis is a cultural shift, a shift in our way of conceiving architecture: back again from architecture as utility to architecture as communication; from architecture as service to architecture as art. Just as the Picturesque broke up architectural composition into a sequence of images, so Post-Modernism has deconstructed tectonic form into a multiplicity of signals. In other words, it is not so much Post-Modern as Post-Functional. During the late 1970s this Post-Functional style, in protean guise, became something of a new orthodoxy in England.[224] By 1986 Venturi himself had emerged as architect of the National Gallery extension in Trafalgar Square. There had been a few signposts in the sixties: Sir Basil Spence's arcaded courts at Sussex University (1960 onwards);[225] Darbourne and Darke's brick-tiered housing estate in Lillington Gardens, London (1961-70).[226] But it was in the mid-seventies that Post-Modernism took off. Post-Modern vernacular, like the Hill-

212 Andrew Derbyshire, Hillingdon Civic Centre (1976). Post-Modern vernacular.

ingdon Civic Centre (1976; Andrew Derbyshire of Robert Matthew, Johnson-Marshall and Partners)[212]: red bricks, broken bays, hipped tile roofs – Victorian Modern Gothic gone Post Modern.[227] Post-Modern Classicism, like Boyd Auger's offices at Clifford's Inn, Holborn (1982).[228] Post-Modern pragmatism: romantic-like Ted Cullinan's church at Barnes (1978–82);[229] or opportunist, like Col. Seifert's Fire Station in Shaftesbury Avenue, London (1984–5).[230] Post-Modern eclecticism, like the Ealing Civic Centre (1983; Building Design Partnership)[213]: red bricks, slate roofs, corbelled balconies, echoes of Norman Shaw, Pierrefonds and Carcassonne.[231] All part of the search – still experimental, still confused – for 'a new architecture of humanism'.[232]

'Post-Modernism,' explains Philip Johnson, 'is ... a legitimisation of some feelings that reach beyond the puritanism of modern architecture. It suggests that the ideology of the Modern Movement is dead; that we want to get away from the modernism of modern architecture. What Post-Modernism is really doing is legitimising eclecticism ... I am ... a functionalist; but ... also an eclectic.'[233] For Mies, 'Beauty was truth and truth beauty – a thing I have always hated John Keats for, and always will, because as Nietzsche very properly replied: "Art is with us that we not perish from truth." ... Art is artifice, the opposite of truth: it's invention, it's lying, it's cheating the eye, it's subverting the psyche. That's what art is ... Relativism [is] the only absolute.'[234]

266

What distinguishes Post Modern from Modern is not its occasional use of historical references, but the way in which design is employed as an instrument of pleasure and as a means of communication. In that sense, Post-Modernism is as old as the Rolls-Royce radiator. Modernism – at least in its more dogmatic moods – had attempted to equate utility and beauty. Post-Modernism adds the persuasion of semiology to the impact of functional form. In that respect, the whole Post-Modern phenomenon involves a reversion to pre-modern visual values. It begins with the inevitability of subjective design; it ends with the enjoyment of atectonic forms. Traditional aesthetics in untraditional guise: style, yes; the styles, no – or at least not necessarily.

The Modernists had attempted to establish a functionalist vernacular, a standard language of form based on the universal intelligibility of industrial technology. Alas, it was what theorists call auto-referential: architects like Buckminster Fuller ended up talking to themselves. The public knew all along that there was more to architecture than functional form.[235] When the functionalist consensus collapsed – in the '60s, in America; in the '70s in England – it was replaced by just the sort of pluralistic diversity which had succeeded the collapse of the Gothic Revival a hundred years previously, and the disintegration of Palladianism one hundred years before that.[236]

In fact the dilemma is much the same today as it was for the mid-Victorians; how to make use of an earlier language – with its disciplinary form and associative force – without succumbing to the dread disease of

213 Building Design Partnership, Ealing Civic Centre (1983). Post-Modern eclecticism.

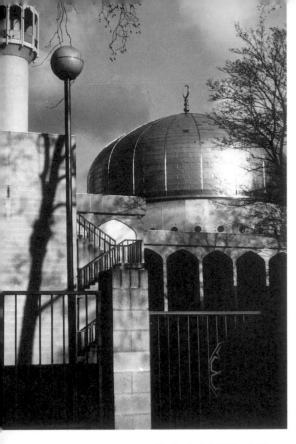 

214 Sir Frederick Gibberd, The
Mosque, Regent's Park, London
(1973). Post-Modern pastiche.

215 Norman Foster, Hong Kong and Shanghai
Bank (1980–6). Techno-Romanticism.

historicism.[237] Current wisdom suggests that the answer lies in 'symbolic depth' rather than pastiche: Stirling's Staatsgalerie, Stuttgart (1977–84)[217] rather than Gibberd's Regent's Park Mosque (1973)[214]. Of course, such distinctions merely re-phrase the Puginian dilemma – principle or prototype? In that respect Modernist critics[238] have had to concede a good deal of the Post-Modern[239] argument. They concede the necessity of subjectivity, of some form of eclecticism: an architecture of the future in a fusion of past and present. That is the common ground between Late-Modernists and Post-Modernists; neo-classicists and neo-vernacularists; community architects, critical regionalists[240] and romantic or opportunist pragmatists. We are all Post-Functionalists now.

Of course English Modernism is not entirely dead: it lives on, in all its tectonic purity, in the work of Norman Foster (Sainsbury Centre, University of East Anglia, 1978).[241] But even Foster – the prophet of High Tech; the last apostle of formal perfection – has been infected by techno-romanticism, as in the Hong Kong and Shanghai Bank (1980–86)[215];[242]

he has even begun to make concessions to context: as in his Mediathèque, Nîmes (1984–7).[243] And even High Tech – as in the Pompidou Centre, Paris (Piano and Rogers 1971–7)[244], the INMOS Factory, Newport, Mon (Rogers 1982)[245] and Lloyds of London (Rogers 1978–86)[216][246] – even High Tech has abandoned the mythology of objective form for the subjective rhetoric of tectonic discourse. Whether the High Tech is overtly functional (as in Arup's Bush Lane House, London, 1976) or overtly Post-Functional (as in Farrell's 'Dec Tech' TV-AM, London, 1980–3),[247] the myth of objectivity has finally been abandoned. The functionalist bogey seems to have been exorcised at last.

James Stirling's progress is instructive: a steady retreat from the late-Brutalism of his Leicester University Engineering Building (Stirling and Gowan 1959–63)[248] and Florey Building, Queen's College, Oxford (1971).[249] Increasingly, the fiction of function has been forgotten. Tectonic elements assume a rhetorical role. Modernism has become, like every other style, both symbolic and expressive. Of course, there have been hiccups along the way: his Cambridge History Faculty Library (1964–8) – like the Florey Building – turned out to be a veritable 'masterpiece of leaks'.[250] But in the 1980s Stirling seemed to hit a winning streak.

The Staatsgalerie at Stuttgart (1977–84)[217][251] combines Neo-Classical formality with Corbusian free-planning; neo-vernacular polychromy and fenestration with structural metaphors and Post-Functional symbols. There are echoes here of Schinkel's Altes Museum and Klenze's Walhalla,

216 Richard Rogers, Lloyds of London (1978–86). High Tech rhetoric.

217 J. Stirling and M. Wilford, Staatsgalerie, Stuttgart (1977–84). Post-Functional symbols.

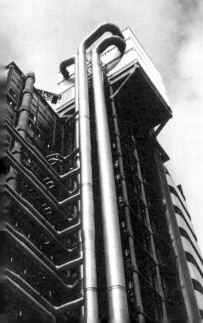

decked out with High Tech trickery. The jokey rustication is a sly caricature of Giulio Romano. The stumpy Doric columns parody Playfair's Neo-Classicism at Cairness, Aberdeenshire (1789; 1791–7).[252] Stirling himself calls this sort of thing 'monumental formalism'.[253] Summerson calls it 'social functionalism', to distinguish it from High Tech.[254] Modernists *and* Post-Modernists name him as their man; but the Post-Modernists have the better claim. Unlike Sir Denys Lasdun – an unreconstructed Modernist – Stirling is a Modernist who has come to terms with the world-wide Post-Modernist mood. And he manages to outflank the pundits by putting his quotations in quotation marks. The rationalism of function has become the rhetoric of Post-Functionalism. At Stuttgart – and in London's Tate Gallery extension (1982–7) – Stirling builds not quite as Lutyens built, but as Lutyens might have built had he lived now.[255]

Well, where do we stand today? In effect, we have turned the corner. With architects as different as Jeremy Dixon and Terry Farrell, we can look forward with a degree of optimism. Pluralist societies – be they Imperial Rome, the Venetian Republic, or Victorian England – naturally develop a plurality of culture, and thus eventually, eclecticism of style. Hence the architectural eclecticism of our late twentieth-century western world: nineteenth-century mimetics plus twentieth-century semiotics; pluralism multiplied by mass-communication.

Since the mid-eighteenth century, we have seen the pendulum swing back and forth: from Palladian authority to Picturesque freedom; from Pugin's universal Gothic to late Victorian Progressive Eclecticism; and, finally, from the Modern Movement's dogmatic functionalism, to Post-Modernism's liberal eclecticism. Only a radical – indeed cataclysmic – social change will shift that pendulum back again. Such an event would be – in the literal sense – totalitarian: the product of a monolithic culture. Post-Modernism will continue to have its critics[256] – after all, it reflects our current cultural incoherence. But eclecticism in some form or other is surely here to stay. The hybridity of Post-Modernism is merely an index of the heterogeneity of modern communities. Total styles are the product of simple societies or totalitarian regimes. Eclecticism – not necessarily historical in form – is the vernacular of sophisticates, the language of freedom.[257] In a sense we are all Post-Modernists now, because we are all Post-Functionalists. Even Punk Vernacular – New Wave Romanticism – puts fun back into function.[258] The quest for objectivity in design has been very largely abandoned. We have had to re-learn what the nineteenth century painfully discovered: architecture begins where function ends.[259]

In a famous essay, *The Architecture of Humanism* (1914), Geoffrey Scott set out to destroy for all time four fallacious bases of architectural judgement: the Mechanical Fallacy (tectonic criteria), the Ethical Fallacy (moral criteria), the Romantic Fallacy (associational criteria) and the Biological Fallacy (evolutionary criteria). In their place he set up aesthetic criteria, based on Crocean notions of 'Humanist values' in art. In so doing, he created a fifth fallacy: the Aesthetic Fallacy – namely the view that aesthetic appeal alone must be the criterion of architectural excellence. That view has in turn been attacked by the Modernists who attempted to introduce yet another yardstick – social purpose – as the principal yardstick of architectural goodness. Their fallacy was the Purposive Fallacy. But good architecture cannot be restricted to any single set of criteria. Associational factors, tectonic factors, purposive factors, moral factors, evolutionary factors, *and* aesthetic factors, all have their part to play. Great architecture synthesises them all. It is commodity, and firmness, as well as delight. And great architects achieve equipoise between all three.[260]

A building designed with style derives that style from two sources. In the first instance it bears the circumstantial marks of time and place: material, conceptual, utilitarian. In the second it betrays the personal imprint of its designer. An historical style is thus the accumulation of innumerable acts of design, expressed in the language of available circumstance, then codified as a system of aesthetics. But that code is culturally determined: when cultures fragment, codes are necessarily fractured. Hence today, the inevitability of plurality; hence too the associated dilemmas of eclecticism.

Out of these dilemmas will emerge the Post-Functionalism of the twenty-first century. Whatever its form, it is likely to combine elements of rationality (in structure); elements of functionality (in purpose); elements of symbol and metaphor (through semiotic ornament – intrinsic or extrinsic); elements of memory (through association); elements of contextuality (through environmental planning). In other words, its intelligibility will operate on several complementary levels. And from this confluence of factors will emerge – given the will, and given the resources – Architecture. We can end with an optimistic cliché: the Modern Movement is dead; long live modern architecture!

Notes and References

Principal Abbreviations

A.: *The Architect* (1868–1926); thereafter united with *Building News.*

A.A.: *Annales Archéologiques* (1844–70).

A.A. Papers/Notes/Sketchbook/Jnl./Qtly./Files.: *Architectural Association Papers/Notes/Sketchbook/Journal/Quarterly/Files.*

A.D.: *Architectural Design* (1930–).

A.J.: *Architect's Journal* (1919–).

A.R.: *Architectural Review* (1896–).

Archaeol. Jnl.: *Archaeological Journal* (1844–).

B.: *The Builder* (1843–1966); thereafter known as *Building.*

B.N.: *Building News* (1855–1926); thereafter united with *The Architect.*

Boase: F. Boase, *Modern English Biography* (1892–1921).

Burl. Mag.: *Burlington Magazine* (1903–).

C.E.A.J.: *Civil Engineer and Architect's Journal* (1837–67).

C.L.: *Country Life* (1897–).

D.N.B.: *Dictionary of National Biography* (1885–).

E.: *The Ecclesiologist* (Cambridge Camden Society, 1842–68).

G.L.C.: Greater London Council.

G.M.: *Gentleman's Magazine* (1731–1868).

I.L.N.: *Illustrated London News* (1843–).

L.C.C.: London County Council.

N.M.R.: National Monuments Record.

Qtly. Rev.: *Quarterly Review* (1809–1967).

R.I.B.A. Trans./Papers/J.: *Royal Institute of British Architects Transactions/Papers/Journal* (1842–).

R.S.A. Jnl.: *Royal Society of Arts Journal* (1852–).

Ruskin, *Works*: *The Works of John Ruskin*, ed. E. T. Cook and A. Wedderburn, 39 vols. (1903–12).

S.A.H.: Society of Architectural Historians.

Sat. Rev.: *Saturday Review* (1855–1938).

S.P.A.B.: Society for the Protection of Ancient Buildings.

Preface

1 *The Listener* LXV (1961), 300.

1 The Consequences of the Picturesque

1 See, for example, E. H. Gombrich, 'Style', in *Encyclopaedia of the Social Sciences* xv (New York, 1968), 352–61.

2 G. G. Scott, *A Plea for the Faithful Restoration of our Ancient Churches* (1850), 76; and *B.* viii (1850), 170, 197; W. Morris, 'Restoration', *Athenaeum* (1877), 807: the Manifesto of the SPAB.

3 R. Wittkower, 'Individualism in Art and Artists: a Renaissance Problem', *Jnl. Hist. Ideas* xxii (1961), 291–302; 'Imitation, Eclecticism and Genius', *Aspects of the 18th Century*, ed. E. R. Wasserman (Baltimore, 1965), 143 *et seq.*; 'Genius: Individualism in Art and Artists', in *Dictionary of the History of Ideas* ii (New York, 1973), 287–312.

4 See C. Jencks, *The Language of Post-Modern Architecture* (1977 edn).

5 Compare Flitcroft's lakeside Pantheon (1756) at Stourhead with Claude's *Coast View of Delos with Aeneas* or his *View of Delphi with a Procession.* Henry Hoare II noted: for the Pantheon, 'the view of the Bridge, Village and Church altogether will be a charming Gaspard view at the end of that Water' (K. Woodbridge, *Landscape and Antiquity. Aspects of English Culture at Stourhead, 1718–1838*, Oxford, 1971). There are other echoes too, of course – e.g. Gothic symbols of English liberty (M. Kelsall, 'The Iconography of Stourhead', *Jnl. Warburg and Courtauld Institutes* xlvi, 1983, 133–43).

6 Vitruvius, *De Architectura*, bks. iii–iv. For attempts to invent a new Order, see *Dictionary of Architecture*, ed. W. Papworth, (A.P.S., 1852–92), s.v. 'Order of Architecture'.

7 J.-F. Blondel, *Cours d'architecture* iv (Paris, 1773), liv–v. R. Middleton, 'J.-F. Blondel and the "Cours d'architecture"', *Jnl. S.A.H.* xviii (1959), 140–48, suggests the influence of Boffrand's *Livre d'Architecture* (Paris, 1743).

8 C.-N. Ledoux, *L'Architecture considerée sous le rapport de l'art, des moeurs et de la legislature* (Paris, 1804). See G. Hersey, 'Association and Sensibility in 18th century Architecture', *Eighteenth-Century Studies* iv (1970–71), 71–89. In 1852, Leon Vaudoyer christened this *l'architecture parlante* (*Le Magasin Pittoresque* xx, 1852, 388). More recently the term 'expressionist architecture' has been used.

9 Colen Campbell refers to the Palatial, Temple and Theatrical styles, as well as the styles of Vitruvius and

Inigo Jones (*Vitruvius Britannicus*, li, 1717).

10 C. Hussey, 'Shugborough, Staffs.', *C.L.* cxv (1954), 510–13, 590–93, 676–9.

11 For ancient gardens see R. Bradley, *Survey of Ancient Husbandry and Gardening … collected from Cato, Varro, Columella, Virgil … and other Greeks and Romans* (1725) and R. Castell, *Villas of the Ancients* (1728): the plan of Pliny's garden at Laurentium is not unlike Chiswick. For Renaissance gardens, see E. MacDougall, '*Ars Hortularum*: 16th century Garden Iconography and Literary Theory in Italy', in D. Coffin, ed., *The Italian Garden* (Dumbarton Oaks, 1972): the exedra at Chiswick is compared to the gardens of Duke Mattei on Monte Celio in Rome. Rousham has been compared to the gardens of the Villa Barberigo at Valzansibio, near Padua (S. Lang, 'The Genesis of the Landscape Garden', in N. Pevsner, ed., *The Picturesque Garden*, Dumbarton Oaks, 1974, 27); Claremont to the Vatican Belvedere; and Chiswick – 'a memory theatre of architectural and garden history' – to the Teatro Olimpico at Vicenza (J. Dixon Hunt, *Garden and Grove: the Italian Renaissance Garden in the English Imagination, 1600–1750*, 1986, 189, 199).

12 A. Gerard, *An Essay on Taste* (1759), 33. 'Beauty is, at least in part, resolvable into association' (*ibid.*, 1754 edn, 43). 'Differences of taste are unavoidable … The constitution of human nature renders this … inevitable' (*ibid.*, pt. IV, i, 200, 202). See M. Grene, 'Gerard's *Essay on Taste*', *Modern Philology* xli (1943), 45–58; J. Archer, 'Character in English Architectural Design', *Eighteenth-Century Studies* xii (1979), 339–71 and 'The Beginnings of Association in British Architectural Esthetics', *ibid.*, xvi (1983), 241–64.

13 T. Whateley, *Observations on Modern Gardening* (1777).

14 *Observations* (1793 edn), 154–5. For an explanation of this argument, see J. Dixon Hunt, 'Emblem and Expression in the 18th century landscape garden', *Eighteenth-Century Studies* iv (1970–71), 294–317. 'Allusion was now replaced by effusion and mythography by empathy' (R. Williams, 'Making Places', *Jnl. of Garden History* iii, 1983, 384). See J. Dixon Hunt, *Garden and Grove, op. cit.*, 222, 259.

15 'Utility must often take the lead of beauty, and convenience be preferred to picturesque effect' (H. Repton, *Inquiry into the changes of Taste in Landscape Gardening*, 1806, 41). 'Real comfort, and … ideas of picturesqueness, are incompatible' (H. Repton, *Observations on the Theory and Practice of Landscape Gardening*, 1803, 111). See J. Dixon Hunt, 'Sense and Sensibility in the Landscape Designs of Humphry Repton', *Studies in Burke and His Time* xix (1978), 3–28.

16 See E. Tuveson, *The Imagination as the Means of Grace: Locke and the Aesthetics of Romanticism* (Berkeley and Los Angeles, 1960); M. Kallick, *The Association of Ideas and Critical Theory in 18th Century England* (The Hague, 1970); P. Kivy, *The Seventh Sense: A Study of Francis Hutcheson's Aesthetics and its Influence on 18th Century Britain* (New York, 1976).

17 'The Pleasures of the Imagination'. *Spectator* (1712).

18 F. Hutcheson, *Inquiry Concerning Beauty, Order, Harmony and Design* (1726); ed. P. Kivy, 1973, IV, i, 40. Shaftesbury took the opposite view: he argued for innate beauty instinctively recognised (*Characteristicks*, 1737, III, 2, ii, 411, 414).

19 D. Hume, 'Of the Standard of Taste' (1757), in *Essays Moral, Political and Literary* (1876 edn), 136.

20 E. Burke, *A Philosophical Inquiry into the Origin of our Ideas of the Sublime and the Beautiful* (ed. J. T. Boulton, 1958), 58–9, 72, 101, 130, 143.

21 C. Perrault, *A Treatise of the Five Orders in Architecture*, Trans. J. Jones (1708).

22 A. Alison, *Essays on the Nature and Principles of Taste* (1871 ed.), 229.

23 Alison, *Essays* (Edinburgh, 1790), 2.

24 *ibid.*, 127–8, 133; (1825 ed.), 179, 187–8.

25 See R. Scruton, *The Aesthetics of Architecture* (1979).

26 See M. H. Abrams, *The Mirror and the Lamp: Romantic Theory and the British Tradition* (Oxford, 1953), 162–3, 167–70, 177–81, 366 n. 86.

27 D. Hume, *Treatise of Human Nature*, 10, 12–13.

28 J. Heely, *Letters on the Beauties of Hagley, Envil and the Leasowes* i (1777), 172 *et seq.*

29 R. Wittkower, *Architectural Principles in the Age of Humanism* (1949; 4th edn, 1973), 150–54. For the notion of 'anachronical accumulation' – turning paradigm into syntagm – see P. Junod, 'Future in the Past', *Oppositions* xxvi (1984), 148–63.

30 A. Smith, *Moral Sentiments* (1759), 300.

31 Bishop Hurd, *Idea of Universal Poetry* (1765).

32 *Edinburgh Rev.* xviii (1811), 1 46. See also his article on 'Beauty' in *Encyclopaedia Britannica*, supp. 1816. Cf. E. F. Carritt, *Philosophies of Beauty* (1931); M. Kallick, *The Association of Ideas and Critical Theory in 18th Century England* (The Hague, 1970). 'And what is Education', asked James Arbuckle in 1726, 'but stocking a Child's Brain with Chains of Images' (quoted in Kallick, *op. cit.*, 36). It was through the idea of inbred universal associations that Reynolds, Kames and Burke attempted to reconcile subjectivity of taste with absolute standards of beauty (Kallick, *op. cit.*, 141–2, 146, 159, 181, 213). For the influence of such ideas on Kant's thinking, see T. A. Gracyk, 'Kant's Shifting Debt to British Aesthetics', *Brit. Jnl. of Aesthetics* xxvi (1986), 204–17.

33 W. Gilpin, *Three Essays on Picturesque Beauty* (1792), 32–3.

34 See W. H. Bate, *From Classic to Romantic: Premises of Taste in 18th Century England* (New York, 1961); H. Honour, *Romanticism* (1979); J. Mordaunt Crook, *The Greek Revival: Neo-Classical Attitudes in British Architecture, 1760–1870* (1972).

35 Coleridge, *Biographia Literaria*, ed. J. Shawcross, ii (Oxford, 1907), 222.

36 R. Payne Knight, *An Analytical Inquiry into the Principles of Taste* (1805 edn), 102, 301. Knight took up the associationist viewpoint in a celebrated debate with Uvedale Price, who argued for intrinsic picturesqueness; a debate anticipated in the dispute between Reynolds and Gilpin (W. D. Templeman, 'Sir Joshua Reynolds and the Picturesque', *Modern Language Notes* xlvii, 1932, 446–8).

37 J. Mordaunt Crook, 'Grange Park Transformed', in *The Country Seat*, ed. H. M. Colvin and J. Harris (1970), 223.

38 Quoted in H. J. Paris, 'Rev. W. Gilpin and the Cult of the Picturesque' (B. Litt., Oxford, 1938), 31. See also C. P. Barbier, *William Gilpin: his drawings, teaching and theory of the Picturesque* (Oxford, 1963), 140–3.

39 See E. Gombrich, *Art and Illusion* (1960).

40 R. Payne Knight, *The Landscape* (1794), 35–6.

41 J. Reynolds, *Discourses on Art*, ed. R. R. Wark (San Marino, 1959), Discourse xiii (1786), lines 405 *et seq.*, pp. 241–2.

42 T. Whateley, *Observations on Modern Gardening* (1770). See also M. Baridon, 'Ruins as a mental construct', *Jnl. of Garden History* v (1985), 84–96.

43 For Hulne Priory, see J. Mordaunt Crook, 'Northumbrian Gothick', in *R.S.A. Jnl.* cxxi (1973), 271–83; for the Chichele Tower, see M. McCarthy, in N. Pevsner, ed., *The Picturesque Garden and its Influence outside the British Isles* (Dumbarton Oaks, 1974), 51, n. 60.

44 W. Chambers, *A Dissertation on Oriental Gardening* (1772). Chambers was not the first to recommend Chinese prototypes. In 1753 R. Sayer published *The Emperor of China's Palace at Pekin*. See M. Milder, 'The Emperor of China's Palace at Pekin: a new source of English garden design', *Apollo* cxix (1984), 181–4.

45 W. Gilpin, *Remarks on Forest Scenery* (1791); Knight, *Analytical Inquiry* (1808 ed), 160.

46 W. Chambers, *Treatise on Civil Architecture* (1759 ed), ii.

47 *Treatise* (1791 ed), 108. See E. Harris, 'Burke and Chambers on the Sublime and Beautiful', in *Essays in the History of Architecture Presented to Rudolf Wittkower* (1967), 209 *et seq.*

48 See J. Harris, *Sir William Chambers* (1970), *passim*.

49 R. Morris, *Lectures on Architecture* (1734), 67–8.

50 G. Clarke, 'Grecian Taste and Gothic Virtue', *Apollo* xcvii (1973), 566–71; S. Kliger, *The Goths in England* (Camb. Mass., 1952). The Temple of Modern Virtue was designed as a ruin.

51 Kames, *Elements of Criticism* (1762), ii, 446–7. See I. S. Ross, *Lord Kames and the Scotland of his day* (Oxford, 1972), 280–2.

52 *Boswell's Life of Johnson*, ed. L. F. Powell (Oxford, 1934–64), v, 355.

53 J. Dixon Hunt, 'Sense and Sensibility in the Landscape Designs of Humphry Repton', *Studies in Burke and His Time* xix, no. 1 (1978), 3–28.

54 Knight, *The Landscape*, 14.

55 Repton, *Fragments*, ed. J. C. Loudon (1840), 411–14 and *Sketches* (1794), pl. 7.

56 Similarly W. S. Gilpin, *Practical Hints in Landscape Gardening* (1832), 13. Gilpin – nephew of Rev. W. Gilpin – put this theory into practice at Pitfour, Aberdeenshire (1812 and 1820; dem.1926). John Smith's 'Temple of Theseus on the bleak lake of Pitfour was appropriately labelled a "cold bath house" ', (Tait, *Jnl. Garden Hist.* iii, 1983, 312–32).

57 This had already been suggested by Shenston: 'high hills and sudden deserts are most suitable to castles; and fertile vales, near wood and water, ... for abbeys and religious houses' (W. Shenston, *Works in Prose and Verse*, 1773, ii, 111–12). Similarly, J. Hall, *Essay on the Origin, History and Principles of Gothic Architecture* (Edinburgh, 1813), 146.

58 H. Repton, *Sketches and Hints*, ed. J. C. Loudon (1840). Similar ideas can be found in J. B. Papworth, *Ornamental Gardening* (1818).

59 Repton, *Observations on the Theory and Practice of Landscape Gardening* (1803), 153:ill.

60 Luscombe: *C.L.* cxix (1956), 248–51, 292–5; Endsleigh; *C.L.* cxxx (1961), 246–9, 296–9.

61 Repton, *Fragments* (1840), 440. Alexis de Chateauneuf, in *The Country House*, edited by Lady Mary Fox, suggests that the style of a house might be Greek or Gothic according to whether its owner preferred Homer or Shakespeare (B. xi, 1853, 66).

62 Repton, 'Memoir', quoted in G. Carter, P. Goode and K. Laurie, *Humphry Repton* (Sainsbury Centre, Norwich, 1982), 77.

63 *ibid.*, 78, colour plate 5; Repton, *Fragments* (1816), 14–15 n. Executed by J. A. Repton.

64 Repton, *Design for the Pavillon at Brighton* (1808).

65 Repton, *Inquiry into the Changes of Taste in Landscape Gardening and Architecture* (1806), 41; Carter, Goode and Laurie, *op. cit.*, 85–6.

66 W. Hodges, *Select Views in India* (1785–88); T. and W. Daniell, *Oriental Scenery*, 6 vols. (1795–1808); J. Stuart and N. Revett, *Antiquities of Athens* 4 vols (1762–1816).

67 Repton, *Observations* (1805); ed. Loudon (1840), 129.

68 *ibid.*, 304.

69 *ibid.*, 218.

70 *ibid.*, 218: re Rendlesham Hall.

71 *ibid.*, 303.

72 e.g. J. Plaw, *Rural Architecture* (1785 etc.); C. Middleton, *Picturesque and Architectural Views for Cottages* (1793); J. Malton, *Cottage Architecture* (1798); R. Elsam, *Rural Architecture* (1803); J. Gandy, *Cottages, Cottage Farms and Other Rural Buildings* (1805); F. Goodwin, *Rural Architecture* (1835). Goodwin recommended Italianate for the Lake District. See A. Taylor, 'Francis Goodwin's "Domestic Architecture"', *Architectural History* xxviii (1985), 125–35.

73 J. C. Loudon, *Encyclopaedia of Cottage, Farm and Villa Architecture*, ed. Mrs. J. Loudon (1846), 1113.

74 *Victoria County History: Oxfordshire* xi (1983), 227–8.

75 *C.L.* cvi (1949), 327.

76 See G. Hersey, 'J. C. Loudon and Architectural Associationism', *A.R.* cxliv (1968), 89–92. Hersey's view is modified in S. Lyall, 'Loudon and Associationism', *ibid.*, 308.

77 e.g. 'Cottage Dwellings in Various Styles', *Encyclopaedia* (1867 ed), lxix, lxx, lxxi; 'Gothic' by Messrs. W. and H. Laxton; 'Beau Ideal Villa' (1836 ed): Tudor by C. Barry; 'Anglo-Grecian Villa' (1867 ed), 1220, by E. B. Lamb.

78 Knight, *An Analytical Inquiry into the Principles of Taste* (1808 ed), 160.

79 *ibid.*, 225.

80 *ibid.*, 223. S. P. Cockerell's Sezincote, Glos., follows the same principle.

81 Knight, *Analytical Inquiry, op. cit.*, 162–6, 222–3.

82 See S. Lang, 'Vanbrugh's Theory and Hawksmoor's Buildings', *S.A.H. Jnl.* xxiv (1965), 127–51.

83 W. Duff, *An Essay on Original Genius* (1767); J. L. de Cordemoy, *Nouveau Traité de toute l'architecture* (Paris, 1714 edn.) See S. Lang, 'Richard Payne Knight and the Idea of Modernity', in *Concerning Architecture*, ed. J. Summerson (1968), 85–97; R. D. Middleton, 'The Abbé de Cordemoy and the Graeco-Gothic Ideal: a Prelude to Romantic Classicism', *Jnl. Warburg and Courtauld Institutes* xxv (1962), xxvi (1963).

84 D. Watkin, *Thomas Hope and the Neo-Classical Idea* (1968).

85 Loudon, *Encyclopaedia* (1863 edn), 80.

86 Knight, *Analytical Inquiry*, 223 *et seq.*

87 J. Summerson, *Heavenly Mansions* (1949).

88 See K. Clark, *Civilisation* (1969), 269; H. Honour, *Romanticism* (1979), 73.

89 J. Constable, *Correspondence*, ed. R. B. Beckett vi (1962), 98.

90 Chambers, *Dissertation on Oriental Gardening* (1772), opening. Lord Kames took the same view: 'in gardening ... the emotions raised ... are so faint, that every artifice should be employed to give them their utmost vigour' (*Elements of Criticism*, Edinburgh, 1807 ed, 301).

91 See M. H. Abrams, *The Mirror and the Lamp: Romantic Theory and the Critical Tradition* (New York and Oxford, 1953) and *Natural Supernaturalism: Tradition and Revelation in Romantic Literature* (1971); J. Dixon Hunt, *The Figure in the Landscape: Poetry, Painting and Gardening during the 18th century* (1976). For a helpful summary, see J. Dixon Hunt and P. Willis, eds, *The Genius of the Place: The English Landscape Garden, 1620–1820* (1975).

92 E. S. de Beer, 'Gothic: Origin and Diffusion of the Term; the Idea of Style in Architecture', *Jnl. Warburg and Courtauld Institutes* xi (1948), 148–62.

93 Price, *Essays on the Picturesque*, 2nd ed ii (1810), 268.

94 'Nash had a mind to build ... but a square bit of architecture. I told him however that I must have, not only some of the *windows*, but some of the *rooms* turned to particular points....' (Price to Sir George Beaumont, 18 March 1798, quoted in M. Allentuck, 'Sir Uvedale Price and the Picturesque Garden', in N. Pevsner, ed., *The Picturesque Garden*, Dumbarton Oaks, 1974, 69). See *C.L.* cxi (1952), 33.

95 'The spot from whence the view is taken is in a fixed state to the painter; but the gardener surveys his scenery while in motion; and, from different windows in the same point he sees objects in different situations' (Repton, *Landscape Gardening*, 96). For Hawkstone, see *C.L.* cxxiii (1958), 640–3, 698–701, and cxxiv (1958), 18–21, 72–5, 368–71.

96 Repton, *Fragments* (1816), 168.

97 J. Mordaunt Crook, 'A Vanished Theatrical Masterpiece: Smirke's Covent Garden Theatre', *Country Life Annual* (1970), 102–5.

98 For details, see J. Mordaunt Crook, 'Regency Architecture in the West Country: the Greek Revival', *R.S.A. Jnl.* cxix (1971), 438–51.

99 *Hopper versus Cust on the New House of Parliament* (1837).

100 Buildings in the Egyptian, Greek, Romanesque and Gothic: the university as an architectural museum, archaeological and didactic (D. Watkin, 'Charles Kelsall, the quintessence of neo-classicism', *A.R.* cxl, 1966, 109–21).

101 G. Wightwick, *The Palace of Architecture* (1840), 2: *oratio recta.*

102 ill. *A.A. Jnl.* xlvii (1931), 8.

103 R. Brown, *Domestic Architecture* (1841), pl. xv, 307.

104 Similarly, S. P. Cockerell's Daylesford, Glos. (1788–93), for Warren Hastings, sports a dome with vaguely Oriental profiles.

105 [J. Weale], 'On the Present Condition and Prospects of Architecture in England', *Weale's Quarterly Papers on Architecture* ii (1844), 5–6.

106 Soane, 'R.A. Lectures', reprinted *A.A. Jnl.*, 1928–9.

107 Gandy, 'On the Philosophy of Architecture', *Mag. of the Fine Arts* i (1821), 239–93, 307–79.

108 RIBA.

109 Sir John Soane's Museum.

110 Gandy, 'The Art, Philosophy, and Science of Architecture', i, 219: quoted by B. Lukacher, in *Joseph Michael Gandy* (AA, 1982), 21.

111 *C.L.* cxvii (1955), 1368. Salvin's anti-classical approach can be gauged by his comment on Petworth, Sussex: 'There is only one thing to be done. Pull the whole house down and re-build it' (J. Lees–Milne, *Prophesying Peace*, 1977, 215).

112 [J. Weale], 'On the Present Condition and Prospects of Architecture in England', *Weale's Quarterly Papers on Architecture* ii (1844), 5, 7. Probably referring to Heath's *Picturesque Annual* (c. 1832–41). Appropriately, this volume was dedicated to the would-be rationalist critic, James Fergusson.

113 Repton used this quotation as an epigraph to his *Brighton*, below the text: 'Gardens are works of art rather than nature'.

114 Laugier, *Essai sur l'Architecture* (1753; revised ed. Paris, 1755). A doctrine echoed in George Berkeley's 'appearance of use' (Fraser, *Works of Berkeley*, ii, 136: 'Alciphron or the Minute Philosopher'). See E. R. de Zurko, *Origins of Modern Functionalist Theory* (New York, 1957), 85.

2 Pugin and Ecclesiology

1 J. Soane, *Lectures*, ed. A. T. Bolton (1929), 104.

2 MS. letter, colln. H. M. Colvin.

3 'The masonry is most abominably executed, having no bond in the angles of the turrets to the main walls; the great turrets were [copied] from St Augustine's Gate [Canterbury]; the building is entirely misconceived and built in every part in the slightest manner; flues are introduced in the main pillars of the lantern which never were anything like adequate to support the great weight placed upon them; very great settlements were observable in every part of the building; the whole of the interior decorations are in Wyatt's execrable taste; the ceilings are trifling and the panelling of the dining room and other rooms absolutely foolish. The decoration of the gallery [is] ecclesiastical and bad; the cloister in front of the dining room is plaster and very meagre; all of the oriel windows are likewise cement and plaster; the whole is in a dreadful state of ruin and will shortly fall to pieces' (Pugin Sketchbooks, V & A, 1833).

4 B. Ferrey, *Pugin* (1861), 43, 47; M. Trappes-Lomax, *Pugin* (1932), 47–8. A. Wedgwood, ed., *A. W. N. Pugin and the Pugin Family* (V & A, 1985), 51.

5 A. W. N. Pugin, *True Principles* (1841), 48–50.

6 'Memo ... mouldings too meagre; base mouldings too small; differences of level on buttresses of cloister; glazing of windows, designs too regular; mistaken building centre of cloister; ornament bad [in] centre of gables; bridge [of Sighs] a complete failure; why is [the] lantern made to imitate stone?; finial head great gate very

clever; pinnacles of cloister too small; quatrefoils [on] top of turrets too large; arches under groining too meagre' (Pugin Sketchbooks, V & A, 1833).

7 Pugin, *True Principles*, 51–2. 'The mechanical part of Gothic architecture is pretty well understood, but it is the principles which influenced ancient compositions, and the soul which appears in all the former works, which is so lamentably deficient' (Pugin, *Contrasts*, 1841, 43).

8 Pugin, *Apology*, (1843), 1–2. Similarly, the dedication of *Contrasts* 'to the Trade': 'Designs wanted: A Moorish fish market with a literary room over; an Egyptian marine villa; a castellated turnpike gate; a gin temple in the baronial style; a dissenting chapel in a plain style to serve occasionally as a lecture or reading room; a monument to be placed in Westminster Abbey – a colossal figure in the Hindoo style would be preferred, and no regard need be paid to locality; a Saxon cigar divan ...' In 1835 he noted in his diary: 'The present condition of architecture is deplorable. Truth reduced to the position of an interesting but rare and curious relic' (Wedgwood, *Pugin etc., op. cit.*, 33).

9 Pugin, *Apology*, 5

10 *ibid.*, 2.

11 *ibid.*, 5–7.

12 Wedgwood, *Pugin etc, op. cit.*, 111: 30 July 1847.

13 'When Pagan ideas triumphed over Christian principles, *inconsistency* was for the first time developed in architectural designs. Previous to that period, architecture had always been a correct type of the various systems in which it was employed; but from the moment the Christians adopted the fatal mistake of reviving classic design, the principles of architecture have been plunged into miserable confusion' (Ferrey, *Pugin*, 353).

14 Pugin, *True Principles* (1841), 51–2. 'In pointed architecture the elevation is *raised from the plan*, ... in Anglo-classic the *plan* is made to suit the *elevation*' (Pugin, *Orthodox Jnl.* 9 Nov. 1839, 317).

15 Pugin, *True Principles*, 56; Pugin, *Apology*, 37. 'In short, Catholicism is so interwoven with every thing sacred, honourable, or glorious in England, that three centuries of puritanism, indifference, and infidelity, have not been able effectively to separate it ... It clings to this land ... What! an Englishman and a protestant! Oh worse than parricide ...' (*ibid.*, 50).

16 A. Wedgwood, ed., *A. W. N. Pugin and the Pugin Family* (1985), 103: 5 Jan. 1841.

17 Pugin, *Apology*, 10–11.

18 M. Girouard, *C.L.* cxxviii (1960), 1226–9. See also A. Wedgwood, ed., *A. W. N. Pugin and the Pugin Family* (1985), 120: 25 June 1843.

19 It was designed for 'a warden and confrator, both in priests' orders; six chaplains or decayed priests, a sacrist, twelve poor brethren, a schoolmaster and an unlimited number of poor scholars'. The buildings consisted of 'a chapel, school, lodging for the warden, common hall, kitchen, chambers and library ... lodgings for the poor brethren, and a residence for the schoolmaster' (Pugin, *Present State of Ecclesiastical Architecture*, 1843, 87). Nearby Alton Towers is only partly Pugin's work: Morris thought its exterior 'gimcrack' (Morris, *Letters*, ed. N. Kelvin, Princeton, i, 1984, 292: 26 March 1876).

20 Pugin, *True Principles*, 1.

21 *B.* viii (1850), 134.

22 Pugin, *Orthodox Jnl.* 9 Nov. 1839, 318. See also

Samuel Huggins, *B.* vii (1849), 356 and viii (1850), 209.

23 Mrs Stanhope's dress in Trollope's *Barchester Towers* (1857) was designed on Puginian principles: 'she well knew the great architectural secret of decorating her constructions, and never descended to construct a decoration'.

24 See J.L. Petit on the meaningless distinction between decorated construction and constructed decoration (*B.* xix, 1861, 370).

25 P. Stanton, *Pugin*, (1971), 11; Pugin, *Present State* (1843), 108. 'God forbid that I should presume to introduce novelty ... The restoration of Catholic antiquity is all that I seek; and I must disclaim any personal merit ... beyond that which would be due to one who had reprinted an excellent but almost forgotten book' (Pugin, *Orthodox Jnl.* 9 Nov. 1839, 316).

26 Pugin, *Apology*, 22.

27 D. Gwynn, *Lord Shrewsbury, Pugin and the Catholic Revival* (1946), 122.

28 Trappes-Lomax, *Pugin*, 314–15.

29 Pugin, *Apology*, 39.

30 Ruskin, *Works* IX, 72: *Stones of Venice*, i. For a general discussion, see M. Bright, 'A Reconsideration of Pugin's Architectural Theories', *Victorian Studies* xxii (1979), 151–72.

31 Ferrey, *Pugin*, 106, 315. Of course elements of this view derive from eighteenth-century French rationalism, e.g. 'nothing is beautiful but what is true' (N. Boileau, *Art Poétique*, quoted in P. Collins, *Changing Ideals in Modern Architecture*, 1965, 198).

32 'The history of architecture is the history of the world ... The beliefs and manners of all people are embodied in the edifices they raised; it was impossible for any of them to have built consistently otherwise than they did ... each style was the type of their Religion, customs and climate' (Pugin, *Apology*, 4–5). Hence Pugin planned a treatise on *Natural Architecture* (*ibid.*, 15).

33 [W.H. Leeds], 'Architectural Revivalism and Puginism', *Fraser's Mag.* xxviii (1843), 605.

34 'As soon as Pugin tried to institute a synthesis between the extrinsic meanings of religious symbolism and the intrinsic meanings of construction, function and material, the semantic precision of the word "real" was under threat' (C. Brooks, *Signs of the Times: Symbolic Realism in the Mid-Victorian World*, 1984, 161).

35 Pugin's *Earnest Address on the Establishment of the English Catholic Hierarchy* (1851) was attacked by Catholic clerics (*The Rambler* viii, 1851, 45–6) and praised [by Benjamin Webb] in *Morning Chronicle*, 4 March 1851, 6. His unpublished 'Apology for the separated Church of England' would have caused still greater dispute. For the controversy from a Catholic viewpoint, see E. Sheridan Purcell in Ferrey, *Pugin*, 386 *et seq.*; reviewed [by Benjamin Webb], *Saturday Rev.* xii (1861), 121–3.

36 'Puginism is identical with Puseyism', wrote J.M. Capes (*The Rambler* viii, 1851, 41–6); 'Pugin ... judged [the Church] by a Protestant test, viz. by her accordance or disagreement with his personal tastes in externals' (*ibid.* v, 1850, 366–75). In that he agreed with Beresford Hope. 'Mr. Hope's anti-Catholicism', Capes noted, 'is of the aesthetic species. He is a Protestant on ritualistic and architectural grounds'. 'Oratorianism is his enemy' (*ibid.* vii, 1851, 323–37). Hope's 'Oratorianism and

Ecclesiology', *Christian Remembrancer* xxi (1851), 141–65, supported the Puginian approach against the developmental ecclesiology of the Oratorians. He may even have hoped for Pugin's return to Anglicanism (*E.* x. N.S. vii, 1850, 302 and xiii, N.S. x, 1852, 353).

37 For the background to Cotton College, see R. Addington, ed., *Faber* (1974).

38 Pugin to E. J. Willson, 1839 (Stanton, *Pugin*, 59).

39 The West doors, however, echo Lichfield, or the Chapter House at York.

40 e.g. at St. Marie's, Rugby (1846–7). Pugin 'has had the laudable courage to put a saddlebacked head to the tower' (*E.* ix, N.S. vi, 1849, 370).

41 Assisi, Perugia, Arezzo, Cortona, Florence, Pistoia (Trappes-Lomax, *Pugin*, 115).

42 Pugin, *True Principles*, 53.

43 Stanton, *Pugin*, 121.

44 'I have seen most glorious things, far beyond my expectations; the restoration of the Ste. Chapelle . . . is worthy of the days of St. Louis. I never saw Images so exquisitely painted' (A. Wedgwood, ed. *A. W. N. Pugin and the Pugin Family*, 1985, 108: 30 May 1844).

45 Stanton, *Pugin*, 7. He believed that Pugin fell into the trap of regarding architecture as end rather than means: 'Our rules and our rubrics have been altered to meet the times, and hence an obsolete discipline may be a present heresy' (Newman, *Idea of a University*, 1852).

46 Stanton, *Pugin*, 97 *et seq.* The consecration in 1846 was an international event: A. N. Didron, editor of *Annales Archéologiques*, and A. Reichensperger, editor of *Kölner Domblatt*, both attended. See *The Tablet* 1846, 568–9.

47 J. F. White, *The Cambridge Movement: the Ecclesiologists and the Gothic Revival* (Cambridge, 1962). The Irish Ecclesiological Society was founded in 1842. See also N. Yates, *The Oxford Movement and Anglican Ritualism* (1983).

48 A. G. Lough, *Influence of J. M. Neale* (1962) and *J. M. Neale: Priest Extraordinary* (1978). His romantic views are summed up in his poem 'The Good Old Times of England' (1843). He may have been the original 'Mr. Falconer' in Peacock's *Gryll Grange* (1860).

49 C. C. J. Webb, 'Benjamin Webb', *Church Qtly. Rev.* lxxv (1913), 329–48. Webb was a stabilising influence on the society: 'Neale with all his genius was not judicious' (*Sat. Rev.* 12 Dec. 1885). See also obit. by Beresford Hope, *Guardian* 2 Dec. 1885.

50 H. W. and I. Law, *The Book of the Beresford Hopes* (1925). Hope was a more moderate churchman than Neale, e.g. J. M. Neale, *Extreme Men: a letter to A. J. B. Beresford Hope* (1865).

51 'It is well known that I never was a ritualist . . . [though] my name is a byword for that with which I never had any sympathy' (H. P. Liddon, *Pusey*, ix, 211–12: 1860, 1866). Pusey's family chapel at Pusey, Oxfordshire, retained the appearance of a Georgian drawing room.

52 'Newman never went into architecture . . . Keble was a latitudinarian, if not a utilitarian, in architecture' (Mozeley, *Reminiscences*, i, 217). Fr. J. B. Dalgairns noted in 1842 that Newman's monastery at Littlemore was 'a very cheap but not nasty place, very like almshouses, very anti-Puginian: after Oscott it will look quite low' (R. D. Middleton, *Newman and Bloxam: an Oxford Friendship*, 1947, 58).

53 Newman, *Letters* xii, 222; xiii, 460. For Newman v. Pugin, see J. Patrick, 'Newman, Pugin and Gothic', *Victorian Studies*, xxiv (1981), 185–207. 'In details Pugin is perfect, but his altars are so small you can't have a Pontifical High Mass at them, his tabernacles so low that you can scarce have an Exposition, his east windows so large that everything is hidden in the glare, and his screens so heavy that you might as well have the function in the sacristy for the seeing of it in the congregation' (Newman, *Letters and Diaries*, xii, 213–5: 6 June 1848).

54 See Parker's obituaries, *B.* xlvi (1884), 189, 211; *B.N.* xlvi (1884), 225–6. For Freeman's obit., see *B.N.* lxii (1892), 424.

55 For membership lists, see W. A. Pantin, 'The Oxford Architectural and Historical Society', *Oxoniensia* iv (1939), 174–94. Its leading architect, J. P. Harrison, designed All Saints, Hursley, Hants. (1846–48) for Keble.

56 'What can an Architectural Society have to do with Altar Cloths?' (S. L. Ollard, 'The Oxford Architectural and Historical Society and the Oxford Movement', *Oxoniensia* v. 1940, 154, 157). Several R.C. converts, e.g. J. M. Capes, managed to remain members of the Committee.

57 [M. S. Lawson, ed.], *Letters of J. M. Neale* (1910), 70. Speaking in Oxford, Hope emphasised Cambridge's 'priority of onwardness' (*E.* vii, N.S. iv, 1847, 90). By moving to London the Ecclesiological Society opened itself to Oxford Men, notably the Rev. William Scott and Sir Stephen Glynne.

58 'We take our stand on the ground held by Andrews, Bancroft, Laud, Wren, Montagu, and their fellow confessors, and we claim, with them, for the English church, the revival of all the vestments and ornaments to which, it can be proved, she is justly entitled' (*Hierugia Anglicana*, ed. J. Fuller Russell, 1849, 9). 'It was the golden time of "retrograding transcendentalism' as the hard heads called the Anglo-Catholic sympathy' (G. W. E. Russell, *Mr Gladstone's Religious Development*, 1899, 21).

59 F. Close, *The Restoration of Churches is the Restoration of Popery: Proved and Illustrated from the Authenticated Publications of the 'Cambridge Camden Society'* (1844), 4.

60 B. F. L. Clarke, *Church Builders of the Nineteenth Century* (1969), 78.

61 *E.* xii, N.S. ix (1851), 152.

62 Florence Nightingale attended the consecration service at Leeds in 1841: 'it was quite a gathering for Puseyites from all parts of England. Papa heard them debating whether they should have lighted candles before the Altar, but they decided no, because the Bishop of Ripon would not like it – however they had them in the evening and the next morning when he was gone . . . Dr. Hook has the regular Catholic jerk in making the genuflexion every time he approaches the altar' (B. Cook, *Life of Florence Nightingale* i, 1913, 55). Thirty years later, however, St. Peter's seemed a mere 'Castle of Otranto in ecclesiastical disguise' (J. T. Micklethwaite, *Church Furniture and Arrangement*, 1908 edn. 33; reprinted from *Church Builder*, 1899–1905). See also N. Yates, *Leeds and the Oxford Movement* (Thoresby Society, 1975). For the ritual context of church design, cf. G. W. O. Addleshaw and F. Etchells, *The Architectural Setting of Anglican Worship* (1948), 203–22; J. F. White,

Protestant Worship and Church Architecture, Theological and Historical Considerations (New York, 1964).

63 *E.* i (1842), 134.

64 *E.* v, N.S. ii (1846), 52–3.

65 E. A. Freeman, *Principles of Church Restoration* (1846), 7.

66 Whewell also suggested the nave at Exeter or the chapter house and nave at York; in Germany, Cologne and Strasbourg; in France, the choir at Amiens and St. Ouen at Rouen (Whewell, *Architectural Notes on German Churches and Notes in Picardy and Normandy*, 1835).

67 'The moment the *flat* or four-centred arch was introduced, the spirit of Christian architecture was on the wane. *Height* or the vertical principle, emblematic of the resurrection, is the very essence of Christian architecture' (Pugin, *True Principles*, 7, n. 1). 'During the ... Norman era, the Catholic church was forming her architectural language: in the Tudor period she was unlearning it' (*A Few Words to Church Builders*, 6). For a recent assessment of the Decorated style, see J. Bony, *The English Decorated Style: Gothic Architecture Transformed, 1250–1350* (1979).

68 e.g. his 'eclectic use of the Perpendicular' at Ramsgate (*E.* ix, NS vi, 1849, 370).

69 *E.* xxxii, NS xxix (1868), 315–6.

70 *E.* xv, NS xii (1854), 4; S. T. Madsen, *Restoration and Anti-Restoration* (Oslo, 1976), 25.

71 By 1860 the Incorporated Church Building Society had aided 1197 new churches, 697 rebuildings, 2376 enlargements and 1,092,206 extra seats (G. K. Brandwood, 'Church Building and Restoration in Leicestershire 1800–1914', Ph.D. Leic. 1984, 127).

72 *E.* xiii, N.S. x (1852), 276. Eg., I. J. Lockhead, 'Gilbert Scott, Benjamin Montfort and the Building of Christ Church Cathedral', *Bull. New Zealand Art History* iv (1976) 2–15.

73 Designed by an expatriate architect, F. Wills of Exeter, author of *Ancient English Ecclesiastical Architecture, and its Principles applied to the Wants of the Church at the Present Day* (New York, 1850).

74 The Rev R. H. Cox, the incumbent, travelled from England with the working drawings (B. F. L. Clarke, *Anglican Cathedrals outside the British Isles*, 1958, 7).

75 e.g. Streatham (Tite) and Wilton (T. H. Wyatt).

76 'Do you really suppose that nine tenths of our subscribers care one straw for foreign matter? or that a country Priest, wanting real practical information, will endure to be put off with Cologne or Paris ... [Foreign items are] turning us from a first-rate practical into a third-rate Archaeological Magazine' (Neale to Webb, 12 Dec. 1846, in [M.S. Lawson, ed.], *Letters of J. M. Neale*, 1910, 100). 'The French articles only prejudice people against us' (*ibid.*, 155: 21 Sept. 1850).

77 See obit., *E.* xvi, N.S. xiii (1855), 137–40.

78 T. F. Bumpus, *London Churches* ii [1908], 193n. By 1866 Lord Shaftesbury was horrified by the 'theatrical gymnastics' at St. Alban's, Holborn, and the 'clouds upon clouds of incense' (S. Leslie, *The Oxford Movement*, 1933, 76).

79 Hope, *An Essay on the Present State of Ecclesiological Science in England* (Oxford, 1846).

80 Pugin, *Present State*, 86.

81 *E.* iv, NS i (1845), 184.

82 *E.* i (1842), 91; obit. *A.* i (1869), 10. See also *D.N.B.*

83 *E.* xv, N.S. xii (1854), 3. At proof stage Beresford

Hope changed the title of his Oxford paper of 1846 (see n. 79) from 'Art' to 'Science' (Hope Collection, Trinity College Library, Cambridge).

84 A. G. Lough, *J. M. Neale: Priest Extraordinary* (1975), 60; 1844.

85 Close, *Restoration of Churches* ..., 17. 'Such *Restoration* of Churches as the Cambridge Camden Society would effect, not only *tends to*, but *actually* is POPERY!' (*ibid.*, 18).

86 P. Maurice, *Popery of Oxford* ..., 53n. Newman's church was said to be modelled on St. Giles' church, Oxford, or on Mozeley's church at Moreton Pinkney, Northamptonshire (T. Mozeley, *Reminiscences*, 1884, i, 346; J. Rothstein, 'Newman at Littlemore', *A.R.* xcviii, 1945, 176–7; P. Howell, 'Newman's Church at Littlemore', *Oxford Art Jnl.* vi, 1983, (i), 51–5). The *Ecclesiologist* called it 'the first unqualified step to better things that England had long witnessed; the first building for many a long year erected showing itself to be not so much a sermon house, as a temple of the MOST HIGH' (*E.* iv, N.S. i, 1845, 32–3).

87 *E.* viii, N.S. v (1848), 387.

88 'Supposing you do one day get every old thing back again – copes, lecterns, rood-lofts, candlesticks, and the abbey-lands into the bargain; what will it be but an empty pageant, like the tournament of Eglinton Castle, separated from the reality of Catholic truth and unity by the abyss of three hundred years of schism?' (Montalembert, *Letters to ... Rev. [J. M. Neale]*, Liverpool, 1844). See also *E.* iv, N.S. i (1845), 25, 114.

89 Pugin, *Present State*, 115, 131, 137, 152–3. An estimated 350 Anglican clergymen went over to Rome between 1833 and 1860 (P. Adams, 'Converts to the R.C. Church in England, c. 1830–70', B.Litt., Oxon., 1977, 3).

90 'Mr Pugin was a son of *our* Church, against whom he turns the weapons *she* has given him: his knowledge was acquired in *our* school. We accept his argument. We grant that a relish for the beauty of Catholic architecture is a symptom of Catholic soundness' (T. Mozeley, reviewing *Contrasts*, in *British Critic*, xxv, 1839, 498).

91 'Now that we have lost him – we have no hesitation in pronouncing [him] the most eminent and original architectural genius of his time' (obit., *E.* xiii, N.S. x, 1852, 352–7).

92 *E.* iii (1843–4), 185. Webb first visited Pugin in 1841 (Stanton, *Pugin*, 127). In 1842 Pugin visited Ely with the Ecclesiological Soc. (Pugin diary, V & A.: 3 May 1842).

93 'A genius, quick, versatile ... full of talent, full of energy', who had reached his peak at St Barnabas, Nottingham, and then declined into a 'mechanical' and 'peculiar crispness'. But 'Mr Pugin is still young and vigorous, and full of talent, and he may yet redeem his mistakes ... let him *realise himself in his own early lessons*' (*E.* v. N.S. ii, 1846, 10–16). See also E. Towle, *J. M. Neale* (1906), 118–19 and *Letters of J. M. Neale*, 86, n. 1. As a result of this attack, F. A. Paley and S. N. Stokes left the Ecclesiological Society for Rome (Stanton, *Pugin*, 186). For Pugin's reply, see *The Tablet* 1846, 64.

94 For Nature 'theologised and sacramentalised', see S. Prickett, *Romanticism and Religion: the Tradition of Coleridge and Wordsworth in the English Church* (Cambridge, 1976). For Keble, Newman and the poeticising of the sacramental principle, see G. B. Tennyson, *Victorian Devotional Poetry: the Tractarian Mode* (1981). For an

example of Tractarian architectural romanticism, see Isaac Williams's poem *The Cathedral* (1838), discussed in O. W. Jones, *Isaac Williams and his Circle* (1971), 37–9.

95 W. Durandus, *Rationale Divinorum Officiorum*, trans. and ed. J. M. Neale and B. Webb (1843), intro. xxvi–xxvii. See also 'Church symbolisms', *Trans. Exeter Diocesan Architectural Soc.* ii (1847), 67–76; B. E. Ferrey, 'Symbolism in Ecclesiology', *Jnl. St. Paul's Ecclesiological Soc.* ii (1886–90), 49–58.

96 Stanton, *Pugin*, 146. Pugin always believed that churches should be 'raised in accordance with the religious rites and mysteries which were to be celebrated in them, and which they *symbolised by their plan, arrangement, structure and decoration*' (Pugin, 'Why This Waste?', *Merry England* vii, 1886, 91–103).

97 Lough, *Neale: Priest Extraordinary*, 51.

98 Didron, reviewing Durandus. *A.A.* viii (1848), 57.

99 Durandus, intro. cxxxiii, *postscript*.

100 For Tractarian aesthetics – art as a religious impulse – see G. B. Thompson, 'Tractarian Aesthetics: Analogy and Reason in Keble and Newman', *Victorian Newsletter* no. LV (1979), 8–10.

101 [Webb] reviewing Eastlake's *Gothic Revival*. *Sat. Rev.* xxxiii (1872), 382–3.

102 [Webb] reviewing Ferrey's *Pugin*, *E.* xxv, N.S. xxii (1861), 305–10, 367–9.

103 E. Sheridan Purcell, in Ferrey, *Pugin*, 311, 352, 419.

104 *B.* i (1843), 69.

105 For Burges's admiration for Pugin, see J. Mordaunt Crook, *William Burges and the High Victorian Dream* (1981), 39, 40–41.

106 Scott, *Personal and Professional Recollections* (1879), 90, 112. *Contrasts* 'vividly exposed the abject meanness which pervaded the architecture of the day'; *True Principles* 'was a gigantic step in advance. It grappled at once with all the fallacies which had corrupted modern architecture, and established a code of rules founded upon common sense, utility and truth'. Firstly, the *Apology* 'showed the necessity of falling back upon our national style, and its ready applicability to any requirement of our day ... Forty years ago no one in building a new church ever have dreamed of making it Gothic, no one now dreams of making it anything else ... the revolution is completed' (Scott, 'On the present position and future prospects of the revival of Gothic architecture', *B.* xv, 1857, 572–3: Yorkshire Architectural Society). For a violent, Protestant counter-attack, see *ibid.*, 597. For a critical reply arguing against any universal style, see *ibid.*, 637; and for a 'plurality of styles', see *B.* xvi (1858), 332.

107 Pugin, *Remarks on ... the 'Rambler'*, (1849), 11.

108 Ferrey, *Pugin*, 422.

109 Stanton, *Pugin*, 108. 'Everything looks plain after Cheadle' (A. Wedgwood, ed., *A. W. N. Pugin and the Pugin Family*, 1985, 115: Nov. 1850).

110 Stanton, *Pugin*, 194.

3 Ruskin and Viollet-le-Duc

1 e.g. N. Pevsner, *Ruskin and Viollet-le-Duc* (1969).

2 *B.* xv (1857), 572–3. 'Mr Ruskin has exercised more influence over the thinking classes of Englishmen than any writer who has made Fine Art his theme' (*A.* iv, 1870, 142). Even C. R. Cockerell called Ruskin 'a master of aesthetics' (*B.* xi, 1853, 114). See also J. D. Jump, 'Ruskin's Reputation in the 1850s: the Evidence of the Three Principal Weeklies', *Publications of the Modern Language Association of America* lxiii, 1948, 678–85).

3 *B.N.* xii (1865), 115, 225; T. G. Jackson, *Recollections* (Oxford, 1950), 55. 'An intellectual king among men ... his mission has been to make the world more beautiful' (Charles Wethered, *On Restoration by Viollet-le-Duc*, 1875: obit., *R.I.B.A. Sess. Papers* 1883–4, 210–17). 'One of the most extraordinary men of his generation. From the time of Vitruvius, no man has written a treatise on architecture which has thrown so much light on the history of architecture' (George Aitchison, *B.* xlvi, 1884, 661).

4 *Daily Telegraph* 31 Aug. 1859.

5 *Companion to the Almanac* 1859, 239.

6 *B.* xi (1853), 654.

7 *E.* x, N.S. vii (1849–50), 353 and xiii, N.S. x (1852), 167.

8 Almost the only time Ruskin mentioned All Saints was to remark: 'I do not altogether like the arrangements of colour in the brickwork'; although he did praise its 'force, vitality and grace', adding: 'having done this, we may do anything' (Ruskin, *Works*, XI, 229–30). Butterfield's polychromy, developed here in 1850–51, probably owed as much to M. D. Wyatt (*Specimens of the Geometrical Mosaic of the Middle Ages*, 1849) as it did to Ruskin. See P. Thompson, 'All Saints, Margaret St., Reconsidered', *Architectural History* viii (1965), 73–87. Butterfield may possibly have known J. C. Lassaulx's *Description of a New Kind of Mosaic Composed of Bricks* (1839) and Lassaulx's polychrome St Arnulph, Nickenich (G. German, *Gothic Revival in Europe and Britain*, 1972, 114–5, pl. 85). Like Butterfield and the ecclesiologists, Street was also looking for a new type of town church: 'Instead of Kentish rag one should have ... clean hewn ashlar, and for plaster we should have ... gorgeous fresco and glittering marble' (Street, 'On the Proper Characteristics of a Town Church', *E.* xi, N.S. viii, 1850, 227–33). Other suggested prototypes were S. Pierre, Chartres, and the ruined Augustinian church in Rue Malpalm, Rouen. At this date Street regarded Butterfield's St Augustine's, Canterbury, as 'perfect'. For ecclesiological attitudes to polychromy, see also *E.* xii, N.S. ix (1851), 348.

9 'The relative majesty of buildings depends more on the weight and vigour of their masses, than on any other attributes of their design: mass of everything, of bulk, of light, of darkness, of colour, not mere sum of any of these, but breadth of them; not broken light, nor scattered darkness, nor divided weight, but solid stone, broad sunshine, starless shade' ('Ruskin, 'Lamp of Power', *Works* VIII, 134). See E. N. Kaufman, ' "The weight and vigour of their masses": mid-Victorian country churches and "The Lamp of Power" ', in J. Dixon Hunt and Faith M. Holland, eds., *The Ruskin Polygon* (Manchester, 1982), 94–121.

10 *E.* xx, N.S. xviii (1859), 185; Hope, *The English Cathedral of the Nineteenth Century* (1861), 234–5.

11 It was the elder Didron who made sure that the winning design would be thirteenth century French (*B.N.* xv, 1868, 31; *A.A.* xiv, 1854, 385). Competition drawings: Lille Diocesan Archives and R.I.B.A. Details: *A.A.* xvi (1856) and *E.*xvii, N.S. xiv (1856), *passim*.

12 Both Wild and Wyatt – at Wilton church (1840–42) and at Christ Church, Streatham (1840) – had worked in a pre-Renaissance, 'round-arched' style, or 'rundbogenstil': a mixture of Early Christian, Lombard and Romanesque. Possible models for Wild's Wilton church are San Michele, Pavia (T. Hope, *An Historical Essay on Architecture*, 1835) and Santo Carcere, Catania (H. Gally Knight, *Saracenic and Norman Remains* [1840], pl. x). At St. Johanneskirche, Maobit, Berlin, (1832), Schinkel employed North Italian quattrocento rather than Lombardic Romanesque. Wild's Anglican church at Alexandria, Egypt (1842) is more strikingly Lombardic. During the 1840s English attitudes towards Italian Gothic had changed dramatically, from curiosity to reverence. Compare R. Willis, *Remarks on the Architecture of the Middle Ages, especially of Italy* (1835), and B. Webb, *Sketches of Continental Ecclesiology* (1848), with T. Hope, *Essay on Architecture* (1835) and H. Gally Knight, *Ecclesiastical Architecture of Italy from the Time of Constantine to the Fifteenth Century*, (1842–4). See also *B.* iii (1845), 326–7; iv (1846), 334; v (1847), 468; vi (1848), 577.

13 See J. Mordaunt Crook, 'Early French Gothic', in *Influences in Victorian Art and Architecture*, ed. S. Macready and F.H. Thompson (Soc. of Antiquaries, 1985), 49–58.

14 See J. Unrau, 'A Note on Ruskin's Reading of Pugin', *English Studies* Aug. 1967, 335–7.

15 *E.* xxii, N.S. xix (1861), 310, 367.

16 Ruskin, *Works* VIII, 59.

17 For Ruskin's attacks on Venetian Baroque, see *Works* XI, 135, 145, 150, 297 (S. Zobenigo and S. Maoise); XI, 431–2 (Scalzi); XI, 428 (S.M. della Salute); XI, 397 (church of the Ospedaletto); XXIV, 440(Pal. Rezzonico); XI, 381–2 (S. Giorgio). He had praise for the Pal. Grimani (*Works* XI, 43–4; XVI, 466n.). But its facility of execution and its 'doggerel' proportions only emphasised the emptiness of the mandarin elite which applauded it, and the degradation of the slaves who produced it (*Works* VIII, 9–10; X, 189n.; XI, 18–19, 74–5).

18 'No style of noble architecture *can* be exclusively ecclesiastical. It must be practised in the dwelling before it can be perfected in the church, and it is the test of all noble style that it should be applicable to both' (*Works* X, 123: *Stones of Venice* ii).

19 Ruskin, *Works* XII, 89.

20 *Works* IX, 72: *Stones of Venice* i.

21 *Works* VIII, 61: *Seven Lamps* ii.

22 *Works* XX, 216: *Aratra Pentelici* i (1870).

23 *Works* XXIII, 87–8: *Val D'Arno* vi (1873). Cf. Laugier's doctrine of 'apparent utility'. There is circumstantial evidence that Ruskin knew of Lodoli's theories, if not Laugier's (M. Lutyens, *Effie in Venice* 1972, 117 *et seq*).

24 It is significant that there are no architectural cross-sections in Ruskin's writings, and few plans.

25 Ruskin, *Works* IX, 106; *Stones of Venice* i.

26 'The suggestion of a mode of structure or support other than the true one' (*Works* VIII, 60: *Seven Lamps*, ii).

27 'It gradually became manifest to me that the sculpture and painting were, in fact, the all in all of the thing to be done; that these, which I had long been in the careless habit of thinking subordinate to the architecture, were in fact the entire masters of the architecture; and the architect who was not a sculptor or a painter, was nothing better than a framemaker on a large scale ... What we call architecture is only the association of [sculpture and painting] in noble masses, or the placing of them in fit places. All architecture other than this is, in fact, mere *building*; and though it may sometimes be graceful ... or sublime ... there is in ... it no more assertion of the powers of high art, than in the gracefulness of a well-ordered chamber or the nobleness of a well-built ship' (*Works*, VIII, 10–11: *Seven Lamps*, 2nd ed., preface).

28 e.g. *Works*, IX, 45, 58: *Stones of Venice*, i.

29 *Works* XII, 83–5, and *Stones of Venice*, i.

30 *Works* IX, 70: *Stones of Venice*, i.

31 *Works* VIII, 230: *Seven Lamps*, vi.

32 *Works* VIII, 184: *Seven Lamps*, iv.

33 *Works* VIII, 218: *Seven Lamps*, v.

34 Hence his wilful misunderstanding of Pugin. He failed even to respond to Pugin's linking of Gothic architecture and seamanship: 'I cannot imagine him living by the sea ... I cannot conceive anything more adverse to Gothic pinnacles than its wild rough-level unity' (Ruskin to W. H. Harrison, 30 Oct. 1851, quoted in M. Hardman, 'The Prose and Ideas of John Ruskin', Ph.D. Cantab. 1975, 63).

35 e.g. R. Willis, *Remarks on the Architecture of the Middle Ages, especially of Italy* (1835); W. Whewell, *Architectural Notes on German Churches, etc.* (1842 ed.).

36 Ruskin, *Works* XXIV, 277: *St Mark's Rest*, viii.

37 W. Worringer, *Form in Gothic* (1912); *Abstraction and Empathy* (1908; trans. New York, 1963). For admirable accounts of Ruskin's architectural theory, see J. Unrau, 'Ruskin's Architectural Writings' (D.Phil., Oxford, 1969); *Looking at Architecture with John Ruskin* (1978); *Ruskin and Venice* (1984).

38 'A foolish person builds foolishly, and a wise one sensibly; a virtuous one beautifully; and a vicious one basely' (*Works* XIX, 389: *Queen of the Air*, iii). 'The right question to ask respecting all ornament is simply this: was it done with enjoyment – was the carver happy while he was about it?' (*Works* VIII, 218: *Seven Lamps*, v).

39 *Works* XI, 46: *Stones of Venice* iii.

40 e.g. *Works* XXIV, 406–7 (letter to Count Zorgi); XX, 96–7 ('The Relation of Art to Use'); XIX, 24 ('The Study of Architecture in Our Schools').

41 *Works* XVI, 184 ('Inaugural Address'). For a similar attack on the inadequacy of 19th c. art, see *Works* XII, 169: review of Lindsay's *Christian Art*.

42 L. Tolstoy, *Recollections and Essays*, trans. A. Maude (1937), 188.

43 *B.* iii (1845), 145.

44 *B.* viii (1850), 97, 257; A. Clifton-Taylor, *The Pattern of English Building* (1962).

45 *C.E.A.J.* (1849), 360 and (1851), 543–4.

46 *B.* ix (1851), 733 and x (1852), 37, 168, 180, 197.

47 See climatic statistics in J. D. Rosenberg, *The Darkening Glass: a portrait of Ruskin's Genius* (1961), 214 n. 7.

48 *B.N.* v (1858), 589.

49 *Works* VIII, 252: *Seven Lamps*, vii. 'Choose a style, and . . . use it universally' (*Works* VIII, 214: *Seven Lamps*, v).

50 *Works* VIII, 258: *Seven Lamps*, vii. Norman and Lombardic were too 'barbarous'.

51 *Works* X, 264: *Stones of Venice*, ii.

52 *E.* xiv, N.S. xi (1853), 424.

53 See J. Mordaunt Crook, 'Ruskinian Gothic' in J. Dixon Hunt and F. M. Holland, eds., *The Ruskin Polygon* (Manchester, 1982), 68–71.

54 What style 'ought, at present, to be consistently adopted by our architects [?] I have no doubt that the only style proper for modern Northern work, is the Northern Gothic of the Thirteenth Century, as exemplified in England, pre-eminently by the cathedrals of Lincoln and Wells, and in France by those of Paris, Amiens, Chartres, etc.' (*Works* VIII, 12–13: *Seven Lamps*, 2nd. edn., preface).

55 *Works* XVI, 469: Ruskin agreed with Street, 15 Feb. 1859.

56 *Works* XI, 230: *Stones of Venice*, iii. For Ruskin's definition of 'Surface Gothic', see *Works* X, 261–2, 265: *Stones of Venice* vi.

57 e.g. *Works* X, 164, 431: *Stones of Venice*, ii, pls. x, xx.

58 e.g. *Works* X, 164, 262, 431: *Stones of Venice* ii, pls. x, xii, xx. See S. A. Fergusson, 'Victorian and Medieval Sources for the Early Churches of G. F. Bodley' (M. A. Courtauld, 1979).

59 D. Verey, 'G. F. Bodley', in *Seven Victorian Architects*, ed. J. Fawcett and N. Pevsner (1976), 84.

60 B. Read, *Victorian Sculpture* (1982), 239–41.

61 C. L. Eastlake, *A History of the Gothic Revival* (1872); ed. J. Mordaunt Crook (Leicester, 1978), appendix no. 248.

62 Godwin, 'Modern Architects and their Work', *B.N.* xxiii (1872), 167.

63 *B.N.* xxiv (1866), 679, 792; xv (1868), 11, 29, 147.

64 Details have been traced to Sta. Maria Maggiore, Bergamo; the Castello di Corte, Mantua; and the Palazzo Sagredo, the Palazzo Foscari and the Ca' d'Oro, Venice (C. Simon, 'George Somers Clarke', M. A. Courtauld, 1983). Somers Clarke also designed a warehouse for the London Printing and Publishing Co., West Smithfield (1860; dem.), in red brick, with abstracted Franco-Flemish details. See *B.N.* vi (1860), 663, 894–5: ills.; *E.* xxiii, N.S. xx (1862), 333; *B.* xix (1861), 161: ill. Motifs have been traced to the Hotel Chambellan, Dijon, the Town Hall at Franeker, Friesland, and the Town Hall at Veere (Simon, *op. cit.*).

65 For Woodward (1815–61), see W. Papworth, ed., *Dictionary of Architecture* (1852–92); *B.* xix (1861), 436; *Irish Builder* iii (1861), 563; D. S. Richardson, 'Gothic Revival in Ireland' (Ph.D., Yale, 1974); F. O'Dwyer and J. Williams, 'Benjamin Woodward', in *Victorian Dublin*, ed. T. Kennedy (Dublin, 1980). E. Blau, *Ruskinian Gothic. The Architecture of Deane and Woodward, 1845–61* (Princeton, 1982). For Thomas Deane (1792–1871), see *B.* xxix (1871), 804; E. Blau, 'The Earliest Work of Deane and Woodward', *Architectura* ix (1979), 172–92. For Thomas Newenham Deane (1828–99), see *B.* lxxvii (1899), 471; *B.A.* lii (1899), 343; *R.I.B.A.J.*, 3rd series vii (1899), 48–9. See also C. P. Curran, 'B. Woodward, Ruskin and the

O'Sheas', *Studies* (Dublin), xxix (1940), 255–68 and *Irish Times* 16–17 May 1967. For Thomas Manley Deane (1851–1933), see *B.* lxxvii (1899), 471.

66 O'Dwyer and Williams, *op. cit.*, 40: ill.; Blau, *Ruskinian Gothic*. 12–26.

67 *B.* x (1852), 483; O'Dwyer and Williams, *op. cit.*, 43: ill.

68 Ruskin, *Works* XVI, xliv. Some of the carvings seem to have been designed by Lizzie Siddal and J. E. Millais (O'Dwyer and Williams, *op. cit.*, 58); the college surveyor, John McCurdy, supervised the work (*B.* lxxvi, 1899, 5).

69 Ruskin, *Works* XVIII, 149–50. 'One of the greatest masterpieces of the Gothic Revival, the finest secular building the movement ever produced' (Osbert Lancaster, *Cornhill Magazine*, May 1944). For contemporary praise, see *Dublin Builder* iii (1861), 563. Some of the motifs derive from the Palazzo dei Pergoli Intaglisti, the Palazzo de' Cornari, the Palazzo Dario and Casa Visetti, Venice (*B.* ix, 1851, 170–71, 202, 330–31, 530–31; xi, 1853, 420). See Blau, *Ruskinian Gothic, op. cit.* 31 *et seq.*

70 H. M. and K. D. Vernon, *A History of the Oxford Museum* (Oxford, 1909); Blau, *Ruskinian Gothic, op. cit.*, 48–92; J. Mordaunt Crook, 'Ruskinian Gothic', *op. cit.*, 65–93. Ruskin helped to design one of the windows, besides paying for several more (H. W. Acland and J. Ruskin, *Oxford Museum*, 1859, 88, 106; W. G. Collingwood, *Ruskin*, 1893, i, 194); twin lancet window, ill. *A.* (1872), 4–5. He seems also to have designed part of Skidmore's metal bracketing (Ruskin, *Works* XIV, xlvi). Ruskin's only other executed design was a window – partly the work of Edmund Oldfield – in Scott's St. Giles, Camberwell (E. T. Cook, *Ruskin*, 1911, i, 159). Woodward defeated, among others, E. M. Barry, H. B. Garland, E. Ellis and J. W. Papworth. Most of the designs were Italianate. Barry was the front runner, and according to one account the rightful winner. See [Beresford Hope], *Sat. Rev.* i (1856), 208–9; *A.* lxxx (1908), 266. Barry's designs were exhibited at the R. A. in 1855, nos. 1236, 1272.

71 For this society, see *Oxoniensia* iv (1939), 174–94.

72 J. Morris, ed., *The Oxford Book of Oxford* (Oxford, 1978), 254.

73 Initially Ruskin thought it 'though by no means a first rate design, yet quite as good as is likely to be got in these days, and on the whole good' (*Works* XVI, xliii). Skidmore's iron supports, however, had in part to be replaced (Vernon, *op. cit.*, 70), and most of the carving remained unfinished (*Works* XVI, lxii; XX, 16, 524–5; XXII, 523–6). The interior capitals were eventually completed by two carvers called Mills and Holt, working for Farmer and Brindley, in 1906–15 (Vernon, *op. cit.*, 85–6). Only one mural – by the Rev R. St. J. Tyrwhitt – was executed, in a lecture room on the North side. The Curator's House (*B.N.* v, 1859, 11–12) was dem. *c.*1950. Rossetti drew a sad allegory of Woodward's martyrdom at the hands of the university ('Sir Galahad and an Angel', or 'Alma Mater and Mr Woodward': V. Surtees, *Paintings and Drawings of D. G. Rossetti*, Oxford, 1973, n. 96). The total estimate had been less than £30,000; the cost more than £60,000 (O'Dwyer and Williams, *op. cit.*, 58). The sculptured porch, designed by Hungerford Pollen for Thomas Woolner, was never built (A. Woolner, ed., *Thomas Woolner*, 1913, 194;

Ruskin, *Works* XVI, liii and XXVIII, 366). O'Shea ended up carving caricatures of his academic superiors in the guise of parrots and owls. This famous episode is described at length in *Works* XVI, xlix. The University authorities seem to have objected to 'the unnecessary introduction of cats' (*Works* XVI, 231). '"What are you carving there, Shea?" "Monkeys, your honour; I'm carving the Darwinian theory"' (Obit. of Sir H. Acland, *British Medical Jnl.* 27 Oct. 1900, 1283).

74 He believed art was 'impossible' in Manchester's 'devil darkness' (Ruskin, *Works* XXXIV, 37, 521, 603).

75 'No state of society ... ever does away with the natural pre-eminence of one man over another' (*Works* XVI, 121; VIII, 167; IX, 260). For a discussion of Ruskin's politics, see P. D. Anthony, *John Ruskin's Labour: a Study of Ruskin's Social Theory* (Cambridge, 1984) and R. Hewison, ed., *New Approaches to Ruskin* (1982).

76 Eastlake, *Gothic Revival*, ed. J. Mordaunt Crook (Leicester, 1978), 312–5: appendix no. 177.

77 *B.* xvii (1859), 290, 296, 323–6, 339. See also *B.N.* v (1859), 427.

78 *B.* xvii (1859), 290.

79 *E.* xxi, N.S. xviii (1860), 178.

80 *E.* xxii, N.S. xix (1861), 162. The executed version was much simpler than the competition design: the upper windows lost their Venetian ogee mouldings, and the curious clock tower became a traceried gable, probably modelled on the sacristy at Assisi. Waterhouse may have borrowed this idea from R. N. Shaw, *Architectural Sketches from the Continent* (1853). See C. Cunningham, in *Alfred Waterhouse* (R.I.B.A., 1983), 18. See also *B.* xxiii (1865), 135–6; *R.I.B.A. Papers* 1864–65, 165 *et seq.*

81 Ruskin, *Works* XVIII, lxxv.

82 P. Henderson, ed., *Letters of William Morris* (1950), 303.

83 '13th c. Gothic suffused with the feeling of the present age' (*B.* xxvi, 1868, 259–61, 317). See also F. Jenkins, 'Manchester Town Hall', *C.L.* cxli, 1967, 336–9; J. H. G. Archer, ed., *Art and Architecture in Victorian Manchester* (Manchester, 1985).

84 *R.I.B.A.J.* 3rd series, i (1894), 23.

85 In O. Shipley, ed., *The Church and the World* (1868), 581. 'I do not for one moment wish to deny the wonderful massiveness, beauty, and strength of the larger Italian works ... but the details of Italian Gothic are worse than useless. For the most part they are executed in marble, which requires just as different a treatment to stone as stone does to brick' – whereas 'modern Italian Gothic' confounds the mouldings of all three (*B.* xxv, 1867, 386).

86 *E.* xxii, N.S. xix (1861), 354; xxiii, N.S. xx (1862), 16. He had previously made much of the adaptability of Italian Gothic (eg. *E.* xvi, N.S. xiii, 1855, 299–305; *B.* xvii, 1859, 146–8, 170–71).

87 J. Mordaunt Crook, *William Burges and the High Victorian Dream* (1981), 175–9.

88 In Shipley, *op.cit.*, 582.

89 *E.* xxiii, N.S. xx (1862), 336–7.

90 See also Street, 'Thirteenth century Architecture: France', R.A. lecture 28 Feb. 1881 (*Memoir*, ed. A. E. Street, 1888, 420–21).

91 Street, *Unpublished Notes and Reprinted Papers*, ed. G. C. King (1916), 317–29.

92 *B.* xxv (1867), 386.

93 *B.* xii (1865), 577, 605.

94 *B.* xix (1861), 403. Burges is here echoing Beresford Hope, *The English Cathedral of the Nineteenth Century* (1861), 45.

95 *R.I.B.A. Trans.* xxxiv (1884), 221.

96 Viollet-le-Duc, *Dictionnaire* ii (1859), 309.

97 Cited in G. German, *The Gothic Revival in Europe and Britain* (1972), 163.

98 Street, *Unpublished Notes, op. cit.,* 172.

99 J. Mordaunt Crook, *Burges, op. cit.,* 195–208.

100 *ibid.*, 238–9.

101 *B.N.* xiv (1867), 337. 'Perhaps a touch of eccentricity, but better that ... than cold imitative mediocrity' (J. Thorne, in *Companion to the Almanac* 1867, 178).

102 *B.N.* xiii (1866), 800.

103 J. Mordaunt Crook, *Burges, op. cit.,* 305–6.

104 Viollet-le-Duc, *Habitations Modernes* (1875–7).

105 J. Mordaunt Crook, 'William Burges and the Dilemma of Style', *A.R.* (1981), 6–15.

106 J. Mordaunt Crook, *Burges, op. cit.,* 246–52. See also B. Whelan, 'What Might Have Been', *Merry England* iii (1884), 144–52: 'it is little less than a national catastrophe' that it remained unbuilt. 'In spite of all the changes of style and fashion ... it remains a marvel and an inspiration even yet' (*B.N.* lxvi, 1894, 72).

107 For accusations of plagiarism, see *B.N.* xvii (1869), 265, 393, 435, 468; *A.* i (1869), 206, 276, 290, 302 and xxv (1881), 369; *B.* xxvii (1869), 840 and xxx (1872), 907.

108 See H. Suzuki, 'Josiah Conder and England', *Kenchikushi Kenyu* xl (1976–79), 1–15.

109 See S. Moore, *C.L.* clxxxv (1984), 1572–4.

110 Richardson's Lululaund, Herts. (1886), seems almost a tribute to Burges. Summerson sees in Richardson's work 'the reflected glamour of [Burges's] dramatised archaeology', plus Syrian influence (through Voguë's books) and Romanesque (through Vaudremer and Labrouste in Paris). See *R.I.B.A.J.* xliv (1936–7), 143. For more Burgesian influence – via Trinity College, Hartford, Connecticut (1872–82) – see M. Schuyler, 'The Work of F. H. Kimball', *Architectural Record* viii (1897), 479–518 and F. R. Kowsky, *The Architecture of Frederick Charles Withers* (Middleton, Conn. 1980).

111 J. Mordaunt Crook, *Burges, op. cit.,* 82–3.

112 Viollet-le-Duc, *Entretiens* i (1863), 450.

113 'In Pointed architecture all is structural' (A. Bartholomew, *Specifications for Practical Architecture*, 1841, preface). Willis's definitive studies of vaulting were available in French from 1843 (*Review Générale de l'Architecture* iv, 1843, *et seq*).

114 e.g. Rondelet, Labrouste, Delorme, Durand, Cordemoy, Frézier. See N. Pevsner, *Ruskin and Viollet-le-Duc* (1969).

115 Viollet-le-Duc, *Entretiens* i, 186–7.

116 *ibid.*, ii, 64.

117 See D. Porphyrios, 'The "End" of Styles', *Oppositions* viii (1977), 119–33.

118 Viollet-le-Duc, *Dictionnaire* iv (1859): s.v. 'construction', translated as *Rational Architecture*; *B.* lxviii (1895), 181.

119 D. Verey, 'Woodchester Park', in H. Colvin and J. Harris, *The Country Seat* (1970), 237–43. Bucknall translated *Histoire d'une Maison* (1874), *Histoire d'une forteresse* (1875), *Histoire de l'habitation humaine* (1876) and *Entretiens sur l'architecture* (1877–81). His St Francis of Assisi, Chester, (1862) collapsed (*The Tablet*

1862, 631; 1863, 797), and he spent the later part of his life abroad.

120 'Simply wonderful' (*G.M.* ccxcv, 1863, 675); 'wonderful monument of human knowledge and human industry' in O. Shipley, ed., *The Church and The World*, 1868, 582).

121 *G.M.* ccxv (1863), 677. 'Luckily very few people could read his French, and therefore it did very little harm. He is very logical, but his premises are wrong' (*A.* x, 1873, 323).

122 B. Foucart *et al.*, *Viollet-le-Duc* (Grand Palais, Paris, 1980), 248–59.

123 'We should say it was very much ... in the shape of a medieval kitchen ... in fact, just as if it had walked out of the pages of M.V.-le-Duc' (*B.N.* xv, 1868, 480); i.e. Viollet-le-Duc, *Dictionnaire* iv (1860), 462. The kitchen had already appeared in A. Lenoir, *Architecture Monastique* ii (1856), 350, pl. 495, of which Burges had a copy. The metal-framed chairs at Cardiff Castle are copied from Viollet-le-Duc, *Mobilier* i (1858), s.v. 'chaise', Basil Champneys and James Brooks were also guilty of 'cribbing': see R. D. Middleton, 'Viollet-le-Duc's Influence on 19th c. England', *Art History* iv (1981), 203–19.

124 *B.* xxxi (1873), 1001: following a paper on Pierrefonds at the R.I.B.A. by Phéné Spiers. Burges's criticisms were supported by Horace Jones and C.F. Hayward. For a powerful defence by B. Bucknall, see *A.* xi (1874), 28–9.

125 Viollet-le-Duc, *Entretiens*, Discourse X, trans. B. Bucknall (1877–81), pt. i, 446 *et seq.*

126 *R.I.B.A.J.* iv (1947–48), 515; 'Viollet-le-Duc and the rational point of view', in *Heavenly Mansions* (1948), 135–58.

127 *A.* x (1873), 323; *Gazette des architectes et du bâtiment* ii (1864), 134–5: ill.

128 See R. Middleton and D. Watkin, *Neo-Classical and Nineteenth-century Architecture* (New York, 1980), 336 *et seq.*

129 'Style is the manifestation of an ideal established on a principle' (Viollet-le-Duc, *Dictionnaire*, viii, 1866, 478).

130 Middleton and Watkin, *op. cit.*, 36: ill. See also P.-M. Auzas, ed., *Actes du Colloque International Viollet-le-Duc, Paris, 1980* (Nouvelles Éditions Latines, Paris, 1982).

131 Quoted in Middleton and Watkin, *op. cit.*, 378. For Ruskin's praise of the *Dictionnaire*, see *Works* XXIII, 465.

132 G. E. Street, *Brick and Marble in the Middle Ages. Notes on a Tour in North Italy* (1874 ed.), 4, 9.

133 *ibid.*, 366. 'I am not by any means a blind enthusiast about Italian architecture'. Italian Gothic 'never produced anything perfect both in detail and mass' (*ibid.*, 381).

134 *ibid.*, 361.

135 *ibid.*, 363, 369, 370–71.

136 Street, 'Thirteenth Century Architecture: Italy': R.A. lecture; reprinted in A. E. Street, *Memoir of G. E. Street* (1888), 397–8. It even embodied alien influences from the East, hence 'the Venetian love of the ogee arch ... a most vitiated perversion' (Street, *Brick and Marble*, *op. cit.*, 367). 'I did not find one finial in Venice which was satisfying' (*ibid.*, 218); 'I have only seen one good Gothic staircase in Venice. This is in the Casa Galdini' (*ibid.*, 223: ill.).

137 *ibid.*, 365.

138 *ibid.*, 368–9.

139 *ibid.*, 380.

140 St. Mark's: 'Very outré ... It is quite vain to describe this in formal architectural terms. The colour is so magnificent that one troubles oneself but little about the architecture ... all architectural lines of moulding are entirely lost, and nothing but a soft swelling and undulating sea of colour is perceived ... yet the mystery of colour does for it even more than the mystery of size does for Köln or Beauvais, Milan, Toledo, or Bourges' (*ibid.*, 153–5).

141 Sta. M. Maggiore: *ibid.*, frontispiece.

142 Cathedral and Palace of the Jurisconsults: *ibid.*, 266, ill. and 269, ill.

143 The Broletto: *ibid.*, 340, ill., 380.

144 'Our buildings are, in nine cases out of ten, cold, colourless, insipid, academical studies ... The puritanical uniformity of our coats and all our garments is but a reflection from the prevailing lack of love of art or colour of any kind. A rich colour is thought vulgar, and that only is refined which is neutral, plain and ugly' (*ibid.*, 400, 406).

145 *ibid.*, 20.

146 Street, 'Thirteenth Century Architecture: Italy', *op. cit.*, 399. See also Street, 'On Colour as Applied to Architecture', *Associated Architectural Societies Reports and Papers* iii (1855), 348–66; 'The Study of Foreign Gothic Architecture, and its Influence on English Art', in O. Shipley, ed., *The Church and the World* (1868), 397–411.

147 [Beresford Hope], *Sat. Rev.* ii (1856), 68–9. Italian Gothic, he quipped, had previously been regarded as oxymoronic, like the poetry of the Stock Exchange.

148 Street, 'True Principles of Architecture and the Possibility of Development', *E.* xiii, N.S. x (1852), 253.

149 D. B. Brownlee, *The Law Courts: the Architecture of G. E. Street* (Camb., Mass., 1984).

150 The style was first hinted at in Street's paper, 'On the Proper Characteristics of a Town Church', *E.* xi, N.S. viii (1850), 227–33, and first adumbrated in his church at Boyne Hill, Maidenhead (1854–56). See N. Jackson, 'The Un-Englishness of G. E. Street's church of St James-the-Less', *Architectural History* xxiii (1980), 86–94. See also Street's scheme for rebuilding Wren's St. Dionis Backchurch, in 'the peculiar style of British pointed which he has made his own' (*E.* xxi, N.S. xviii, 1860, 88–9; S. Humphrey, 'St. Dionis Backchurch: Victorian Proposals', *London Topographical Record* xxiv, 1982, 131–45).

151 'By-and-by, Street's candid mind and clear intellect realized that workaday Italian Gothic was for England a caprice, and he bravely returned to the purity and elasticity of the Edwardian [Gothic] style, only retaining ... the greater variety of materials in marble and brick and mosaic which modern commerce and processes had made available' (Beresford Hope, obituary of Street, *R.I.B.A. Trans.* 1883–84, 199–203).

152 N. Pevsner, *London* i (1973 ed.), 321.

153 H.-R. Hitchcock, *Architecture: 19th and 20th centuries* (1963 ed.), 186.

154 See C. L. V. Meeks, 'Churches by Street on the Via Nazionale and the Via del Barberino', *Art Quarterly* xvi (1953), 213–28; R. Dorment, 'Burne-Jones's Roman Mosaics', *Burl. Mag.* cxx (1978), 73–82; H. A.

Millon, 'G. E. Street and the Church of St Paul's in Rome', in H. Searing, ed., *In Search of Modern Architecture: a tribute to H.-R. Hitchcock* (New York, 1982), 85–101.

155 According to Ruskin, colour in nature never followed form: 'The stripes of a zebra do not follow the lines of its body or limbs, still less the spots of a leopard. I hold this, then, for the first great principle of architectural colour; let it be visibly independent of form') (*Works* VIII, 177: *Seven Lamps*, iv). Street, however, believed that marble veneering was 'rather likely to be destructive of good architecture because it was sure to end in an entire concealment of the real construction of the work' (Street, *Brick and Marble, op. cit.*, 400).

156 Because of its synthesis of 'Roman, Lombard, and Arab' (Ruskin, *Works* IX, 38: *Stones of Venice* i).

157 N. Smith, 'Imitation and Invention in Two Albert Memorials', *Burl. Mag.* cxxiii (1981), 232–3, also suggests Arnolfo di Cambio's Ciborium at S. Paolo fuori le Mura, Rome. For comments by Kenneth Clark, see *C.L.* lxiv (1928), 520, 598, 633. 'Italian Gothic as such, must not be used in England, but ... the study of it is necessary to the perfecting of our revival ... I never fell into the Italian mania' (Scott, *Personal and Professional Recollections*, 1879, 157–63, 204, 373).

158 Scott, *Lectures on Medieval Architecture* ii (1879), 318.

159 'A style which I may call my own invention ... It is simply a thirteenth or fourteenth century, secular style with the addition of certain Scottish features, peculiar to that country in the sixteenth century, though in reality derived from the French style of the thirteenth and fourteenth centuries' (Scott, *Recollections, op. cit.*, 272). See also *B.* xxvii (1869), 257.

160 'Modified Venetian Gothic' (Eastlake, *Gothic Revival*, ed. J. Mordaunt Crook, Leicester, 1978, appendix no. 156). See also M. Girouard, *C.L.* cxli (1967), 1230–33, 1302–5.

161 *B.* xvii (1859), 118.

162 *B.N.* xiii (1867), 461 and x (1864), 117.

163 Scott to Palmerston, 23 July 1859: Broadlands MSS. GC.SC/18/1–6. *Ex inf.* Dr. I. Toplis.

164 Scott, *Secular and Domestic, op. cit.*, 205.

165 Scott, *Recollections, op. cit.*, 178. Scott's premiated design (no. 116A) is ill. in *B.N.* iii (1857), 855, along with his explanation. For Street's defeated design, see *I.L.N.* 24 Oct. 1857, 142; ill. For Woodward's, see *B.N.* iii (1857), 501; *I.L.N.* xxxi (1857), 348: ill.; *B.* xv (1857), 270–71, 563: ill.

166 Scott had experimented with 'a sort of Basilican style' at St. Michael, Cornhill, London, and at Lord Hill's chapel, Hawkstone, Shropshire. When Palmerston rejected Gothic, Scott 'conceived the idea of generating what would be strictly an Italian style out of ... the Byzantine of the early Venetian palaces, and ... the earliest renaissance of Venice ... Byzantine, in fact, toned into a more modern and usable form'. Palmerston called it a 'regular mongrel affair', and insisted on 'ordinary Italian' (Scott, *Recollections, op. cit.*, 192–9). For a full account of the Foreign Office controversy, see D. Brownlee, 'That "regular mongrel affair", G. G. Scott's, design for the government offices', *Architectural History* xxviii (1985), 159–82.

167 Scott, *Recollections, op. cit.*, 271. 'This is not copybook stuff, it is improvisation on to the drawing board. To fail to appreciate this is to fail hopelessly to understand Victorian architecture' (J. Summerson, *Victorian Architecture: Four Studies in Evaluation*, 1970, 42). Girouard justly calls St Pancras 'a masterpiece in spite of its absurdities' (*C.L.* cxli 1967, 1233). For contemporary criticisms, see *B.N.* xxi (1871), 96–7; xxvi (1874), 437. See also J. Simmons, *St. Pancras Station* (1968).

168 H.-R. Hitchcock, 'Ruskin and American Architecture', in J. Summerson, ed., *Concerning Architecture* (1967), 166–208. Basil Ransome 'had heard of the great memorial Hall ... the ornate, overtopping structure, which was the finest piece of architecture he had ever seen. He thought there was rather too much brick about it, but it was buttressed, cloistered, turreted, dedicated, superscribed, as he had never seen anything; though it didn't look old, it looked significant' (Henry James, *The Bostonians*, Penguin ed., 209).

169 Quoted by D. H. Dickenson, *The Daring Young Men* (Bloomington, Indiana, 1953), 117.

170 *B.* xxxii (1874), 437, 439; ills.

171 *A.R.* lxix (1931), 1. See also G. Stamp, 'Victorian Bombay', *A.A.R.P.* (1977), 22–7 and 'British Architecture in India', *R.S.A Jnl.* cxxix (1980–81), 357–79.

172 'The architecture we endeavoured to introduce is inconsistent alike with the reckless luxury, the deforming mechanism, and the squalid misery of modern cities; among the formative fashions of the day, aided, especially in England, by ecclesiastical sentiment, it indeed attained notoriety; and sometimes behind an engine furnace, or a railroad bank, you may detect the pathetic discord of its momentary grace, and, with toil, decipher its floral carvings choked with soot. I felt answerable to the schools I loved only for their injury' (*Works* XVIII, 150: *Sesame and Lilies*, iii).

173 'I am proud enough to hope ... that I have had some direct influence on Mr. Street. But I have had indirect influence on nearly every cheap villa builder between [Denmark Hill] and Bromley; and there is scarcely a public house near the Crystal Palace but sells its gin and bitters under pseudo-Venetian capitals copied from the Church of the Madonna of Health or of Miracles. And one of my principal notions for leaving my present house [and fleeing to Brantwood] is that it is surrounded everywhere by the accursed Frankenstein monsters of, indirectly, my own making ... For Venetian architecture developed out of British moral consciousness I decline to be responsible' (Ruskin, *Works* X, 458–9: 16 March 1872). This statement was made in reply to a review in the *Pall Mall Gazette* by Coventry Patmore. Patmore had suggested that Ruskin's direct influence was bad: 'a preference for Venetian over English Gothic ... the underrating of expressional character in architecture, and the overrating of sculptural ornament, especially of a naturalistic and imitative character, and ... an exclusiveness which limited the due influence of some ... noble styles of architecture'. He thought Ruskin's indirect influence – what Graham Hough called the Ruskinian 'revolution in sensibility' – was, however, beneficial (G. Hough, *The Listener*, 30 May 1963, 921). In the preface to the third edition of *Seven Lamps* (1874) Ruskin wrote: 'I would rather ... that no architects had ever condescended to adopt one of the views suggested in this book, than that any should have made the partial use of it which has mottled our manufactory chimneys with black and red brick, dignified our banks and drapers shops with Venetian

tracery, and pinched our parish churches into dark and slippery arrangements for the advertisement of cheap coloured glass and pantiles.' In particular he cited a public house in Ealing: 'the modern brickwork would have been in no discord with the tomb of the Can Grande, had it been set beside it in Verona. But this good and true piece of brickwork was the porch of a public house, and its total motive was the provocation of thirst, and the encouragement of idleness' (*Works* X, 11–12).

174 *B.* xviii (1860), 821: ill.

175 *Art Jnl.* 1862, 57–9, reviewing R. Rawlinson, C.E., *Designs for Factory, Furnace and Other Tall Chimneys* (1862): fig. 4 is modelled on a campanile at Verona. See also *B.* xv (1857), 281: ill. Rawlinson built chimneys at Great Birkenhead Docks and at West Ham, London.

176 Ruskin, *Works* XII, 78: *Architecture and Painting*, ii.

177 *B.* xxix (1871), 426–7; A. Gomme, M. Jenner and B. Little, *Bristol: An Architectural History* (1979); C. Crick, *Victorian Buildings in Bristol* (1975).

178 *The Listener* xi (1948), 857–8.

179 Also another block by Clegg and Knowles, 101 Portland St. (1870), on the corner of Princess St. (*B.* xxviii, 1870, 849: ill.).

180 Like 'a Victorian Gothic river steam-boat' (Hitchcock, A.R. c, 1949, 61 *et seq.*).

181 *ibid.*; N. Taylor, *Monuments of Commerce* (1968), 50–55. As late as 1901 Aitchison exhibited a view of this building – perhaps the perspective by D. Varry, 1864 (*B.N.* xi, 1864, 134: ill.; R.I.B.A.). It was described as in the 'semi-circular style ... associated with ... Deane and Woodward' (*B.N.* lxxx, 1901, 583).

182 P. Collins, *Changing Ideals in Modern Architecture, 1750–1950* (1965), 115. A link between the curtain wall, the wall-veil and Semper's theory of the priority of textile art has also been suggested (J. Rykwert, *The Necessity of Artifice*, 1982, 130).

183 Kerr, 'The Battle of the Styles', *B.* xviii (1860), 293–4: by 1860, 'Latitudinarianism had served its purpose ... copyism was almost extinct and precedent a dead letter'. See M. M. Ohman, 'Latitudinarianism: an Architectural Theory and its Application in English and American Architecture, from 1840 to 1895' (Ph.D. Missouri, Columbia, 1973).

4 The Architect's Dilemma

1 J. A. Froude, 1864: 'We live in times of disintegration' (W. H. Dunn, *James Anthony Froude* i, 1961, 72). Frederick Harrison, 1869: 'There is abroad a strange consciousness of doubt, instability and incoherence' (O. Chadwick, *The Secularisation of the European Mind*, 1975, 125). Cardinal Manning, 1871: 'Faith is gone, morals are going ... The end of this must be anarchy or despotism' (*ibid.*). John Morley, 1874: Our age 'is characteristically and cardinally an epoch of transition in the very foundations of belief and conduct' (*ibid.*). For doubts by Macaulay, Froude and Huxley, see W. E. Houghton, *The Victorian Frame of Mind* (New Haven, Conn., 1957).

2 'We are passing through a period of disintegration and differentiation', and 'art cannot escape'. 'The whole force of our economic system is against spontaneous art'. Hence the 'revolving kaleidoscope of dead styles' (Walter Crane, 'The Architecture of Art', *B.N.* lii, 1887, 267–70).

3 The subtitle to James Malton's *Essay on British Cottage Architecture* (1795) tried to solve this particular conundrum by explaining it as 'an attempt to perpetuate in Principle, that peculiar mode of Building which was originally the effect of Chance'.

4 G. G. Scott, *Secular and Domestic Architecture, present and future* (1858), 263.

5 E. Beckett, *A Book on Building* (1880 ed.), 61.

6 Viollet-le-Duc, *Entretiens sur l'architecture* i (1863), 179; trans. B. Bucknall, i (1877), 177.

7 'That ... single word "style" lies at the root of the evil ... Architecture at present is in no condition at all. The conflict of styles proves that, strictly speaking, Europe has no architecture. This is probably the first time in the history of art that it has come to a period of universal confusion. It is at the present moment governed by no laws. Formerly it had fixed principles ... Architecture was like a language – it went through successive developments ... But now it has no laws ... The whole profession is founded upon nothing ... It cannot be that Greek art is ... right for certain things, and right in its way, and that Pointed art is suited for certain purposes, and right in its way. This, which affects to be Liberalism is, to use the nomenclature of another subject, Indifferentism. It is the recourse of intellectual idleness and critical incapacity ... There must be an exclusive [mode] in the architecture of every period of society or civilisation. [Architecture was once the inevitable way of building] it fulfilled the order of nature ....' (*Sat. Rev.* viii, 1859, 609–10).

8 'This notion of a new style, a style analogous to those of the past but different in constructive principle and in ornamental expression, pervades the entire architectural history of the century' (J. Summerson, '1851 – a New Age, a New Style', in H. Grisewood, ed., *Ideas and Beliefs of the Victorians*, 1949, 64). For the origins of this rejection of the past – 'gnosiological idealism' – in the writings of Konrad Fiedler, see P. Junod, *Transparence et Opacité* (Lausanne, 1976). See Fiedler's *On the Nature and History of Architecture* (1878), trans. C. Reading (Lexington, Kentucky, c.1950) and *On Judging Works of Visual Art* (1876), ed. H. Schaefer-Simmern (Berkeley, 1949).

9 Lindsay, *Sketches of the History of Christian Art* (1847), i: cclvii; ii, 29–30n. For discussions of this important work, see J. Steegman, 'Lord Lindsay's History of Christian Art', *Jnl. Warburg and Courtauld Institutes* x (1947), 123–31; H. Brigstock, 'Lord Lindsay and the "Sketches of the History of Christian Art"', *Bull. John Rylands Library* lxiv (1981), 27–60.

10 Lindsay, *Progress by Antagonism* (1864). The idea was taken up again in 1865 by J. S. Aitkin of Manchester, who predicted the inevitability of a New British Style based on synthesis – the dialectical offspring of thesis and antithesis – the synthesis of Gothic and Classic (*B.* xxiii, 1865, 378–9).

11 *B.* ix (1851), 223.

12 *B.* xi (1861), 430.

13 Donaldson, 'On a New Style in Architecture', 'The Education of the Architect', *B.* v (1847), 492. A theme echoed in R.I.B.A. prize essays, 1842–3 (*C.E.A.J.*, x, 1843, 255–6).

14 *Land and Building News* ii (1856), 57.

15 Ruskin, *Works* XII, 173: review of Lindsay's *Christian Art*.

16 *Works* XIII, 23: 'The Study of Architecture in Our Schools'.

17 J. Mordaunt Crook, 'William Burges and the Dilemma of Style', *A.R.* clxx (1981), 6–15.

18 Scott, *Secular and Domestic Architecture, op. cit.*, 192; *B.* viii (1850), 197.

19 *B.* xi (1853), 193–4.

20 Donaldson, *Preliminary Discourse* (1842), 28–30. For Donaldson and his successors at University College London, and their contemporaries at King's College, London, see J. Mordaunt Crook, 'Architecture and History', *Architectural History* xxvii (1984), 555–78.

21 RA lectures, 1860 onwards, summarised in J. Mordaunt Crook, 'Sydney Smirke: the architecture of compromise', in *Seven Victorian Architects*, ed. J. Fawcett and N. Pevsner (1976), 64–5.

22 *B.* lxi (1891), 138.

23 *B.* lxxii (1897),369: RIBA; *B.* lxxiv (1898), 147–9: R.A.

24 *B.* lxxvi (1899), 84: RIBA.

25 *B.* lxx (1896), 252: RIBA.

26 *B.* lxviii (1895), 81: RA.

27 *R.I.B.A. Sess. Papers* 1864, 97–107.

28 *B.* lxxii (1897), 114–5: RA.

29 *B.* l (1886), 334, 351: RA.

30 *B.* lxxiv (1898), 252: RA.

31 *B.* lxxiv (1898), 149, 614: photo.

32 The scene of their encounter is now the Birds Eggs Store.

33 G. H. Guillaume, *B.N.* xi (1864), 871. Scott called these the 'retrospective' and the 'prospective' elements (Scott, *Secular and Domestic Architecture, op. cit.*, 272).

34 For Brunel, see L. T. C. Rolt, *Isambard Kingdom Brunel* (1957) and A. Pugsley, ed., *The Works of I. K. Brunel: An Engineering Appreciation* (New York,1976).

35 *Qtly. Rev.* cxiv (1863), 289–331: review of Samuel Smiles, *Lives of British Engineers*, 3 vols. (1862).

36 'The Victorians believed in fairies, and found them in the engineers' (H. S. Goodhart-Rendel, *English Architecture Since the Regency*, 1953, 103).

37 Fergusson, *History of the Modern Styles of Architecture* (1862), 25, 55. This develops in specific terms the theoretical framework of his *Historical Inquiry into the True Principles of Beauty in Art more especially with Reference to Architecture* (1849).

38 Fergusson, *Modern Styles, op. cit.*, 129. The historic 'styles are so essentially different, both in principle and detail, that if one is right, the rest must be wrong – if, indeed, all are not so; [yet] we find the same architect forced . . . to build . . . in all the styles, thus contradicting himself every hour'. Indeed architects are 'like men fishing for stars whose reflection they see in the stagnant waters of a former world' (Fergusson, *True Principles of Beauty, op. cit.*, 145, 154).

39 *Macmillan's Mag.* xxv (1871–2), 250–56.

40 J. Mordaunt Crook, 'The Pre-Victorian Architect: Professionalism and Patronage', *Architectural History*, xii (1969), 62–78.

41 *Qtly Rev.* cxiv (1863), 289–331.

42 J. M. Binnie, *Early Victorian Water Engineers* (1981), 134. Hawkesley also designed the Mannerist Vyrnwy dam tunnel (1884).

43 *B.* lxxi (1896), 312: ill. Barry described his build-

ing as follows: 'The architectural façade is simply treated in the Italian Renaissance manner, and it is intended to convey the notion of strength and solidity, characteristic of the civil engineer and his work' (*B.* lxvii, 1895, 470). For the growth and status of the engineering profession see J. Ahlstrom, *Engineers and Industrial Growth* (1982).

44 'How characteristic of the sentiments of the time was this flight from the workshop to fairyland' (Goodhart-Rendel, *op. cit.*, 170). See M. J. Wiener, *English Culture and the Decline of the Industrial Spirit, 1850–1980* (Cambridge, 1981).

45 For Brunel's house, see C. Brunel Noble, *The Brunels* (1938), 187.

46 *Qtly. Rev.* cxiv (1863), 289–331.

47 J. Fergusson, *Illustrated Handbook of Architecture* (1855), 55.

48 Fergusson's advice was rejected by the Office of Works over Street's Gothic Law Courts, but accepted over James Williams's classical G.P.O. in St. Martin's-le-Grand (W. H. White, *Architecture and Public Building: their Relation to School, Academy and State in London and Paris*, 1884, 182).

49 'There are distinct signs of progress everywhere . . . People are no longer content with churches or dwelling houses of plain walls, pierced with holes, but ornamental art is demanded everywhere. They want men to think, men to appreciate, and men to demand, and when that combination takes place progress is inevitable. With progress we shall very soon be independent of Gothic, Greek, or any other style of art . . . the next ten years will witness such progress in architecture as will make it worthy of the nation and of the world' (RIBA Papers, 1866–67, 13–14: *oratio recta*).

50 *Architectural Mag.* iv (1837), 277–87.

51 *C.L.* clxvi (1979), 2374–7, 2454–7.

52 Pugin to Shrewsbury, Oct. 1844 (Phoebe Stanton, 'Welby Pugin and the Gothic Revival', Ph.D., London, 1950, 348.

53 A. Barry, *The Architect of the New Palace at Westminster* (1868), 54: 1 Aug. 1845; F. Eisenlohr, *Ausgeführte oder zur Ausführung bestimmte Entwürfe* (Karlsruhe [1852–9]; G. German, *The Gothic Revival in Europe and Britain* (1972), 10, 149, pl. 84. These stations were also admired by Reichensperger and Lassus (*A.A.* ix, 1849, 349; xiii, 1853, 259).

54 B. Ferrey, *Pugin*, 258.

55 Pugin to Hardman, 1851 (Stanton, Ph.D., *op. cit.*, 464–5). 'in terms of art and taste it is utterly ridiculous, but it is imaginative and there is something . . . great and . . . simple about the execution . . . With every step you take in this building you sense the immense power of the English. It is a toy which cost 25 millions, and a toy in which several cathedrals could do a waltz' (Prosper Merrimée, 1850: P. Leon, *Merrimée*, Paris, 1962, 318). Morris thought it 'wonderfully ugly' (Morris, *Works* xxii, 429).

56 Hitchcock, 'Early Victorian Architecture, 1837–51', *R.I.B.A.J.* xliv (1936–37), 992.

57 *Marble Halls*, ed. M. Darby and J. Physick (V and A, 1973), no. 116; M. D. Wyatt and J. B. Waring, *A Handbook for the Medieval Courts* (1854); M. D. Wyatt, *Views of the Crystal Palace and Park, Sydenham* (1854); Drawings: V. and A., P. and D., Box 85. For Fergusson's Nineveh Court, see *B.N.* l (1886), 115.

58 *Building Chronicle* i (1854), 29, 31, 80, 184. For

an enthusiastic and optimistic view, see W. B. Adams, 'Industrial Exhibition', *Westminster Rev.* iv (1851), 346–74.

59 Quoted by P. Thompson, *The Listener* 7 July 1966, 15.

60 *B.* viii (1850), 153–4, 566–7 and xxi (1863), 200–201. See also N. Pevsner, *Some Architectural Writers of the Nineteenth Century* (1972), 192 and A. T. Bolton in *A.A. Jnl.* xxvii (1912), 63

61 *B.* viii (1850), 219.

62 *B.* xv (1857), 570.

63 Ruskin, *Works* IX, 455–6: Stones of Venice, i. Garbett agreed with Ruskin that marble veneering was not a sham: it no more makes 'a wall look like solid marble than a suit of armour makes a man look solid iron' (*B.* xi, 1853, 51).

64 For some of his later eccentricities, see *B.N.* lxi (1891), 8 and *B.N.* lxiv (1893), 786. He claimed to have invented colour photography (*B.* xi, 1853, 682). For Garbett on Salisbury Cathedral, see *B.* xxvi (1868), 473–4 and *B.* lxxiii (1897), 113.

65 *E.* xii, N.S. ix (1851), 269 *et seq.*

66 *B.* ix (1851), 85–6.

67 Ruskin, *Works* VIII, 66n.: *Seven Lamps*, ii.

68 *ibid.*, 66.

69 'Answer to Mr Garbett', *Works*, IX, 455–6. For Ruskin on the Crystal Palace, see also G. Wihl, *Ruskin and the Rhetoric of Infallibility* (New Haven, 1985), 168–82.

70 Pugin, 'Why This Waste?', *Merry England* vii (1886), 91–103. 'We approve highly of cast iron for constructive purposes while we denounce it as the meagre substitute for masons' skill' (Pugin, *Apology* 40–41). Cast iron lacks 'that play of light and shade consequent on bold relief'; it is 'a source of continual repetition subversive of the variety and imagination exhibited in pointed design' (Pugin, *True Principles* 26–7).

71 Ruskin, *Works*, VIII, 156–7: *Seven Lamps*, iv.

72 Fergusson, 'The Effect on Architecture of the Building for the Great Exhibition', *B.* ix (1851), 52–3.

73 Fergusson, *Illustrated Handbook of Architecture* (1855), intro.

74 C. Hussey, *Lutyens* (1953), 194.

75 The architect's object 'is to arrange the material of the engineer not so much with regard to economical as to artistic effects, and by light and shade, and outline, to produce a form that in itself shall be permanently beautiful' (Fergusson, *Illustrated Handbook of Architecture*, i, 1855, xxviii–ix). 'A brewer's dray and a gentleman's carriage bear the same relation to each other that the brewery does to the ornamental villa' (Fergusson, *True Principles of Beauty in Art*, 1849, 105).

76 Fergusson, *True Principles of Beauty in Art* (1849), 149.

77 Fergusson, *Handbook, op. cit.*, i (1855), xxxvi.

78 Fergusson, *History of the Modern Styles of Architecture* (1862), 491.

79 *ibid.*, 476, 478, 480, 483. He thought the Crystal Palace lacked 'sufficient decoration' to make it artistic, and sufficient 'solidity … to make it really architectural'. Here, however, was a potential new style: the problem lay in the 'immense amount of thought' involved in working it out (*B.* xxi, 1863, 161–4). Sydney Smirke took a similar line: 'The mere dry, unimpassioned beauty resulting from the quality of fitness, however it may satisfy the engineer, will hardly suffice

to meet the aspirations of the architect [for] as artists … we require something more' (Sydney Smirke, R.A. lectures, 1860 onwards, quoted in J. Mordaunt Crook, 'Sydney Smirke: the architecture of compromise', in *Seven Victorian Architects*, ed. J. Fawcett and N. Pevsner, 1976, 64–5).

80 Fergusson, *Handbook, op. cit.* i (1855), lvii.

81 O. Herderer, *Klenze* (Munich, 1964), 379.

82 Viollet-le-Duc, *Dictionnaire* viii (1866), 494.

83 R. Middleton and D. Watkin, *Neo-Classical and 19th century Architecture* (New York, 1980), 370.

84 C. H. Driver, *B.N.* xxxvi (1879), 141. 'Architecture attempts things higher than keeping out the wet … Engineering is an essential *part* of architecture … Architecture includes … engineering … as much as grammar includes … orthography'. To involve architects in such matters would be a maldistribution of labour – like forcing 'professors … to teach schoolboys'. Architecture and engineering will both progress, but separately: 'Growth perfects a sheep; growth perfects a goat; but no process converts a sheep into a goat' (E. L. Garbett, *B.* ix, 1851, 35–6).

85 'The Engineer and the Architect', *B.N.* lxx (1896), 363–4.

86 *A.* xxxvii (1882), 367.

87 'Church restoration the seductions of antiquity – have robbed our rising generation of architects of what should have been their inalienable property in art, and another fast-rising profession have appropriated it. We mean the use of iron, artificial stone, new modes of construction, and the thousand appliances and inventions science has thrown in our way' (G. H. Guillaume, in *B.N.* xxvi, 1874, 412; xxvii, 1874, 45).

88 *Marble Halls, op. cit.*, no. 55: ill.

89 *ibid.*, no. 136: exhibited in London and Paris, 1859, 1862, 1867.

90 'A vital Art movement [is] rapidly developing … it will presently enable Art to burst into the full vigour of a new life … The musty rules of dead Architecture … are rapidly becoming disowned, and these shackles and fetters of the imagination will soon be struck off … Why should architects be the only men to stand still … Giants in science, we are pigmies in art … [But] it is much easier to perceive the inconsistencies of modern practice than to point a way to remedy them' (*B.* xx, 1862, 537–8, 633, 701). He is a sanguine man is Mr. Reade; his suggestions might well 'produce an edifice novel in appearance, yet it would not be … a "new style" …' (*Art Jnl.* 1861, 242).

91 *B.* lxxi (1896), 10: ill.; *B.N.* lxx (1896), 76, 93: ills.

92 For Pickett's *Metallurgic Architecture* (1844), see P. Collins, *A.R.* cxxx (1961), 267. Pickett set up the Iron Architectural and Engineering Co., with a capital of £500,000, to develop his inventions (*B.* xxii, 1864, 373).

93 W. B. Adams, 'Architecture: Adaptation of Iron', *Westminster Rev.* li (1849), 104–45.

94 RIBA MSS, Council Minutes: 12 Jan. 1846.

95 *E.* xiii, NS ix (1852), 248.

96 See G. German, *The Gothic Revival in Europe and Britain* (1972), 116, 148. 'C'est de l'architecture antediluvienne, plus monstreuse et plus bossue que les mastodantes les plus rebarbatifs' (*A.A.* xii, 1853, 229). For Boileau's iron-ribbed church of Notre Dame de

France, Leicester Place, Soho (1865–68; dem.), see *Survey of London* xxxiv (1966), 484, pl. 22a. For examples of his designs, see R. Middleton and D. Watkin, *Neo-Classical and Nineteenth Century Architecture* (New York, 1980), 366–71.

97 Brunel asked M. D. Wyatt for assistance: 'Are you willing to enter upon the work *professionally* in the subordinate capacity ... as my *assistant* for the ornamental details?' (C. Harvie, G. Martin and A. Scharf, *Industrialisation and Culture, 1830–1914,* 1970, 257: 31 Jan. 1851).

98 *Companion to the Almanac* 1855, 235.

99 Scott, *Secular and Domestic Architecture, op. cit.,* 109–11.

100 *C.E.A.J.* 1866, pl. 38; S. Muthesius, 'The Iron Problem in the 1850s', *Architectural History* xiii (1970), 58–63.

101 [H. Heathcote Statham], *B.* lxvii (1894), 91–2.

102 For Semper, see J. Rykwert, 'Semper and the Conception of Style', in *The Necessity of Artifice* (1982), 122–30; M. Podro, *The Critical Historians of Art* (1982), 46 *et seq.*; and W. Herrmann, *Gottfried Semper: in search of architecture* (Camb., Mass., 1985).

103 Fergusson himself went some way towards bridging this gap with his intermediate designation of 'Technic Aesthetic' (Fergusson, *Historical Inquiry into the True Principles of Beauty in Art,* 1849, 104–6). But he later abandoned this (Fergusson, *History of Modern Styles,* 1862, 25).

104 *B.N.* liv (1888), 171; *B.* xlvii (1884), 821.

105 'The End of Iron Architecture', *B.N.* lxix (1895), 729–30.

106 Dr Acland, *E.* xvi, NS xiii (1855), 249. For Skidmore's theories, see *E.* xv (1854), 124 and xvii (1856), 221–2, 333–8.

107 *B.N.* vi (1859), 338.

108 *E.* xxii, NS xix (1861) 25–6. Munby visited the museum with Acland in 1860: 'We all agreed that the least successful part is the ironwork, elegant as it is: the shafts and arches have nothing for roof but glass, which gives no background and seems to need no support' (D. Hudson, *Munby: Man of Two Worlds,* 1972, 65).

109 S. Muthesius, 'The Iron Problem in the 1850s', *Architectural History* xiii (1970), 58–63. [Benjamin Webb] thought it confused 'the distinction between building and engineering'; its architects should have been 'satisfied with the proper subordinate development of the capabilities of [iron] in construction (*Bentley's Qtly Rev.* i, 1859, 143–82).

110 *Instrumenta Ecclesiastica* ii (1856), pls. 19–26.

111 *E.* xvii, NS xiv (1856), 280–81, 338.

112 Ruskin, *Works* VIII, 27: *Seven Lamps* ch. i: aphorism 4.

113 Hope, *The English Cathedral of the Nineteenth Century* (1861), 6–7.

114 Quoted in German, *Gothic Revival, op.cit.,* 164.

115 H. Heathcote Statham regarded the Forth Bridge as 'admirable', but Tower Bridge as 'one of the most objectionable structures ... in London' (*B.* lxxiv, 1898, 255: AA). For details of the Forth Bridge, see *Engineering* 28 Feb. 1890.

116 In 1878 Jones proposed an arched span bascule bridge (*Marble Halls, op. cit.,* no. 121, p. 175: ill.); Wolfe Barry preferred an additional, higher span, allowing pedestrian access and wider opening. Jones died in 1887, so the Gothic detail may well be by Wolfe Barry. The style stemmed initially from Government conditions. See also T. Crosby, *The Necessary Monument,* 1970.

117 H. Heathcote Statham, *Modern Architecture* (1897), 172–3; ill., frontispiece.

118 Aitchison, 'Iron as a Building Material', *RIBA Sess. Papers* (1864), 97–107; *B.* lxii (1892), 456 and lxxvi (1899), 84. He forced his RA students to design lamp-posts (*B.* li, 1886, 929).

119 O. Jones, 'On the Influence of Religion on Art' (Architectural Soc., 1835; reprinted 1863). See M. Darby, 'Owen Jones and the Eastern Ideal' (Ph.D., Reading, 1974).

120 M. Darby and D. Van Zanten, 'Owen Jones' Iron and Glass Buildings of the 1850s', *Architectura* 1974, i, 53–75.

121 *R.I.B.A. Papers* 1863–64, xxiv–v; in response to J. P. Seddon's lamentation on 'this age of eclecticism'.

122 *Marble Halls, op. cit.,* no. 126: ill.; *B.* xxiv (1866), 318; F. D. Klingender, *Art and the Industrial Revolution,* ed. A. Elton (1968), 104: ill.

123 *A.* xix (1878), 57, 215.

124 'The End of Iron Architecture', *B.N.* lxix (1895), 729–80: 'Iron construction is more and more in vogue; but iron architecture, till science shows us how to modify the nature of iron, is given up as hopeless'.

125 *B.N.* xxxviii (1880), 624–5. Still *in situ* in an alley between Chancery Lane and the Law Courts (J. M. Robinson, *The Wyatts,* 1980, pl.126). 'Though not an ill-tempered man', noted Morris, Street 'dearly loves a row' (W. Morris, *Collected Letters,* ed. N. Kelvin, i, Princeton, 1984, 588).

126 Street, *An Urgent Plea for the Revival of True Principles of Architecture in the Public Buildings of the University of Oxford* (1853), 4–5; *B.* xi (1853), 403–4.

127 Street, quoted in C. Stewart, *The Stones of Manchester* (1956), 90.

128 *B.* xxxviii (1860), 661.

129 *E.* xiii, NS x (1852), 247–62 and xiv, NS xi (1853), 70–77.

130 Street, *Brick and Marble, op. cit.,* 406.

131 For Lord Crawford, in the 'Italico-Lombard style' (Iona S. Lindsay, 'Dunecht House', MA Edin., 1980, 26).

132 Discussion following J. A. Picton, 'Iron and Mild Steel as Building Materials', *RIBA Trans.* (1879–80), 149–61; *B.N.* xxxviii (1880), 624–5; *A.* xxiii (1880), 370. For cast iron façades in New York, see *B.N.* xvi (1869), 458, 463: ills.; C. Singer, ed. *A History of Technology* v (Oxford, 1958), 471: ill.

133 White, 'Ironwork: its Legitimate Uses and Proper Treatment', *RIBA Trans.* (1865–6), 15–30.

134 *B.N.* xxxviii (1880), 624–5. 'If ever architecture should become iron, it would cease to be architecture' (*B.* lxii, 1892, 456).

135 *RIBA Trans.* (1865–6), 15–30. Similarly H. Heathcote Statham: 'The idea that iron is to revolutionise modern architecture I hold ... to be a complete fallacy, based on bad reasoning and on a confusion between engineering and architecture. Architecture will remain the art of producing beautiful and expressive structures, and not economic or merely utilitarian ones; and whenever it relinquishes that aim, it will cease to be architecture ... and there will be an end to it as an art' (Statham, *Modern Architecture,* 1897, 275).

288

136 Hope, *The Common Sense of Art* (1858), 11.

137 *Times Literary Supplement* 27 Feb. 1976, 211.

138 Quoted in P. Thompson, *Butterfield* (1971), 97, re St. John, Clevedon. 'One thing we can be sure of – our character is as completely stamped, and will be as clearly read by posterity, in our buildings, as we now read the refinement of Greece in her ruined temples' (A. Christie, *B.* xi, 1853, 733).

139 R. Kerr, *The Gentleman's House* (1864), ed. J. Mordaunt Crook (1972), 342. To dub nineteenth century architecture 'Victorian' was not only 'preposterous in its prematurity' but indicated 'a tendency to finality' which was 'fatal to all originality and improvement' (*B.* xxii, 1864, 66).

140 Architectural Exhibition catalogue, 1850.

141 W. Pater, *Appreciations* (1922 ed.), 261.

142 Brunt, 'Cast Iron in Decorative Architecture', *The Crayon* xi (1859), 15–20. 'For the last fifty years we [have] had dishes in all styles.... Such inconsistency and ... incoherence were never witnessed before. [Were] it not a great sign of the times, we would think that the architects were mad. But architecture has [always] been the faithful picture of every stage of civilisation, and ... the nineteenth century is [an age of] transition....' When the 'new style' comes, it will be 'international.... A style of architecture is, and always has been, a collective production' (G. A. Heller, 'Thoughts of a Mechanic about a New Style', *B.* xx, 1862, 590–91).

143 Brunt, 'On the Present Condition and Prospect of Architecture', *Atlantic Monthly* lviii (1886), 379–84.

144 'Future historians of architectural progress will probably distinguish the present as the Competition era' (*B.N.* lxiv, 1893, 429). See G. Morgan, 'On Public Competitions for Architectural Designs', *RIBA Trans.* viii (1858), 156 and T. Porter, 'Architectural Competitions', *ibid.*, xxx (1880), 65–108; J. Bassin, 'The Competition System: Architectural Competitions in Nineteenth Century England' (Ph.D., Indiana, 1975); R. H. Harper, *Victorian Architectural Competitions: an index to British and Irish Architectural Competitions in The Builder, 1843–1900* (1983).

145 J. Fergusson, *History of the Modern Styles of Architecture* (1862), 488–90; *B.* xxi (1863), 161–4.

146 For a swingeing attack, see R. Kerr in *RIBA Trans.* xxxiv (1884).

147 *B.* l (1886), 113.

148 'It does not require a man or set of men ... to invent a new style.... What we require is that architects have the moral courage to refrain from borrowing, and be content to think, to work, and to improve bit by bit what they have got.... The demand, however, must arise from the public, and cannot come from the profession' (Fergusson, *Modern Styles, op. cit.*, 488–90).

149 ills.: *B.N.* xxxix (1880), 64, 588; xli (1881), 72.

150 'The eclecticism of the present is barren and fruitless'; re-birth will come only 'as part of a change as wide and deep as that which destroyed feudalism ... the greater part of what we call architecture is but an imitation of an imitation of an imitation' (Morris, *Gothic Architecture*, 1893, 59, 65).

151 *A.* xxiii (1880), 397–8. Similarly *B.* xxxviii (1880), 554.

152 'Nothing's more striking ... than the absence of true creative power ... we have produced no national style, nor do we seem likely at present to do so.... But for the present we may well console ourselves for the deadness of the creative power in the vigour of the critical faculty ... and ... in [our] minute acquaintance with the history of past styles ... we may find some amends for the want of one of our own' (G. G. Scott Jnr., *Essay on ... English Church Architecture*, 1881, 1–2).

153 Fergusson, *True Principles of Beauty in Art* (1849), 161, 164. He might, however, have fallen back on Cromwell's dictum: 'None goes so far as he who knows not whither he is going'.

154 *B.N.* xv (1868), 86.

155 Fergusson, *Modern Styles, op.cit.*, 329.

156 See Marianne North, *Recollections*, 3 vols. (1892–3). The architect and artist were friends.

157 'We are weighted now with a thousand precedents thrust upon us through our modern familiarity with styles of past ages and different countries. We can never again work out our own original bent with the straightforward faith and ardour of those who knew no style but their own, and had no precedents and examples to disturb their singleness of aim' (H. Heathcote Statham, *B.* l, 1886, 114). 'We cannot go back'; we have to accept 'the hugeness of the present system and its complexity' (G. A. T. Middleton, *B.N.* xlvii, 1884, 738).

158 Fergusson, *Observations on the British Museum, National Gallery and National Record Office* (1849).

159 *Marble Halls, op. cit.*, 6–7, competition designs under the motto 'Dulcius ex Asperis'. His unexecuted scheme for the National Gallery (RIBA Drawings C/F, 117: RA 1850, no 1192) suggests a mind steeped in archaeology. The villa he designed in Newstead Road, Wimbledon (dem.) was rather less elaborate, but in its own way equally traditional. His scheme for the Albert Memorial (1864) has yet to be located. In 1856 he designed a new civic centre for Singapore: 'Mr Fergusson had a splendid opportunity of putting into practice his theories of a new style.... We regret he has let the occasion slip.... The building which he offers is merely a large edifice of the sort of deteriorated Italian with which we are already familiar in steel engravings of Anglo-Indian cities' (*Sat. Rev.* iii, 1857, 10; Architectural Exhibition, 1856–7, no. 12).

160 Fergusson, *Modern Styles, op. cit.*, 251.

161 Morris, 'The Revival of Architecture', *Fortnightly Rev.*, May 1882, reprinted in *Architecture, Industry and Wealth*. 'We have no style of our own at present. The Victorian style is [the style] of Ancoats', Manchester (Morris, in *B.N.* lxv, 1893, 539).

162 Cited by P. A. Dale, *The Victorian Critic and the Idea of History* (1977), 1–3. In 1831 J. S. Mill noted that 'the idea of comparing one's own age with former ages ... was ... the dominant idea [of the age]' (Mill, *Essays on Literature and Society*, ed., J. Schneewind, 1965, 28). 'Our age is retrospective', explained Emerson, 'It builds on the sepulchres of the fathers. It writes biographies, histories and criticism'. 'That is just what we are doing', noted the *Building News* (*B.N.* li, 1886, 371).

163 Acton, *Lectures on Modern History* (1960 ed.), 35–6. See also J. H. Buckley, *The Triumph of Time* (Camb., Mass., 1967); E. E. Shils, *Tradition* (1981).

164 H. Heathcote Statham, Jubilee survey, *B.* lii (1887), 927–9. See W. Hazlitt, 'Why Distant Objects Please' (1821) in *Selected Writings* (1970), 148–79.

165 See F. Meinecke, *Historism: the Rise of a New Historical Outlook*, trans. J. E. Anderson (1972); T. W.

Heyck, *The Transformation of Intellectual Life in Victorian England* (1982); W. Kingston, *Innovation: the creative impulse in human progress* (1977).

166 'Thus, as the source of that extended receptiveness which distinguishes the nineteenth century, the demand for character seems also to stand as the guarantee of its formal anarchy, for by its simple recognition, liberalised in its sympathies and enfranchised of time, the architect was now heir to all the ages, and for him not only the whole of nature but the whole of history had become present – and available' (C. Rowe, 'Character and Composition; or Some Vicissitudes of Architectural Vocabulary in the Nineteenth Century', *The Mathematics of the Ideal Villa and Other Essays* (Camb., Mass., 1976, 69).

167 *Works* XXXVI, 115: Ruskin to Henry Acland, 24 May 1851.

168 E. Troelstsch, *Neue Rundschau* (1922), cited in A. K. Thorlby, *The Romantic Movement* (1966), 83.

169 D. Watkin, *C. R. Cockerell* (1974), 105.

170 *Victorian Studies* xviii (1974), 134.

171 'The Epic', preceding and succeeding *Morte D'Arthur* (1842).

172 C. Ricks, *Tennyson* (1972), 244 *et seq.*

173 Speaking of *Demeter and Persephone* (1889), he noted: 'when I write an antique like this I must put it into a frame – something modern about it. It is no use giving a mere *rechauffé* of old legends' (*ibid.*, 290).

174 *A.* xxv (1881), 37.

175 Gottfried Semper went further: 'Monuments of architecture are in fact nothing but the aesthetic expression of social, political and religious institutions' (quoted in N. Pevsner, *Architectural Writers, op. cit.*, 261). Norman Shaw disagreed: 'We hold that the art of architecture is on precisely the same footing as painting and sculpture' (T. G. Jackson and R. N. Shaw, eds., *Architecture: a Profession or an Art?*, 1892, 9).

176 e.g. E. B. Lamb: 'It would be absurd to say that precedent should be entirely disregarded, as in so doing, unless we produce a complete revolution in Architecture, we should at once destroy all character and association' (Lamb, *Studies of Ancient Domestic Architecture*, 1846, 5).

177 *Times Literary Supplement* 27 Feb. 1976, 211.

5 Modern Gothic

1 Colln. C. Petherick.

2 *R.I.B.A.J.* lvi (1949), 25–9; *A. and B.N.* cxcv (1949), 359–62, 381–4.

3 'Gothic has become the popular art' (*Art Jnl.* 1863, 92).

4 Burgesian Early French 'called forth a legion of imitators, who easily caught up some of the tricks of the style, but lacked altogether the skill needed to turn it to any good use, and who covered the land with buildings which for downright ugliness surpass all others even in this age of ugly buildings. No one was stronger in his condemnation of these things than Mr Burges himself, but they did not shake his faith in his favourite style' (J. T. Micklethwaite, in *The Academy* xix, 1881, 325–6).

5 'Their proceedings are about as reasonable as ... those of a man who, failing to write a poem, should claim originality by trying to alter the orthography of a language' (Burges, in Shipley, ed., *Church and World*, 1868, 582). 'There is much truth in the accusation of Prof. Kerr that there is an incredible worship of ugliness amongst us' (W. M. Mitchell, in *B.N.* xxiv, 1873, 584–5). In 1858 Scott was already objecting to 'that intentional queerness and artistic ugliness with which some of our young architects labour to produce' (Scott, *Secular and Domestic Architecture*, 275).

6 *R.I.B.A. Papers* 1873–74, 215–8; *B.* xxxi (1873), 384.

7 M. Girouard, *The Victorian Country House* (1979 edn.), 199. For Teulon's Shadwell Park, Norfolk (1859–60), see *C.L.* cxxxvi (1964), 18–21, 98–102.

8 e.g. also Teulon's churches at Silverton (*E.* xxi, N.S. xviii, 1860, 187, 193) and Agar Town, London (*ibid.*, 324). His earlier churches are more Puginian, e.g. St Thomas, Hastings (*E.* xx, NS xvii, 1859, 69; *B.* xv, 1857, 351; Eastlake, *Gothic Revival. op. cit.*, appendix no. 145); or St Thomas, Wells (*E.* xvii, NS xiv, 1856, 72; *B.* xvii, 1859, 841; *B.N.* iii, 1857, 140).

9 T. F. Bumpus, *London Churches* ii [1908], 327–9. 'All Teulon's perverse elements combined in a harsh Hallelujah' (I. Nairn, *London*, 1966, 217). The *Ecclesiologist* noted that Elvetham's 'eccentricity' included French and Saracenic motifs (*E.* xxi, NS xviii, 1860, 55). See also M. Saunders in *The Architectural Outsiders*, ed. R. Brown (1985), 132–52, 218–26.

10 *B.* xxvii (1869), 720; *A.* ii (1869), 114.

11 He was much praised by the *Building Chronicle* (e.g. i, 1854, 97–8: Preston Town Hall design), and by the *Land and Building News*, but consistently condemned by the *Ecclesiologist*. He was blamed for pursuing 'originality at the expense of standards of architectural style' (*E.* xiii, NS x, 1852, 58–9). For his principles of Picturesque originality, see *B.N.* vi (1860), 439.

12 *Catalogue of Designs: New Houses of Parliament.* In 1839 Lamb also entered a design in the St George's Hall, Liverpool, competition.

13 E. B. Lamb, *Studies of Ancient Domestic Architecture ... with some brief Observations on the Application of Ancient Architecture to the Pictorial Composition of Modern Edifices* (1846).

14 *B.* xiv (1856), 409; *B.N.* iii (1857), 44.

15 Broadlands, MSS., G.C./DO/4, enc.2 (I. L. Toplis, 'The Foreign Office', Ph.D. Thames Polytechnic, 1980, 114).

16 *B.* xxii (1864), 188–90: ill. Lamb's clients were mainly Nonconformist Liberals. But, on the advice of Sir Philip Rose, he was chosen by Disraeli to reconstruct Hughenden Manor, Bucks. (1862 onwards). See *C.L.* cxiii (1953), 1604–7, 1698–1701; Disraeli Papers, Hughenden, Rose Papers, R/I 11/C2: *ex inf.* Dr G. Stamp; *B.* xxxii, 1874, 908, 1070. For Lamb's 'eccentric' Bath Hotel on the corner of Green Park and Piccadilly, with its 'weighty, quasi-Gothic window heads [and] projecting keystones', see *E.* xxiii, NS xx (1862), 333–6; *Companion to the Almanac* 1862, 278.

17 *B.* xxiv (1866), 779: ill; J. Summerson, *Victorian Architecture: Four Studies in Evaluation* (New York, 1970).

18 *B.* xvii (1859), 492.

19 'One of the strangest churches which it has ever fallen to our lot to notice'; the transepts look like 'paddle-

boxes ... entered by amorphous arches'; the Sedilia are 'of a bulk whch defies computation'; the stained glass is 'worse ... than we could have thought possible' (*E*. xi, NS viii, 1850, 195–7). W. H. Leeds, however, speaking from a low church point of view, thought it a nice example of economy of force (*Companion to the Almanac*, 1850, 233–4). Designed in 1849, it was later extended by William White (*B.N*. lxii, 1892, 519). See *Survey of London* xli (1983) 135–9, pls. 62–3. Lamb had been recommended by Lady Frankland Russell of Thirkleby Park, Yorks.

20 This 'most affected and *outré*, and at the same time, ineffective, of all our ecclesiastical architects' (*E*. xvi, NS xiii, 1855, 38: re Leiston church, Suffolk. For its 'Puginian' polychromy, see *B*. xii, 1854, 462). Lamb's church at West Hartlepool (1850–54) was dismissed as 'one of those uncouth and grotesque combinations of incongruous architectural *tours de force*, which it requires the inartistic and withal presumptuous mind of Mr Lamb to conceive. Such a mass of absurdities, as the apse of the eastern triplet, the horrific chimney, the octagonal central tourelle, the beacon turret with its "wide awake" capping, and the out-corbelled battering termination of the West Tower ... can, we should imagine, be hardly equalled elsewhere' (*E*. xvi, NS xiii, 1855, 38).

21 *B*. xxiii (1865), 170; *Scotsman* 17 Feb. 1865. For Pilkington's work in Edinburgh, see *Buildings of Scotland: Edinburgh* (1984), *passim*.

22 E.I[ngress]. B[ell], *The Year's Art* (1883), 152.

23 *The Sacristy* iii (1873), 28. For a similar attack by Bodley, see *B*. xlviii (1885), 294–6. Sir Edmund Beckett produced similar arguments with similar vehemence (Sir E. Beckett, *A Book of Building*, 1880 ed., 106–7).

24 'Beauty no more depends on crockets, pinnacles, foliage and encaustic tiles, than it does upon violently coloured bricks, the straight-sided arch, or drain pipes instead of marble ... Art consists neither in prettiness nor ugliness ... but in beauty and feeling' (Burges, in Shipley, ed., *Church and World*, 1868, 597–8).

25 J. Stevens Curl and J. Sambrook, 'E. Bassett Keeling', *Architectural History* xvi (1973), 60–69; *C.L*., clxxx (1986), 1030–31.

26 *B.N*. xi (1864), 826 and xxxiii (1877), 302–3. 'Eccentric rather than beautiful ... an elaborate mistake – good intention and excellent work misapplied; unsatisfactory, but suggestive' (*Companion to the Almanac*, 1865, 165).

27 *A*. xxxvi (1886), 294; *B.N*.xi (1864), 864 and xvii (1869), 121.

28 Pevsner, *London*, ii, 244.

29 *B.N*. xi (1864), 333.

30 Some critics have seen in Ruskin's admiration of Gothic, a respect for sexual potency. See D. Senstroem, 'John Ruskin and the Nature of Manliness', *Victorian Newsletter* no. xi (1971), 147–201. Gothic building at its best 'looks as if it had been built by strong men' (*Works* X, 268: *Stones of Venice*, ii). 'The square and circle are pre-eminently the areas of power ...; and these, with their relative solids, the cube and the sphere, and the relative solids of progression ... the square and cylindrical column, are the elements of utmost power in all architectural arrangements' (*Works* VIII, 110: *Seven Lamps*, iii).

31 O. Jones, *The Grammar of Ornament* (1856 edn),

pl. 98 (by Christopher Dresser), conclusion.

32 Sir E. Beckett, *A Book on Building* (1880 edn), 96–7.

33 Quoted by Dudley Harbron, in *A.R*. xcii (1942), 63. For obits., see *B*. lxxix (1900), 39; *B.N*. lxxix (1900), 40; *R.I.B.A.J.* vii (1900), 450.

34 T. Harris, *Victorian Architecture: a Few Words to Show that a National Architecture adapted to the ... Nineteenth Century is Attainable* (1860), 3, 5. 'Iron and glass ... have succeeded in giving a distinct and marked character to the future of architecture ... The architecture of the nineteenth century cannot be expected to reach its full development in our time, but the future of that style, the Victorian style ... is assured' (*Examples of the Architecture of the Victorian Age and Monthly Review of the World's Architectural Progress*, 1862, 55–8). See also P. F. R. Donner [N. Pevsner], 'A Thomas Harris Florilegium', *A.R*. xciii (1943), 51–2; D. Harbron, 'Thomas Harris', *A.R*. xcii (1942), 63–6: Goodhart-Rendel, in *R.I.B.A.J.* xliv (1936–37), 675.

35 Harris, *Victorian Architecture, op. cit.*; *B*. xviii (1860), 673, ill.

36 'The so-called Victorian architecture may be described as a violation of all canons of good taste, combined with ... total disregard [for] the just principles of construction' (Burges, in Shipley, ed., *Church and World*, 1868, 576).

37 T. Harris, *Victorian Architecture, op. cit.*, 3–4.

38 *E*. xxii, NS xx (1861), 13. The *Ecclesiologist* condemned his Phillips' ceramic depot, New Bond St., but approved his Gilbey's wine store, near the Pantheon, Oxford St. (*E*. xxiii, NS xx, 1862, 333–6). When Harris produced a design for a club house combining Gothic and Classic forms, the same journal commented: this 'will not settle the controversy of styles' (*E*. xxiv, NS xxi, 1863, 166).

39 *Survey of London* xl (1981), 302–3, pl. 83a; *B.N*. iv (1858), 980 and v (1859), 165, 167, 223, 247, 272–3, 318, 341.

40 e.g. Phillips' Ceramic Establishment, New Bond St., or Osler's glass gallery in Oxford St. (*Art Jnl.* 1862, 173).

41 *B*. xxxii (1874), 111: ill.

42 See also Bedstone Court, Shropshire (1884) 'in an Early English half-timbered style ... to which has been imported a Jacobean feeling' (*B*. xlvii, 1884, 839, 856: ills.); or Stokesay Court, Shropshire (1888–91) for J. Dent Alcroft, an attempt to carry on where Smithills Hall, Lancs., and Pooley Hall, Warwicks., left off (*B*. lxvii, 1894, 91–2).

43 *B.N*. xxix (1875), 530: ills.

44 'No *invention* of a new style is possible', but 'we can invent a new construction, and the new system will grow out of it' (*A.R*. xcii, 1942, 63 and xcii, 1943, 51). See *B.N*. lxvii (1894), 135–6.

45 T. Harris, *Three Periods of English Architecture* (1894), 87.

46 Quoted in K. Clark, *The Gothic Revival* (1964 ed.), 206.

47 Goodhart-Rendel, *English Architecture Since the Regency* (1953), 134–5.

48 When he visited Sta. Anastasia, Verona, in 1854 he was delighted to find 'that what he did in simplicity as his own development of Gothic principles had been done before him' (Benjamin Starey, quoted in P. Thompson, *Butterfield*, 1971, 92).

49 See P. Thompson, *Butterfield*, (1971).

50 Butterfield's details are more often English – from East Anglia and the Midlands – than Italian. At All Saints, Margaret St., the carved bosses have been traced to Warmington, Northants. (Thompson, *Butterfield, op. cit.*, 456). At St Alban's Holborn (1862–3), the mouldings of the nave arcade are modelled on Tintern Abbey. At Keble College (1868–82) the pattern – if not the scale – of his brickwork is closer to Norfolk than to North Italy. And in his secular buildings he regularly made use of Georgian vernacular sash windows. Towards the end of his life he told Bumpus: 'I have remained firmly English' (*A.* lxiii, 1900, 226).

51 Recalled by G. H. Fellows-Prynne, in *A.A. Notes* xv (1900), 60.

52 For the West front of Queen's Gate, Thompson suggests the Kloster Kirch at Chorin; Bumpus suggests the brick churches near Toulouse, e.g. Montgiscard, Villefranche and Villenouvelle (Bumpus, *London Churches*, ii, 307).

53 [B. Webb] in *Bentley's Quarterly Rev.* i (1859), 143–82 and *Sat. Rev.* iii (1857), 426–7; v (1858), 447–9; vi (1858), 303–5; viii (1859), 96–7.

54 C. Brooks, *Signs of the Times* (1984), 168.

55 Butterfield's buildings at Merton College, Oxford, (since altered), were condemned for their 'fantastic striving after every strange and unheard of form' [? E. A. Freeman], *Sat. Rev.* xxxvii (1874), 808–9.

56 *E.* xi, NS viii (1850), 209.

57 *E.* xx, NS xvii (1859), 185. 'The crudeness of the juxtaposition of colours, as in the voussoirs of the arches, and the stiffness and disproportion, not to say grotesqueness, of form in the ornamental scrolls and foliage and patterns, are positively distressing to the eye ... [The pulpit is] a perversely ingenious confusion of coarse contrasts' ([Benjamin Webb], *Sat. Rev.* vii, 1859, 630–82). The patterns of tile and brick were thought to be 'abrupt ... disproportionate and ungainly' (*E.* xx, NS xvii, 1859, 186).

58 Cardinal Wiseman similarly attacked Pre-Raphaelite ugliness in art (*B.* xi, 1853, 649). Bumpus continued the tradition, describing Butterfield's talent for 'masterly ... grotesque ugliness' (Bumpus, *London Churches*, ii, 272–4). Summerson developed this view into a 'sadistic' interpretation in *Heavenly Mansions* (1949).

59 Thompson, *Butterfield, op.cit.*, 33.

60 [C. Patmore] in *Sat. Rev.* iv (1857), 583–4.

61 [B. Webb], 'The Art Exhibition of 1859', *Bentley's Qtly Rev.* i (1859), 592.

62 *Companion to the Almanac* 1864, 142.

63 See e.g. *B.N.* xxvii (1874), 336 and xxviii (1875), 536.

64 *Oxoniensia* iv (1939), 187.

65 *B.N.* xlix (1885), 1023. Cecil Bradshaw Roper commented on Keble's 'essentially modern ... spirit' (*B.N.* lvii, 1889, 518).

66 M. Girouard, *C.L.* cxlvi (1969), 1042–6.

67 At the RIBA: quoted in C. Stewart, *The Stones of Manchester* (1956), 106.

68 *B.* xxvii (1869), 358; xxviii (1870), 418–9; xxxi (1873), 544, 547; ill.; Eastlake, *Gothic Revival, op. cit.*, appendix no. 318.

69 W. R. Lethaby, *Philip Webb and his Work* (Oxford, 1935), 162.

70 M. Girouard, *Alfred Waterhouse and the Natural History Museum* (1981), 42–4; S. A. Smith, 'Waterhouse', in *Seven Victorian Architects*, ed. N. Pevsner and J. Fawcett (1976), 112. T. Roger Smith hailed it as a portent of the 'evolution of a new English architecture – original and good' (*B.* lxxvi, 1889, 219–22 and lxi, 1891, 274–7).

71 P. Howell, 'Letters from J. F. Bentley to C. Hadfield', *Architectural History* xxiii (1980), 100.

72 Pevsner, *London*, ii, 258.

73 *B.* xxxii (1874), 409.

74 *E.* xxiii, NS xx (1862), 1–16.

75 Scott, *Recollections, op. cit.*, 228.

76 The cornice is Sienese, the upper windows Venetian – after the Ca' d'Oro, and the Palazzo Pisani – and the lower windows Veronese (Stewart, *Stones of Manchester, op. cit.*, 84). See also shops by J. H. Chamberlain, at 28–9 Union St., Birmingham (1856; dem.), ill. T. Harris, *Examples of Architecture of the Victorian Age* (1862).

77 'Astonishing for its date ... for novelty and invention [it] can give a stone and a beating to most of the buildings that nowadays are dug up as "epoch-making"' (Goodhart-Rendel in *R.I.B.A.J.* xlvi, 1938–39, 877).

78 Scott, *Recollections, op. cit.*, 228. 'All our movements are in excess, and we seem for the time [being] at least, to be all at sea' (*ibid.*, 226–7). 'We seem as a nation to have lost that instinctive eye for beauty which it is quite clear that our forefathers possessed. This defect spoils nine-tenths of the works of our day in whatever style' (Scott, *B.* xv, 1857, 572–3).

79 Morris, *Collected Works*, ed. May Morris, xxii (1914), 234, 315–8, 322, 328–9; xxiii (1915), 147.

80 *B.N.* xxvi (1874), 690.

81 'No age has ever deliberately invented a "new style"; in fact it is morally impossible to do so' (Scott, *Secular and Domestic, op. cit.*, 204).

82 R. Kerr, *The Gentleman's House* (1864); ed. J. Mordaunt Crook, (1972), 368, 378.

83 'Crude Architecture', *A.* vi (1871), 1–3.

84 See [B. Webb] in *Bentley's Quarterly Rev.* i (1859), 143–82 and *Sat. Rev.* iii (1857), 426–7; v (1858), 447–9; vi (1858), 303–5; vii (1859), 96–7; [B. Webb], 'Domestic Architecture', *Bentley's Quarterly Rev.* ii (1860), 474–517 and *Sat. Rev.* xiv (1862), 509–10; [B. Webb] reviewing Eastlake's *Gothic Revival, Sat. Rev.* xxxiii (1872), 315–6 and Eastlake's *Hints on Household Taste, ibid.*, xxxv (1873), 255–6.

85 [Benjamin Webb] commented on Butterfield's decline; he thought Keble 'the degradation of the style' compared with All Saints, Margaret St.: 'the original work of modern English art' (*Sat. Rev.* xxxiii, 1872, 382–3).

86 e.g. J. D. Sedding, *B.N.* xxx (1876), 267.

87 'Late Gothic – Shall it be Revived?', *B.N.* xxxiii (1877), 609–10.

88 Sedding called for a 'hearty revival' of its latest and flattest forms ('The Revival of the Later Styles of English Gothic', *B.N.* xxxiii, 1877, 680–82. See also 'Perpendicular Architecture', *B.N.* xxxviii (1880), 650–53). As late as 1880 Seddon was still invoking the spirit of Viollet-le-Duc and refusing to touch Queen Anne: 'I can't dabble with dirt' (*B.N.* xxxviii, 1880, 178, 237). Norman Shaw's 'Queen Antics' might be making his fortune, but such architectural absurdities were 'treason to the profession' (*B.N.* xxxviii, 1880, 297).

89 *B.* xciii (1907), 385–6. Designed by Prior, with Randall Wells as site clerk, incorporating concrete construction reinforced with iron and steel.

90 Wells had previously been clerk to Lethaby at Brockhampton church. See *A.R.* cxxxvi (1964), 366–8.

91 Goodhart-Rendel, however, thought that Champneys's use of an ecclesiastical plan for secular purposes on this occasion, amounted to 'mortal sin' (*A.A. Jnl.* xxxvii, 1921, 41).

92 e.g. Wilson's unexecuted designs for St Andrew, Boscombe, Hants. (*B.* lxix, 1895 154 and lxx, 1896, 16; ills.); or Sedding's lodge at Flete, Holbeton, Devon (1887).

93 'The greater part of what passes for the Gothic of today is as dross, compared with the best, nay the better, Gothic revival work of the 70s and 80s' (W. D. Caröe, *A.A. Jnl.* xxi, 1906, 187).

94 'The Gothic of France is very beautiful and expressive of French thought; but to transplant it to England is as absurd as to suppose the English language could ever convey the beauties of Molière, or French the character of the writings of Shakespeare' ('O.O.O.', in *B.* xxi, 1863, 447). See also *B.* xvii (1864), 500; *B.N.* xii (1865), 638 and xiii (1866), 617.

95 'The time for a reaction from exclusively French or Italian types has at length arrived' (*E.* xxiv, NS xxi, 1863, 127–8). Designed initially in 1861, revised in 1863 and c. 1868, All Saints became progressively more English and less Continental in style (*B.* xxii, 1861, 124 and xxviii, 1870, 891).

96 'On reading these exchanges [between architect and patron] one realises that the late Victorian return to historicism owed as much to declining courage as to increased sensitivity' (Thompson, *Butterfield, op. cit.*, 354).

97 *E.* vi, NS iii (1846), 100.

98 *R.I.B.A.J.* 3rd series, xvii (1910), 314–15.

99 *B.* lviii (1890), 314, 465: 'a mere repetition ... of a medieval church'.

100 R. A. Cram, *Church Building* (1899; Boston, 1924), 46, 66–7.

101 *A Few Words to Church Builders* (1844); J. E. White, *The Cambridge Movement* (1962), 87; K. Clark, *Gothic Revival* (1964 ed.), 154.

102 G. G. Scott, *A Plea for the Faithful Restoration of our Ancient Churches* (1850), 93.

103 Ruskin, *Works* IX, 229–33; *Stones of Venice*, i.

104 G. G. Scott, Jnr., *Modern Village Churches* (1873); *Church Architecture* (1872); 'Modern Town Churches', *Building World* iv (1880), 422–4 and v (1880), 11–14, 51–4.

105 Goodhart-Rendel, *English Architecture Since the Regency*, 216. The best analysis of Bentley's masterpiece, Westminster Cathedral (1895–1903), is by Hope Bagenal, in *A.A. Jnl.* xxxiv (1919), 111–14.

106 J. Summerson, *Architectural Association* (1947), 24.

107 N. Pevsner, *Yorkshire: North Riding* (1966), 322.

108 'Pendlebury ... and Hoar Cross ... had a long-lasting influence on Bodley's pupils. Leonard Stokes developed the structural innovations of [Pendlebury] at St Clare's, Sefton Park, while the luxuriant model of Hoar Cross ... was often copied by Sir Ninian Comper, Sir Walter Tapper, F. C. Eden and Edward Warren' (M. Richardson, *Architects of the Arts and Crafts Movement*, 1983, 113).

109 H. S. Goodhart-Rendel, 'Temple Moore', *A.R.* lix (1926), (i), 11–17.

110 G. F. Bodley, *Modes in Which Religious Life and Thought may be influenced by Art* (1881), 4–5.

111 J. Summerson, *Heavenly Mansions* (1949), 156.

112 G. F. Bodley, 'On Some Principles and Characteristics of Ancient Architecture, their Application to the Modern Practice of Art', *B.* xlviii (1885), 275.

113 'There is a lot of highly Anglican carving, meaning about as much as most hymns ... There are long richly moulded arcades of arches of small span! Oh! so nicely detailed' (Goodhart-Rendel card index: Herringlow, Staffs., NMR). *Ex inf.* R. Halsey.

114 G. Stamp, 'G. G. Scott Jnr.' (Ph.D., Cambridge, 1979), 342.

115 A. Quiney, *J. L. Pearson* (1979).

116 *B.* xlii (1882), 508. 'Simply [a] medieval cathedral repeated' (*Companion to the Almanac*, 1881, 143). In 1885 young C. R. Ashbee noted: 'It seems fine and yet out of place somehow ... It all resolves itself into the question which, if I become an architect I must solve, Will Nineteenth Century Gothic do?' (A. Crawford, *C. R. Ashbee*, 1985, 213).

117 *B.* lxxvii (1899), 31.

118 B. F. L. Clarke, *Church Builders of the Nineteenth Century* (1969 edn.), 212.

119 Goodhart-Rendel, *English Architecture Since the Regency*, 221.

120 For Comper, see J. Betjeman, *A.R.* lxxxv (1939), 79–82; P. F. Anson, *Pax* (1937; 1950).

121 Obit. *R.I.B.A.J.* xlii (1934–35), 1157–60.

122 For Bodley's RIBA Gold Medal speech, in which he still pleads for a single style – Gothic – see *A.* lxxviii (1907), 258. For the sensitive restoration of his own home, Water Eaton Manor, Oxford, see H. Avray Tipping, *C.L.* xxii (1907), 666–74.

123 *C.L.* liii (1923), 308.

124 Goodhart-Rendel, 'Oxford Buildings Criticised', *Oxoniensia* xvii–xviii (1952–3), 211.

125 *R.I.B.A.J.* xxxv (1923), 470–92. 'The Gothic Revival ... began well and became better, and opened the door to a living development of vital architecture. Street used plate-glass windows at the Law Courts, and Butterfield devoted all his ingenuity of design to Keble College Chapel. Then the whole thing was plunged back again into the antiquarian obsolescent darkness of the fifteenth century, where the ecclesiastical mind sticks to-day' (*ibid.*, 511).

126 K. E. Kirk, *The Story of the Woodard Schools* (1937).

127 Goodhart-Rendel, 'Temple Moore', *A.R.* lix (1926), (i), 11–17.

128 V. E. Cotton, *The Book of Liverpool Cathedral* (Liverpool, 1964); J. Thomas, 'Liverpool Cathedral', in R. Dixon, ed., *Sir G. Scott and the Scott Dynasty* (South Bank Polytechnic, 1980).

129 J. M. Richards and J. Summerson, *The Bombed Buildings of Britain* (1942), 114.

130 Goodhart-Rendel, *English Architecture Since the Regency*, 249–52. For C. H. Reilly's analysis, see *C.L.* liv (1924), 1042–51; lv (1925), 123; lvi (1925), 103, 397. For Hope Bagenal's, see *A.A. Jnl.* xxxvi (1920–21), 140–2 and xl (1924), 129–30.

131 In the 1870s, the Church of England was completing churches at the rate of one per week. In the diocese of Manchester only two churches were built

between 1890 and 1898, as against fifteen in 1880–89 and twenty-one in 1870–79 (*A.* cxiii, 1900, 3).

132 G. Stamp, 'New British Churches between the wars', *C.L.* clxix (1981), 238–40; N.F. Cachemaille-Day, 'Ecclesiastical Architecture in the Present Age', *R.I.B.A.J.*, 3rd series, xl (1932–3), 825–38. Even Sir Reginald Blomfield appreciated its links with Albi: 'those dear echoes of the past that linger in the memory like half-remembered music' (Blomfield, *Modernismus*, 1934, 168).

133 *A. & B.N.* cxxxi (1932), 342–4: ills. (with Hilda Mason).

134 *A. & B.N.* cxxxii (1932), 168–72: ills.

135 Library and chapel: ills. *B.* lxv (1893), 226, 280.

136 H. Wilson *et al.*, *J. D. Sedding* (1892), 12. He regarded Holy Trinity, Sloane St. as 'a perfect treasure house of the finest modern art'; there one is 'looking on Sedding's face' (*ibid.*, 8). 'Sedding ... was a Gothic man who rocked and nearly wrecked the Gothic boat, going all out for the "late and debased" and once, at Clerkenwell, actually landing himself in the *quattrocento*' (J. Summerson, *The Turn of the Century: Architecture in Britain around 1900*, Glasgow 1976, 13). For a brief memoir of Sedding, by the Rev. E. F. Russell, see J. D. Sedding, *Garden Craft Old and New* (1901), intro. For Sedding's views, see 'Religion and Art', in *Art and Handicraft* (1893), 38; 'Design' in *Arts and Crafts Essays* (1893), 410.

137 Even in 1849 his *Seven Lamps* had contained seeds of doubt. 'The stirring which has taken place in our architectural aims and interests within these last few years', he wrote, 'is thought by many to be full of promise: I trust it is, but it has a sickly look to me. I cannot tell whether it be indeed a springing of seed or a shaking among bones.' Thirty years later he added a bleak footnote: 'I am glad to see I had so much sense thus early – if only I had had just a little more, and stopped talking' (*Works* VIII, 194n.: 'Lamp of Life', iii).

138 'We had gone a long and weary way from Ely Cathedral to Gower St., from Giotto to Joshua Reynolds, from Beowulf to the Rape of the Lock ... Nevertheless, out of this dreariness came that intellectual Rebellion ... the Gothic Revival'. But until the Socialist revolution, 'nothing is possible in architecture but jerry-built houses for the masses and vulgar Victorian architecture for the well-to-do and rich' (W. Morris, 'The Gothic Revival' (1884), in *Unpublished Lectures*, ed. E. D. Le Mire, Detroit, 1969, 70, 80–83, 85–7).

139 'A Goth' [J. P. Seddon], *B.N.* lviii (1890), 585. See also *B.N.* xlvii (1884), 771–5.

140 *B.* lii (1887), 927–9.

141 Burges had 'assimilated the medieval spirit more fully ... than either Street or Scott' (*B.* liii, 1887, 290–91); he had enjoyed an 'insight ... into the very bones and marrow of medieval art', but it was just 'a revival and nothing more' (E. J. Tarver, 'Architectural Style', *B.* xlviii, 1885, 644–6).

142 'After spending millions of pounds we came to the conclusion that it had been to no purpose. The Gothic revival, for all practical purposes, is dead ... When it came to building, especially in places like the City, we found it would not answer' (W. R. Lethaby, *Philip Webb and His Work*, Oxford, 1935, 76).

143 *A.A. Jnl.* xxxii (1917), 121.

144 *A.A. Jnl.* xxxvii (1921), 2–3.

145 *R.I.B.A.J.* xlii (1934–5), 311.

146 Goodhart-Rendel, *English Architecture Since the Regency* 220, referring to Caröe – perhaps to St David's, Exeter: 'an extremely vulgar and objectionable design ... low sprawling nave ... fittings [however] better than the church ... The style is "New Art" with Gothic affinities' (Goodhart-Rendel church index, N.M.R.). He called Edmund Sedding's St Peter, Shaldon, nr. Teignmouth (1893), 'of all freaks the freakiest. New Art gone mad' (*ibid*). Pevsner similarly called Atkinson's shop at 24, Bond St. (1926, by Vincent Harris; now Ferragamo Ltd.) 'a successful freak' (Pevsner, *London* i, 604).

147 *The Globe* 13 Jan. 1874.

6 Progressive Eclecticism

1 H.-R. Hitchcock, *Modern Architecture: Romanticism and Reintegration* (1929).

2 One day his wife, Lady Mildred – a daughter of Lord Salisbury and sister of the future Prime Minister – tumbled into a fountain on the terrace at Bedgebury. Beresford Hope re-fixed his monocle, strolled back into the house, and rang the bell for the footman: 'go and pick her ladyship out of the fountain' (H. W. and I. Law, *The Book of the Beresford Hopes* 1925, 195).

3 *B.* liii (1887), 665; *B.N.* xlvi (1884), 491, 496–9 and liv (1888), 417. 'An amateur, though not an ordinary one. For there are amateurs and amateurs' (*B.* xlvii, 1884, 413).

4 'I would have imagined myself measuring swords with Gladstone, or Disraeli, or Carlyle, or Tennyson, or Montalembert. Now I shall die a second rate notoriety ... "the rich Mr Beresford Hope"' (Law, *op. cit*, 126, 232). For his sadness – e.g. at the death of Burges, Street, Benjamin Webb and J. M. Neale — see *B.N.* liii (1887), 648. Ritualists attacked him as a trimmer: for 'ratting' on his allies by putting politics before religion and aesthetics before faith: for degrading the Ecclesiological Society 'from a pioneer of Church progress into a mere dilettante club for talking about crockets and Munich glass' ('A Rat Behind the Arras', *Church Times* 8 Dec. 1866, 411).

5 *B.N.* liii (1887, ii), 675.

6 *A.* xxxviii (1887), 259.

7 *Athenaeum* no. 3131 (1887), 571.

8 *A.* xxxviii (1887), 265–6.

9 *E.* xxiii, NS xx (1862), 229; Hope, *The Condition and Prospects of Architectural Art* (1863), 13.

10 [Beresford Hope] reviewing Fergusson's *Handbook*, *Sat. Rev.* i (1856), 234–6.

11 *ibid.*

12 *E.* xxiii, NS, xx (1862), 229.

13 [Beresford Hope] reviewing the 1862 Exhibition, *Qtly. Rev.* cxiii (1863), 176–207.

14 He favoured 'Cismontane Gothic for Cismarine England'. 'The absolute Gothic of Italy is surely out of court', on climatic grounds. But 'its diversity of materials, and ... colour' were there for the taking, thanks to 'the conjoint action of chemistry and commerce, and the increased facilities of transport and

working'. Let not the architect 'be afraid of the new colours which God had given' him. Instead, let him 'make proof of his daring'. The Gothic of the future would be northern in origin – Hope preferred Decorated or Middle Pointed ('the golden mean') to Early French; Early English he thought too 'prim' – but enriched by the diversity and colour of southern types (Hope, *The English Cathedral of the Nineteenth Century*, 1891 ed., 33, 44, 62).

15 *Sat. Rev.* i (1856), 234–6.

16 Hope, *The Common Sense of Art* (1858), 10.

17 *ibid.*, 11.

18 *E.* vii, NS iv (1847), 90.

19 Hope, *Common Sense of Art*, 13.

20 *Sat. Rev.* i (1856), 234–6.

21 Hope, *Common Sense of Art*, 14.

22 *ibid.*, 21.

23 *Sat. Rev.* i (1856), 234–6.

24 Hope, *Common Sense of Art*, 14; Hope, *Public Offices and Metropolitan Improvements* (1857), 24.

25 'Still more ridiculous is to call such childish archaeological exercises eclecticism. When you have learnt to feel the refinement of the Greek, the strength of the Roman, and the common sense of the Goth – when you can see how to harmonise principles without becoming a slave to precedents, then you may lay claim to the title of eclectic' (E. W. Godwin, 'Modern Architects and their Work', *B.N.* xxii, 1872, 13).

26 [Beresford Hope] reviewing the Oxford Museum competition, *Sat. Rev.* i (1856), 208–9. Similarly Ruskin: 'the work of young artists ... should be full of failures; for these are the signs of efforts' (*Works* III, 623; *Modern Painters* i).

27 *A.* xxxviii (1887), 265–6.

28 Hope, *Public Offices and Metropolitan Improvements*, 34.

29 Hope, *English Cathedral of the Nineteenth Century* (1861), 31–2. For [Benjamin Webb's] review, see *Sat. Rev.* xi (1861), 643–4.

30 *B.* xxxiv (1876), 18. Less eloquently, 'the new school of eclecticism' was defined as those who 'collect all collectable examples as stock-in-trade – and systematise them and analyse them in order to utilise them' (*A.* xxix, 1883, 85).

31 [Benjamin Webb] reviewing *Common Sense of Art*, *Sat. Rev.* vii (1859), 96–7.

32 V. Cousin, *Eclecticism* (1839); *The True, the Beautiful and the Good* (trans. 1853; originally lectures at the Sorbonne); R. Middleton, 'The Rationalist Interpretations of Classicism of Leance Reynaud and Viollet-le-Duc', *A.A. Files* xi (1986), 29–48.

33 A. C. Quatremère de Quincy, *Dictionnaire d'architecture encyclopédie méthodique* (Paris, 1788–1825), iii, pt. 2, s.v. 'Type'.

34 *Revue Générale de l'Architecture* (1853); trans. *B.* xiii (1855), 89–90.

35 *B.* lxiii (1892), 8.

36 *Discourses*, trans. B. Bucknall i (1889), 455.

37 'The Plague of Art' recalls the motto used by Lassus in the Lille Cathedral competition. Lassus was a dogmatic anti-latitudinarian: 'The situation is grave ... in the state of anarchy into which art is now reduced ... there remains ... only one anchor of safety, unity of style; and as we have no art belonging to our own time – everyone is convinced of it and deplores it – there is only one thing for us to do: ... choose one [style] ...

not ... to copy ... but ... to compose' (*E.* xvii, NS xiv, 1856, 284–7, 322–2, 414–31; xviii, NS xv, 1857, 46–9, 89–91).

38 *B.* xiii (1855), 90.

39 *B.N.* iv (1858), 617.

40 'Our architecture must embrace within its pale, the semi-circular, the semi-ellipse, the segmental and the pointed arches, but it would reserve a strong preference for the pointed ... We need a master mind which can grasp the great principles which pervade all good art, and which out of the immense fund of material left us by the Greek, the Roman, the Byzantine, the Medieval and Oriental decorators, can sift out all that which is good and out of it generate a perfect style worthy of the highest efforts of which our art is capable' (Scott, *Secular and Domestic Architecture*, 270). This book was dedicated to Beresford Hope, 'who has ... taken a leading position among those who, in different countries of Europe, are labouring in the revival of their indigenous architecture, as the nucleus on which to develop that of the future'.

41 J. Mordaunt Crook, *William Burges and the High Victorian Dream* (1981), 103–5, 110–11.

42 'The present period is one of architectural anarchy'; a combination of Classic and Gothic might 'lead to the formation of an original style, fitted to ... our present high state of civilisation' (*Architectural Magazine* v, 1838–9, 658).

43 'The Anglo-Classic style ... awaits ... an infusion ... of ... the fire and energy ... [of] Gothic' (*B.* xi, 1852, 573).

44 'Our ... architecture is ... a confused assemblage of many styles ... a ship entangled amidst unknown shoals'; evolutionary eclecticism might supply a solution to 'the difficulties which beset this transitional period' (*RIBA Papers* 1866, 152).

45 P. Metcalf, *James Knowles* (1980), 218–9.

46 'Cosmos, we hope, will presently come out of ... CHAOS' (*A.* iv, 1870, 1).

47 J. T. Emmett, *Six Essays*, ed. J. Mordaunt Crook (1972).

48 R. Kerr, *The Gentleman's House*, ed. J. Mordaunt Crook (1972).

49 T. Hope, *An Historical Essay on Architecture* (1835), 561.

50 *Sat. Rev.* i (1856), 208–9.

51 *E.* xxii, NS xix (1861), 25–6.

52 *Macmillan's Magazine* xxv (1871–72), 250–56. Fergusson was speaking of Fowke's defeated design, in similar style, for the Natural History Museum.

53 *Qtly. Rev.* cxiii (1863), 176–207.

54 *ibid.*, cxiii (1862), 179–219; *Sat. Rev.* xi (1861), 340.

55 'Primarily French of the Tudor period, and Scotch only by modification ... an uncivilised style [which] ought never to be brought into juxtaposition with anything more highly cultivated than the beautiful heather braes of Loch Lomond' (R. Kerr, *Gentleman's House*, 377).

56 See *RIBA Trans.* 1st ser. xv (1864–5), appendix 1–3.

57 Hope acted as referee (*Companion to the Almanac*, 1865, 119).

58 *Gent's Mag.* NS xiv (1863), 600–6.

59 *Qtly. Rev.* cxii (1862), 179–219.

60 Metcalf, *Knowles*, 129–43.

61 'It ... unites some of the leading forms of Italian

with the picturesque, the freshness, and the variety of medieval work' (*B.N.* xii 1865, 726; *B.* xxi, 1863, 531–3: ill.).

62 'Look at the Renaissance house in Upper Brook St. erected for Mr Samuel (C. O. Parnell, *c.* 1860; *I.L.N.* 17 Nov. 1860, 455: ill.), with its high roof and varied skyline. Look at the house in course of construction for Messrs. Longman in Paternoster Row (J. Griffith and H. Dawson, 1861–3, *B.N.* x, 1863, 182–5: ill.) with its high French roofs and carved stone work; look at the ... Westminster Palace [Hotel] (A. and W. Moseley, Victoria St., 1857–61; *B.* xvi, 1858, 245–7: ill.) and London Bridge Hotel (H. Curry, 1861–62; *B.* xix, 1861, 427–9: ill.) ... and look at Montagu House (for the Duke of Buccleugh, by W. Burn, 1859–62; *B.N.* ix, 1862, 416: ill.) and many others' (Hope, *The Condition and Prospects of Architectural Art*, Architectural Museum, 1863, 15–18). Hope himself played a part in this. Hope House, Piccadilly, had dormers, mansards, and lots of 'Frenchified finery' (*B.N.* ii, 1856, 77; designed by P. C. Dusillion of Paris; executed by T. L. Donaldson, 1848–51; later the Junior Athenaeum; *B.* vii, 1849, 433–4, 498–9: ill.). Hope also employed Carpenter and Slater to rebuild his country seat, Bedgebury, Kent (1688; enlarged 1836), in the style of Clagny and Choisy (J. Newman, *West Kent and the Weald*, 1969, 340; Hope, 'The Skyline of Modern Domestic Buildings', *RIBA Trans.* 1863–64, 103).

63 J. L. Petit, *Church Architecture* (1841).

64 *B.* xiv (1856), 83, 115, 117, 120.

65 Petit, 'On the Revival of Styles', *B.* xix (1861), 350–52, 369–72 (Architectural Exhibition).

66 See A. Saint, *R. N. Shaw* (1976), 24 *et seq.* Similarly, Ashfield and Pouncefoot Lodges, Broadlands, Hants. (designed 1868; erected 1870). See *C.L.* clxix (1981), 261: ills. West Lodge, Trentham, Staffs. (1859) is even earlier, and possibly also by Nesfield (T. Mowl and B. Earnshaw, *Trumpet at a Distant Gate*, 1985, 173). R. Phéné Spiers singled out Nesfield's lodge in Regent's Park (dem.) as 'a brilliant example of ... material architecture, in which the economic and stylistic treatment was turned to account' (*B.N.* lii, 1887, 679).

67 M. Girouard, *C.L.* cxlvi (1969), 1640–3, 1694–7.

68 Bodley's vicarage at Valley End, Windlesham, also dates from 1866; his houses in Malvern Link (executed with help from Philip Webb) were completed in 1869. His River House, 3 Chelsea Embankment (Bodley and Garner, 1879) echoes Kew directly (G. Stamp, *The English House, 1860–1914*, 1980, 12–13).

69 H. S. Goodhart-Rendel, *English Architecture Since the Regency* (1953), 150.

70 Cited in M. Girouard, *Sweetness and Light* (Oxford 1977), 24. Webb was 'probably the architect who first decided upon adapting and combining the vigour of the thirteenth century with the internal comfort and dignity of the eighteenth century' (E. J. Tarver, 'Architectural Style', *B.*, xlviii, 1885, 644–6). E.g. Webb's classical interiors at 1a Holland Park (W. Crane, *Ideals in Art*, 1905, 131, 258: ill.). See also M. Swenarton, 'Philip Webb's Classicism', *Building Design* 25 May 1984, 20–22.

71 W. R. Lethaby, *Philip Webb*, 75.

72 *ibid.*, 24, 130.

73 *ibid.*, 136.

74 M. Girouard, *C.L.* cxxvii (1960), 1382–5. See also Webb's studio house for Val Prinsep in Holland Park

(*B.N.* xxxix, 1860, 511: ill.).

75 See also Balne vicarage, Yorks. (1853), and other prototypes in *Instrumenta Ecclesiastica* (1847; 1856).

76 Photos. and description by Scawen Blunt, *C.L.* xvi (1904), 738–48.

77 'One of the most *important* works of our time is a little entrance lodge at Kew Gardens ... As a work of Art it is perfect, and [Nesfield] in this his first public work, struck a chord which still vibrates through the architectural world ... from this little building ... nearly all that is best in our misnamed Queen Anne work receives its impulse' (E. I[ngress] B[ell], 'Architecture in 1882', in *The Year's Art*, 1883, 150–52).

78 e.g. at Greenwich (*B.N.* xxviii, 1875, 206). See D. Gregory-Jones, 'Towers of Learning', *A.R.* cxxiii (1958), 393–8.

79 *B.* xxxiii (1875), 1145; *B.N.* xxxi (1876), 120. Thackeray's 'Queen Anne' house was on Palace Green, Kensington.

80 When 'Greek' Thomson met G. G. Scott Jnr. at dinner with J. J. Stevenson in 1871, he noted Scott's 'black knee breeches, black silk stockings, high heeled shoes and large buckles – blue coat, yellow vest, white neck cloth with stiffer and frilled shirt' (R. McFadzean, *Life and Work of Alexander Thomson*, 1979, 271). See also *A.* xv (1876), 368.

81 'L'Art pour L'Art' was a phrase coined by Victor Cousin. The *Saturday Review* blamed Théophile Gautier (*Sat. Rev.* xxxv, 1873, 273–4). See R. Snell, *Théophile Gautier* (Oxford, 1982).

82 He was in fact referring to Dresser's abstracted leaf and flower patterns (Burne-Jones Papers, Fitzwilliam Museum: letter to E. R. Robson, *c.* 1863).

83 See 'The Ballad of Bedford Park', in *St James's Gazette* 17 Dec. 1881.

84 *B.N.* xxviii (1875), 333, 457, 587, and xxx (1876), 33, 35, 55–6. See also [? Beresford Hope], 'The Queen Anne Craze' *Sat. Rev.* xl (1875), 142–3. For Seddon's views see his *Progress in Art and Architecture* (1852). His attitude was somewhat compromised by his own address: No. 1, Queen Anne's Gate. Similarly Butterfield lived in an Adam-style house by Leverton in Bedford Square; Pearson in an Adam house in Mansfield St.; Street at 14, Cavendish Place; Scott in a house by Sir Robert Taylor in Spring Gardens. Bodley, Garner and G. G. Scott Jnr. all lived in Church Row, Hampstead.

85 *B.* xxxiv (1876), 18.

86 *A.* ix (1873), 271. Compare a contemporary statement of the progress of the Gothic Revival (*B.N.* xviii, 1870, 314) with modern accounts of the development of Queen Anne (*C.L.* cxlii, 1967, 1654–8 and clxiv, 1978, 1602–5, 1722–5).

87 *B.N.* xxxiv, (1878), 268–9 and xxxviii (1880), 124.

88 In 1878 the *Building News* even devoted an editorial to the Five Orders (*B.N.* xxxv, 1878, 687), and in 1880 there appeared a new edition of *The Works in Architecture of Robert and James Adam* (*B.N.* xxxiv, 1880, 614, 620–21).

89 *A.* viii (1875), 254–5: 'Free Classic Architecture'.

90 J. J. Stevenson, 'On the recent reaction of taste in English architecture', RIBA conference, 1874 (*A.* xi, 1875, supp. 9).

91 *B.N.* xxviii (1875), 651. This is a remarkably early use of the term: the building to which it was (rather improbably) applied was Bodley and Garner's

School Board Offices on the Embankment, London (*B.N.* xxix, 1875, 10–13: ills.).

92 *B.N.* xxviii (1875), 709.

93 *B.N.* xxxii (1877), 2.

94 *A.* ix (1873), 271.

95 e.g. *B.N.* xxxiii (1887), 101; xxxv (1878), 585; xxxvi (1879), 201; xxxvii (1879), 299–300.

96 *Sat. Rev.* xxxvi (1873), 123–4.

97 'A renaissance of the Renaissance, a Gothic game played with Neo-Classical counters, not very different from the game that had been played all over Europe three centuries before. The nineteenth-century players were more conscious than the sixteenth-century players had been of their audience, more often tempted into picturesque poses, into unnecessary virtuosity. On the other hand they were much less gross than their Elizabethan ancestors, coached [as *they* had been] by clumsy Germans High and Low' (Goodhart-Rendel, *English Architecture Since the Regency*, 171–2).

98 D. Bassett, '"Queen Anne" and France', *Architectural History* xxiv (1981), 83–91.

99 Stevenson, *House Architecture*, i, 215.

100 Robson, *School Architecture*, 322–3.

101 *A.* xxvii (1882), 231–2: ed.

102 'Whatever was admirable about the quaint old houses of the middle of the eighteenth century was simply a survival of the Gothic times; the rest was ... a mere token of a narrow, pinched bourgeoisdom' (Morris, 'The Gothic Revival', 1884, in *Unpublished Lectures*, ed. E. D. LeMire, Detroit, 1969, 80–83). 'It was not the differentia of the Queen Anne style that was its attraction; all that is a mere bundle of preposterous whims; it was the fact that in the style there was yet left some feeling of the Gothic' (Morris, 'The Revival of Architecture', *Fortnightly Rev.* May 1868, reprinted in *Architecture, Industry and Wealth*, 1902).

103 *B.N.* liii (1887), 43.

104 e.g. 'Free Classic' wallpaper (*B.N.* lv, 1888, 468: ill.).

105 See S. Wickman, *Japonisme: The Japanese Influence on Western Art since 1858* (1981).

106 'The Style of the Future', *B.N.* xxviii (1875), 425. For William H. White's caricature of the style – a parody of François Premier – see *A.* xi (1874), 62: ill.

107 *RIBA Trans.* xxxiv (1888).

108 J. P. Seddon, after H. Conybeare (*A.* xi, 1874, 146).

109 'Sham antique'; 'child's play' (*B.* xliv, 1883, 597); 'occasional lapses into superabundance' (Barr Ferree, 'Architecture in London', *Architectural Record*, v, 1895–6, 1–30). Gilbert's house (no. 19, now 39) was paid for out of the profits of *Patience*.

110 *B.* lxxiii (1897), 102.

111 H. Muthesius, *The English House*, trans. J. Seligman (1979), 36. Lutyens recalled that Ernest George 'took each year three weeks holiday abroad and returned with overflowing sketch books. When called on for a project he would look through them and choose some picturesque turret or gable from Holland, France or Spain and round it weave his new design. Locations mattered little and no provincial formation influenced him, for at that time terra-cotta was the last word in building' (quoted in C. Hussey, *The Life of Sir Edwin Lutyens*, 1950, 17). According to his last pupil, Darcy Braddell, 'when commissioned to design a building, [George] would ask what style was required – Gothic?

"Queen Anne"? Modern?' (J. Lees-Milne, *Prophesying Peace*, 1977, 49).

112 *B.* lii (1887), 863; *B.N.* lii, (1887), 714; *B.A.* xxxviii (1893).

113 Begun by Bodley (*B.* xxx, 1872, 489; xxxiii, 1875, 704); extended by Robson (*B.* l, 1886, 387, 404) and Edis (*B.* lxi, 1891, 291; *A.* liii, 1895, 417: ill.). See also *B.N.* xxix (1875), 13: ills.; *A.* ix, 1873, 248: ill.; *B.* xliii (1882), 849: ill.

114 Saint, *Shaw*, op.cit., 219

115 *B.N.* xxviii (1875), 248. William White had already spotted that the question of truth was really a red herring: 'Truthfulness has nothing to do with "style" as such ... we [Goths] have no right to lay a sole claim to universal truthfulness' (*B.* xv, 1857, 402).

116 *B.N.* xlv (1883), 633. 'Ruskinism is solemnly, irremediably dead. If an educated man, placed in a picture gallery, were found chattering today of the holiness of toil and the dignity of prayer; if, instead of appealing to the sense of sight, he were to demand the exercise of every other sense, he would claim only the attention of the hypocrite' ('A Sane Critic', *New Review* Jan. 1876). 'Is it not time that some one published a book on the absurdities of Ruskin?' (*B.* lxxiii, 1897, 152).

117 J. Edwards, *London Street Improvements, 1855–97* (1898); *Survey of London* xxxi (1963), 71–4 and xxxiii (1966), 297–300; J. Summerson, 'London: the Artefact', in *The Victorian City*, ed. J. Dyos and M. Wolff (1973), ii, 311–32.

118 *B.N.* xxiii (1872), 25.

119 Seddon, 'The Modern Architect and His Art', *B.N.* xlvii (1884), 771–5: A.A.

120 Sedding, *The Artist*, 1 April 1883, 115–7: A.A.

121 Sedding, 'English Schools of Art – Old and New', *B.N.* xlix (1885), 1021–5. Sedding claimed that 'all styles [were] inspired of God', but his preferences were clearly Gothic (*B.N.* li, 1886, 378). For Sedding's own brand of eclecticism, as in his unexecuted designs for St Dyfrig's, Cardiff, see H. Heathcote Statham, *Modern Architecture* (1897), 77–8: ill.

122 *B.N.* li (1886), 479 and lii (1887), 670–71.

123 Quoted in Saint, *Shaw*, op. cit., 218–9.

124 Scott, *Recollections*, op. cit., 372.

125 *B.N.* liii (1887), 197: ed.

126 *B.N.* liv (1888), 450.

127 'The Progress of Architecture', *A.* xvi (1876), 379: ed.

128 'Vitality in Architecture', *A.* xviii (1877), 15: ed.

129 *B.N.* xlvii (1884), 733.

130 Statham: *B.N.* xlvi (1884), 121.

131 Godwin: *B.* xlvi (1884), 1–2.

132 *B.* xlix (1885), 1: ed.

133 H. C. Boyes, 'What Style Next?', *B.* xxxiv (1876), 1100. 'No one can safely predict the style [of the future]' (*Encyclopaedia Britannica*, 9th ed., ii, 1875, 153–4, signed T. Hayter Lewis and G. E. Street).

134 *B.* xxiii (1865), 795–8.

135 *B.* xxiv (1866), 831; *RIBA Reports* 1866–67, 9.

136 *B.* xxv (1867), 334.

137 *B.* xlvi (1884), 714.

138 'The style is really original, showing in a successful combination some of the best characteristics both of Gothic and Italian [Renaissance] design' (*B.* xxix, 1871, 838–9; see also *B.* xxviii, 1870, 877: ill.).

139 *B.N.* xxiii (1872), 35. Similarly Gilbert Scott: 'Classic and Gothic will probably run on for many years collaterally ... till at length ... they will unite in a style infinitely more Gothic than Classic' (Scott, *Secular and Domestic Architecture*, 1858, 277).

140 B. liii (1887), 589–90: Statham.

141 H. Hucks Gibbs, in *RIBA Trans.* NS iv (1888), 58.

142 *B.N.* liv (1888), 417.

143 *B.N.* xxix (1875), 22. Hope called this a parody of the Haarlem Butter Market (*Sat. Rev.* xl, 1875, 142–3), but it was also a parody of the Hotel d'Ecoville, Caen (*B.N.* xxx, 1876, 218, 220: ill.).

144 J. Mordaunt Crook, 'T. G. Jackson and the Cult of Eclecticism', *In Search of Modern Architecture*, ed. H. Searing (New York, 1982), 102–20.

145 *Art Jnl.* 1887, 209.

146 Champneys, 'Victorian Architecture and Originality', *B.A.* xxviii (1887), 435–7; 'The Architecture of Queen Victoria's Reign', *Art Jnl.* 1887, 203–9, Gerard Manley Hopkins noted a similar eclecticism in the poetic diction of William Morris: 'the language [of these poems] is a quaint medley of the Middle Ages and "Queen Annery", a combination quite of our age and almost even of our decade' (C. C. Abbott, ed., *Correspondence of G. M. Hopkins and R. W. Dixon*, 1935, 82–3).

147 Champneys, 'Style', *Trans. Nat. Assocn. for the Advancement of Art and its Application to Industry* i (1888), 166–74. 'At present we are off the track, in the absence of Scott, Street, Burges and Godwin. We have gone astray. The great designers who were their later contemporaries, and who shared their powers and zeal, are silent, and prefer retirement ... The profession may be advanced, but the art will be forgotten'. Examinations have become absorbed in technicalities: students would be better employed in trying to discover 'wherein lay the power of such great designers as Burges, Street, Godwin, Thomson, or Cockerell' (Beresford Pite, *B.N.* lix, 1890, 667: *oratio recta*).

148 *B.N.* xliv (1893), 627.

149 *B.N.* lxv (1893), 502.

150 B. lxvii (1894), 350: *oratio recta*.

151 *A.A. Jnl*, xxiii (1908), 78.

152 *B.N.* lviii (1890), 923.

153 B. xlviii (1885), 1, 721.

154 'Without exactly saying that one would have wished to see it carried out, one must admit that it is a very clever combination' (Statham, *Modern Architecture*, *op. cit.*, 67: ill.).

155 *B.N.* lviii (1890), 151.

156 *B.N.* lxviii (1895), 225, 326, 646.

157 *B.N.* lxviii (1895), 573.

158 'We are at the very brink of the grave ... the art of architecture is almost entirely dead' ('Life, Death and the Futurity of Architecture', *B.N.* xlvi, 1884, 121–4, 160–62, 223–5: Birmingham Architectural Association).

159 'Changes of Architectural Fashion', *B.N.* lxii (1892), 229: ed.

160 'As Others See Us', *B.N.* lxix (1895), 215–6: ed. See also *B.N.* lxx (1896), 1: ed. Perhaps they were thinking of the Jacobean Margarine works at Southall, Middx., by Bird and Whittenbury of Manchester (*B.N.* lxix, 1895, 299). Looking back over the past half-century, the *Building News* saw chiefly the architecture of Philistinism: 'a vulgar race for wealth, and the osten-

tatious spending of it'. The great church-building and school-building movements were over. 'The power of building beautiful houses has not left us.' But the mass of architecture, public and secular, was corrupt. 'Art is the appeal of mind to mind; but ostentation is only the appeal of pocket to pocket' (*B.N.* lxvi, 1894, 1, 72, 523).

161 Barr Ferree, 'Architecture in London', *Architectural Record* v (1895–6), 1–30.

162 *B.N.* xlix (1885), 183 and lix (1890), 807.

163 'A Great English chronicle', *Macmillan's Mag.*, Jan. 1896. See also 'The Ugliness of Modern Life', *Nineteenth Century*, Jan. 1896.

164 B. Whelan, 'The Oldest of the Arts', *Merry England* iii (1884), 144–52.

165 'Style is ... unison and harmony, between the mental and aesthetic powers, between constructive science and aesthetic expression. [But today] architecture is becoming dust, [thanks to the disintegration of] religious ... social and moral unity' (B. lxiv, 1893, 66; *B.N.* lxiv, 1893, 627: letter to Aitchison following Daly's receipt of the RIBA Gold Medal).

166 T. G. Jackson, 'The Commonplace of Architecture', *B.N.* xlviii (1885), 443. See also *B.N.* l (1886), 689.

167 G. F. Terry, '"Present Worth" of Architecture as a serious life's pursuit', *B.N.* lvii (1889), 725–6. Terry's lecture, to the Society of Architects, was 'very well received by the architectural profession'. Its confessional theme was taken up by popular papers like the *Daily News*. In 1896 the *Builder* proposed a tax on pilasters ('The Persistent Pilaster', *B.* lxx, 1896, 43–4).

168 B. lxx (1896), 32.

169 B. lxv (1893), 357.

170 'Sensational Architecture', *B.N.* lvii (1889), 827. Ornament, in preference to proportion or harmony, is the 'vulgar error' responsible for 'the costly ugliness of our streets ... It is impossible to believe that any one ... ever looks at it without a shudder ... It lies in wait and hits you in the eye from every suburban porch, and fires whole volleys at you from the walls in our main streets' (F. Baggally, 'Common Errors in Architectural Design', *B.* lxxvi, 1899, 61–4: Sheffield). When in 1895 the RIBA staged a symposium on 'Simplicity in Architecture', Walter Crane was unable to attend, but sent a telegram: 'Sorry cannot come ... Count me against architectural confectionary and fidgetty façades'. Halsey Ricardo suggested that 'buildings, like the drama, should be pregnant – condensed – in their ornamentation'. Champneys came out against forced originality. Statham called for positive, not merely negative, simplicity; Young for 'simplicity, but no poverty'; William White for 'repose'; E. R. Robson for 'reticence' (B. lxviii, 1895, 122–4).

171 e.g. *B.N.* xxvi (1874), 69 and l (1886), 251: *A.* xiii (1875), 1 and xvi (1875), 19, 32, 44; B. xlvi (1884), 726–31.

172 *B.N.* lxvi (1894), 603–5: ill. See also Crane's 'Triumph of Labour', *B.N.* lx (1891), 621: ill.

173 W. Crane, *William Morris to Whistler* (1911), 90; 'The Architecture of Art', *B.N.* lii (1887), 269–70 and 'The Applied Arts in Relation to Common Life', *B.N.* lii (1887), 791–2; H. Holiday, 'Modernism in Art', *B.N.* lviii (1890), 427–31; B. lviii (1890), 212–4; Halsey Ricardo, *B.N.* lxviii (1895), 225, 326, 646.

174 Jackson, 'The Obstacles Opposed to the Advancement of Architecture by Architects them-

selves', *Trans. Nat. Assocn. for the Advancement of Art and its Application to Industry* i (1888), 199.

175 R. Blomfield, *A Short History of Renaissance Architecture in England* (1900 ed.), 296: *oratio recta*. Town planners had been making a similar point for some time: if Victorian London was ever to match Haussman's Paris, 'the Gothic landmarks must fall; the rectangle and the lintel must supersede the curve, the zig-zag and the point' (*B.A.* ix, 1873, 3).

176 R. Blomfield, 'The Outlook of Architecture' (1913), in *The Touchstone of Architecture* (Oxford, 1925), 63, 67–8, 70. 'I think that we English architects lay too much stress on originality, quaintness, and that pernicious quality picturesqueness. Are we not false to our great art, when we prefer picturesqueness before dignity, and quaintness before grandeur, complexity before simplicity, and originality before perfection? ... it seems to me that we might with advantage strive to attain grandeur, dignity, simplicity, strength, rather than strain our powers to produce the quaint, the novel, and the picturesque ... Public edifices ought to have a certain stateliness ... The artist ... must disindividualise himself ...' ('G.L.S.', *B.*, lxi, 1891, 44–5).

177 His architectural theories are 'preposterous clap-trap', based on a Romantic – and fallacious – analogy between architecture and nature. 'Nature, in regard to her physical forms, has nothing whatever to do with architecture ... Architecture is a highly artificial and conventional form of art, the business of which is to impart dignity and expression to structure ... the main forms of architecture arise out of structural and mechanical conditions of an entirely artificial nature ... Of planning and structure Mr Ruskin knows nothing ... The public are beginning ... to find him out ... Enough of such twaddle' ('Revised Ruskin', *B.* lxi, 1891, 57–8: ed.).

178 e.g., T. Hayter Lewis and R. Langton Cole, *Companion to the Almanac* 1887, 129; 1891, 289–90.

179 Designed in conjunction with S. H. Hamp, C. B. Young and A. H. Mackmurdo. See A. S. Gray, *Edwardian Architecture* (1985), 58–60.

180 *B.N.* xxxix (1875), 363–4: ills.

181 *B.N.* xxxii (1877), 512, 646: ills.

182 *B.* liii (1887), 1–3: ill.; *B.N.* liii (1887), 10; *C.L.* cxix (1956), 329–30; *Survey of London* xli (1983), 17 *et seq.*

183 R. Langton Cole, *Companion to the Almanac* 1893, 290; 1894, 289.

184 *B.N.* lxii (1892), 101, 425; discussion with Owen Fleming.

185 In 1880 Hope seized the presentation of the RIBA Gold Medal to J. L. Pearson as a chance to mount one last assault on the iniquities of Queen Anne: neither Gothic dame nor Greek goddess, but a veritable Vampire Queen, a harlot clothed in meretricious rubbish; how different to 'that magnificent, severe virgin, *Ars Gothica*' (*RIBA Trans.* 1879–80, 195; *A.* xxii, 1880, 397–8).

186 R. Kerr, *The Gentleman's House*, ed. J. Mordaunt Crook (1972), 342. In W. H. Mallock's *New Republic* (1877), Mr Rose (Walter Pater) is talking to Mr Luke (Matthew Arnold). To Mr Luke's astonishment, Mr Rose looks forward to an architecture of the future, composed 'of no style in particular, but a renaissance of all styles'.

187 *A.* xxxviii (1887), frontispiece: from Beresford Hope's inaugural address as PRIBA, 1865.

7 From Neo-Classicism to Imperial Baroque

1 For what follows, see J. Mordaunt Crook, *The Greek Revival: Neo-Classical Attitudes in British Architecture, 1760–1870* (1972); *The Age of Neo-Classicism* (Arts Council, 1972); E. Kaufman, *Architecture in the Age of Reason* (1955); R. Rosenblum, *Transformations in Late Eighteenth-century Art* (1967); D. Wiebenson, *Sources of Greek Revival Architecture* (1969).

2 For a different view, arguing for the separation of Neo-Classicism and Romanticism, see H. Honour, *Neo-Classicism* (1968); *Romanticism* (1979). For an attempt at integration, under the neologism 'Romantic Classicism', see H.-R. Hitchcock, *Architecture: 19th and 20th Centuries* (1958)

3 J. Mordaunt Crook, 'Sir Robert Smirke: a centenary florilegium', *A.R.* cxliii (1967), 208–10.

4 J. Mordaunt Crook, *The British Museum* (1971).

5 J. Rykwert, 'Lodoli on Function and Representation,' *A.R.* clx (1976), 21–6. For comparisons with Laugier and Cordemoy, see W. Herrmann, *Laugier* (1962).

6 Haldane Lectures (1874), quoted in R. McFadzean, *Alexander Thomson* (1979), 222.

7 Address to the Glasgow Institute of Architects (1871), quoted in McFadzean, *op. cit.*, 256.

8 'The laws of architecture ... [are not] the rules of a game ... [They] do not consist of a series of arbitrary contrivances. They were not invented by men, but were discovered by them' (Haldane Lectures, McFadzean, *op. cit.*, 263). 'The laws which govern the universe, whether aesthetical or physical, are the same which govern architecture. We do not contrive rules – we discover laws' ('An Inquiry into the Appropriateness of the Gothic Style', 1866, quoted in McFadzean, *op. cit.*, 200).

9 Haldane Lectures, McFadzean, *op. cit.*, 265.

10 'His enthusiasm for the abstract possibilities of his art ... His grimly intellectual insistence on the power of dead-weight construction to achieve the most titanic results, was too vital a thing in its realisation to be obscured by adventitious excrescences. His work is effective out of all proportion to its size ... Thomson naturally thought in the Grand Manner' (Sir R. Blomfield, *A.R.* xv, 1904, 181–95).

11 *B.N.* xiv (1867), 374.

12 Haldane Lectures, McFadzean, *op. cit.*, 266. 'The aesthetic faculty appears to serve three purposes – the perceptive, the selective, and the creative' (*ibid.*, 262).

13 R. C. Rome, *The Union Club* (1948).

14 F. G. Waugh, *The Athenaeum Club* (c.1900); F. R. Cowling, *et al.*, *The Athenaeum* (1975).

15 W. H. Leeds, *The Travellers' Club House ... and the Revival of the Italian Style* (1839).

16 J. Mordaunt Crook, *The Reform Club* (1973).

17 Sir C. Petrie, *The Carlton Club* (1955).

18 C. Firebrace, *The Army and Navy Club* (1934).

19 e.g. Parnell's Sansovinesque Whitehall Club, at 47 Parliament St. (1865–66).

20 *Survey of London* xxx (1963), 496–509.

21 *B.* xiv (1856), 13; R.A.

22 *Sat. Rev.* iii (1857), 474–5.

23 *A.* xi (1874), 121; *B.* lxv (1893), 375; A.A. For Donaldson and Kerr, see J. Mordaunt Crook, 'Archi-

tecture and History', *Architectural History* xxvii (1984), 555–78. When in 1863 Samuel Huggins set out his *Chart of the History of Architecture*, he predicted that 'The Style of the Future' would be eclectic classicism (*B.* xxxi, 1863, 670).

24 C. Stell *Nonconformist Chapels and Meeting Houses in Central England* (R.C.H.M., 1986).

25 H. Hobhouse, *Thomas Cubitt, Master Builder* (1971), ch. 18.

26 Goodhart-Rendel, *English Architecture Since the Regency* (1953), 115. For a more favourable view, see A. E. Richardson, *C.L.* cxxxii (1962), 14.

27 *B.* xxxiv (1876), 600; *R.I.B.A.J.* 1876–7, 217–8.

28 See D. Linstrum, 'Cuthbert Brodrick; an interpretation of a Victorian architect', *R.S.A. Jnl.* cxix (1971), 72 *et seq.*; *Marble Halls*, ed. M. Darby and J. Physick (1973), no. 83, p. 130–31.

29 e.g. town halls at Bolton (W. Hill, 1866–73), Portsmouth (W. Hill, 1886–90) and Morley (G. A. Fox, 1895); Philadelphia City Hall (J. McArthur Jnr., 1871–1901); Parliament House, Melbourne (Kerr and Knight, 1856); Parliament House, Adelaide (Wright and Taylor, 1880s); Durban Town Hall (P. Dudgeon, 1883–5: *A.* lxxi, 1904, 49: ill.) and Cape Town City Hall (Reid and Green, 1893). See D. Linstrum, *West Yorkshire: Architects and Architecture* (1978), 339–43. Ruskin conceded that the base of the building was 'of fair Roman composition', but he regarded the tower as 'an abortion', put up by 'snobs or charlatans' (*Works* XXIV, 725).

30 Scott to Palmerston, 23 July 1859 (Broadlands MSS., C.C./S.C./18/1–6.); I. L. Toplis, 'The Foreign Office' (Ph.D. Thames Polytechnic, 1980), 102. 'The fenestration of Barry's Reform Club echoes through Bayswater; the garden front of the Travellers' inspires terraces in the Ladbroke area' (J. Summerson , 'London, the Artefact', in *The Victorian City*, ed. J. Dyos and M. Wolff, 1973, ii, 313).

31 Disraeli, *Tancred* (1845), Bk. i., ch 10. For an attack on 'Modern Town Houses', see Capt. Marryat, *Olla Podrida* (1840). 'Everything comes to an end', quipped Sydney Smith, 'even Wimpole St.'. For an assessment of the Italianate phase in housing development, see H.-R. Hitchcock, *Early Victorian Architecture* i (1954), 408–55; a 'sequel to the Georgian story, although like most sequels markedly inferior in interest'.

32 *B.N.* lxi (1891), 270.

33 W. Papworth, *The Renaissance and Italian Styles of Architecture in Great Britain* (1883); L. Scott, *The Renaissance of Art in Italy* (1883); A. Schütz, *Architecture and Decoration of the Italian Renaissance* (1883); J. Kinross, *Details from Italian Buildings, chiefly Renaissance* (1883); R. P. Pullan, *Studies in Architectural Styles* (1883).

34 *R.I.B.A.J.* 3rd series, viii (1900), 77.

35 *A.* xxix (1883), 263–4.

36 Winning designs, ills.: *B.* xlvii (1884), 326–7, 460; *B.N.* xlvii (1884), 168–9, 310–11, 357, 628–9, 674–5.

37 'Merely commonplace, from base to cornice, without a spark of genius in it'; its order 'out of proportion'; its balustrades vitiated by 'three different scales'; its roofline 'all over pots and pepper castors'; in plan and composition 'little short of a disgrace'. So much for 'the most important building of this generation'. Here was a 'great architectural opportunity

thrown away' (*B.* xlix, 1885, 248, 451–2).

38 Modified designs, ill.: *B.* xlviii (1885), 488–9, 492–3; *B.N.* xlviii (1885), 532–3, 535–6, 620–21, 720–21, 978–9, and lx (1891), 260–61, 364.

39 *Hansard*, 9 April 1885, col. 1170; *B.N.* xlviii (1885), 573.

40 W. H. White, *A Protest Against the Amended Designs for the Proposed Admiralty and War Office* (1885), 9.

41 Bodleian, Harcourt MSS., dep. 90, f. 47: 24 Nov. 1892. *Ex inf.* Dr N. Bingham.

42 *A.* xxxiv (1885), 166.

43 The 'current idea of the picturesque [is] ... ruinous to Classic architecture on a grand scale' (*A.* xxxii, 1884, 161).

44 R. Phéné Spiers, *The Orders of Architecture* (1891); a long series of detailed articles by G. A. T. Middleton which appeared in *B.N.* lxvii–lxx (1895–6), *passim*, and formed the basis of G. A. T. Middleton, and R. W. Carden, *Ornamental Details of the Italian Renaissance* (1901). 'Forty or fifty years ago, the leaders of the Gothic revival took up arms against the Orders, and thought and talked as if they had slain them. Yet here they are again, as active as ever!' (*B.* lxi, 1891, 39: ed.). 'I fancy I see a ... growing fondness for the good old Classic column' ([J. P. Seddon], *B.N.*, lxiv, 1893, 654). See also 'The Whirligig of Time', *B.* lxxii (1897), 10.

45 See G. Stamp and C. Amery, *Victorian Buildings in London* (1980), 151–2.

46 *B.N.* lxxx (1901), 255. The style was widely considered at the time to be 'an acquired taste'; it was greeted with 'laughter' in the House of Commons, and incomprehension in the streets (*B.N.* lviii, 1890, 153, 654).

47 C. Aslet, *The Last Country Houses* (1982), 120; *B.* lxxvii (1899), 32: ills.

48 Obit. by Hippolyte J. Blanc, *A.A. Notes* xvi (1901), 99–102. When in 1901 the RIBA was asked to nominate a short list of architects for the government buildings in Whitehall, Brydon received the vote of every member of Council (*B.* lxxx, 1901, 529–30).

49 Quoted by Beresford Pite, in *B.N.* lxxix (1900), 868–70: RIBA.

50 *B.N.* l (1886), 690; *B.* xlviii (1885), 616: ill.; revised version, *B.N.* lii (1887), 173.

51 Brydon, 'The English Classic Revival of the 17th and 18th centuries', *B.N.* lvi (1889), 263–4.

52 *A.A. Notes* xiii (1898), 172.

53 *B.* xiv (1856), 85–7: ill. and 317–8; *B.N.* v (1859), 110.

54 D. J. Bassett, 'The French Renaissance Revival in British Architecture, 1824–1914' (Ph.D., Edin., 1979), 7, 324. See also M. Girouard, 'The Wren Revival at Wellington', *C.L.* cxxv (1959), 1372–3.

55 i.e. Mansart at Balleroy and Berny. See Bassett, *op. cit.*, 327. For Kinmel, see M. Girouard, 'Kinmel Park', *C.L.* cxvi (1969), 542–5, 614–7; E. Hubbard, *Clwyd* (1986), 280–4. Brydon had been working with Nesfield at the time (*B.* xliv, 1888, 269).

56 'An English Classical style as truly the embodiment of the civilisation and life of the people as any Gothic that ever existed, a living, working, architectural reality, as much a part of England as its literature or its great school of painting' (*B.* lvi, 1889, 170).

57 *A.A. Notes* iii (1887), 93. By comparison the Queen Anne synthesis seemed 'loud ... vulgar and ...

un-English' (*B.* lx, 1871, 130: 'The English Renaissance of the eighteenth century': AA), and Beresford Pite's 'free classicism' seemed positively chaotic (*R.I.B.A.J.* 3rd series, viii, 1900, 92). See also *B.* lxxiv (1898), 81.

58 *B.* lvi (1889), 170: e.g. Scamozzi's Venetian window.

59 *R.I.B.A.J.* 3rd series viii (1900), 92. See also 'A.D. 1890', *A.A. Notes* i (1890), 74–5.

60 Guildhall extension (*B.* lxii, 1892, 38, 428: ill.); Technical School (*B.* lxx, 1896, 368); Picture Gallery and Library (*B.* lxxiii, 1897, 328: ill., and lxxiv, 1898, 408, 442); Pump Room and Roman Baths (*B.* lxvi, 1894, 198, 446: ill., and lxviii, 1895, 394); Council Chamber (*B.* lxxiii, 1897, 30: ill.). See also *A.R.* xviii (1905), 3–9, 51–9, 147–54.

61 *B.N.* lxi (1891), 270, 844 and lxii (1892), 58, 128.

62 *The Builder Album of R.A. Architecture* (1896), pl. xxxv; *Academy Architecture* ix (1896), 57.

63 ills.: *B.* lxxvi (1899), 300 [Parliament Square] and lxxviii (1900), 444 [courtyard]; *B.N.* lxxvi (1899), 452–3 [Parliament Square], 480–81 [with Scott and Barry's buildings]; *A.* lxi (1899), 320 [surroundings]. See also *B.* xciii (1907), 19 [exterior] and xcv (1908), 100 [courtyard].

64 *B.* lxxviii (1900), 444: ill.

65 The Charles St and Home Office towers were never built; Tanner was responsible for detailing the St James's Park façade.

66 Goodhart-Rendel, *English Architecture Since the Regency*, 200–201. 'It is not an eighteenth-century copy, but it is sufficiently eighteenth century not to be vulgar' (C. H. Reilly, *Some Architectural Problems of Today*, 1924, 10).

67 Obit. by J. M. Brydon, *R.I.B.A.J.* 3rd series, viii (1900), 44–7; by W. H. Seth-Smith, *A.A. Notes* iv (1900), 17–71.

68 *B.* lxiii (1892), 297.

69 W. Young, *Town and Country Mansions and Suburban Houses* (1879), 7.

70 *B.* lxiii (1892), 397.

71 *A.* liii (1895), 209, 225, 273; ills.; *B.N.* lx (1891), 489 and lxi (1892), 345.

72 The Marble Hall was designed in an eclectic Indian style (Mughal and Hindu), with advice from Caspar Purdon Clarke, Director of the V. and A., on a neo-Baroque plan (C. Aslet, 'Elvedon, Suffolk', *C.L.* clxxv, 1984, 672–6).

73 'The largest Classic building of the time in the kingdom' (*B.N.* lii, 1887, 625). Winning design, *B.N.* xliii (1882), 37: ill.

74 C. H. Reilly thought it a popular building merely because it was so obvious: 'When you have glanced at it from the top of a passing omnibus you have seen it all. It will not bear looking into' (Reilly, *Architectural Problems of Today*, op. cit., 10).

75 W. Young, *The Municipal Buildings, Glasgow* (Glasgow, 1890), 17, 20.

76 Designs (partly by Clyde Young), ill. *B.* xcii (1907), 666 and xciii (1907), 648; *A.R.* xx (1906), 302.

77 They echo, besides St Paul's, Wren's 1698 scheme for Whitehall (*Wren Society* viii, 1931, 9).

78 One derivative is Aston Webb and Ingress Bell's Royal United Services Institute, Whitehall (1893–95). See *B.* lxiv (1893), 368 and lxv (1893), 208: ills; *B.N.*

lxiv (1893), 752: ill. C. H. Reilly thought the Institute of Chartered Accountants Belcher's 'best building', but one which had much 'influence for harm among the half-learned' (*C.L.* lvi, 1924, 944).

79 *B.N.* li (1891), 171 258–9: ill. See also *B.* lxi (1891), 96–7; *A.* xlvi (1891), 106–7, 238: ill.; *British Architect* xxxiv (1891), 131.

80 *B.N.* lxxxvii (1907), 605: ill.

81 ills.: *B.N.* xcviii (1910), 12; *B.* xcviii (1910), 39, 42; *A.R.* xxviii (1910), 54–61. 'It is big and bold and strong. It is well made, its composition is satisfactory and it is weathering to a beautiful colour. But it has no distinction. It is better than Joe Beckett, but not as good as Carpentier. Its columns are the ordinary unfluted columns of commerce, while its entrance porch might be the entrance to a new Whitehall hotel – in Bloomsbury' (Reilly, *Architectural Problems*, op.cit., 10).

82 Summerson also sees the influence of the recently built Palais des Beaux Arts, Lille, by Bérard and Delmas (J. Summerson, *The Turn of the Century*, 1976, 16).

83 e.g. warehouses, Austin Friars (1879): ills., *B.N.* lvi (1889), 813.

84 *B.N.* lxi (1891), 128.

85 *B.N.* lxxx (1901), 583. For ills. of Webb's winning design, see *B.N.* lxi (1891), 180. Spanish influence was also visible in designs submitted by Emerson, Colcutt and even T. G. Jackson. Young, Deane and Macartney stayed Baroque or Palladian. For Emerson and Webb, see *B.N.* lxi (1891), 178, 217, 377, 716; for Colcutt and Belcher, *ibid.*, 251, 414, 428, 462; for Young and Deane, *ibid.*, 286; for Macartney and Jackson, *ibid.*, 322, 377. Digby Wyatt's *Architect's Notebook* (1872) had opened up Spanish Renaissance to English eyes; A. N. Prentice's *Renaissance Architecture and Ornament in Spain* (5 vols. 1893) supplied detailed ills. for the first time ('The Picturesque Architecture of Spain', *B.* lxv, 1893, 369–70). By 1892 [J. P. Seddon] was noting that a 'Spanish craze' had replaced the 'Dutch and Flemish mania' (*B.N.* lxiii, 1893, 302).

86 Summerson, *Turn of the Century*, op. cit., 17.

87 *B.* lxxxi (1901), 438: ill.

88 *B.* lxxxi (1901), 378, 464; *A.R.* x (1901), 212: ill.

89 *A.R.* x (1901), 211: ill.

90 RIBA Drawings W1.5/31/1.

91 For Webb's winning design, see *A.R.* x (1901), 200 and supp.; *B.* lxxxi (1901), 388–9.

92 130 HC. 45, 24 Feb. 1904, 873: *ex. inf.* Dr N. Bingham. Heathcote Statham, editor of the *Builder*, preferred his own scheme: *B.* lxxx (1901), 359–61, 413.

93 e.g. Adrian Berrington's 'Imperial Way' (1912), a mighty avenue which was to wend its way from Buckingham Palace, via a re-constituted South Bank, to St Paul's Cathedral, Guildhall and the Mansion House (ills.: *B.* cii, 1912, 11–13, 666–9 and civ, 1913, 13–14); schemes by A. E. Richardson *et al.* for Trafalgar Square (*A.R.* xxiv, 1908, 55–7: ills.) and Piccadilly Circus (*B.* ciii 1912, 46: ills.; cviii, 1915, 568: ills.); and F. W. Speaight's plans for Park Lane and Marble Arch (F. W. Speaight, *The Marble Arch: A Suggestion by a Citizen of London*, 1905) and Horse Guards Parade and St James's Park (Speaight, *The Horse Guards' Parade: A Suggested Improvement*, 1909; *A.R.* xxiii, 1909, 115–8).

94 See *B.* lxxxviii (1905), 455–6. Initial elevation by T. Raffles Davison, RIBA Drawings X10/4/7; ill.: *Academy Architecture* xxvii (1905), 12; *B.* lxxviii (1905),

468; perspective by Robert Atkinson, incorporating alterations: R.I.B.A. Drawings X10/4/9; *B*. xcix (1910), 128: ill.; *Academy Architecture* xxxviii (1910), 13: ill. See also R. Hyde and J. Hoole, *Getting London in Perspective* (1984), pl. 153.

95 *The Times* 23 Oct. 1912, p. 5: ill.; 24 Oct. 1913, p. 6. For comparisons between Blore's façade and Webb's, see *B*. ciii (1912), 496–8; civ (1913), 538; cv (1913), 517; cvii, 1914, 196; *B.N.* ciii (1912), 535, 614.

96 In planning both the Mall and Admiralty Arch, Aston Webb owed much to the perception of a young government architect named Richard Allison (obit. *B*. cxcv, 1958, 577 and *R.I.B.A.J.* lcvi, 1959, 145). *Ex inf.* Dr N. Bingham.

97 *B*. xciii (1907), 362: ill. and xcv (1908), 304: ill. A 'new Greek' revival had been hailed as early as 1887: the art of 'perfected trabeation' (*B.N.* lii, 1887, 67–8).

98 *B*. xci (1906), 249.

99 *B*. xci (1906), 634: ill.; G. Stamp, *London 1900* (*A.D.* Profiles, xiii, 1978), 394. For Peach's career, see A. S. Gray, *Edwardian Architecture* (1985), 297–80.

100 Goodhart-Rendel, *English Architecture since the Regency*, 201; Summerson, *Turn of the Century*, 18. Also short-listed in the preceding competition were: Belcher (Mannerist), Hare (Franco-Palladian), Florence (Neo-Grec), Baggally (Georgian Baroque *à la* Newgate) and Brydon (Cockerellian). See *B.N.* lxxix (1900) *passim*: ills.

101 Goodhart-Rendel, *English Architecture Since the Regency*, 209–10.

102 See *A.R.* xviii (1905), 28–31; xxi (1907), 257–67; xxxii (1912), 261–89: ills.

103 *B*. lxxxviii (1905), 682; *B.A.* lxiii (1905), 456. 'Clever, cosmopolitan, slightly vulgar, the art of E. A. Rickards is the architectural champagne of the period' (Summerson, *Turn of the Century*, 23). See also H. V. Lanchester and A. Fern, *The Art of E. A. Rickards* (1920).

104 It was originally intended to house a natural history museum and reading room (*Academy Architecture*, xxix, 1906, 24: ill.; *B*. xc, 1906, 590: ill.).

105 Cave began as an Arts and Crafts man and a sensitive neo-Georgian, e.g. Bengeo House, Hertford (L. Weaver, *Small Country Houses of Today*, i, 1922, ed., 167–70: ills.).

106 It replaced a Flemish Renaissance structure of 1888 by W. O. Mylne (*B.N.* liv, 1888, 59: ill.). One of England's first reinforced concrete structures was Henry Tanner's Baroque Post Office (1907–11) near St Bartholomew's Hospital (i.e. the King Edward Building, see *R.I.B.A.J.* 3rd series, xviii, 1911, 149–77). The Portland stone Baroque of H. N. Hawkes's Agriculture and Fisheries Building in Whitehall Place (1910–14) is similarly skin-deep: it clothes a steel skeleton and reinforced concrete frame. At this date, building regulations required external walls to carry their own weight. F. W. Troup, (offices for Spicer Bros, New Bridge St., London, 1913) and J. J. Burnet (Kodak Building, Kingsway, London, 1911) were almost alone in using facing materials to express the steel skeleton underneath (A. S. Gray, *Edwardian Architecture*, 1985, 66, 357).

107 For all three, see A. S. Gray, *Edwardian Architecture* (1985).

108 See *B*. xcviii (1910), 296: ill. and xcvi (1909), 218: ill. Some thought this was indeed 'a new style – the Ugly Style' (*A.R.* xxvii, 1910, 334). Walter Thomas's Liver Building on Pier Head, Liverpool (1908–11), perhaps.

109 *A.R.* lii (1922), 160.

110 C. H. Reilly, *Some Architectural Problems of Today* (1924), 148.

111 *The Architect's and Builder's Jnl.* (1911).

112 Starting from a Gothic viewpoint, Westlake had come to a similar conclusion: 'What is the cause [of stylistic multiplicity]? Is it that there is no dominant thought requiring a dominant idiom, no great and leading poetical aspiration in us, no really important idea for us as a nation to represent? ... this is the first century of the world's civilisation unmarked by any dominant architectural style ... we ... speak many languages ... [but] we lack a mother tongue ... there is neither dominant idea nor dominant idiom ... [so] what is the architect to do?' He must accept 'the necessity of the position in which we live' – that is, he must accept the stylistic plurality consequent on cultural plurality, and simply make architecture out of that. 'Wren and Inigo Jones did this, as Burges and as Pugin did' (Westlake, 'Fashion in Architecture and the Kindred Arts', *B.N.* lxii, 1892, 223–4).

113 H. Heathcote Statham, *Modern Architecture* (1897), 24–6. Statham dismissed Lethaby's dream of a revived vernacular as wishful thinking (*B*. lxix, 1895, 326: ed.; *ibid*., 334–5: RIBA). 'We curse the nineteenth century too much ... [Even if it is not] a great architectural age', it deserved better than the blanket condemnation of the Goths. It is no good complaining 'Architecture is dead! Architecture is dead!' 'Why not try to make it live?' 'Instead of laying hold of the details of some past style', we should say, 'What have I got to express in this – how can I make it a symbolism of something ... instead of going to the past for symbols' (*B*. lxxiii, 1897, 369).

114 e.g. *C.L.* cxli (1967), 54, 70: ills.

115 *C.L.* xviii (1905), 414. Also the exterior of Homewood, Herts. (1901), and on both the exterior and interior of Abbotswood, Glos. (1901–2).

116 *C.L.* xiii (1903), 602–11: ills.; cxli (1967), 70.

117 C. Hussey, *C.L.* lxxi (1932), 316–22, 378–84: ills.

118 e.g. *C.L.* cxlv (1969), 711: ill.

119 A. S. G. Butler, *The Architecture of Sir Edwin Lutyens* iii (1950), 22.

120 C. Hussey, *The Life of Sir Edwin Lutyens* (1953), 133 *et seq.*; *C.L.* clxxv (1984), 181

121 *C.L.* xxxviii (1910), 54.

122 Butler, *Lutyens, op. cit.*, i (1950), 33; D. Linstrum, *West Yorkshire: Architects and Architecture* (1978), 89–90.

123 RIBA MSS.: Lutyens to Baker, 1911 (Herbert Baker Colln.); partly quoted in *Lutyens* (Arts Council Exhibition catalogue, 1931), 108–9 and Linstrum, *op. cit.*, 91. There are more hints of Lutyens's debt to Sanmichele in the Midland Bank, Piccadilly (see C. H. Reilly, in *C.L.* lvi, 1924, 605).

124 C. Hussey, *C.L.* lxxvii (1935), 374–9, 400–405: ills.

125 C. Hussey, *C.L.* c (1946), 28–31, 74–7: ills.

126 Pevsner and Sherwood, *Oxfordshire* (1974), 703.

127 For changing attitudes towards Lutyens, compare Pevsner, 'Building with Wit, the architecture of Sir Edwin Lutyens', *A.R.* cix (1951), 217–25; J. Summerson, review of the *Lutyens Memorial Volumes, R.I.B.A.J.* Aug. 1951, 390–91; Frank Lloyd Wright, *ditto, Build-*

ing, July 1951, 260–62; R. Gradidge, *Dream Houses* (1980) and *Edwin Lutyens: Architect Laureate* (1981).

128 L. Weaver, *C.L.* xxx (1911), 374–80: ills.

129 A. S. G. Butler, *C.L.* xcviii (1945), 200–205, 244–7: ills.

130 Hussey, *Lutyens*, 218. 'I look at the big house ... [as] a centre for all the charity that should begin at home and cover henwise with wings of love all those near about her that are dependent and weaker and smaller'.

131 L. Weaver, *C.L.* xxxviii (1915), 680–88; lxxxix (1941), 232: ills.

132 The *British Architect* argued for Italian, as did *The Times*; the *Architects' and Builders' Jnl.* for Greek; and the *Builder* for English Renaissance: Britain's 'natural means of expression'.

133 The Viceroy, Lord Hardinge, advocated a mixture of Palladian and Pathan, a blend of Indian symbolism and Renaissance composition. So did Herbert Baker. And so did Hardinge's predecessor, Lord Curzon: he cited the fusion of Moorish and Renaissance elements in Southern Spain.

134 Hussey, *Lutyens*, *op.cit.*, 247.

135 For detailed analyses, see R. Byron, 'New Delhi', *A.R.* lxix (1931), 1–10; *Lutyens* (Arts Council Exhibition Catalogue, 1981), 32–43, 162–84; R. G. Irving, *Indian Summer: Lutyens, Baker and Imperial Delhi* (1981).

136 Hussey, *Lutyens*, *op. cit.*, 280.

137 *ibid.*

138 R. Byron, 'New Delhi', *C.L.* lxix (1931), 710. Or as Herbert Read put it: behind 'every dictator, there is a bloody Doric column' (quoted in *A.R.* clxxvi, 1984, X. 68–70).

139 *R.I.B.A.J.* 3rd series, lii (1945), 123.

140 Hussey, *Lutyens*, *op. cit.*, 123–4. Hence Hussey's conclusion that Lutyens was 'the last master of humanist architecture' (*ibid.*, 473).

8 From Modern to Post-Modern

1 B. Hillier, *John Betjeman: a life in pictures* (1984), 48. 1925 was the year of Gropius's Bauhaus building in Dessau.

2 L. Weaver, *Small Country Houses of Today* i (1910; 1922 ed.), 5.

3 *ibid.* (1922 ed.), 16. He was thinking of Coneyhurst at Ewhurst, Surrey (1886). Webb was always ahead of the field. When in the early 1890s young Lutyens first caught sight of Joldwynds, he exclaimed: 'that's good ... I wonder who the young man is?' (C. Hussey, *The Life of Sir Edwin Lutyens*, 1950, 26).

4 'It is impossible to foresee the kind of style that will spring from the determined efforts of contemporary arts and crafts ... It is up to the next generation to sort out what exactly our style was' (Muthesius, 'The Meaning of the Arts and Crafts', 1907, in *Form and Function*, ed. T. Benton *et al.*, 1975, 39). The term 'Arts and Crafts' was coined in 1888 by its first historian, J. T. Cobden-Sanderson, for an exhibition held at the New Gallery in Regent St. See J. T. Cobden-Sanderson, *The Arts and Crafts Movement* (1905).

5 Most famously in the case of Whistler v. Ruskin.

6 e.g. C. Nicholson, *Recent English Ecclesiastical Architecture* (1912).

7 For all these, see A. S. Gray, *Edwardian Architecture* (1985).

8 'We presume this is a new house, though it [Crooksbury, Surrey, 1889–1914] is made to look very much like an old one both in style and in the manner of drawing'. Anyway, 'it is decidedly picturesque ... pretty and homelike. The author [of Munstead Corner, Surrey, 1891] seems to be making a reputation for the treatment of this class of picturesque small country house' (*B.* lx, 1891, 427, 468).

9 *C.L.* clxvii (1980), 489, 574; *A.R.* xxv (1909), i, 143–50; *A. and B.J.* 27.7 (1910), 84, 87–91.

10 See also Stokes's own house, Littleshaw, Camp Rd., Woldingham, Surrey (1902–4): T. Raffles Davison, *Modern Homes* (1909), 106–12.

11 e.g. Bishopsgate Institution (1892–3); Whitechapel Art Gallery (1899–1901); Horniman Museum (1896–1900; 1910); Great Warley church, Essex (1904); Cliff Towers, Salcombe, Devon (ill.: *B.* lxxv, 1898, 843).

12 M. Girouard, *C.L.* cxlvii (1970), 494–7, 554–7.

13 'The local tradition in building is the crystallization of local need, material and ingenuity. When the result is so perfect, that is to say, when the adaptation of means to ends is so satisfactory that it has held good for a long time, and that no local need or influence can change it for the better; it becomes a style, and remains fixed until other conditions arise to disturb it' (Gertrude Jekyll, *Old West Surrey*, 1904, 5–6).

14 W. Morris, *Works*, ed. May Morris, xxii (1914), 429.

15 H. Muthesius, *The English House*, trans. J. Seligman (1979), 162.

16 See J. D. Kornwolf, *Baillie Scott and the Arts and Crafts Movement* (1972), *passim*. 'I have come to the conclusion,' Reginald Blomfield told T. G. Jackson in 1906, 'that the Arts and Crafts Movement has done more harm than good to Architects' (R. Blomfield, *Memoirs of an Architect*, 1932, 114). 'The study of building and materials is to the architect [only] what the study of anatomy is to the sculptor' – merely a preliminary to composition (R. Blomfield, *The Mistress Art*, 1908, 102). 'The popularity and attractiveness of silver-grey oak and multi-coloured birch, of cottagey casements divided up with thick leads, of rough, soft roofing tiles warped in the burning, were greedily seized, not as an enrichment of, but as a substitute for, architecture' (Goodhart-Rendel, *English Architecture Since the Regency*, 184).

17 'A great many Edwardian architects became terrified of the age they lived in, and ran to ground in the burrows of antiquity' (*ibid.*).

18 L. Weaver, *Small Country Houses of Today* ii (1919), 38, 40.

19 'Modern civilisation rests on machinery, and no system for the endowment, or the encouragement, or the teaching of art can be sound that does not recognise this ... [However] machinery in so far as it destroys human Individuality is bad, in so far as it develops it is good ... Machinery untamed ... that is the barbarism we have now to fight' (A. Crawford, *C. R. Ashbee: Architect, Designer and Romantic Socialist*, 1985, 116, 160, 419).

20 C. R. Ashbee, *Craftsmanship in Competitive Industry* (Campden, 1908), 9.

21 See F. MacCarthy, *The Simple Life: C. R. Ashbee in the Cotswolds* (1980).

22 *C.L.* clxviii (1980), 1551–5: colour ills.; A. Crawford, ed., *By Hammer and Hand: the Arts and Crafts Movement in Birmingham* (Birmingham, 1984). For Arts and Crafts aesthetics see C. Neve, 'Arts and Crafts Movement', *C.L.* cliv (1973), 1048–9.

23 W. R. Lethaby, A. Powell and F. L. Griggs, *Ernest Gimson. His Life and Work* (1924): ills.

24 W. R. Lethaby, 'Towns to live in', in *Form in Civilisation* (Oxford, 1957), 25.

25 Mackintosh was as much a product of the English Arts and Crafts Movement as he was of the Scottish vernacular tradition; and his reputation was European rather than British. See T. Howarth, *C. R. Mackintosh and the Modern Movement* (1952); R. Macleod, *C. R. Mackintosh* (1968).

26 See P. Davey, *Arts and Crafts Architecture: the Search for Earthly Paradise* (1980), 137. The department was headed by W. E. Riley (A. S. Gray, *Edwardian Architecture*, 1985, 312–3). Statham noted in 1897 that the designs of London's fire stations – unlike the regular mixed classicism of Stokes's London post offices – were 'too broken up', too lacking in 'simplicity' (H. Heathcote Statham, *Modern Architecture*, 1897, 150).

27 e.g. Lea Cottage and Stoneywell Cottage, Markfield, Leicestershire (1898–9). See L. Weaver, *Small Country Houses of Today* ii (1919), 15–21; G. Stamp and A. Goulancourt, *The English House, 1860–1914* (1986), 128–9.

28 'The actual building [at Markfield] was done by Mr Detmar Blow ... captaining a little band of masons' (L. Weaver, *Small Country Houses of Today*, ii, 1919, 16). 'The buildings look as solid and lasting as the pyramids, and though they are built with almost stern rudeness, yet they look gracious and homelike' (H. Wilson, 'The Arts and Crafts Society's Exhibition', *A.R.* vi, 1879, 214).

29 Quoted by C. Aslet, *C.L.* clxiv (1978), 118. Rodmarton was finished in 1928, by Norman Jewson.

30 'Rodmarton is magnificent, but it is a dead-end: a medieval house created in a medieval way in one of the last pockets of feudalism in England' (Davey, *Arts and Crafts Architecture*, 1980, 152).

31 Quoted in G. Naylor, *The Arts and Crafts Movement* (1971), 9.

32 L. Weaver, *Small Country Houses of Today* ii (1919), 94. He was referring to the Cloisters by Baillie Scott in Avenue Rd., Regent's Park. See also C. Aslet, 'Rhapsodies on a Tudor Theme', *C.L.* clxvii (1980), 1394–7: Bailifscourt, Sussex (1935); Crowhurst Place, Sussex (1918 onwards); Old Surrey Hall, Lingfield (1922). For Tudorbethan houses – and garages ('The Garage Desirable') – by Blunden Shadbolt, Maurice Webb, etc., see P. A. Barron, *The House Desirable: a handbook for those who wish to acquire homes that charm* (1929).

33 W. R. Lethaby, *Architecture* (1911), conclusion.

34 H. Muthesius, *The English House*, trans. J. Seligman (1979), 163.

35 Goodhart-Rendel, *English Architecture Since the Regency* (1953), 17, 254, 256.

36 *A.R.* xviii (1905), 27.

37 D. Simpson, *C. F. A. Voysey* (New York, 1979).

When Voysey first exhibited at the R.A. in 1895 – Perrycroft, Colwall, Herefs. – his designs seemed 'primitive' and 'odd-looking'. Like Baillie-Scott's work in the same year, it seemed 'a protest' against the 'smugness' of Queen Anne (*B.N.* lxviii, 1895, 648).

38 C. F. A. Voysey, 'Ideas in Things', in *The Arts Connected with Building*, ed. T. Raffles Davison (1909), 120. See also, Voysey, *Reason as the Basis of Art* (1906); *Individuality* (1915); 'The Quality of Fitness in Architecture', *Craftsman* xxiii (1912), 174–82; 'The Aesthetic Aspects of Concrete Construction', *The Architect and Engineer* lvii (1919), 80–82.

39 *A.R.* lxx (1931), 91.

40 H. Muthesius, *The English House*, trans. J. Seligman (1979), 196.

41 Muthesius, *English House, op. cit.*, 63. See also P. Davey, 'Arts and Crafts Gardens', *A.R.* clxxix (1985), (9), 32–7. Robert Lorimer – 'the Scottish Lutyens' – visited Munstead Wood and sent out a rapturous description to a friend in Australia: 'It looks so reasonable, so kindly, so perfectly beautiful that you feel that people might have been making love and living and dying there, and dear little children running about for the last – I was going to say, thousand years, anyway six hundred. They've used old tiles which of course helps, but the proportion, the way the thing's built (very long coursed rubble with thick joints and no corners) in fact it has been built by the old people of the old materials in the old "unhurried" way but at the same time "sweet to all modern uses" ...' (Quoted in P. Savage, *Lorimer and the Edinburgh Craft Designers*, 1980, 25).

42 See T. Raffles Davison, *Port Sunlight* (1916), viii: 'a combination of the practical and the artistic ... How fortunate the workpeople who are enabled to live under such ideal conditions!'

43 See S. Beattie, *A Revolution in Housing* (1980).

44 e.g. Avon Tyrrell, Hants. (1891–93); High Coxlease, Lyndhurst, Hants. (1900–1901). See Muthesius, *English House, op. cit.*, 37–8; G. Rubens, *W. R. Lethaby* (1986), 111–21, 145–8.

45 'All architecture ... worth the name, is one vast symbolism. "Symbolism controlled by and expressive of structure" might be the definition of Architecture' (W. R. Lethaby, *Scrips and Scraps*, ed. A. H. Powell, 1975, 19).

46 'Co-operative human intelligence is totalised in [Gothic]. The time is the architect, the nation is the building ... the greatest productions of architecture are ... a sort of deposit or geological formation ... each race deposits a stratum: each individual contributes a stone' (*Notre Dame*, quoted by Lethaby in 'Modern Building Design', *B.* lxix, 1895, 312).

47 'Architectural beauty ... [grows] from within outward, out of the necessities and character of the dweller ... out of ... unconscious truthfulness and nobleness without even a thought for ... appearance' (quoted, *ibid.*)

48 'Noble architecture ... must be practised in the dwelling before it can be perfected in the church' (Ruskin, *Works*, x, 123: *Stones of Venice* ii).

49 'The art that is to come will not be an esoteric mystery shared by a little band of superior beings: it will be a gift of the people to the people ... A building is made up of millions of hammer-strokes, chisel-strokes, and movements of the hand. Because a man sits in an

office and makes a design, it does not follow that you get a fine building' (quoted by Lethaby, *B.* lxix, 1895, 313).

50 Lethaby, *B.* lxix (1895), 312: *oratio recta*. In Baroque, he believed, that balance was upset: 'delight' at the expense of 'commoditie'. 'Architecture is not an appearance, a wreathing of vapour evolved by an individual magician waving a wand in a vacuum; it is the solid and permanent embodiment of great cooperative toil' (Lethaby, 'The Architecture of Riot', *B.* cxxiv, 1923, 893: review of G. Scott, *Architecture of Humanism*).

51 *A.R.* i (1897), 52, 266.

52 To compare columns and trees was to turn a poetic analogy into a category mistake (*B.* lxix, 1895, 326).

53 *B.* lxxi (1896), 308: A.A.

54 Lethaby, 'Modern Building Design', *B.* lxix (1895), 335.

55 Lethaby, 'The Problem of Modern Architecture', *B.* lxxi (1896), 307: *oratio recta*.

56 Lethaby, 'A National Architecture', *B.* cxv (1918), 229.

57 Lethaby, *Art and Workmanship* (Birmingham, 1930), 3. Similarly Warington Taylor to E. R. Robson: 'style means copyism, the test of good work would be the absence of style' (quoted in D. Watkin, *English Architecture*, 1979, 177).

58 Henry Cole of the Victoria and Albert Museum had openly admired the '36 Colt Navy revolver. Such artefacts have always polarised formalists and functionalists (*A.R.* clxxv, 1984, (v), 5).

59 'If we agree that a plum pudding were a machine to eat, it would not be made by designing it like a wheel or screw, but by making it to function properly for its purpose' (Lethaby, 'Engineering and Architecture', *B.* cxl, 1931, 54): i.e. that a plum pudding should be made to *taste* well, not *look* well.

60 Lethaby, 'A National Architecture', *B.* cxv (1918), 300.

61 *ibid.*, 261.

62 *ibid.*, and 300.

63 *ibid.*, 262.

64 *ibid.*, 300.

65 *ibid.*, 229.

66 Lethaby, 'Art and Workmanship', *The Imprint* Jan. 1913.

67 Lethaby, 'Architecture as Form in Civilisation', in *Form in Civilisation* (Oxford, 1957), 7.

68 Lethaby, 'Of the "Motive" in Architectural Design', *A.A. Notes* iv (1889), 24.

69 Lethaby, 'A National Architecture', *B.* cxv (1918), 319.

70 *ibid.*, 363.

71 *ibid.*, 406.

72 *ibid.*, 442.

73 *ibid.*, Alas, to be artless is to be art-less. Lutyens was wiser when he noted that architectural tradition 'consists in our inherited sense of structural fitness, the evolution of rhythmic forms by a synthesis of needs and materials, and the avoidance of arbitrary faults by the exercise of common sense coupled with sensibility.... The best old work was composed' (Hussey, *Lutyens*, 1953, 557).

74 Lethaby, 'What shall we call beautiful?' in *Form in Civilisation* (Oxford, 1957), 126: 1918.

75 The phrase 'modern movement' was probably first used by Mackintosh in 1903 in a letter to Fritz Warndörfer, although the epithet 'modern' was current before that date, e.g. O. Wagner, *Moderne Architektur*, 3 vols. (Vienna, 1896–1902).

76 Lethaby, 'Architecture as Engineering', *B.* cxxxvi (1929), 252. See also *A.R.* lxv (1929), 271–2.

77 Lethaby, 'Architecture as Engineering', *B.* cxxxvi (1929), 301.

78 Lethaby, 'Art and the Community', *B.* cxxxvi (1930), 56.

79 See B. C. Brolin, *The Failure of Modern Architecture* (1976), 14 *et seq.*

80 Lethaby, 'Art and the Community', *B.* cxxxvi (1930), 310. 'Style properly is an expression from within; "style", falsely so called, is imposed from without – an imposition indeed. This is what is wrong with our modern approach to building problems' (*ibid.*, 487).

81 *ibid.*, 488.

82 Lethaby, 'Engineering and Architecture', *B.* cxl (1931), 54. The Modern Movement had become 'only another design humbug to pass off with a shrug – ye old modernist style – we must have a style to copy – what funny stuff this art is' (Quoted in R. Macleod, *Style and Society*, 1971, 67).

83 *C.L.* lxx (1931), 3027.

84 M. Fry, *Autobiographical Sketches* (1975), 136.

85 In 1933 Frederick Towndrow stated that there were 'only about a dozen really scientific [i.e. Modern] buildings in this country, and only about half a dozen architects – if that – who understood the philosophy or ideals of the movement.' He lists Emberton's Yacht Club at Burnham, and offices for Beck and Pollitzer at Southwark Bridge; two houses by George Checkley at Cambridge; Connell's 'High and Over'; the new BBC studios; Robertson's Horticultural Hall; Tait's Freemasons' Hospital, Ravenscourt Park; and Holden's Piccadilly Line underground stations (*The Listener* x, 1933, 127–8).

86 Viollet-le-Duc, *Entretiens*, i, 99.

87 'The modern movement in architecture represents not new knowledge, but a wilful loss of knowledge on a scale unprecedented in the history of art' (R. Scruton, *The Times* 22 March, 1983, 12).

88 All the following quotations are from *Towards a New Architecture*, trans. F. Etchells (1927).

89 Quoted in S. Gardiner, *Le Corbusier* (1974), 14. See Le Corbusier, 'In the Defence of Architecture' (1929); reprinted in *Oppositions* iv, Oct. 1974.

90 Maxwell Fry in *The Listener* x (1983), 127.

91 'This is the greatest discovery in modern thought, a discovery never the old architects dreamed of, for they did not have our modern machines to give them the clue' (F. Towndrow, *The Listener* x, 1933, 128).

92 Gropius, 1919 Programme (T. Benton *et al.*, *Form and Function* 1975, 78–9). See B. Adler and J. L. Martin, 'The Bauhaus', *The Listener* xli (1949), 485–6, 527–9; G. Naylor, *The Bauhaus* (1968); F. Whitford, *Bauhaus* (1984). For a different viewpoint, see J. Rykwert, 'The Dark Side of the Bauhaus', in *The Necessity of Artifice* (1982), 44–9.

93 'The reality of our century is technology: the invention, construction and maintenance of machines.... Everyone is equal before the machine ... there is no tradition in technology, no class-consciousness' (Moholy-Nagy, 'Constructivism and the Pro-

letariat', 1922, cited in Whitford, *Bauhaus*, 1984, 128).

94 See Whitford, *Bauhaus* (1984), 180. 'All things in this world are a product of the formula *function times economics*' (Meyer, 1928, cited in H. M. Wingler, *The Bauhaus*, Camb. Mass., 1969, 153).

95 See also L. Moholy-Nagy, *The New Vision* (trans. D. M. Hoffmann, New York, 1932), and *Vision in Motion* (Chicago, 1947); R. Kostelonetz, ed., *Moholy-Nagy* (1970); S. Moholy-Nagy, *Moholy-Nagy: Experiment in Totality* (New York, 1950).

96 S. Cantacuzino, *Wells Coates* (1978), 13, 16. See also J. M. Richards, 'Wells Coates', *A.R.* cxxiv (1958), 357–60.

97 See J. M. Richards, *The Functional Tradition* (1958).

98 Pevsner calls it 'the most advanced British building of its date', an epitome of 'the dignity of labour and the might of the machine', adding: 'Why is it not just as famous as Peter Behrens' turbine factory of 1909?' (Pevsner, 'Nine Swallows – No Summer', *A.R.* xci, 1942, 109). Certainly its is functional: the factory was designed for a firm specialising in water pipe boilers; the tower contained hydraulic accumulators; the facings are of industrial bricks; the lintels of cast iron; the roofs of glazed steel; even the battered buttresses owe their shapes to lateral presures and the necessities of their functions (*B.* lxxxi, 1901, 34–5; xci, 1906, 634; ills.). Creswell claimed 'the design attempts to give candid architectural expression to engineering workshops'. But his Vauxhall Motor Co. factory at Luton, Beds. (1907–15) is Neo-William-and-Mary.

99 In the early 1980s, Charles Jencks designed Post-Modernist suits with their lapels doubled.

100 Cantacuzino, *op. cit.*, 24

101 *ibid.*

102 A. Connell, quoted in A. Jackson, *The Politics of Architecture* (1970), 56. In 1938 the MARS Group's 'New Architecture' exhibition catalogue described it as 'one of those periodic *plateaux* which occur in the historical ascent of every intellectual movement' (*New Architecture*, 1938, 6). Several architects were excluded from the Group as insufficiently 'modern': Howard Robertson, Grey Wornum, Oliver Hill, Lewis Wamsley, Oswald Milne, Joseph Emberton (Cantacuzino, *op.cit.*, 47). Connell broke with the Group over his neo-classical design for Newport Civic Building (1936). The group finally dissolved in 1957. See D. Lasdun in *Architect's Year Book* viii (1957), 57–60.

103 *The Listener* x (1933), 130. 'The engineer makes the structure, and the architect arranges it to achieve maximum usefulness [not beauty].'

104 *A.A. Jnl.* April 1938. See also W. Coates, in *Unit One: the Modern Movement in English Architecture, Painting and Sculpture*, ed. H. Read (1934), 108. Unit One was based on the Mayor Gallery in Cork St., London, see *Unit One: Spirit of the '30s* (Mayor Gallery, 1984).

105 Coates, *Unit One, loc. cit.*

106 *A.R.* July 1933. See also J. Pritchard, *View from a Long Chair: the Memoirs of Jack Pritchard* (1984).

107 Quoted in *A.R.* clxxvi (1984), x, 68–70.

108 Cantacuzino, *Wells Coates*, 102.

109 P. Carter, 'Sayings of Mies van der Rohe', *A.D.* March 1961.

110 'A bicycle shed is a building; Lincoln Cathedral is a piece of architecture ... the term architecture applies only to buildings designed with a view to aesthetic appeal' (N. Pevsner, *Outline of European Architecture*, 1943 etc; intro).

111 G. Scott, *Architecture of Humanism* (1961 ed.), 120: an echo of Ruskin's fourth aphorism in *Seven Lamps*, i.

112 A. Loos, 'Ornement et crime' [1908], in *L'Esprit nouveau* 2 (Nov. 1920), 159–68. Loos believed that 'only a very small part of architecture belongs to art: the tomb and the monument'. He accepted only half of Ruskin's theory of ornament as pleasure – the craftsman's pleasure. He failed to see that such pleasure might be reciprocal between craftsman and client or spectator.

113 Quoted by P. Fuller, in *W. R. Lethaby: Architecture, Design, Education*, ed. S. Backemeyer and T. Gronberg (1984), 40.

114 However precise the technology, Nervi reminds us, 'there always remains a margin of freedom sufficient to show the personality of the creator or, if he be an artist, to allow that his creation, even in its strict technical obedience, becomes a real and true work of art' (quoted in R. Arnheim, *The Dynamics of Architectural Form*, Berkeley, 1977, 256). Similarly Sir Giles Gilbert Scott in *R.I.B.A.J.*, 3rd series, xlii (1934–5), 908.

115 *A.A.Jnl.* lii (1937), 294 'Forms ... do not ... somehow come from the programme. Where forms come from, as any art historian knows, is a very great mystery indeed. They come from the artist's personality, his totality of experience, and how they come is a problem of the psychology of art ... of which astonishingly little is known' (J. Summerson, *R.I.B.A.J.* lxiv, 1957, 313). Similarly Pevsner: 'A style in art belongs to the world of mind, not the world of matter' (*An Outline of European Architecture*, 1953 ed., 22–3).

116 *B.N.* lxviii (1895), 828.

117 'Architectural judgement is not merely an optional addition to the architect's psychology. It is an essential expression of his rational nature. To imagine a world purged of all aesthetic preoccupations, is to imagine a world with neither concepts nor eyes' (R. Scruton, *The Aesthetic Understanding*, 1983, 188).

118 e.g. F. R. S. Yorke claimed in 1934 that architects need make no attempt 'to discover a new style, or new shapes': all they need is functional propriety and structural purity (Yorke, *The Modern House*, 1934; *The Modern House in England*, 1937; [and F. Gibberd], *The Modern Flat*, 1937). Later on he is less dogmatically mechanistic: by 1939 he was conceding that there had been an initial 'tendency to over-emphasize the expression of structure ... at the expense of appearances' (Yorke and C. Penn, *A Key to Modern Architecture*, 1939). But as late as 1964, Chermayeff was still arguing for a Science of Environmental Design – computerised now – as the basis of objective form: 'Beauty', in Eric Gill's words 'will look after itself' (S. Chermayeff and C. Alexander, *Community and Privacy: Towards a New Architecture of Humanism*, 1964 ed., 20). See also S. Chermayeff and A. Tzonis, *Shape of Community* (1971).

119 Corbusier, 'The vertical garden city', *A.R.* lxxix (1936), 10.

120 *A.J.* lxxxi (1935), 435.

121 R. Furneaux Jordan, 'Lubetkin', cxviii (1955), 36–44. Lubetkin was commenting on Russian architecture, in *A.R.* lxxi (1932), 201.

122 *A.R.* clxxi (1982), 5–6. In Bevin House,

Finsbury, 'new symbolic forms [were] synthesized with sound construction and a well researched study of needs' (J. Lubbock, in *New Statesman* 27 July 1982, 24–5).

123 *A.R.* cix (1951), 135.

124 Lubetkin, 'Architectural Thought Since the Revolution', *A.R.* lxxi (1932), 207. Similarly, F. Towndrow: in future, people will ask 'not whether the buildings are beautiful, but whether they are fit for their function' (*Listener* x, 1933, 128).

125 *A.R.* cix (1951), 135. 'An artist isn't there to please himself but is an agent of his time' (*The Observer* 7 March 1982).

126 'Public and private usefulness, and the happiness and preservation of mankind, are the aims of architecture.... Thus one should not strive to make a building pleasing, since if one concerns oneself solely with the fulfilment of practical requirements, it is impossible that it should not be pleasing' (J. N. L. Durand, *Précis des leçons d'architecture* i, 1802, 18).

127 'Beauty ... consists in the ... use of ... forms ... perfectly adapted to their purpose' (Viollet-le-Duc, *Entretiens*, vi, 1863, trans. B. Bucknall, i, 1877, 183).

128 Yorke and Gibberd, *The Modern Flat*, (1937), 83–7.

129 *ibid.*, 88–90.

130 A. Cox, 'Highpoint Two', *Focus* ii (1938), 79.

131 *A.R.*, lxxxiv (1938), 166.

132 See J. M. Richards, 'The condition of architecture and the principle of anonymity' in *Circle*, ed. J. L. Martin *et al.* (1937), 184.

133 *A.R.* lxv (1929), 17.

134 Quoted in L. Esher, *A Broken Wave* (1981), 85.

135 E. Waugh, *Decline and Fall* (1928). Waugh credited Silenus with the design of a chewing-gum factory, presumably Messrs. Wrigley, Wembley (1927).

136 M. Fry, *Autobiographical Sketches* (1975), 147.

137 *A.A. Jnl.* lii (1937), 63. 'Corbusier ... is one of those men who are born old-fashioned. I think he has the worst Victorian ethical view of architecture' (*R.I.B.A.J.* xxxv, 1928, 585–6).

138 J. M. Richards, intro. to F. R. S. Yorke, *The Modern House in England* (1937; 1948), 2. See also, P. Fleetwood-Hesketh, *Thirties Society Jnl.* i (1980), 16.

139 Compare Crabtree's Peter Jones with Mendelsohn's Schocken store at Chemnitz, Germany (1928–29). The Savoye House at Poissy-sur-Seine (1929–30: Le Corbusier and P. Jeanneret) was replicated all over England. Frederick Towndrow denied this: 'There is no such thing as a "modern style" ... style implies the idea of an accepted external expression which may be imposed upon the organic nature of the subject. The scientific school ... is not committed in any way to the use of reinforced concrete, or white plaster, or horizontal windows, or angular shapes, or flat roofs. These, where they occur, should be the result of causes in service and structure ... one may have a building that is no less modern because it has stone walls and a tiled roof.... Flat roofs are employed not because they look 'modern' but because ... they are cheaper and more serviceable' (*The Listener* x, 1933, 128). Accusations of copyism were, however, really beside the point. 'What did it matter if they said you were imitating Mies or Gropius or Corbu. It was like accusing a Christian of imitating Jesus Christ' (T. Wolfe, *From Bauhaus to Our House*, 1983, 73).

140 W. Coates, *Unit One*, ed. H. Read (1934), 108.

141 J. M. Richards and S. Chermayeff, *A.J.* lxxxi (1985), 189–90.

142 With reference to the Barcelona Pavilion. See A. Drexler, ed., *The Architecture of the Ecole des Beaux Arts* (New York, 1977), 36–7.

143 A. Trystan Edwards, 'The dead city', *A.R.* lxxvi (1929), 137.

144 C. Hussey, *Lutyens*, 542: 1933.

145 e.g. 'Torilla', Hatfield (F. R. S. Yorke, 1934–5), had hardly any insulation; no cavity walls or roofspace; inaccessible plumbing, and wiring buried in concrete. The walls cracked and the windows rusted (*The Times* 7 May 1984).

146 See Blomfield, *Modernismus*, 58.

147 'Architecture is the art of form, of rhythm, and proportion, and ... its problem is to translate into terms of ordered beauty the requirements of civilised life as it moves from age to age.... The spirit of Classical architecture does not rest in orders and entablatures, but in a clearness of conception that controls the whole design from first to last and excludes everything that is not essential to the expression of the dominant idea' (R. Blomfield, *French Architecture and its Relation to Modern Practice*, Zaharoff Lecture, Oxford, 1927, 16–17). Palladio held little attraction for him; Wren and Mansart were his heroes (R. A. Fellows, *Sir Reginald Blomfield*, 1985). For reviews of Blomfield's *Modernismus* (1934), see *A.J.* lxxix (1934), 363 (by E. Maxwell Fry); B. cxlvi (1934), 667; *Times Literary Supplement*, 1 March 1934, 140; *R.I.B.A.J.* 1934, 704 (by W. Vernon Crompton).

148 Blomfield, *Modernismus*, 72, 76–7; *R.I.B.A.J.* xxxv (1928), 513–4.

149 Ruskin, *Works*, ix, 72: *Stones of Venice*, i.

150 Muthesius, 'The Problem of Form in Engineering', 1913 (T. Benton *et al.*, *Form and Function*, 1975, 117).

151 'Beauty has been defined by some as fitness for purpose. It is a good slogan ... but it is quite untrue. It is blatantly untrue in its extreme form: fitness equals beauty, and it is not even correct in the more moderate form: no beauty without fitness' (N. Pevsner, *Visual Pleasures From Everyday Things*, Council for Visual Education, 1946, 12).

152 H. Read, *Art and Industry* (1934), 101. Similarly, T. L. Donaldson: 'True beauty cannot be apart from convenience. The most beautiful will be the most convenient, but the converse proposition is not a corollary thereto' (*Maxims*, 1847, liii; *A.* lxxxv, 1904, 39).

153 Blomfield, *Modernismus*, 164; 'Is Modern Architecture on the Right Track?', *The Listener* x (1933), 124. Similarly, Goodhart-Rendel: 'Utilitarianism is an aesthetic negative which will die out of art when its work of destruction is accomplished' (*English Architecture Since the Regency*, 283).

154 'The fact is that the perception of expediency of proportion can but rarely affect our estimates of beauty, for it implies a knowledge which we very rarely and imperfectly possess' (Ruskin, *Works*, IV, 110: *Modern Painters*, ii). Ruskin had absorbed Laugier's distinction between 'apparent utility' and constructive use: he distinguished between 'apparent' and 'constructive' proportion (*ibid.*, 102–3).

155 Architecture is the 'art of ordered building.... The Art *par excellence* of abstract form, which can make its impact on the emotions by sheer rhythmical form

and composition of forms' (R. Blomfield, *Memoirs of an Architect*, 1932, 115).

156 M. Golossov designed a 'House of Labour' in Moscow in iconic form, to look like a dynamo's cog-wheel (R. Blomfield, *Modernismus*, 53).

157 J. Summerson, 'Architecture', in *The Arts Today*, ed. G. Grigson (1935), 284.

158 R. Blomfield, *Modernismus*, 74. In other words, a misapplication of metaphor: the Romanesque and Gothic styles embodied metaphors of their own arcuation; Modernist buildings were metaphors of machines.

159 The phrase seems to have been coined by Alfred Barr. For an alternative critique of Johnson's thought – and a reply by Johnson – see P. Eisenman, 'Behind the Mirror: on the writings of Philip Johnson', *Oppositions* x (1977), 1–19.

160 See L. Menear, *London's Underground Stations* (Tunbridge Wells, 1983).

161 Wallis, Gilbert and Partners had already made mass concrete modernistic, e.g. East Surrey Water Works, Purley (T. P. Bennett, *Architectural Design in Concrete*, 1927, 11–12, pl. lvi).

162 In conversation with the author, 1983. Pevsner called the Hoover Factory 'perhaps the most offensive of ... modernistic atrocities' (Pevsner, *Middlesex*, 1951, 180). But by 1977, Philip Johnson confessed: 'With the benefit of fifty-year hindsight, those former "enemies" now look more interesting, more rich in associations, in metaphor, in decorative abundance, than the [Modern] style which we espoused' (*Oppositions* x, 1977, 17).

163 Admitted by Sir James Richards, in 'The Hollow Victory', *R.I.B.A.J.* 3rd series lxxix (1972), 192–7. Interior decoration helped to change attitudes: 'A few short years have vastly altered the public attitude towards function and modern design. It has taken its place in the long succession of styles' (*C.L.* lxix, 1931, 200). 'Treated as a style and not as a religion [Modernism] has great capabilities' (Goodhart-Rendel, 'Growing Pains', *A. and B.N.* cxxv, 1931, 302).

164 The Battersea designs were originally prepared by Messrs. C. S. Allott and Son, consulting engineers, and Messrs. Halliday and Agate, architects. Scott was consultant architect for the exterior. Summerson calls Scott's styling 'a case of misapplied skill' (*The Times* 17 Dec. 1983). But for a nice example of that skill applied in miniature, compare Scott's classical GPO telephone kiosks of 1927 ('K.2') and 1935 ('K.6') with Bruce Martin's formless version of 1968 ('K.8').

165 'Structure alone [is] not sufficient ... [we require] the indication of it; the human mind [can] not grasp it unless it [is] focussed. The architect ... gives expression to the organic idea of structure' (F. E. Towndrow, *R.I.B.A.J.* xxv, 1928, 520–21).

166 J. Betjeman, 'Christmas', *Collected Poems* (1962), 189. See *A. and B.N.* cxxvi (1931), 105–23; *B.* cxliv (1931), 753–4.

167 F. Pick, intro. to W. Gropius, *The New Architecture and the Bauhaus*, trans. P. Morton Shand (1935; 1945), 8–9. Similarly Charles Holden: 'I regard the present phase of extreme simplicity as comparable to a piece of ground which is allowed to be fallow for the benefit of future crops. In the meantime our architecture is gaining in significance by the elimination of non-essentials' (*The Listener* x, 1933, 125).

168 e.g. Hill's Midland Hotel, Morecombe (1932–3) and Scott's Royal Shakespeare Theatre, Stratford-on-

Avon (1928–32). For Hill, see R. Gradidge in *A.D. Profiles* xxiv (1980), 30–43.

169 If Lutyens' Queen's Dolls' House represents 'the most educated taste of today, the most educated taste of today wants a dose of something ... the public demand for imitative antiques ought to be regarded by the State as on all fours with the public demand for cocaine, and dealt with accordingly' (Goodhart-Rendel, 'Yesterday and Tomorrow', *A.A. Jnl.* xl, 1924, 95–8). For his criticism of Regent St., see *A.A. Jnl.* xli, 1926, 108. For a friendly caricature, see *ibid.*, xlii, 1926, 18.

170 *A.A. Jnl.* liv (1938), 100; A. Cox, 'An Open Letter to H. S. Goodhart-Rendel', *Focus* i (1938), 26.

171 Clark, 'Ornament in Modern Architecture', *R.I.B.A.J.* 3rd series, xlii (1934–5), 167–9 and *A.R.* xciv (1943), 147–50. Sir Raymond Unwin took a similar line: 'Let every building be convenient and well equipped with efficient apparatus, certainly; but that is the beginning not the end of design. It is the special function of the architect to transform the sanitary family stables or economical human warehouse into homes, with all the ... comfort and beauty which that old English word implies' (*The Listener* x, 1933, 213).

172 *R.I.B.A.J.* 3rd series i (1942–3), 75, 97, 99, 101. See also 'Rebuilding Britain', *A.R.* xciii (1943), 85–112.

173 Lethaby, 'A National Architecture', *B.* cxv (1918), 213, 340, 423, 441–3. In 1922 Lethaby founded the Modern Architecture Constructive Group to fulfil these ideals (G. Rubens, *W. R. Lethaby, His Life and Work, 1857–1931*, 1986, 295–6: manifesto). In 1938 Anthony Cox echoed the same sentiments: 'Freedom lies in the knowledge of necessity' (quoted in L. Esher, *A Broken Wave*, 1981, 41).

174 Fry, 'The Future of Architecture', *Architect's Year Book* i (1945), 7–10.

175 e.g. R. Tubbs, *Living in Cities* (1942).

176 e.g. R. Tubbs, *The Englishman Builds* (1945); Sir Charles Reilly, *Architecture as a Communal Art* (Council for Visual Education, 1944; 1946).

177 *A.A.Jnl.* lxv. (1949–50), 33.

178 *R.I.B.A.J.* 3rd series lii (1945), 215.

179 L. Esher, *A Broken Wave* (1981), 303–4. Osbert Lancaster, however, hailed it as 'the end of the Modern Movement in Architecture', the healthy sign of a New Empiricism (*The Listener* xlvi 1951, 638–40). For the Festival Hall, see J. M. Richards' critique in *A.R.* June (1951), 355–8.

180 'The Festival Style belongs firmly and squarely in the world of the New Towns, to the piazzas and pedestrian precincts, the espresso bars and community centres, to the blocks of council flats and rows of little houses and, above all, to the office buildings of the idea it expressed most, that of the post-war Welfare State' (Sir Roy Strong, in *A Tonic to the Nation: the Festival of Britain, 1951*, ed. M. Banham and B. Hillier, 1976, 9).

181 *Architects' Year Book* ii (1947), 148.

182 *A Tonic to the Nation, op. cit.*, 12.

183 *A.R.* cxvi (1954), 142.

184 L. Esher, *A Broken Wave* (1981), 272.

185 Alton Estate, East (1952–55) and West (1954–58). See T. Dannat, *Modern Architecture in Britain* (1959), 130–33; *The Times* 29 August 1984 (Colin Lucas, obit.); B. Cherry and N. Pevsner, *London ii, South* (1983), 689–90.

186 e.g. A. Colquhoun, W. Howell, C. St John Wilson, P. Carter. Several combined to form the

Architects' Co-Partnership.

187 The term was first coined in 1950 by Hans Asplund (*A.R.* cxx, 1956, 72); it was publicly adopted by Peter Smithson in 1953 (*A.D.* xxiii, 1953, 342). See R. Banham, *The New Brutalism: Ethic or Aesthetic?* (1966), 10.

188 'Probably the only instance that we have in England where the constructivist theory has been reasonably demonstrated in building – as distinct from pure engineering works and machines. So far as I can discover, the structure of this building is quite logical; there has been no sacrifice of utility to art or novelty, and . . . no cost was allowed over and above the ordinary necessities of the subject. This building seems to bear out the constructivist theory as to absolute economy, and the engineer's dictum – which physics and biology would seem to substantiate – that the line of beauty is the line of least resistance' (F. Towndrow, *Architecture in the Balance*, 1933, 140). Emberton – 'the quality of beauty is directly related to efficiency' – remained a committed Functionalist, e.g. 1929: 'beauty will come, it is born of efficiency, it is God's reward for virtue – in architecture anyhow' (R. Ind, *Emberton*, 1983, 47).

189 A. and P. Smithson, *The Heroic Period of Modern Architecture* (1965; 1980) 5.

190 R. Banham, 'Apropos the Smithsons', *New Statesman* lxii (1961), 317–8.

191 R. Wittkower, 'Systems of Proportion', *Architects' Year Book* v (1953), 9–18. K. Clark believed that if Geoffrey Scott had read Wittkower on Alberti, he would never have believed in a non-symbolic, hedonist or purely aesthetic theory of Renaissance architecture (*A.R.* cix, 1951, 69).

192 A. and P. Smithson, *Without Rhetoric: an Architectural Aesthetic, 1953–72* (1973), 2, 6, 14. For Hunstanton, see P. Johnson in *A.R.* Sept (1954), 148–62. For the Smithsons' Economist Building, St James's St., London (1961–4), see *A.D.* xxxv (1965), 61–86; *The Economist* 13 July 1961.

193 It is 'difficult . . . for us to think like this, for the Modern Movement . . . was puritanical – equating the hard with the good – and it committed us to attitudes . . . we find unnatural to shake off' (*Without Rhetoric, op. cit.*, 36, 69, 74, 77). See also A. and P. Smithson, *Ordinariness and Light* (1970), and *A.D.* xlii (1972), 91-7.

194 'The New Brutalism', *A.J.* cxx (1954), 336. See also *A.D.* xxiii (1953), 238–48 and *A.R.* cxv (1954), 274.

195 A. Jackson, *The Politics of Architecture* (1970), 184. For a neutral description, see T. Dannatt, *Modern Architecture in Britain* (1959), 117–20.

196 P. Murray and S. Trombley, *Modern British Architecture since 1945* (RIBA, 1984), 22.

197 *A.D.* April 1957. See also R. Banham, 'The New Brutalism', *A.R.* cxviii (1955), 355–61 and a review by A. and P. Smithson, *A.J.* cxliv (1966), 1580, 1590–91.

198 L. Esher, *A Broken Wave* (1981), 110. The team – including E. J. Blyth, N. W. Engleback, W. Chalk, J. A. Roberts, W. J. Sutherland, J. W. Szymaniak, and R. Herron – was led by Jack Whittle, Sir Leslie Martin, Geoffrey Horsfall and Sir Hubert Bennett who retired in 1971 to become a property developer (*A.J.* cxlv, 1967, 999–1018; *B.* ccxx, 1971, 83). At the time Jencks hailed the Hayward Gallery as the triumph of 'Adhocism' over the 'moribund aesthetic' of traditional Modernism (*A.R.* xcliii, 1968, 27–30). For Terry Farrell's scheme to encase the whole complex in a Post-Modern skin, see *The Times* 15 Oct. 1985.

199 *A. and B.N.* cxxiii (1930), 12.

200 A. and P. Smithson, *The Heroic Period of Modern Architecture* (1981), 70.

201 A. and P. Smithson, *Urban Structuring* (1967), 18. See also 'Team 10', *A.D.* xxx (1960), 149–50, 175 *et seq.* and A. Smithson, ed., *Team 10 Primer* (1968).

202 W. Gropius, 'Architecture in a Scientific Age', *The Listener* xlvi (1951), 296. The recantation was only partial: he still believed in anonymous architecture, collective and mechanised.

203 For Seifert's progress in London from Late Modern – e.g. Centre Point (1963–7), Nat. West Tower (1981), London Bridge House (c.1963), and the Penta, Park Tower and Royal Garden Hotels (1972–3) – to Post-Modern – e.g. Shaftesbury Avenue fire station (1984–5) – see *The Times* 21 Nov. 1984.

204 e.g. London University's Institute of Education, Bloomsbury (1975–9). For an explanation of Lasdun's approach, see *A.R.* cxxviii (1960), 214–7 and cxxxvii (1965), 269–80 (Royal College of Physicians, Regent's Park, 1960–64), and *A.R.* clxi (1977), 1–70 (National Theatre, South Bank, 1967–76). For Lasdun's credo, see *R.I.B.A.J.* Sept (1977), 179, 366-7: 'You cannot have form in architecture which is unrelated to human needs; and you cannot serve human needs, in terms of architecture, without a sense of form and space. Architecture . . . only makes sense as the promoter and extender of human relations. But it has to communicate through the language of form and space if it is to be considered an art. . . . [Today] the results are not always pretty. Nor need they be. Architecture has other things to do besides consoling'.

205 For retrospective polemic, criticising, e.g., Erno Goldfinger's Fleming House, Elephant and Castle (1959) and Trellick Tower, N. Kensington (1968) – see C. Booker, 'Collectivism by Design', *Daily Telegraph* 21 Feb. 1979. The centres of Edinburgh (e.g. New Club, Prince's St., dem. 1966) and Shrewsbury (e.g. Lloyds Bank, dem. 1968) are just two examples of ill-advised redevelopment.

206 Banham, *The New Brutalism* (1966), 132–3.

207 *ibid.*, 134.

208 M. Fry, *Art in a Machine Age* (1969), 168–71.

209 Pevsner, *Yorkshire, West Riding* (1967 ed.), 448, 466.

210 *Observer* 8 Nov. 1981 (S. Gardiner); *The Times* 21 Feb. 1985 (C. Knevitt); N. Taylor, 'The Failure of Housing', *A.R.* cxlii (1967), 341–59. Michael Foot called them, belatedly, 'insults to the working class' (*Observer* 17 Jan. 1982). For psychological and socio-political polemics, see O. Newman, *Defensible Space* (1973); C. Jameson, *Notes for a Revolution in Urban Planning* (1978); C. Ward, ed., *Vandalism* (1973).

211 See P. Cook, ed., *Archigram*, (1973).

212 e.g. Knightsbridge Barracks (Spence, 1967–9); National Theatre (Lasdun, 1967–77); New Scotland Yard (Chapman, Taylor and Gale, 1962–6); R.C. Cathedral, Liverpool (Gibberd, 1959–68); Trowbridge Estate, East London; Dept. of the Environment, Marsham St. See *Sunday Times* 30 Dec. 1984; *The Times* 28 Aug. 1984. The architects and engineers of Liverpool Cathedral eventually forfeited £1.3 million in settlement of a negligence claim (*The Times* 12 Feb. 1986). 'At least

the Modern Movement has built-in obsolescence' (S. Jenkins, *Sunday Times* 3 June 1984).

213 e.g. Liverpool: Netherley and 'The Piggeries', Everton (The Haigh, Canterbury and Crosby Heights, 1961 onwards, chief architect: R. Bradbury); Basford Flats and Balloon Woods, Nottingham (*The Times* 1 March, 1985).

214 ill., *A Tonic for the Nation*, ed. M. Banham and B. Hillier (1976), 143.

215 See *The Spectator* 4, 11 May 1985 and *The Times* 30 April, 1984 (B. Appleyard); 1 May 1984 (R. Scruton); 7 May 1984 (F. Mount). The inquiry coincided with a speech by the Prince of Wales at a banquet at Hampton Court – held to celebrate the RIBA's 150th anniversary – in which he vigorously attacked Modernism, and in doing so won popular acclaim: 'Whatever the outcome of the inquiry, the Modernist cause is now lost' (J. Lubbock, *New Statesman* 8 June 1984, 29). For James Stirling's post-Miesian designs see *The Guardian* 14 May 1986; *Sunday Telegraph* 17 May 1987.

216 See, for example, U. Eco, *A Theory of Semiotics* (Bloomington, 1976); G. Broadbent, R. Bunt and C. Jencks, *Signs, Symbols and Architecture* (Wiley, 1980); E. Leach, *Culture and Communication* (Cambridge, 1976); E. Gombrich, *The Sense of Order* (Oxford, 1979); C. Rowe, *The Mathematics of the Ideal Villa and Other Essays* (Cambridge, Mass., 1976); G. Baird and C. Jencks, eds., *Meaning in Architecture* (1969); M. Tafuri, *Theories and History of Architecture* (1968; 1976).

217 M. Fry, *Art in a Machine Age* (1969), 134.

218 P. Collins, *Changing Ideals in Modern Architecture* (1965), 199.

219 As suggested in L. Esher, *A Broken Wave* (1981).

220 'Our post-modern Age of Western History' (A. Toynbee, *An Historian's Approach to Religion*, 1956, 146). The term first appears in J. Hudnut, *Architecture and the Spirit of Man* (1949), 119. Richard Sheppard's Churchill College, Cambridge (1959 onwards) prompted Pevsner to accept 'the existence of a new style, successor to my International Modern of the 1930s, a post-modern style ... the legitimate style of the 1950s and 1960s' (*The Listener* lxxvi, 1966, 955).

221 e.g. Johnson's Sunderlandwick Hall, Yorks. (1982), ill. *The Times* 29 Aug. 1984 and 18 Sept. 1984 (letter by G. Power). Also Terry's 'Palladian' riverside development at Richmond (1984–7), described by Sir Hugh Casson as 'Beggar's Opera Georgian' (*Observer* 7 Dec. 1984; *The Times* 11 Nov. 1984); and houses for M. Heseltine and D. and A. McAlpine (F. Russell, ed., *Quinlan Terry*, A.D. 1981; J.M. Robinson, *The Latest Country Houses*, 1984). Terry's Neo-Georgian Sandringham Court in Dufours Place, Soho, continues traditional forms and techniques without evolutionary intent. For Erith's opinions and designs – e.g. King's Walden Bury, Herts. (1969–71) – see L. Archer, *Raymond Erith, Architect* (Burford, 1985), and notes by N. Cooper (*A.J.* 22 Sept. 1976, 518–21) and J. Cornforth (*C.L.* 7 Oct. 1976, 987–8).

222 e.g. the work of Robert Adam (C. Aslet, 'A Way Forward for Classicism', *C.L.* clxxvii, 1985, 622–4). For the concept, see C. Jencks, 'Post-Modern Classicism: the New Synthesis', *A.D.* 5/6 (1980).

223 e.g. D. Porphyrios, ed., *Classicism is Not a Style*, *A.D.* lii (1982), 5, 51–7.

224 R. Gradidge, *The Times* 30 March 1984. 'We

have now entered a period of evolution where there are no absolutes' (*ibid.*, 18 May 1984). For a general discussion, see 'The Great Debate: Modernism versus the Rest', *R.I.B.A. Trans.* iii (1983). In 1976 Peter Eisenman suggested 'post functional' as a preliminary label for 'a new consciousness in architecture which I believe is potentially upon us' (*Oppositions* vi, 1976, ed.).

225 I. Nairn and N. Pevsner, *Sussex* (1965), 499–500.

226 C. Amery and L. Wright, *The Architecture of Darbourne and Darke* (1977).

227 G. Stamp, *A.R.* clxv (1979), 84–9.

228 See B. Auger, 'A Return to Ornament?', *A.R.* cxl (1976), 77–80.

229 Or the Sainsbury Building at Worcester College, Oxford (1983: MacCormac, Jamieson and Pritchard). Cullinan calls his approach 'a delicate and sophisticated modernism' (*The Times* 12 Sept. 1984). Darley and Davey define it as 'a pragmatic meeting of Modernism and the Picturesque' (*The Times* 18 May 1984).

230 *The Times* 21 Nov. 1984.

231 Gradidge, *The Times* 30 March 1984.

232 Sir Philip Dowson, *The Times* 18 May 1984, echoing Chermayeff.

233 *Oppositions* x (1977), 18.

234 Quoted in S. Games, *Behind the Façade* (1985), 86–7.

235 'Where is there a precedent for popular hatred against a whole architectural style even after it has been around for some three-quarters of a century and dominant for roughly half that time?' (C. Jameson, *The Times* 13 Oct. 1984). For a subtler approach, see V. Scully, *Modern Architecture: the Architecture of Democracy* (1961).

236 *A.R.* clxxiii (1983), 15.

237 'How in an increasingly industrialised world to avoid the anomie of meagre functionalism, and the bogus remedy of saccharine revivalism' (W. Curtis, 'Principle v. Pastiche', *A.R.* clxxvi, 1984, viii, 11–21, 46). 'An architecture that is constantly aware of its own history, but constantly critical of the seductions of history' (A. Colquhoun, 'Three Kinds of Historicism', *Oppositions* xxvi, 1984, 39).

238 e.g. W. Curtis and R. Banham in *A.R.* clxxvi (1984), viii, *passim*.

239 Especially C. Jencks, *The Language of Post-Modern Architecture* (1977; 4th ed., 1984) and *Late Modern Architecture* (1980), bibliography.

240 The term was coined by A. Tzonis and L. Lefaivre in *Architecture in Greece* xv (1981), and developed by K. Frampton in *The Anti-Aesthetic*, ed. H. Foster (1983; reprinted as *Postmodern Culture*, 1985).

241 *A.R.* clxiv (1978), 345–62.

242 *The Times* 3 April 1986; *A.R.* clxxix (1986), iv, *passim*.

243 *Sunday Times* 28 Oct. 1984.

244 *A.R.* clxi (1977), 271–94: 'high-quality civil engineering ... without pretentious play-acting at machine aesthetics ... [but also a monument] to *ideas* of impermanence ... [controlled by] a fixed image' (R. Banham). Rogers may have been inspired by the Maison de Verre at 31 Rue St Guillaume (1928) by Pierre Chareau. On a smaller scale, the Oxford Ice Rink (N. Grimshaw and Partners, 1983) translates nautical imagery into High Tech terms: it is functional, but not

utilitarian; imagistic rather than symbolic (*A.R.* clxxvii, 1985, iii, 38–45).

245 Here Banham sees 'the facts of electronic life' expressed in rhetorical form: if not 'beauty', then 'at least a kind of formal perfection' (*A.R.* clxxii, 1982, 26–38).

246 *A.R.* clxix (1981), 278–82 and clxxx (1986), (10). 'Modernism has come back ... but ... chastened and transformed.... Engineering is one way of designing things, architecture is another. The triumph of Lloyds, paradoxically, is that it is so often difficult to tell them apart. Nevertheless ... in the last resort, *alles ist Architektur*' (R. Banham, *A.R.* clxxx, 1986, (10), 55–6).

247 *A.R.* clxxiii (1983), (6), 28–43.

248 *A.R.* cxxxv (1974), 253–60: 'a functional building that looks functional ... [unlike] the architecture of the 'twenties, almost invariably more cubist than practical ... [but moderated by] romantic dash ... and ... a desire for visual harmony' (J. Jacobus).

249 *A.R.* clii (1972), 260–77: 'On the whole the buildings don't cheat ... [but Stirling is] beginning to find [this] particular formal discipline restrictive' (M. Girouard).

250 *Sunday Times*, 17 March 1985. Banham, however, admired the 'dumb insolence' of its exterior, and considered the 'glass pyramid ... a reasonable, responsible environmental device, not a formalist extravagance.... Style and detailing derive intrinsically from the building itself, not extrinsically from some more or less accurate apprehension of contingent cultural factors' (*A.R.* cxliv, 1968, 328–41).

251 *A.R.* clxxvi (1984), (12), 19–22, 35, 42; P. Cannon-Brooks, 'The Post-Modern Art Gallery Comes of Age', *International Jnl. of Museum Management and Curatorship* iii (1984), 159–81.

252 J. Mordaunt Crook, *The Greek Revival* (1972), pl. 85. Another possible source is Ehrensvärd's Dock-yard Gateway at Karlskrona (*The Age of Neo-Classicism*, 1972, pl. 103a).

253 *The Times* 8 Nov. 1984.

254 J. Summerson, 'Vitruvius Ludens.', *A.R.* clxxiii (1983), 19–21.

255 'Vitruvius Ridens', *A.R.* clxxxi (1987), (6), 45–6.

256 In ferocity of language the Modernist critics of Post-Modernism rival the Gothic critics of Queen Anne. Summerson calls it 'drivel or poison' (*R.S.A.Jnl.* cxxx, 1982, 658–9). Lubetkin damns its 'decadence', 'chaos' and 'intellectual sterility'; its 'tribal magic'; its use of 'titbits from the dustbin of history' – all the fault of 'Manhattan wits' and 'Cambridge lecturers' (on receiving the RIBA Gold Medal, 29 June 1982: see *R.I.B.A.Trans.*, Nov. 1982). Four years later Arata Isozaki became the first Post-Modern Gold Medallist and Rod Hackney the first Post-Modern P.R.I.B.A.

257 'Nothing to my mind could be a worse imposition than to have some individual, even temporarily, deliberately fix the outward forms of his concept of beauty upon the future of a free people or even a growing city' (Frank Lloyd Wright, quoted in *A.R.* clxxi, 1982, 6).

258 See E. M. Farelly, ed. 'The New Wave', *A.R.* clxxx (1986), (8), *passim*, and following debate.

259 Fergusson, Lutyens and Goodhart-Rendel made almost identical observations on this point (J. Fergusson, *Illustrated Handbook of Architecture*, 1855, intro.; C. Hussey, *Lutyens*, 1953, 194; H. S. Goodhart-Rendel, *English Architecture Since the Regency*, 1953, 253). Compare Venturi, 1978: architecture is 'shelter with decoration on it' – i.e. the 'decorated shed' (quoted in T. Wolfe, *From Bauhaus to Our House*, 1983, 139).

260 Using rather different language, Fergusson came to a similar conclusion in 1849: great architecture equalises Technic, Aesthetic and Phonetic elements (J. Fergusson, *True Principles of Beauty in Art*, 1849, 140).

Bibliography

I Periodicals

Academy Architecture (1889–1932)

American Association of Architectural Bibliographers, Papers (1965–)

Annales Archéologiques (Paris, 1844–81)

Annals of the Fine Arts (1817–20)

Architect (1869–1926); thereafter united with the Building News

Architect's Year Book (1946–74)

Architectural Association Notes/Journal/Files (1890–)

Architectural History (1958–)

Architectural Magazine, ed. J. C. Loudon (1834–8)

Architectural Record (1891–)

Architectural Review (1896–)

Art History (1978–)

The Art Union (1839–48); continued as The Art Journal (1849–1912)

Associated Architectural Societies' Reports and Papers (1850–61)

Athenaeum (1828–1931); thereafter incorporated with The Nation

Bartlett Society, Transactions (1962–73)

Bentley's Quarterly Review (1859–60)

British Almanac and Companion (1827–1913)

British Architect (1874–1919)

Builder (1843–1966); continued as Building (1966–)

Building News (1855–1926); thereafter united with the Architect

Bulletin of the John Rylands Library (Manchester, 1914–)

Burlington Magazine (1903–)

Cambridge Camden Society, Transactions (1840–45)

Catholic Magazine (1838–42)

Christian Remembrancer (1819–40; 1840–68)

Church Builder (1862–1904)

Civil Engineer and Architect's Journal (1837–67)

Country Life (1897–)

Critical Review (1756–1817)

Ecclesiologist [Cambridge Camden Society] (1842–68)

Eclectic Review (1805–68)

Edinburgh Review (1802–1929)

Fraser's Magazine (1830–82)

Garden History (1972–)

Garden History, Journal. of (1981–)

Gentleman's Magazine (1731–1868)

History of Ideas, Journal of (1939–)

Illustrated London News (1843–)

Library of the Fine Arts (1831–33)

The Listener (1929–)

Macmillan's Magazine (1860–1907)

Merry England (1883–95)

National Association for the Advancement of Art, Transactions (1888–90).

Newcomen Society, Transactions (1922–)

Nineteenth Century (1887–1900); continued as Nineteenth Century and After and Twentieth Century

Oppositions (1973–)

Orthodox Journal (1813–46)

Oxoniensia (1936–)

Quarterly Review (1809–1967)

The Rambler (1848–62)

Repository of Arts (1809–29); published by R. Ackermann

Revue Générale de l'Architecture (Paris, 1840–88)

R.I.B.A. Transactions/Papers/Journal (1842–)

Royal Society of Arts, Journal (1873–)

The Sacristy (1871–72)

St. Paul's Ecclesiological Society, Transactions (1881–1938)

Saturday Review (1855–1938)

Society of Architectural Historians, U.S., Journal (1941–)

Studies in Architectural History (1954–55)

Surveyor, Engineer and Architect (1840–42); continued as Architect, Engineer and Surveyor (1843)

The Tablet (1840–)

The Times (1785–)

Victorian Studies (Bloomington, 1965–)

Warburg and Courtauld Institutes, Journal (1937–)

Westminster Review (1824–1914)

II Separate Works

Abrams, M. H., The Mirror and the Lamp: Romantic Theory and the Critical Tradition (Oxford, 1953)

— Natural Supernaturalism (New York, 1974)

Ackerman, J. S., Palladio (1966)

Acland, H. W. and Ruskin, J., The Oxford Museum (1859)

Acton, Lord, Lectures on Modern History (1906; 1960)

Addington, R., ed., Faber, Poet and Priest: Selected Letters (1974)

Ahlston, J., Engineers and Industrial Growth (1982)

Alexander, C., Notes on the Synthesis of Form (Harvard, 1964)

Alison, Rev. A., Essays on the Nature and Principles of Taste (Edinburgh, 1790; 1811)

Allen, B. Sprague, Tides in English Taste, 1619–1800, 2 vols. (Cambridge, Mass., 1937)

Allen, C. Bruce, Cottage Building, ed. J. Weale, et al. (1880).

Alloway L., *This Is To-Morrow* (Whitechapel Art Gallery, 1956)

Allsopp, B., *Towards a Humane Architecture* (1977)

Amery, C., ed., and Wright, L., *The National Theatre* (1977)

— *The Architecture of Darbourne and Darke* (1977)

Ames, W., *Prince Albert and Victorian Taste* (1967)

Anson, P. F., *Fashions in Church Furnishings, 1840–1940* (1960)

Antal, F., *Classicism and Romanticism* (1966)

Anthony, P. D., *John Ruskin's Labour: a study of Ruskin's Social Theory* (Cambridge, 1984)

Appleyard, B., *Richard Rogers* (1986)

Archer, J. H. G., *Edgar Wood – a Manchester Art Nouveau Architect* (Manchester, 1966)

— ed., *Art and Architecture in Victorian Manchester* (Manchester, 1985)

Archer, L., *Raymond Erith* (Burford, 1985)

[Architectural Association] *Joseph Michael Gandy* (1982)

— *'Greek' Thomson* (1984)

Arnell, P. and Bickford, T., *James Stirling: Buildings and Projects, 1950–82* (1984)

Arnheim, R., *The Dynamics of Architectural Form* (Berkeley, 1977)

[Arts and Crafts Exhibition Society] *Arts and Crafts Essays* (1893)

Art and Craft (1897)

[Arts Council] *The Age of Neo-Classicism* (1972)

— *Thirties* (1979)

— *Lutyens* (1981)

— *Le Corbusier* (1987)

Ashbee, C. R., *Craftsmanship in Competitive Industry* (Campden, 1908)

— *Should We Stop Teaching Art?* (1911)

— *Where the Great City Stands: a Study in the New Civics* (1917)

Aslet, C., *The Last Country Houses* (1982)

— *Quinlan Terry: The Revival of Architecture* (1986)

Aslin, E., *The Aesthetic Movement* (1981)

Atkinson, R. and Bagenal, H., *Theory and Elements of Architecture* (1926)

Atwell, D., *Cathedrals of Entertainment* (1980)

Auzas, P. M., ed., *Actes du Colloque International Viollet-le-Duc, Paris, 1980* (Paris, 1982)

[Avery Library] *Avery Obituary Index of Architects* (Columbia University, 1980)

Backemeyer, S. and Gronberg, J., eds., *W. R. Lethaby* (1984)

Baird, G. and Jencks, C., eds., *Meaning in Architecture* (1969)

Baker, H., *Architecture and Personalities* (1944)

Banham, M. and Hillier, B., eds., *A Tonic to the Nation. The Festival of Britain, 1951* (1976)

Banham, R., *Theory and Design in the First Machine Age* (1960; revised 1980)

— *Guide to Modern Architecture* (1962)

— *The New Brutalism: Ethic or Aesthetic?* (1966)

— *The Architecture of the Well-Tempered Environment* (1969)

— *Design by Choice* (1981)

— *A Concrete Atlantis: U.S. Industrial Building and European Modern Architecture* (M.I.T., 1986)

— Foster, M. and Butt, L., *Foster Associates* (1979)

Barbier, C. P., *William Gilpin: his drawings, teaching and theory of the Picturesque* (1963)

Barnard, J., *The Decorative Tradition* (1973)

Barr, A. W. C., *Public Authority Housing* (1958)

Barr, J., *Anglican Church Architecture* (1843)

Barron, P. A., *The House Beautiful* (1929)

Barry, Rev. A., *The Architect of the New Palace of Westminster* (1868)

— *Life and Works of Sir Charles Barry* (1870; reprinted 1972)

Bartholomew, A., *Specifications for Practical Architecture* (1841; ed. F. Rogers, 1873)

Barzun, J., *Classic, Romantic and Modern* (1943; revised, New York, 1961)

Bate W. J. *From Classic to Romantic, Premises of Taste in 18th century England* (Cambridge, Mass., 1946)

Bayer, H., Gropius, W. and Gropius, I., eds., *Bauhaus 1919–28* (1938; 1975)

Beattie, S., *A Revolution in London Housing: L.C.C. housing architects and their work, 1893–1914* (1980)

Beaver, P., *The Crystal Palace, 1851–1936* (1970)

Beckett, E. [Lord Grimthorpe], *A Book on Building* (1880)

Belcher, J., *Essentials in Architecture* (1907)

Benevolo, L., *History of Modern Architecture* (1971)

Bennett, A., Lanchester, H. and Fern, A., *The Art of E. A. Rickards* (1920)

Bennett, T. P., *Architectural Design in Concrete* (1927)

Benton, J. and Benton, C., eds., *Form and Function ... 1890–1939* (1975)

Berlin, Sir I., *Historical Inevitability* (1954)

— *Four Essays on Liberty* (Oxford, 1969)

Billings, R. W., *The Power of Form Applied to Geometrical Tracery* (1851)

Binnie, J. M., *Early Victorian Water Engineers* (1981)

[Blackie and Sons] *Villa and Cottage Architecture* (1868, etc.)

Blau, E., *Ruskinian Gothic: the Architecture of Deane and Woodward, 1845–61* (Princeton, 1982)

Blomfield, Sir R., *The Mistress Art* (1908)

— *The Touchstone of Architecture* (Oxford, 1925)

— *French Architecture and its Relation to Modern Practice* (Oxford, 1927)

— *Memoirs of an Architect* (1932)

— *Modernismus* (1934)

— *Richard Norman Shaw* (1940)

Blondel, J. F., *Cours d'architecture* (Paris, 1771–7)

Bloxam, M. H., *Principles of Gothic Ecclesiastical Architecture* (1838; 1882)

Blunt, Sir A., *Artistic Theory in Italy, 1450–1600* (Oxford, 1966)

— *Nicolas Poussin*, 2 vols. (1967)

— *et al., Essays in the History of Architecture presented to R. Wittkower* (1967)

Boase, T. S. R., *English Art, 1800–70* (Oxford, 1959)

Bodley, G. F., *Modes in Which Religious Life and Thought may be Influenced by Art* (1881)

Boë, A., *From Gothic Revival to Functional Form* (Oxford, 1957)

Bonta, J. P., *Architecture and its Interpretation* (1979)

Boudon, P., *Lived-in Architecture* (1972)

Bradbury, R., *The Romantic Theories of Architecture of the 19th century in Germany, England and France* (New York, 1934)

Bradley, J. L., ed., *Ruskin: the critical heritage* (1984)

Bradley, R., *Survey of Ancient Husbandry and Gardening* (1725)

Brandon-Jones, J., *et al., C. F. A. Voysey* (Brighton, 1978)

Brett, L. [Lord Esher] *Landscape in Distress* (1965)

— *A Broken Wave: the Rebuilding of England, 1940–1980* (1981)

—*Our Selves Unknown: an autobiography* (1985)

Britton, J., *Architectural Antiquities*, 5 vols. (1807–26)

—*Cathedral Antiquities*, 14 vols. (1814–35)

Broadbent, G., Bunt, R. and Jencks, C., eds., *Signs, Symbols and Architecture* (Wiley, 1980)

Brolin, B. C., *The Failure of Modern Architecture* (1976)

—*Flight of Fancy: the Banishment and Return of Ornament* (1985)

Brooks, C., *Signs of the Times* (1984)

Brooks, H. Allen, *The Prairie School* (Toronto, 1972)

—ed., *Writings on Wright* (Cambridge, Mass., 1983)

Brown, Prof. R., *Domestic Architecture* (1841)

Brown, R., ed., *The Architectural Outsiders* (1985)

Brownlee, D. B., *The Law Courts: the Architecture of G. E. Street* (Cambridge, Mass., 1984)

Buckley, J. H., *The Victorian Temper* (Cambridge, Mass., 1951)

—*The Triumph of Time* (Cambridge, Mass., 1967)

Bumpus, T. F., *London Churches, ancient and modern* (1883); 2 vols. [1908]

Burges, W., *Art Applied to Industry* (1865)

—*Architectural Drawings* (1870)

Burke, E., *A Philosophical Enquiry into the Origin of our Ideas on the Sublime and the Beautiful* (1757); ed. J. T. Boulton (1958)

Burnett, J., *A Social History of Housing, 1815–1970* (1980)

Butler, A. S. G., *The Substance of Architecture* (1926)

—*The Architecture of Sir Edwin Lutyens*, 3 vols., (1950)

[Cambridge Camden/Ecclesiological Society] *A Few Words to Church Builders* (1841)

—*A Few Words to Church Wardens* (1846 ed.)

—*Instrumenta Ecclesiastica* (1847; 1856)

—*A Handbook of English Ecclesiology* (1847)

Cantacuzino, S., *Wells Coates* (1978)

Carritt, E. F., *A Calendar of British Taste from 1669 to 1800* (1949)

Carter, G., Goode, P. and Laurie, K., *Humphry Repton, Landscape Gardener* (1982)

Carter, P., *Mies van der Rohe at Work* (1974)

Castell, R., *Villas of the Ancients* (1728)

Caumont, Arcisse de, *Abécédaire ou rudiment d'archaeologie*, 3 vols., (Paris, 1850–62)

Chadwick, G. F., *The Works of Sir Joseph Paxton* (1961; reprinted 1985)

—*The Park and the Town: public landscape in the 19th and 20th centuries* (1966)

Chadwick, Sir O., *The Mind of the Oxford Movement* (1962, ed.)

—*The Victorian Church*, 2 vols. (1966; 1970)

—*The Secularisation of the European Mind* (1975)

Chambers, F. P., *History of Taste* (New York, 1932)

Chambers, Sir W., *A Treatise on Civil Architecture* (1759); ed. J. Gwilt (1825)

—*A Dissertation on Oriental Gardening* (1772)

Chermayeff, S. and Alexander, C., *Community and Privacy: Towards a New Architecture of Humanism* (1964, ed.)

—*Design and the Public Good*, ed. R. Plunz (M.I.T., 1982)

—and Tzonis, A., *Shape of Community* (1971)

Cherry, G. E. and Penny, L., *Holford* (1986)

Choisy, F. A., *Histoire de l'architecture*, 2 vols. (Paris, 1899)

Church, R. W., *The Oxford Movement, 1833–45* (1891 ed.)

Clark, H. F., *The English Landscape Garden* (1948)

Clark, Sir K. [Lord Clark] *The Gothic Revival, an Essay in the History of Taste* (1964 ed.)

—*Ruskin Today* (1964)

Clarke, Rev. B. F. L., *Church Builders of the 19th century* (1938; revised 1969)

—*Anglican Cathedrals outside the British Isles* (1958)

Clarke, M. and Penny, N., *The Arrogant Connoisseur, Richard Payne Knight* (Manchester, 1982)

Clifford, D., *A History of Garden Design* (1962)

Close, Rev. F., *The Restoration of Churches is the Restoration of Popery* (Cheltenham, 1853)

Clutton, H., *Domestic Architecture of France* (1853)

Cobden-Sanderson, T. J., *The Arts and Crafts Movement* (1905)

Coe, P. and Reading, M., *Lubetkin and Tecton: Architecture and Social Commitment* (Bristol, 1981)

Coffin, D., ed., *The Italian Garden* (Dumbarton Oaks, 1972)

Cole, D., *The Work of Sir Gilbert Scott* (1980)

Coleman, A., *Utopia on Trial: Vision and Reality in Planned Housing* (1985)

Collingwood, R. G., *Philosophy of Art* (1925)

—*The Idea of Nature* (Oxford, 1945)

Collingwood, W. G., *Ruskin*, 2 vols. (1893)

Collins, P., *Concrete: the Vision of a New Architecture* (1959)

—*Changing Ideals in Modern Architecture, 1750–1950* (1965)

—*Architectural Judgement* (1971)

Colquhoun, A., *Essays in Architectural Criticism: Modern Architecture and Historical Change* (Cambridge, Mass., 1981)

Colvin, H. M., *A Biographical Dictionary of British Architects, 1600–1840* (1978)

—and Harris, J., *The Country Seat: Studies presented to Sir John Summerson* (1970)

Comino, M., *Gimson and the Barnsleys* (1980)

Conner, P., *Oriental Architecture in the West* (1979)

Conrad, P., *The Victorian Treasure House* (1973)

Conrads, U., ed., *Programmes and Manifestos on 20th century Architecture* (1970)

Cook, E. T., *Ruskin* (1911)

Cook, P., *Architecture: Action and Plan* (1967)

—ed., *Archigram* (1973)

Cordemoy, J. L. de, *Nouveau traité de toute l'architecture* (Paris, 1706; 1714)

Cotton, J., *Suggestions in Architectural Design: prefaced with Thoughts on Architectural Progress* (1896)

Cousin, V., *Exposition of Eclecticism*, trans. G. Ripley, (1839)

—*The True, the Beautiful and the Good*, trans. O. W. Wright (Edinburgh, 1854)

Cram, R. A., *The Gothic Quest* (1907)

—*Church Building* (1899; Boston, 1924)

Crane, W., *Ideals in Art* (1905)

—*William Morris to Whistler* (1911)

Crawford, A., ed., *By Hammer and Hand: the Arts and Crafts Movement in Birmingham* (Birmingham, 1984)

—*C. R. Ashbee: Architect, Designer and Romantic Socialist* (1985)

Creese, W., *The Search for Environment* (New Haven, Conn. 1966)

Crick, C., *Victorian Buildings in Bristol* (Bristol, 1975)

Croce, B., *Aesthetics as Science of Expression*, trans. D. Ainslie (1955 ed.)

Crook, J. Mordaunt, *Victorian Architecture: a Visual Anthology* (1971)
— *The British Museum* (1972)
— *The Greek Revival: Neo-Classical Attitudes in British Architecture, 1760–1870* (1972)
— *The Reform Club* (1973)
— *William Burges and the High Victorian Dream* (1981)
— ed., *The Strange Genius of William Burges* (Cardiff, 1981)
— and Port, M. H., *The History of the King's Works* vi (1782–1851), ed. H. M. Colvin (1973)
— and Lennox-Boyd, C. A., *Axel Haig and the Victorian Vision of the Middle Ages* (1984)
Crosby, T., *The Necessary Monument* (1970)
Cruikshank, D., ed., *Timeless Architecture* (1985)
Culler, A. D., *The Victorian Mirror of History* (Yale, 1986)
Cullingworth, J. B., *Town and Country Planning in Britain* (1977)
Cunningham, C., *Victorian and Edwardian Town Halls* (1981)
— *et al.*, *Alfred Waterhouse* (R.I.B.A., 1983)
Curl, J. Stevens, *Victorian Architecture: its practical aspects* (Newton Abbot, 1973)
— *The Egyptian Revival* (1982)
Curry, R. J. and Kirk, S., *Philip Webb in the North* (Middlesborough, 1984)
Curtis, W. J. R., *Modern Architecture Since 1900* (1982)
Dale, A., *James Wyatt* (1936; revised 1956)
Dale, P. A., *The Victorian Critic and the Idea of History: Carlyle, Arnold, Pater* (Cambridge, Mass., 1977)
Dannatt, T., *Modern Architecture in Britain*, intro. J. Summerson (1959)
Darley, G., *Villages of Vision* (1975)
Davey, P., *Arts and Crafts Architecture: the search for earthly paradise* (1980)
Davie, W. Galsworthy, *Architectural Sketches in France* (1877)
Davies, P., *Splendours of the Raj: British Architecture in India, 1660–1947* (1984)
Davis, T., *The Architecture of John Nash* (1960)
— *John Nash* (1966)
— *The Gothick Taste* (1975)
Davison, T. Raffles, ed., *The Arts Connected with Building* (1909)
Dean, D., *The Thirties* (1983)
Dellheim, C., *The Face of the Past* (Cambridge, 1982)
De Zurco, E. R., *Origins of Functionalist Theory* (1957)
Dixon, R. and Muthesius, S., *Victorian Architecture* (1978)
— ed., *Sir G. Scott and the Scott Dynasty* (South Bank Polytechnic, 1980)
Dobai, J., *Die Kunstliteratur des Klassizismus und der Romantik in England, 1700–1840*, 3 vols. (Berne, 1974–7)
Donaldson, T. L., *Preliminary Discourse* (1842)
Doxiadis, C., *Ekistics* (1969)
Draper, J. W., *18th century English Aesthetics, a bibliography* (Heidelberg, 1931)
Dresser, C., *Modern Ornamentation* (1886)
Drexler, A., ed., *The Architecture of the Ecole des Beaux-Arts* (New York, 1977)
[Drummond, H.] *The Principles of Ecclesiastical Buildings and Ornaments* (1851)
Duff, W., *An Essay on Original Genius* (1767)
[Dulwich Picture Gallery], *Soane and After* (1987)
Dunnett, J. and Stamp, G., *Erno Goldfinger* (Architectural Association, 1983)

du Prey, P. de la Ruffinière, *John Soane: the Making of an Architect* (Chicago, 1982)
Durand, J. N. L., *Recueil et parallèle des edifices de tout genre, anciens et modernes* (Paris, 1801)
— *Précis des Leçons d'Architecture* (Paris, 1802–9)
Dyos, H. J. and Wolff, M., eds., *The Victorian City*, 2 vols. (1973)
Eastlake, C. L., *Hints on Household Taste* (1868); ed. J. Gloag (1970)
— *A History of the Gothic Revival* (1872); ed. J. Mordaunt Crook (Leicester, 1970; revised, 1978)
Eco, U., *A Theory of Semiotics* (Bloomington, 1976)
Eden, W. A., *The Process of Architectural Tradition* (1942)
Edis, R. W., *Decoration and Furniture of Town Houses* (1881)
Edwards, A. Trystan, *The Things Which Are Seen* (1921)
— *Good and Bad Manners in Architecture* (1924)
— *Architectural Style* (1926)
Egbert, D. D., *Social Radicalism in the Arts* (New York, 1970)
Eichner, H., ed., *'Romantic' and its Cognates: the European History of a Word* (Toronto, 1972)
Eitner, L. E. A., *Neoclassicism and Romanticism, 1750–1850*, 2 vols. (Englewood, 1970)
Elkin, S., *Politics and Land-Use Planning – the London Experience* (1974)
Emmett, J. T., *Six Essays* (1891); ed. J. Mordaunt Crook (1972)
Fain, J. T., *Ruskin and the Economists* (Nashville, Tenn., 1956)
Fairchild, H. N., *The Noble Savage: a Study in Romantic Naturalism* (New York, 1928)
Farr, D., *English Art, 1870–1940* (Oxford, 1978)
Fawcett, J. and Pevsner, N., eds. *Seven Victorian Architects* (1976)
Fellows, R. A., *Sir Reginald Blomfield*, (1984)
Fergusson, J., *An historical inquiry into the true principles of Beauty in Art, more especially with reference to Architecture* (1849)
— *Observations on the British Museum, National Gallery and National Record Office* (1849)
— *History of the Modern Styles of Architecture*, ed. R. Kerr (1872)
Ferrey, B., *Recollections of A. W. Pugin and his father Augustus Pugin* (1861); ed. C. Wainwright (1978)
Ferriday, P., ed., *Victorian Architecture* (1964)
Fiedler, K., *On Judging Works of Visual Art* (1876), ed. H. Schaefer-Simmern (Berkeley, 1949)
— *On the Nature and History of Architecture* (1878), trans. C. Reading (Lexington, Kentucky, c. 1950)
Finch, N., *Style in Art History* (Metuchen, 1974)
Fischer, E., *The Necessity of Art* (1959; trans. Harmondsworth, 1963)
Fishman, R., *Urban Utopias in the 20th century* (New York, 1977)
Fitch, J. Marston, *Walter Gropius* (New York, 1961)
— *Architecture and the Esthetics of Plenty* (New York, 1961)
Fletcher, Sir B., *History of Architecture*, 19th edn., ed. J. Musgrave (1987)
Forty, A., *Objects of Desire: Design and Society, 1750–1980* (1986)
Foster, H., ed., *The Anti-Aesthetic: Essays on Postmodern Culture* (Washington, 1983)

Foucart, B., *et al.*, *Viollet-le-Duc* (Grand Palais, Paris, 1980)

Foulston, J., *Public Buildings erected in the West of England* (1838)

Frampton, K., *A Concise History of Modern Architecture* (1973)

— *Modern Architecture and the Critical Present* (A.D., 1982)

— *Modern Architecture: a critical history* (1980; 1985)

Franciscono, M., *Walter Gropius and . . . the Bauhaus* (Urbana, 1971)

Frankl, P., *The Gothic: Literary Sources and Interpretations through Eight Centuries* (Princeton, 1960)

— *Principles of Architectural History* (1914; trans., Cambridge, Mass., 1968)

Freeman, E. A., *Principles of Church Restoration* (1846)

Fry, E. Maxwell, *Fine Building* (1944)

— *Art in a Machine Age* (1969)

— *Autobiographical Sketches* (1975)

Frye, N., ed., *Romanticism Reconsidered* (1963)

Furst, L. R., *Romanticism in Perspective* (1969)

Games, S., *Behind the Facade* (1985)

Gandy, J., *Designs for Cottages . . . and other Rural Buildings* (1805)

Gant, P., *Viollet-le-Duc* (Paris, 1914)

Garbett, E. L., *Rudimentary Treatise on the Principles of Design in Architecture* (1850; revised 1863)

Gardiner, S., *Le Corbusier* (1974)

Garrigan, K. O., *Ruskin on Architecture* (1973)

Gay, P., *Art and Act* (1976)

Gebhard, D., *C. F. A. Voysey* (Los Angeles, 1975)

Gerard, A., *An Essay on Taste* (1759)

German, G., *The Gothic Revival in Europe and Britain* (1972)

Gibberd, Sir F., *Town Design* (1953)

Gibbs-Smith, C. H., *The Great Exhibition of 1851* (1950)

Giedion, S., *Space, Time and Architecture: the growth of a new tradition* (Cambridge, Mass., 1941; revised 1967)

— *Nine Points on Monumentality* (1943)

— *Mechanisation Takes Command* (1948)

— *Architecture You and Me* (Cambridge, Mass., 1958)

— *The Eternal Present* (1962)

— *Architecture and the Phenomena of Transition* (1970)

Gifford, D., *The Literature of Architecture* (New York, 1966)

Gilpin, Rev. W., *Remarks on Forest Scenery* (1791)

— *Three Essays on Picturesque Beauty* (1792; reprinted 1974)

Girouard, M., *The Victorian Country House* (Oxford, 1971; revised 1979)

— *Sweetness and Light: the 'Queen Anne' movement, 1860–1900* (1977)

— *Victorian Pubs* (1975)

— *Life in the English Country House* (1978)

— *The Return to Camelot: Chivalry and the English Gentleman* (1981)

— *Alfred Waterhouse and the Natural History Museum* (1981)

Gloag, J., *Industrial Art Explained* (1934; 1945)

— *Mr. Loudon's England* (1970)

— and Bridgwater, D., *History of Cast Iron Architecture* (1948)

Gombrich, Sir E., *Art and Illusion* (1960)

— *Meditations on a Hobby Horse* (1963)

— *The Sense of Order: a study in the psychology of decorative art* (1978)

Gomme, A. and Walker, D., *The Architecture of Glasgow* (1968)

Gomme, A., Jenner, M. and Little, B., *Bristol: an Architectural History* (1979)

Goodhart-Rendel, H. S., *Vitruvian Nights* (1932)

— *How Architecture is Made* (1947)

— *English Architecture Since the Regency* (1953)

Goodwin, F., *Rural Architecture* (1835)

Gould, J., *Modern Houses in Britain, 1919–39* (S.A.H. G.B., 1977)

Gradidge, R., *Dream Houses: the Edwardian Ideal* (1980)

— *Edwin Lutyens: Architect Laureate* (1981)

Gravagnuolo, B., *Adolf Loos: theory and works*, trans. C. H. Evans (New York, 1982)

Graves, R. and Hodge, A., *The Long Week-end* (1940)

Gray, A. S., *Edwardian Architecture: a biographical dictionary* (1985)

Grisewood, H., ed., *Ideas and Beliefs of the Victorians* (1949)

Gropius, W., *The New Architecture and the Bauhaus*, trans. P. Morton Shand (1935)

— *The Scope of Total Architecture* (New York, 1955)

— *Apollo in the Democracy* (New York, 1968)

Guiton, J., *The Ideas of Le Corbusier* (New York, 1981)

Gwynn, D., *Lord Shrewsbury, Pugin and the Catholic Revival* (1946)

Haddon, A. C., *Evolution in Art* (1895)

Hakewill, A. W., *Thoughts upon the style of architecture to be adopted in rebuilding the Houses of Parliament* (1835)

Hall, J., *Essay on the Origin, History and Principles of Gothic Architecture* (Edinburgh, 1813)

Halsted, J. B., *Romanticism: selected documents* (1969)

Harbron, D., *Amphion, or the Nineteenth Century* (1930)

— *The Conscious Stone* [E. W. Godwin] (1949)

Hardman, M., *Ruskin and Bradford* (Manchester, 1986)

Harper, R. H., *Victorian Architectural Competitions: an index to British and Irish Architectural Competitions in 'The Builder', 1843–1900* (1983)

— *Victorian Building Regulations* (1985)

Harris, J., Harris, E. and Crook, J. Mordaunt, *Sir William Chambers* (1970)

Harris, T., *Victorian Architecture: A Few Words to Show that a National Architecture adapted to the wants of the 19th century, is attainable* (1860)

— *Examples of the Architecture of the Victorian Age* (1862)

— *Three Periods of English Architecture* (1894)

Hartley, D., *Observations on Man* (1749)

Hartman, G. H., *Beyond Formalism* (1970)

Harvie, C., *et al.*, *Industrialisation and Culture, 1830–1914* (1970)

Hawkes, D. and Taylor, N., *Barry Parker and Raymond Unwin* (1980)

Hawley, H., *Neo-Classicism, Style and Motif* (Cleveland, 1964)

[Hayward Gallery] *Salvator Rosa* (1973)

Head, R., *The Indian Style* (1986)

Helsinger, E. K., *Ruskin and the Art of the Beholder* (Harvard, 1982)

Henderson, P., *William Morris* (1966)

Herrmann, W., *Laugier and 18th century French Theory* (1962)

— *The Theory of Claude Perrault* (1973)

— *Gottfried Semper: in search of architecture* (Camb., Mass., 1985)

Hersey, G. L., *High Victorian Gothic: a study in Associationism* (Baltimore, 1972)

Hewison, R., *Ruskin: the Argument of the Eye* (1976)

— ed., *New Approaches to Ruskin* (1981)

Heyck, T. W., *The Transformation of Intellectual Life in Victorian England* (1982)

Hilton, T., *John Ruskin* i (1985)

Hipple, W. J., *The Beautiful, The Sublime, and the Picturesque in 18th century British Aesthetic Theory* (Carbondale, 1957)

Hitchcock, H.-R., *Modern Architecture: Romanticism and Reintegration* (1929)

— *In the Nature of Materials, 1887–1941: The Buildings of Frank Lloyd Wright* (New York, 1942)

— *Early Victorian Architecture in Britain*, 2 vols. (New Haven, 1954; 1980)

— *Architecture: 19th and 20th Centuries* (Harmondsworth, 1958; 1977)

— and Johnson, P., *The International Style* (New York, 1932; 1966)

— and Bauer, C. K., *Modern Architecture in England* (New York, 1937; reprinted, 1969)

Hix, J., *The Glass House* (Cambridge, Mass., 1974)

Hobbes, T., *Human Nature* (1640)

Hobhouse, H., *Thomas Cubitt: master builder* (1971)

Home, H., [Lord Kames], *Elements of Criticism*, 2 vols. (1762)

Honour, H., *Neo Classicism* (1968)

— *Romanticism* (1979)

Hope, A. J. B. Beresford, *Public Offices and Metropolitan Improvements* (1857)

— *The Common Sense of Art* (1858)

— *The English Cathedral of the 19th century* (1861)

— *The Condition and Prospects of Architectural Art* (1863)

Hope, T., *An historical essay on architecture* (1835)

l'Hôpital, de W., *Westminster Cathedral and its Architect*, 2 vols. (1919)

[Hopper, T.], *Hopper versus Cust on the New Houses of Parliament* (1837)

Hosking, W., *Treatise on Architecture*, ed. A. Ashpital (1867)

Hough, G., *The Last Romantics* (1949)

Houghton, W. E., ed., *The Wellesley Index to Victorian Periodicals, 1824–1900* i (1966); ii (1972); iii (1979)

Howard, E., *Tomorrow: a Peaceful Path to Real Reform* (1898)

— *Garden Cities of Tomorrow* (1902)

Howarth, T., *Charles Rennie Mackintosh and the Modern Movement* (1952; 1977)

Hudnut, J., *Architecture and the Spirit of Man* (Camb., Mass., 1949).

Hume, D. *A Treatise of Human Nature* (1739); ed. P. H. Nidditch (Oxford, 1978)

— *Essays, Moral, Poetical and Literary* (1741); ed. T. H. Green and T. H. Grose (1876)

Hunt, J. Dixon, *The Pre-Raphaelite Imagination* (1968)

— *The Figure in the Landscape: Poetry, Painting and Gardening during the 18th century* (1977)

— *Garden and Grove: the Italian Renaissance Garden in the English Imagination, 1660–1750* (1986)

— ed. *Encounters: Essays on Literature and the Visual Arts* (1971)

— and Willis, P., eds., *The Genius of the Place: the English Landscape Garden, 1620–1820* (1975)

— and Holland, F. M., eds., *The Ruskin Polygon: Essays on*

the Imagination of John Ruskin (Manchester, 1982)

Hussey, C., *The Fairy Land of England* (1924)

— *The Picturesque, Studies in a Point of View* (1927; reprinted 1967; 1976)

— *Sir Robert Lorimer* (1931)

— *The Life of Sir Edwin Lutyens* (1953; reprinted, 1984)

— *English Country Houses: Early, Middle and Late Georgian*, 3 vols. (1954–8; reprinted 1984)

— *English Gardens and Landscapes, 1700–50* (1967)

Hutcheson, F., *An Inquiry into the Originals of our Ideas of Beauty and Virtue* (1724)

— *Inquiry Concerning Beauty, Order, Harmony and Design* (1726); ed. P. Kivy (1973)

Hyde, R. and Hoole, J., *Getting London in Perspective* (1984)

Ind, R., *Emberton* (1983)

Innis, R. E., ed., *Semiotics: an Introductory Reader* (1986)

Irving, R. G., *Indian Summer: Lutyens, Baker and Imperial Delhi* (1981)

Jackson, A., *The Politics of Architecture* (1970)

Jackson, F., *Sir Raymond Unwin: Architect, Planner and Visionary* (1985)

Jackson, Sir T. G., *Modern Gothic Architecture* (1873)

— *Some Thoughts on the Training of Architects* (1895)

— *Recollections*, ed. B. H. Jackson (Oxford, 1950)

Jacobs, J., *The Death and Life of Great American Cities* (1964)

— *The Economy of Cities* (1970)

Jacques, D., *Georgian Gardens: the Reign of Nature* (1983)

James, J., *On the Use of Brick in Ecclesiastical Architecture* (1847)

Jameson, C., *Notes for a Revolution in Urban Planning* (1978)

Jarrett, D., *The English Landscape Garden* (1978)

Jellicoe, Sir G., *et al.*, *The Oxford Companion to Gardens* (Oxford, 1986)

Jencks, C., *Modern Movements in Architecture* (1973; revised 1985)

— *The Language of Post-Modern Architecture* (1977; revised 1984)

— *Late Modern Architecture* (1980)

— *Symbolic Architecture* (1985)

— *What is Post-Modernism?* (1986)

— *Le Corbusier* (1973; 1987)

Jenkins, F. I., *Architect and Patron* (1961)

Jenkyns, R., *The Victorians and Ancient Greece*, (Cambridge, Mass, 1980)

Johnson, P. C. *Machine Art* (New York, 1934)

— *Mies van der Rohe* (New York, 1947; 1979)

— and Barr, A. H., *Modern Architects* (1932)

Johnson, R. J., *Specimens of Early French Architecture* (1864)

Johnson, R. V., *Aestheticism* (1969)

Johnson-Marshall, P., *Rebuilding Cities* (1966)

Jones, B., *Follies and Grottoes* (1953)

Jones, E., *Industrial Architecture in Britain, 1750–1939* (1985)

Jones, E. and Woodward, C., *A Guide to the Architecture of London* (1983)

Jones, O., *The Grammar of Ornament* (1856)

Jones, O. W., *Isaac Williams and his Circle* (1971)

Jones, P., *Hume's Sentiments: their Ciceronian and French Context* (Edinburgh, 1982)

Jordan, R. Furneaux, *Victorian Architecture* (1966)

— *Le Corbusier*, (1972)

Junod, P., *Transparence et opacité* (Lausanne, 1976)

Kallick, M., *The Association of Ideas and Critical Theory in 18th century England* (The Hague, 1970)

Kaufmann, E., *Von Ledoux bis Le Corbusier* (Vienna, 1933)

— *Architecture in the Age of Reason* (Cambridge, Mass., 1955)

— and Raeburn, B., eds., *Frank Lloyd Wright. Writings and Buildings* (New York, 1960)

Kaye, B., *The Development of the Architectural Profession in Britain* (1960)

Kennedy, T., ed., *Victorian Dublin* (Dublin, 1980)

Kerr, R., *The Gentleman's House* (1864); ed. J. Mordaunt Crook (1972)

King, T. H., *The Study Book of Medieval Architecture and Art*, 4 vols. (1858–68)

Kingston, W., *Innovation: the creative impulse in human progress* (1977)

Kinross, J., *Details from Italian Buildings, chiefly Renaissance* (1883)

Kivy, P., *The Seventh Sense: A Study of Francis Hutcheson's Aesthetics and its Influence on 18th century Britain* (New York, 1976)

Kliger, S., *The Goths in England* (Cambridge, Mass., 1952)

Klingender, J. D., *Art and the Industrial Revolution*, ed. Sir A. Elton (1968)

Knevitt, C., *Space on Earth* (1985)

Knight, R. Payne, *The Landscape: a Didactic Poem* (1794)

— *An Analytical Enquiry into the Principles of Taste* (1805)

Kornwolf, J. D., *M. H. Baillie Scott and the Arts and Crafts Movement* (1972)

Kostoff, S. ed., *The Architect* (Oxford, 1974)

Kowsky, F., *The Architecture of F. C. Withers* (Middleton, Conn., 1980)

Ladd, H. A., *The Victorian Morality of Art: an Analysis of Ruskin's Aesthetic* (New York, 1932)

Lamb, E. B., *Studies of Ancient Domestic Architecture* (1846)

Lanchester, H. V. and Fern, A., *The Art of E. A. Rickards* (1920)

Landow, G. P., *The Aesthetic and Critical Theories of John Ruskin* (Princeton, 1971)

Lane, B. M., *Architecture and Politics in Germany, 1918–45* (Cambridge, Mass., 1968)

Lasdun, Sir D., *A Language and a Theme: the Architecture of Denys Lasdun and Partners* (1976)

— ed., *Architecture in an Age of Scepticism* (1984)

Laugier, M. A., *Essai sur l'Architecture* (1753; revised ed. Paris, 1755)

— *Observations sur l'Architecture* (The Hague, 1765)

Law, H. W. and I., *The Book of the Beresford Hopes* (1925)

Leach, E., *Culture and Communication* (Cambridge, 1976)

Le Corbusier [Jeanneret, C.-E.] *Towards a New Architecture* (Paris, 1923; trans. F. Etchells, 1927; reprinted 1946; 1987)

— 'In the Defence of Architecture' (1933); reprinted in *Oppositions* iv Oct., 1974, 93–108

— *The City of Tomorrow and its Planning* (Paris, 1925; trans. F. Etchells, 1929; 1947; 1987)

— *The Radiant City* (Paris, 1933; trans. 1957; 1964)

— *Concerning Town Planning* (Paris, 1946; trans. C. Entwistle, 1947)

— *The Home of Man*, trans. C. Entwistle and G. Holt (1948)

— *The Modulor* (1950; trans. P. de Francis and A. Bostock, 1954)

— *The Marseilles Block* (Souillac, 1950; trans. G. Sainsbury, 1953)

— *My Work* (1960)

Ledoux, C.-N., *L'architecture consideée sous le rapport de l'art, des moeurs et de la législation* (Paris, 1804)

Leeds, W. H., *The Travellers Club House . . . and the Revival of the Italian Style* (1839)

— *Rudimentary Architecture: the Orders and their Aesthetic Principles* (14th ed., 1893)

Léon, P., *Merrimée* (Paris, 1962)

Leslie, S., *The Oxford Movement* (1933)

Lethaby, W. R., *Architecture, Mysticism and Myth* (1892); ed. G. Rubens (1974)

— *Architecture* (1912); ed. B. Ward (Oxford, 1955)

— *Art and Workmanship* (Birmingham, 1930)

— *Philip Webb and His Work* (1935); ed. G. Rubens (1979)

— *Architecture, Nature and Magic* (1956)

— *Form in Civilisation* (Oxford, 1957)

— *Scrips and Scraps*, ed. A. H. Powell (n. d.)

— *About Beauty* (Birmingham School of Printing, 1928)

— , Powell, A. and Griggs, F. L. *Ernest Gimson, His Life and Work* (1924)

Liddon, H. P., *Life of E. B. Pusey*, 4 vols. (1893–7)

Lindsay, Lord, *Progress by Antagonism* (1846)

— *Sketches of the History of Christian Art* (1847)

Linstrum, D., *Sir Jeffry Wyatville* (Oxford, 1972)

— *West Yorkshire Architects and Architecture* (1978)

Liscombe, R. Windsor, *William Wilkins* (Cambridge, 1980)

Locke, J., *Essay Concerning Human Understanding* (1690; 1700)

Lodoli, C. [Memmo, A.], *Elementi d'architettura Lodoliana* (1833)

Loudon, J. C., *Remarks on Hot Houses* (1817)

— *Encyclopaedia of Cottage, Farm and Villa Architecture* (1833); revised by Mrs. J. Loudon (1846; 1867)

Lough, A. G., *The Influence of John Mason Neale* (1962)

— *J. M. Neale: Priest Extraordinary* (1978)

Lovejoy, A. O., *Essays in the History of Ideas* (1948)

Lowenthal, D., *The Past is a Foreign Country* (Cambridge, 1985)

Lugar, R., *Architectural Sketches for Cottages, Rural Dwellings and Villas* (1805)

— *Villa Architecture* (1828)

Lyall, S., *The State of British Architecture* (1980)

Lyon, T. H., *Real Architecture* (1932)

Lyotard, J. F., *The Post-Modern Condition: a Report on Knowledge* (Manchester, 1984)

Macartney, M., *Recent English Domestic Architecture* (1908)

Macaulay, J., *The Gothic Revival, 1745–1845* (1975)

MacCarthy, F., *The Simple Life: C. R. Ashbee in the Cotswolds* (1980)

McCarthy, M., *The Origins of the Gothic Revival* (1987)

McDougall, E. B. ed., *J. C. Loudon and the Early 19th century in Britain* (Dumbarton Oaks, 1980)

MacEwen, M., *Crisis in Architecture* (R.I.B.A., 1974)

McFadzean, R., *The Life and Work of Alexander Thomson* (1979)

McGrath, R., *Twentieth-century houses* (1934)

— and Frost, A. C., *Glass in Architecture and Decoration* (1937)

Mackail, J. W., *Life of William Morris*, 2 vols. (1899)

Macleod, R., *Charles Rennie Mackintosh: architect and artist* (1968; 1983)

—*Style and Society: architectural ideology in Britain, 1835–1914* (1971)

Macready, S. and Thompson, F. H. eds., *Influences in Victorian Art and Architecture* (Society of Antiquaries, 1985)

Madsen, S. T., *Restoration and Anti-Restoration* (Oslo, 1976)

Mainstone, R. J., *Developments in Structural Form* (1975)

Malins, E., *English Landscaping and Literature, 1660–1840* (Oxford, 1966)

Malton, J., *An Essay on British Cottage Architecture* (1798)

—*Designs for Villas* (1802)

Manwaring, E., *Italian Landscape in 18th century England* (New York, 1925; reprinted 1965)

Marks, R. W., *The Dymaxion World of Buckminster Fuller* (New York, 1960)

Markus, T. A., ed., *Order in Space and Society: Architectural Form and its Context in the Scottish Enlightenment* (Edinburgh, 1982)

Marriot, C., *Modern English Architecture* (1924)

Martin, Sir L. *Buildings and Ideas, 1933–83* (Cambridge, 1984)

—*et al., Circle* (1937); reprinted (1971)

Massé H. J, I. J., ed., *The Art Workers' Guild, 1884–1934* (Oxford, 1935)

Maxwell, R., *New British Architecture* (1972)

[Mayor Gallery], *Unit One: Spirit of the '30s* (1984)

Meinecke, F., *Historism: the Rise of a New Historical Outlook*, trans. J. E. Anderson (1972)

Mellor, J., ed., *The Buckminster Fuller Reader* (1970)

Menear, L., *London's Underground Stations* (Tunbridge Wells, 1983)

Metcalf, P., *James Knowles* (Oxford, 1980)

Micklethwaite, J. T., *Modern Parish Churches* (1874)

—*Church Furniture and Arrangement* (1908, ed.)

Middleton, G. A. T. and Carden, R. W., *Ornamental Details of the Italian Renaissance* (1901)

Middleton, R. ed., *The Beaux-Arts and 19th century French Architecture* (1982)

—and Watkin, D., *Neoclassical and 19th century Architecture* (New York, 1980)

Middleton, R. D., *Magdalen Studies* (1936)

—*Newman and Bloxam: an Oxford Friendship* (1947)

Milizia, F., *Principi di Architettura Civile* (1785)

Mill, J. S., *Essays on Literature and Society*, ed. J. Schneewind (1965)

Miller, P., *Decimus Burton* (Building Centre, 1981)

Modiano, R., *Coleridge and the Concept of Nature* (1985)

Moholy-Nagy, L., *The New Vision: From Material to Architecture*, trans. D. M. Hoffmann (New York, 1932, 1939, 1947)

Moholy-Nagy, S., *Moholy-Nagy: Experiment in Totality* (New York, 1950)

Monk, S. H., *The Sublime, a study of critical theories in 18th century England* (New York, 1935; reprinted 1960)

Montgomery-Massingberd, H. and Watkin, D., *The London Ritz* (1980)

Morris, R., *Lecture on Architecture* (1734)

Morris, W., *Collected Works*, 24 vols., ed. M. Morris (1910–15)

—*Selected Writings*, ed. G. D. H. Cole (1934)

—*William Morris, Artist, Writer, Socialist*, ed. M. Morris (Oxford, 1935)

—*Letters*, ed. P. Henderson (1950)

—*Selected Writings and Designs*, ed. A. Briggs (1962)

—*Unpublished Lectures*, ed. E. D. LeMire (Detroit, 1969)

—*Political Writings*, ed. A. L. Morton (1973)

—*Collected Letters*, ed. N. Kelvin, i (Princeton, 1984)

Mowl, T. and Earnshaw, B., *Trumpet at a Distant Gate: the Lodge as a Prelude to the Country House* (1985)

Mozeley, T., *Reminiscences, chiefly of Oxford*, 2 vols. (1884)

Mumford, L., *Technics and Civilisation* (New York, 1934; 1952)

—*Art and Technics* (New York, 1952)

—*The City in History* (New York, 1961)

—ed., *The Roots of Contemporary Architecture* (New York, 1952)

Münz, L. and Künstler, G., *Adolf Loos: Pioneer of Modern Architecture*, intro. N. Pevsner (1966)

Murray, R. and Toombley, S., *Modern British Architecture since 1945* (1984)

Musgrave, C., *The Royal Pavilion* (1959)

Muthesius, H., *Die Neuere Kirchliche Baukunst in England* (Berlin, 1902)

—*Das Englische Haus*, 3 vols. (Berlin, 1908–11; ed. D. Sharp, trans. J. Seligman, 1979)

[National Association for the Advancement of Art], *Transactions: Edinburgh* (1889); *Birmingham* (1890)

Naylor, G., *The Bauhaus* (1968)

—*The Arts and Crafts Movement* (1971)

—*The Bauhaus Reassessed* (1985)

Neale, Rev. J. M. and Webb, Rev. B., *The Symbolism of Churches . . . a Translation of . . . Durandus* (1845; new ed. 1893)

Neale, Rev. J. M., *Letters*, ed. M. S. Lawson (1910)

Nesfield, W. Eden, *Specimens of Medieval Architecture . . . in France and Italy* (1862)

Newman, Rev. J. H. [Cardinal], *Letters and Diaries*, ed. C. S. Dessain (1961)

Newman, O., *Defensible Space* (1973)

Newton, W. G., *The Work of Ernest Newton* (1923)

—*Prelude to Architecture* (1925)

Nicholson, C. and Spencer, C., *Recent English Ecclesiastical Architecture* [1912]

Normand, C. P. J., *Nouveau parallèle des ordres d'Architecture des Grecs, des Romains et des auteurs modernes* (Paris, 1825); trans. A. Pugin (1829); ed. R. A. Cordingley (1951)

Nuttgens, P., *The Landscape of Ideas* (1972)

[Open University], *History of Architecture and Design, 1890–1939*, 24 units (1975–77)

Orbach, L., *Homes for Heroes: British Public Housing, 1915–21* (1977)

Ottolini, W., and Gruner, L., *The Terra-Cotta Architecture of North Italy* (1867)

Palladio, A., *The Four Books of Architecture* ed. I. Ware (1738; reprinted 1965)

Panofsky, E., *Meaning in the Visual Arts* (New York, 1955; revised 1970)

—*Idea: a Concept in Art Theory* (1924; Columbia, S. Carolina, 1968)

Papadaki, S., ed., *Le Corbusier* (New York, 1948)

Papworth, J. B., *Rural Residences* (1818)

—*Hints on Ornamental Gardening* (1823)

—*An Essay on the Principles of Design in Architecture* (1826)

Papworth, W., ed., *Dictionary of Architecture* (Architectural Publication Soc.), 8 vols. (1852–92)

Bibliography

—The Renaissance and Italian Styles of Architecture in Great Britain (1883)

Parker, C., Villa Rustica (1832–41)

Parker, J. H., An Introduction to the Study of Gothic Architecture (1849; 17th ed. 1913)

—A.B.C. of Gothic Architecture (Oxford, 1881; 11th ed. 1900)

Pater, W., Works, 10 vols. (1910 ed.)

Pawley, M., Architecture Versus Housing (1971)

Peisch, L. M., The Chicago School of Architecture (1964)

Perez-Gomez, A., Architecture and the Crisis of Modern Science (M.I.T., 1983)

Perrault, C., A Treatise of the Five Orders in Architecture, trans. J. Jones (1708)

Petit, Rev. J. L., Remarks on Church Architecture, 2 vols. (1841)

Pevsner, Sir N., Pioneers of the Modern Movement. From William Morris to Walter Gropius (1936; reprinted with revisions, as Pioneers of Modern Design, New York, 1949; revised 1960)

—An Enquiry into Industrial Art in England (Cambridge, 1937)

—An Outline of European Architecture (Harmondsworth, 1942; revised, 1968–70)

—Visual Pleasures from Everyday Things (1946)

—The Sources of Modern Architecture and Design (1968)

—Studies in Art, Architecture and Design, 2 vols. (1968)

—Robert Willis (Northampton, U.S.A., 1969)

—Ruskin and Viollet-le-Duc (1969)

—Some Architectural Writers of the 19th century (Oxford, 1972)

—ed., The Buildings of England, Scotland, Ireland, Wales, 52 vols. to date (Harmondsworth, 1951 onwards)

—ed., The Picturesque Garden (Dumbarton Oaks, 1974)

—and Richards, Sir J., The Anti-Rationalists (1973)

—and Metcalf P.,The Cathedrals of England, 2 vols.(1985)

Phillips, L. March, The Works of Man (1911)

Pickett, W. Vose, Metallurgic Architecture (1844)

Pilcher, D., The Regency Style (1847)

Plaw, J., Ferme Ornée or Rural Improvements (1795)

Podro, M., The Critical Historians of Art (1982)

Pollen, A., John Hungerford Pollen (1912)

Poole, W. F., Index to Periodical Literature 6 vols. (1883–1907)

Porphyrios, D., ed., On the Methodology of Architectural History (A.D., 1981)

—Sources of Modern Eclecticism: Studies on Alvar Aalto (1982)

Port, M.H., Six Hundred New Churches: a Study of the Church Building Commission, 1818–56 (1961)

—ed., The Houses of Parliament (1976)

Portoghesi, P., The Presence of the Past (Venice Biennale, 1980)

Powys, A. R., From the Ground Up (1937)

Prentice, A. N., Renaissance Architecture and Ornament in Spain, 5 vols. (1893)

Price, Sir U., An Essay on the Picturesque as Compared with the Sublime and the Beautiful, 2 vols. (1794–8); ed. Sir J. D. Lauder (Edinburgh, 1842)

—A Dialogue on the distinct Characters of the Picturesque and the Beautiful (Hereford, 1801)

Prickett, S., Romanticism and Religion: the Tradition of Coleridge and Wordsworth in the English Church (Cambridge, 1976)

Pritchard, J., View from a Long Chair: the memoirs of Jack Pritchard (1984)

Pugin, A. C. and Willson, E. J. [and Britton, J.] Specimens of Gothic Architecture, 2 vols. (1821–3)

—and Pugin, A. W. N. and Walker, T. L., Examples of Gothic Architecture, 3 vols. (1831–8)

Pugin, A. W. N., A letter to A. W. Hakewill [concerning] the style for rebuilding the Houses of Parliament (1835)

—Contrasts (1836); ed. H.-R. Hitchcock (Leicester, 1969)

—'Lectures on Ecclesiastical Architecture', Catholic Magazine ii (1838), 193–213, 321–37; iii (1839), 17–34, 89–98

—The True Principles of Pointed or Christian Architecture (1841; reprinted, Oxford, 1969)

—The Present State of Ecclesiastical Architecture in England (1843; reprinted Oxford, 1969)

—An Apology for the Revival of Christian Architecture (1843; reprinted, Oxford, 1969)

—Some Remarks . . . relative to Ecclesiastical Architecture and Decoration (1850)

—An Earnest Address on . . . the Re-Establishment of the . . . Hierarchy (1851)

—Photographs from Sketches, ed. S. Ayling, 2 vols. (1865)

Pugsley, A., ed., The Works of I. K. Brunel: An Engineering Appreciation (New York, 1976)

Pullan, R. Popplewell, Studies in Architectural Styles (1883)

Quatremère de Quincy, A.-C., Dictionnaire d'Architecture, 3 vols. (Paris; Liège, 1788–1825)

Quiney, A., J. L. Pearson (1979)

Rawlinson, R., Designs for Factory, Furnace and Other Tall Chimneys (1862)

Read, Sir H., ed., Unit One: the Modern Movement in English Architecture, Painting and Sculpture (1934)

—Art and Industry. The Principles of Industrial Design (1934; revised 1966)

Reade, J. Mellard, Suggestions for the Formation of a New Style of Architecture especially adapted to Civic Purposes (1862)

Reilly, Sir C., Some Architectural Problems of Today (1924)

—Representative British Architects of the Present Day (1931)

—Scaffolding in the Sky (1938)

—Architecture as a Communal Art (1946)

Repton, H., Sketches and Hints on Landscape Gardening (1795)

—Observations on the Theory and Practice of Landscape Gardening (1803)

—Fragments on the Theory and Practice of Landscape Gardening (1816)

Reynolds, Sir J., Discourses on Art, ed. R. R. Wark (1975)

Richards, Sir J., An Introduction to Modern Architecture (Harmondsworth, 1940; revised, 1970)

—The Functional Tradition (1958)

—New Buildings in the Commonwealth, intro. Sir N. Pevsner (1961)

—Memoirs of an Unjust Fella (1980)

—and Summerson, J., The Bombed Buildings of Britain, (1942)

Richardson, Sir A., Monumental Classic Architecture in Great Britain and Ireland during the 18th and 19th centuries (1914)

Richardson, C. J., Observations on the Architecture of England during the Reigns of Queen Elizabeth and King James I (1837)

— *The Englishman's House, from a Cottage to a Mansion* (1870)
— *Picturesque Designs for Mansions, Lodges, Villas, etc.* (1870)
Richardson, M., *Architects of the Arts and Crafts Movement* (1983)
Rickman, T., *An Attempt to Discriminate the Styles of English Architecture* (1819)
Ricks, C., *Tennyson* (1972)
Roberts, A. R. N., *W. R. Lethaby* (1957)
Roberts, J. F. A., *William Gilpin and Picturesque Beauty* (Cambridge, 1944)
Robertson, Sir H., *The Principles of Architectural Composition* (1924)
— *Architecture Explained* (1927)
— *Modern Architectural Design* (1932)
Robertson, M., *Laymen and the New Architecture* (1925)
Robinson, J. M., *The Wyatts: an architectural dynasty* (Oxford, 1979)
— *The Latest Country Houses* (1984)
Robson, E. R., *School Architecture* (1874)
Roethlisberger, M., *Claude Lorrain: Paintings*, 2 vols. (New Haven, 1961); *Drawings*, 2 vols. (Berkeley, 1968)
Rolt, L. T. C., *Isambard Kingdom Brunel* (1957)
— *Telford* (1958)
Rosenberg, J. D., ed., *The Genius of John Ruskin* (1963; revised 1979)
— *The Darkening Glass, a Portrait of Ruskin's Genius* (1963)
Ross, L. S., *Lord Kames and the Scotland of his Day* (Oxford, 1972)
Rossi, A., *The Architecture of the City* (Cambridge, Mass., 1982)
Rowe, C., *The Mathematics of the Ideal Villa and Other Essays* (Cambridge, Mass. 1976)
—, Arnell, P. and Bickford, T., *James Stirling* (1984)
[Royal Academy] *Fifty Years Bauhaus* (1968)
— *Victorian and Edwardian Decorative Art. The Handley-Read Collection* (1972)
[Royal Institute of British Architects] *One Hundred Years of British Architecture, 1851–1951* (1951)
— *Catalogue of Drawings Collection*, ed. J. Lever, 20 vols. (1968–85)
— *Modern British Architecture since 1945* (1984)
Rubens, G., *W. R. Lethaby* (1986)
Ruskin, J., *Complete Works*, ed. E. J. Cook and A. Wedderburn, 39 vols. (1903–9)
— *Diaries*, ed. J. Evans and J. H. Whitehouse, 3 vols. (1956–9)
Russell, Rev. J. Fuller, ed., *Hierugia Anglicana* (1849)
Rykwert, J., *On Adam's House in Paradise, the Idea of the Primitive Hut in Architectural History* (New York, 1972)
— *The First Moderns, the architects of the 18th century* (Cambridge, Mass. 1980)
— *The Necessity of Artifice* (1982).
Saint, A., *Richard Norman Shaw* (1976)
— *The Image of the Architect* (1983)
— *Towards a Social Architecture* (1987)
Santayana, G., *The Sense of Beauty* (New York, 1896)
— *Soliloquies in England* (1922)
Savage, A., *The Parsonage in England* (1964)
— P., *Lorimer and the Edinburgh Craft Designers* (1980)
Saxl, F. and Wittkower, R., *British Art and the Mediterranean* (1948)
Schenk, H. G., *The Mind of the European Romantics* (1966)

Schofield, P. H., *The Theory of Proportions in Architecture* (Cambridge, 1958)
Schopenhauer, A., *The World as Will and Representation*, (1859), trans. E. F. J. Payne, 2 vols. (Colorado, 1958)
Schulze, F., *Mies van der Rohe: A Critical Biography* (Chicago, 1986)
Schütz, G., *Architecture and Decoration of the Italian Renaissance* (1883)
Scott, G., *The Architecture of Humanism: a study in the history of taste* (1914; revised 1924); ed. D. Watkin (1980)
Scott, Sir G. G., *A Plea for the Faithful Restoration of our Ancient Churches* (1850)
— *Remarks on Secular and Domestic Architecture* (1858)
— *Personal and Professional Recollections* (1879)
Scott, G. G. *Modern Village Churches* (1873)
— *An Essay on the History of English Church Architecture* (1881)
Scott, L., *The Renaissance of Art in Italy* (1883)
Scott, M. H. Baillie, *et al.*, *Garden Suburbs, Town Planning and Modern Architecture* (1910)
[Scottish Georgian Society], *Scottish Pioneers of the Greek Revival* (Edinburgh, 1984)
Scruton, R., *Art and Imagination* (1974); revised (1982)
— *The Aesthetics of Architecture* (1979)
— *The Politics of Culture* (Manchester, 1981)
— *Kant* (Oxford, 1982)
— *The Aesthetic Understanding* (1983)
Scully, V., *Modern Architecture: the Architecture of Democracy* (New York, 1961; London, 1968)
— *The Shingle Style Revisited* (1974)
Seaborne, M. and Lowe, R., *The English School, ii, 1870–1970* (1977)
Searing, H., ed., *In Search of Modern Architecture: a Tribute to H.-R. Hitchcock* (New York, 1982)
Sedding, J. D., *Art and Handicraft* (1893)
Seddon, J. P., *Progress in Art and Architecture* (1852)
Serenyi, P., *Le Corbusier in Perspective* (Englewood Cliffs, N. J., 1975)
Sert, J. L., *Can Our Cities Survive?* (1944)
Service, A., *Edwardian Architecture and its Origins* (1975)
— *Edwardian Architecture* (1977)
London 1900 (1979)
Shand, P. Morton, *Modern Theatres and Cinemas* (1930)
— *Building* (1954)
Sharp, D., *Sources of Modern Architecture: a critical bibliography* (1981 ed.)
Sharp, T., *Town and Countryside* (1932)
— *Town Planning* (1940)
Shaw, G. B., *Ruskin's Politics* (1921)
Shaw, R. N., *Architectural Sketches from the Continent* (1858)
— and Jackson, T. G., eds., *Architecture: a Profession or an Art?* (1892)
Shils, E., *Tradition* (1981)
Shipley, Rev. O., ed., *The Church and the World* (1866–8)
Simmons, J., *St. Pancras Station* (1968)
Simpson, D., *C. F. A. Voysey* (1979)
Singelenberg, P., *H. P. Berlage: Idea and Style* (Utrecht, 1972)
Smiles, S., *Lives of the Engineers*, 3 vols. (1862)
Smith, A., *The Theory of Moral Sentiments* (1759; ed. D. D. Raphael and A. L. Macfie, Oxford, 1976)
Smith, P. F., *Dynamics of Urbanism* (1974)

Smithson, A., *Team 10 Primer* (Cambridge, Mass., 1968)
— and P., *The Heroic Period of Modern Architecture* (1965; 1980)
— *Urban Structuring* (1967)
— *Ordinariness and Light* (1970)
— *Without Rhetoric; an Architectural Aesthetic, 1955–72* (1973)
Snell, R., *Théophile Gautier* (Oxford, 1982)
Soane, Sir J., *Designs for Public and Private Buildings* (1828)
— *Lectures on Architecture ... 1809–1836*, ed. A. T. Bolton (1929)
Spaeth, D. and Frampton, K., *Mies van der Rohe* (1985)
Speaight, F. W., *The Marble Arch: a Suggestion by a Citizen of London* (1905)
— *The Horse Guards' Parade: a Suggested Improvement* (1909)
Stamp, G., ed., *Silent Cities* (R.I.B.A., 1977)
— *London, 1900* (A.D. Profiles, xiii, 1978)
— *Britain in the Thirties* (A.D. Profiles, xxiv, 1980)
— *The Great Perspectivists* (1982)
— and Amery, C., *Victorian Buildings in London* (1980)
— and Goulancourt, A., *The English House, 1860–1914* (1980; 1985)
Stanton, P., *The Gothic Revival and American Church Architecture, 1840–56* (Baltimore, 1968)
— *Pugin*, (1971)
Starobinski, J., *The Invention of Liberty* (trans., Geneva, 1964)
— *Emblems of Reason* (1973)
Statham, H. Heathcote, *Modern Architecture* (1892)
Stätz, V. and Ungewitter, G., *The Gothic Model Book* (1858)
Steegman, J. E., *The Rule of Taste from George I to George IV* (1936)
— *Consort of Taste, 1830–70* (1950)
Stevenson, J. J., *House Architecture*, 2 vols. (1880)
Stewart, C., *The Stones of Manchester* (1956)
Stirling, J., *Buildings and Projects, 1950–74* (1975)
Stratton, A., *Elements of Form and Design in Classic Architecture* (1925)
— *The Orders of Architecture* (1931)
Street, A. E., *Memoir of G. E. Street* (1888; reprinted 1976)
Street, G. E., *An Urgent Plea for the Revival of True Principles of Architecture in the Public Buildings of the University of Oxford* (Oxford, 1853)
— *Brick and Marble in the Middle Ages: Notes on a Tour in North Italy* (1855; 1874)
— *Some Account of Gothic Architecture in Spain* (1869, ed.)
— *Unpublished Note Books and Reprinted Papers*, ed. G. G. King (1916)
Stroud, D., *Capability Brown* (1950); revised (1975)
— *The Architecture of Sir John Soane* (1961)
— *Humphry Repton* (1962)
— *George Dance* (1971)
— *Sir John Soane* (1984)
Stuart, J. and Revett, N., *The Antiquities of Athens*, 4 vols. (1762–1816)
Summerson, Sir J., *John Nash* (1935); revised and expanded (1980).
— *The Architectural Association, 1847–1947* (1947)
— *Heavenly Mansions* (1949; New York, 1963)
— *Architecture in Britain, 1530–1830* (Harmondsworth, 1953; revised 1983)

— *Ten Years of British Architecture* (1956)
— *The Classical Language of Architecture* (1963; revised 1980)
— *Victorian Architecture: Four Studies in Evaluation* (New York, 1970)
— *The London Building World of the 1860s* (1973)
— *The Turn of the Century: Architecture in Britain around 1900* (Glasgow, 1976)
— *The Architecture of Victorian London* (Charlottesville, 1976)
— ed., *Concerning Architecture: Essays ... presented to Nikolaus Pevsner* (1968)
— and Williams-Ellis, C., *Architecture Here and Now* (1934)
—, Watkin, D., and Mellinghoff, G.-T., *John Soane* (1983)
Survey of London, 41 vols. to date (1896 onwards)
Sutcliffe, A., ed., *Multi-Storey Living: the British Working-Class Experience* (1974)
Swenarton, M., *Homes Fit for Heroes: the politics and architecture of early state housing in Britain* (1981)
Tafuri, M., *Theories and History of Architecture* (1968; 1976)
— *Architecture and Utopia: Design and Capitalist Development* (trans. Cambridge, Mass., 1976)
[Tate Gallery] *Landscape in Britain, c. 1750–1850* (1973)
Taut, B., *Modern Architecture* (1929)
Taylor, G. L., and Cresey, E., *Architectural Antiquities of Rome* (1821–2)
Taylor, N., *Cambridge New Architecture* (Cambridge, 1964)
— *Monuments of Commerce* (1968)
— *The Village in the City* (1973)
Tennyson, G. B., *Victorian Devotional Poetry: the Tractarian Mode* (1981)
Thompson, E. P., *William Morris: Romantic to Revolutionary* (1955; revised 1977)
Thompson, P., *The Work of William Morris* (1967)
— *William Butterfield* (1970)
— ed., *The High Victorian Cultural Achievement* (Victorian Society, 1967)
— and Pakenham, T., *Architecture: Art or Social Service* (1963)
Thomson, A., 'Glasgow University', *Glasgow Architectural Soc. Proceedings*, (1865–7)
— 'Art and Architecture', *The British Architect* i–ii (1874) reprinted (Manchester, 1874)
Thorlby, A., *The Romantic Movement* (1966)
Tilden, P., *True Remembrances* (1954)
Towle, E. A., *John Mason Neale* (1906)
Towndrow, F. E., *Architecture in the Balance* (1933)
— ed., *Replanning Britain* (1941)
Toynbee, A., *An Historian's Approach to Religion* (1956)
Trappes-Lomax, M., *Pugin, a Medieval Victorian* (1932)
Troeltsch, E., *Writings on Theology and Religion*, ed. R. Morgan and M. Pye (1977)
Tubbs, R., *Living in Cities* (1942)
— *The Englishman Builds* (1945)
Turner, F., *The Greek Heritage in Victorian Britain* (1981)
Turnor, R., *19th century Architecture in Britain* (1950)
Tuveson, E., *The Imagination as the Means of Grace: Locke and the Aesthetics of Romanticism* (Berkeley, 1960)
Twombley, R. C., *Frank Lloyd Wright: his Life and Architecture* (New York, 1979)
Unrau, J., *Looking at Architecture with John Ruskin* (1978)

— *Ruskin and Venice* (1984)

Unwin, Sir R., *Town Planning in Practice* (1909)

— *Nothing Gained by Overcrowding* (1912)

— and Parker, B., *The Art of Building a Home* (1901)

— *Cottage Plans and Common Sense* (1902)

Van Eckhardt, W., *Eric Mendelsohn* (1960)

Venturi, R., *Complexity and Contradiction in Architecture* (1966; 1977)

— , Scott Brown, D. and Izenour, S., *Learning from Las Vegas* (1972)

Vernon, H. M. and K. D., *A History of the Oxford Museum* (Oxford, 1909)

[Victoria and Albert Museum] *Victorian and Edwardian Decorative Art* (1952)

— *Victorian Church Art* (1971)

— *Marble Halls* (1973)

— *High Victorian Design* (1974)

— *Catalogues of Architectural Drawings* (1983 onwards)

Viollet-le-Duc, E. E., *Dictionnaire Raisonné de l'architecture français du XIe au XVIe siècle*, 10 vols. (Paris, 1854–68)

— *Dictionnaire Raisonné du Mobilier Français*, 6 vols. (Paris, 1858–75)

— *Entretiens sur l'architecture*, 2 vols. (Paris, 1863; trans. B. Bucknall, 1877–82)

— *Histoire d'une Maison* (Paris, 1873); trans. B. Bucknall (1874)

— *Histoire d'une Forteresse* (Paris, 1874); trans. B. Bucknall (Boston, 1876)

— *Habitations Modernes*, 2 vols. (Paris, 1875–7)

— *Compositions et Dessins* (Paris, 1884)

Vitruvius, *The Ten Books of Architecture*, trans. H. H. Morgan (New York, 1960)

Voysey, C. F. A., *Individuality* (1915; reprinted 1985)

Wagner, O., *Moderne Architektur*, 3 vols. (Vienna, 1896–1902)

Walden, R., ed., *The Open Hand: Essays on Le Corbusier* (Cambridge, Mass., 1977)

Ward, C., ed., *Vandalism* (1973)

Waring, J. B., *Designs for Civic Architecture* (1850)

Wasserman, E. R., ed., *Aspects of the 18th century* (Baltimore, 1965)

Watkin, D., *Thomas Hope and the Neo-Classical Idea* (1968)

— *The Life and Work of C. R. Cockerell* (1974)

— *Morality and Architecture: the Development of a Theme from the Gothic Revival to the Modern Movement* (Oxford, 1977)

— *The Triumph of the Classical: Cambridge Architecture, 1804–34* (Cambridge, 1977)

— *English Architecture* (1979)

— *The Rise of Architectural History* (1980)

— *The English Vision: the picturesque in architecture, landscape and garden design* (1982)

— *Athenian Stuart* (1982)

Watson, J. R., *Picturesque Landscape and English Romantic Poetry* (1970)

Weale, J., ed., *Quarterly Papers on Architecture*, 4 vols. (1844–5)

Weaver, Sir L., *Houses and Gardens by E. L. Lutyens* (1931; reprinted 1981)

— and Phillips, R. Randal, *Small Country Houses of Today*, 3 vols. (1922–5)

Webb, Rev. B., *Sketches of Continental Ecclesiology* (1848)

Webb, M., *Architecture in Britain Today* (1969)

Wellek, R., *Concepts of Criticism* (New Haven, 1963)

Whateley, T., *Observations on Modern Gardening* (1770)

Whewell, W., *Architectural Notes on German Churches* (1835; 1842)

Whiffen, M., ed., *The History, Theory and Criticism of Architecture* (M.I.T., 1964–5)

White, J. F., *The Cambridge Movement: the Ecclesiologists and the Gothic Revival* (1962)

— *Protestant Worship and Church Architecture* (New York, 1964)

White, W. H., *Architecture and Public Building: their Relation to School, Academy and State in London and Paris* (1884)

— *A Protest Against the Amended Designs for the Proposed Admiralty and War Office* (1885)

Whitney, L., *Primitivism and the Idea of Progress in English Popular Literature of the 18th century*, intro. A. O. Lovejoy (Baltimore, 1934)

Whittick, A., *Eric Mendelsohn* (1940)

— *European Architecture in the 20th c.*, 2 vols. (1950–53)

— and Osborn, Sir F., *The New Towns: the Answer to Megalopolis* (1963)

Wickman, S., *Japonisme: the Japanese Influence on Western Art since 1858* (1981)

Wiebenson, D., *Tony Garnier: the Cité Industrielle* (New York, 1969)

— *Sources of Greek Revival Architecture* (1969)

— ed., *Architectural Theory and Practice from Alberti to Ledoux* (Chicago, 1982)

Wiener, M. J., *English Culture and the Decline of the Industrial Spirit, 1850–1980* (Cambridge, 1981)

Wightwick, G., *The Palace of Architecture* (1840)

Willis, P., ed., *Furor Hortensis: Essays in Memory of H. F. Clark* (Edinburgh, 1974)

Willis, R., *Remarks on the Architecture of the Middle Ages, especially of Italy* (Cambridge, 1835)

— *English Cathedrals* (1842–63; reprinted, 2 vols. 1972)

Wilson, H., *et al.*, *A Memorial of . . . J. D. Sedding* (1892)

Wilson, M., *William Kent* (1984)

Winckelmann, J. J. *Writings on Art*, ed. D. Irwin (1972)

Wingler, H. M., *The Bauhaus* (1969)

Wittkower, R., *Architectural Principles in the Age of Humanism* (1973 ed.)

— *Palladio and English Palladianism* (1974)

— *Idea and Image: Studies in the Italian Renaissance* (1978)

Wolfe, T., *From Bauhaus to Our House* (1982)

Wollheim, R., *Art and its Objects* (New York, 1968)

Woodbridge, K., *Landscape and Antiquity, Aspects of English Culture at Stourhead, 1718–1838* (Oxford, 1971)

Woolner, A., ed., *Thomas Woolner* (1913)

Worringer, W., *Abstraction and Empathy* (1908; trans. New York, 1963)

Wright, F. Lloyd, *Modern Architecture* (Princeton, 1931)

— *The Disappearing City* (New York, 1932)

— *On Architecture*, ed. F. Gutheim, (New York, 1941)

— *When Democracy Builds* (Chicago, 1945)

— *The Future of Architecture* (New York, 1953)

— and Brownell, B., *Architecture and Modern Life* (New York, 1937)

Wyatt, Sir M. Digby, *Views of the Crystal Palace and Park, Sydenham* (1854)

— *An Architect's Note-book in Spain* (1872)

— and Waring, J. D., *A Handbook for the Medieval Courts* (1854)

323

Yates, N., *Leeds and the Oxford Movement* (Thoresby Soc., 1979)
— *The Oxford Movement and Anglican Ritualism* (1983)
— ed., *Kent and the Oxford Movement* (1986)
Yerbury, F. R., *Modern Homes* (1947)
Yorke, F. R. S., *The Modern House* (1934)
— *The Modern House in England* (1937; 1944)
— and Gibberd, Sir F., *The Modern Flat* (1937)
— and Penn, C, *A Key to Modern Architecture* (1939)
Young, A. McLaren, *Charles Rennie Mackintosh* (Edinburgh, 1968)
Young, R. M., *Darwin's Metaphor: Nature's Place in Victorian Culture* (1986)
Young, W., *Town and Country Mansions and Suburban Houses* (1879)
— *The Municipal Buildings, Glasgow* (Glasgow, 1890)
Zevi, B., *Erich Mendelsohn* (1985)

III Articles

Adams, M. B., 'Architects from George IV to George V', *R.I.B.A. Journal* (1912), 598–607, 643–54
Anson, P. F., 'Sir J. N. Comper', *Trans. Scottish Ecclesiological Soc.* (1950)
Archer, J., 'Character in English Architectural Design', *18th century Studies* xii (1979), 339–71
— 'The Beginnings of Association in British Architectural Esthetics', *18th century Studies* xvi (1983), 241–64
Banham, R., 'Historical Studies and Architectural Criticism', *Trans. Bartlett Soc.* i (1962), 35–51.
— 'A Marginal Redefinition of Modern', *Trans. Bartlett Soc.* iv (1965), 27–46.
Baridon, M., 'Ruins as a Mental Construct', *Journal of Garden History* v (1985), 84–96.
Bassett, D., ' "Queen Anne" and France', *Architectural History* xxiv (1981), 83–91
de Beer, E. S., 'Gothic: Origin and Diffusion of the Term: the Idea of Style in Architecture', *Journal of the Warburg and Courtauld Institutes* xi (1948), 148–62
Betjeman, Sir J., 'J. N. Comper', *A.R.* lxxxv (1939), 79–82
Blau, E., 'The Earliest Work of Deane and Woodward', *Architectura* ix (1979), 172–92
Bonnefoi, C., 'Louis Kahn and Minimalism', *Oppositions* xxiv (1981), 3–25
Bradford, T., 'The Brick Palace of 1862', *AR* July (1962), 15–21
Brandon-Jones, J., 'The Work of Philip Webb and Norman Shaw', *A.A. Jnl.* lxxi (1955), 9–21
Bright, H., 'A Reconsideration of Pugin's Architectural Theories', *Victorian Studies* xxii (1979), 151–72
Bright, M. H., 'English Romanticism and the Oxford Movement', *Journal of the History of Ideas* xl (1979), 385–404
Brigstock, H., 'Lord Lindsay and the "Sketches of the History of Christian Art" ', *Bull. John Rylands Library* lxix (1981), 27–60
— 'Lord Lindsay as a Collector', *Bull. John Rylands Library* lxiv (1982), 287–333
Brooks, M., 'The Builder in the 1840s', *Victorian Periodicals Review* xiv (1981), 87–93
Brooks, R. A. E., 'The Development of the Historical Mind', in J. E. Barker, ed., *The Re-Interpretation of Victorian Literature* (Princeton, 1950), 130–53
Brownlee, D., 'That "regular mongrel affair": G. G. Scott's design for the government offices', *Architectural History* xxviii (1985), 159–82
Cachemaille-Day, N. F., 'Ecclesiastical Architecture in ythe Present Age', *R.I.B.A.J.* 3rd series xl (1932–3), 825–38
Clark, G., 'Grecian Taste and Gothic Virtue', *Apollo* xcvii (1973), 566–71
Clark, H. F., '18th century Elysiums', *Warburg Institute Journal* vi (1943), 165–89
— 'The Sense of Beauty in the 18th, 19th and 20th centuries: aesthetic values in English landscape appreciation', *Landscape Architecture* xlvii (1957), 465–9
Clark, K., 'Ornament in Architecture', *R.I.B.A.J.*, 3rd series xlii (1934–5), 167–9
— 'Vitality and Order in Architecture', *R.I.B.A.J.*, 3rd series liv (1946–7), 474–5
Coles, W. A., 'The Architecture of Raymond Erith', *Classical America* iv (Toronto, 1977), 125–52
Colquhoun, A., 'The Modern Movement in Architecture', *British Journal of Aesthetics* ii (1962) 59–65.
— 'Three Kinds of Historicism', *Oppositions* xxvi (1984), 29–39
Crook, J. Mordaunt, 'Sir Robert Smirke: a centenary Florilegium', *AR*, cxlii (1967), 208–10
— 'The Pre-Victorian Architect: Professionalism and Patronage', *Architectural History* viii (1969), 62–78
— 'A Vanished Theatrical Masterpiece: Smirke's Covent Garden Theatre', *C. L. Annual* (1970), 102–5
— 'Regency Architecture in the West Country: the Greek Revival', *R.S.A. Jnl.* cxix (1971), 438–51
— 'Northumbrian Gothic', *R.S.A. Jnl.* cxxi (1973), 271–83
— 'Sydney Smirke: the architecture of compromise', in *Seven Victorian Architects*, ed. J. Fawcett and N. Pevsner (1976), 50–65
— 'William Burges and the Dilemma of Style', *AR* (1981), 6–15
— 'T.G. Jackson and the Cult of Eclecticism', in H. Searing, ed. *In Search of Modern Architecture* (New York, 1982), 102–20
— 'Ruskinian Gothic', in J. Dixon Hunt and F. M. Holland, eds, *The Ruskin Polygon* (Manchester, 1982), 68–71
— 'Progressive Eclecticism: the case of Beresford Hope', *Architectural Design* liii (1983), 56–62
— 'Architecture and History', *Architectural History* xxvii (1984), 555–78
— 'Early French Gothic', *Society of Antiquaries, Occasional Papers* N.S. vii (1985), 49–58
Curl, J. Stevens and Sambrook, J., 'E. Bassett Keeling', *Architectural History* xvi (1973), 60–69
Curran, C. P., 'B. Woodward, Ruskin and the O'Sheas', *Studies* (Dublin) xxix (1940), 255–68
Curtis, W., 'Bertold Lubetkin', *A.A. Qtly* vii, no. 3 (1976), 33–9
Darby, M. and Van Zanten, D., 'Owen Jones's Iron and Glass Buildings of the 1850s', *Architectura* (1974), 53–75
Eisenman, T., 'Real and English: the Destruction of the Box, 1', *Oppositions* 4 Oct. 1974, 5–34
Ettlinger, L. D., 'On Science, Industry and Art. Some

Theories of Gottfried Semper', *AR* cxxxvi (1964), 57–60

Frampton, K., 'The Humanist *versus* Utilitarian Ideal', *AD* xxxviii (1968), 134–6

Gardiner, P., 'Freedom as an Aesthetic Idea', in *The Ideas of Freedom: Essays in Honour of Isaiah Berlin*, ed. A. Ryan (Oxford, 1979), 29–39

Gold, M., 'Sir Owen Williams', *Zodiac* xviii, 11–29

Gombrich, Sir E., 'Style', *International Encylopaedia of the Social Sciences* (New York, 1968), xv, 352–61

— 'The Logic of Vanity Fair, Alternatives to Historicism in the Study of Fashions, Style and Taste', *The Philosophy of Karl Popper*, ed. P. A. Schilpp, ii (Illinois, 1974), 925–57

Goodhart-Rendel, H. S., 'The Work of Sir John Burnet', *Architect's Journal* lvii (1923), 1066–1110

— 'English Gothic Architecture of the 19th century', *R.I.B.A. Journal* xxxi (1924), 321–30

— 'Temple Moore', *AR* (1926), (i), 11–17

— 'English Architecture, 1834–1934', in *The Growth and Work of the R.I.B.A.*, ed. J. A. Gotch (1934)

— 'Rebuilding after the War', *A. and B.N.* clxxii (1942), 123–6, 136–8

— 'The English Home in the 19th century', *Architect's Journal*, cviii (1948), 449–50, 469–70

— 'Rogue Architects of the Victorian Era', *R.I.B.A. J.* lxi (1949), 251–9

— 'Oxford Buildings Criticised', *Oxoniensia* xvii-xviii (1952–3), 200–215

Gregory-Jones, D., 'Towers of Learning', *AR* cxxiii (1958), 393–8

Grierson, H. J. C., 'Classical and Romantic', in *The Background to English Literature* (1934), 256–90

Handley-Read, C., 'High Victorian Design', in *Design, 1860–1960*, ed. P. Thompson (Victorian Soc., 1963), 23–7

Harbron, D., 'J.F. Bentley', *Architect's Journal* lxxxix (1939), 159–60

— 'Thomas Harris', *AR* xcii (1942), 63–6

— 'Queen Anne Taste and Aestheticism', *AR* xciv (1943), 15–18

— 'Edward Godwin', *AR* xcviii (1945), 48 52

Haskell, F., 'A Victorian Monument and its Mysteries' [Albert Memorial], *Revue de l'Art* xxx (1975), 61–76, 104–10

Havens, R. D., 'Simplicity, a Changing Concept', *Journal of the History of Ideas* xiv (1953), 3–32

Hersey, G., 'J.C. Loudon and Architectural Associationism', *AR* cxliv (1968), 89–92

— 'Association and Sensibility in 18th century Architecture', *18th century Studies* iv (1970–71), 71–89

Hinnant, C. H., 'A Philosophical Origin of the English Landscape Garden', *Bulletin of Research in the Humanities* lxxxiii (1980), 292–306

Hitchcock, H-R., 'Victorian Monuments of Commerce', *AR* c (1949), 61–74

— 'Early Victorian Architecture, 1837–51'; 'Late Victorian Architecture, 1851–1900', *R.I.B.A. Journal* xliv (1937), 981–93, 1029–39

— 'The Acclimatisation of Modern Architecture', *A.A.Jnl.* lxii (1946–7), 3–9

— 'Architecture – not Style', *Progressive Architecture* xxx (1949), 12

— 'Early Cast Iron Façades', *AR* cix (1951), 113–16

— 'Ruskin and Butterfield', *AR* cxvi (1954), 285–9

— 'Britain's Contribution to Post-War Architecture',

The Listener 27 Oct., 1955, 696–8

— 'The Imperial Institute, South Kensington', *Kensington Society Annual Report* (1955–6), 26–7

— 'High Victorian Architecture', *Victorian Studies* i (1957), 47–71

— 'G. E. Street in the 1850s', *Journal of the Society of Architectural Historians* xix (1960), 145–72

— 'Brunel and Paddington', *AR* cix (1961), 240–46

Hix, J., 'Richard Turner: Glass Master', *AR* Nov. (1972), 287–93

Howell, P., 'Newman's Church at Littlemore', *Oxford Art Journal* vi (1983), i, 51–5

Hunt, J. Dixon, 'Emblem and Expression in the Landscape Garden', *18th century Studies* iv (1971), 294–317

— 'Sense and Sensibility in the Landscape Designs of Humphry Repton', *Studies in Burke and His Time* xix (1978), 3–28

Hussey, C., 'Humphry Repton', *C. L. Annual* (1952), 44–7

— 'R. Payne Knight: a Regency Prophet of Modernism', *C.L. Annual* (1956), 46–9

Jackson, N., 'The Un-Englishness of G. E. Street's church of St. James-the-Less', *Architectural History* xxiii (1980), 86–94

Jordan, R. Furneaux, 'Lubetkin', *AR* July (1955), 36–44

Jump, J. D., 'Ruskin's Reputation in the 1850s', *Publications of the Modern Language Association of America* lxiii (1948), 678–85

Junod, P., 'Future in the Past', *Oppositions* xxvi (1984), 43–63

Kaufmann, E. Jnr., 'Memmo's Lodoli', *Art Bulletin* (1964), 159–175

Kelsall, M., 'The Iconography of Stourhead', *Journal Warburg and Courtauld Institutes* xlvi (1983), 133–43

Korsmeyer, C. K., 'Relativism and Hutcheson's Aesthetic Theory', *Journal of the History of Ideas* xxxvi (1975), 319–30

Lang, S., 'The Principles of the Gothic Revival in England', *Journal of the Society of Architectural Historians* xxv (1966), 240–67

Liscombe, R. Windsor, 'Economy, Character and Durability: Specimen Designs for Church Commissioners, 1818', *Architectural History* xiii (1970), 43–57

Mc. Kean, C., Cullinan, E. *et al.*, 'Architecture: a local or a universal art', *R.S.A. Jnl.* cxxxv (1987), 103–37

Meeks, C. V. L., 'Picturesque Eclecticism' *Art Bulletin* xxxii (1950), 226–35

— 'Creative Eclecticism', *Journal of the Society of Architectural Historians* xii (1953), 15–18

Middleton, R., 'J.F. Blondel and the Cours d'Architecture', *Journal of the Society of Architectural Historians* (1959), 140–148

— 'The Abbé de Cordemoy and the Graeco-Gothic Ideal: a Prelude to Romantic Classicism', *Journal of the Warburg and Courtauld Institutes* xxv (1962), 278–320 and xxvi (1963), 90–123

— 'Viollet-le-Duc's Influence on 19th century England', *Art History* iv (1981), 203–19

— 'The Rationalist Interpretations of Classicism of Leance Reynaud and Viollet-le-Duc', *A. A. Files* xi (1986), 29–48

Bibliography

Millon, H. A., 'Rudolph Wittkower, *Architectural Principles in the Age of Humanism*: its influence on the Development and Interpretation of Modern Architecture', *Journal of the Society of Architectural Historians* xxxi (1972), 83–91

Muthesius, S., 'The Iron Problem in the 1850s', *Architectural History* xiii (1970), 58–63

Oberg, B. B., 'David Hartley and the Association of Ideas', *Journal of the History of Ideas* xxxvii (1976), 441–54

O'Dwyer, F. and Williams, J., 'Benjamin Woodward' in *Victorian Dublin*, ed. T. Kennedy (Dublin, 1980)

Ollard, S. L., 'The Oxford Architectural and Historical Society and the Oxford Movement', *Oxoniensia* v (1940), 146–60

Pace, G. G., 'Alfred Bartholomew, a Pioneer of Functional Gothic', *AR* xcii (1942), 99–102

Pantin, W. A., 'The Oxford Architectural and Historical Society', *Oxoniensia* iv (1939), 174–94

Patrick, J., 'Newman, Pugin and Gothic', *Victorian Studies* xxiv (1981), 185–207

Pevsner, Sir N., 'The Picturesque in Architecture', *R.I.B.A.J.* lv (1947), 55–61

— 'Revivalisms in Architecture', *The Listener* xliv (1950), 1054–7

— 'How to judge Victorian Architecture', *The Listener* xlv (1951), 91–2

— 'Victorian Thought on Architecture', *The Listener* xlv (1951), 137–9

— 'Victorian Churches and Public Buildings', *The Listener* xlv (1951), 177–9

— 'The Late Victorians and William Morris', *The Listener* xlv (1951), 217–19

— 'Originality: Goodhart-Rendel's defence of the Victorians', *AR* cxv (1954), 367–9

— 'Architecture and William Morris', *R.I.B.A.J.* lxiv (1957), 172–5

— 'Roehampton: L.C.C. Housing and the Picturesque Tradition', *A.R.* cxxvi (1959), 21–35

— 'The Anti-Pioneers', *The Listener* lxxvi (1966), 953–5; lxxvii (1967), 7–9

— 'William Whewell and his architectural notes on German churches', *German Life and Letters* xxii (1968), 39–48

— [as P.F.R. Donner] 'A Harris Florilegium', *AR* xciii (1943), 51–2

Port, M. H., 'The New Law Courts Competition, 1866–7', *Architectural History* xi (1968), 75–93

Redfern, H., 'W. Butterfield and H. Woodyer', *Architect and B. N.* clxxviii (1944), 21–2, 44–5, 58–60; *B. clxvi* (1944), 295

Richards, Sir J., 'The Hollow Victory, 1932–72', *R.I.B.A.J.*, 3rd series, lxxix (1972), 192–7

— 'Twenty Five Years of British Architecture, 1952–77', *R.I.B.A.J.*, 3rd series, lxxxiv (1977), 176–8

Richardson, A. E., 'Architecture', in G. M. Young, ed., *Early Victorian England, 1830–65*, ii (1934), 177–248.

Roberts, H. V. Molesworth, 'L.A. Stokes', *AR* c (1946), 173–7

Rose, E., 'The Stone Table in the Round Church and the Crisis of the Cambridge Camden Society', *Victorian Studies* x (1967), 119–44

Rose, M., 'Habermas and Postmodern Architecture', *Australian Jnl. of Art* v (1986), 113–19.

Rowe, C., 'Neo-Classicism and Modern Architecture',

Oppositions i (1973), 1–26

Rykwert, J., 'Adolf Loos: the New Vision', *Studio International* July/Aug. (1973) 17–21

— [and Middleton, R.] 'Lodoli and Function and Representation', *AR* July (1976), 21–26; 267–8

Schapiro, M., 'Style', in *Anthropology Today*, ed. A.L. Kroeber (Chicago, 1953)

— 'Style, Form and Content', in *Aesthetics Today*, ed. M. Philipson (Cleveland, 1961), 110 *et seq.*

Scruton, R., 'Architectural Aesthetics', *British Journal of Aesthetics* xiii (1973), 327–45

Senstroem, D., 'John Ruskin and the Nature of Manliness', *Victorian Newsletter* no. xi (1971), 147–201

Service, A., 'John Belcher's Colchester Town Hall and the Edwardian Grand Manner', *Essex Archaeology and History* v (1973)

Skempton, A. W., 'Evolution of the Steel Frame Building', *Guild Engineer* x (1959), 37–51

— and H. R. Johnson, 'The First Iron Frames', *AR* cxxxi (1962), 175–86

Smith, N., 'Imitation and Invention in Two Albert Memorials', *Burlington Magazine*, cxxiii (1981), 232–3

Stamp, G., 'Victorian Bombay', *A.A.R.P.* (1977), 22–7

— 'British Architecture in India', *R.S.A. Jnl.* cxxix (1980–81), 357–79

— 'London 1900', *AD* xlviii (1978)

— 'New British Churches between the Wars', *C.L.* clxix (1981), 238–40

Stansky, P., 'Art, Industry and the Aspirations of William Martin Conway', *Victorian Studies* xix (1976), 465–84

Stanton, P., 'Pugin at Twenty One', *AR* cx (1951), 187–90

— 'Some Comments on the Life and Work of A. W. N. Pugin', *R.I.B.A.J.* 3rd series lx (1952), 47–54

— 'Pugin: Principles of Design versus Revivalism', *Journal of the Society of Architectural Historians* xiii (1954), 20–25

Steegman, J., 'Lord Lindsay's History of Christian Art', *Journal of the Warburg and Courtauld Institutes* x (1947), 123–31

Stevens, T., 'Connell, Ward and Lucas', *A. A. Jnl.* lxxii, no. 806, Nov. 1956, 112–13

Summerson, Sir J., 'An Early Modernist: James Wild and his Work', *Architect's Journal* lxix (1929), 57–62

— 'The Work of H. S. Goodhart-Rendel', *Brick Builder* March 1934, 13–17

— 'Architecture', in *The Arts Today*, ed. G. Grigson (1935), 253–88

— 'The Fate of Modern Architecture', *The Listener* xxiv (1940) 1002–3

— 'Norman Shaw', *The Listener* xxv (1941), 493

— 'Bread and Butter and Architecture', *Horizon*, vi (1942), 233–43

— 'Pugin at Ramsgate', *AR* ciii (1948), 163–6

— '1851: A New Age, A New Style', in *Ideas and Beliefs of the Victorians* ed. H. Grisewood (1949), 63–70

— 'Soane: the Case-History of a Personal Style', *R.I.B.A.J.* lviii (1951), 83–91

— 'A Question of Taste', *The Listener* xlvi (1952), 175–6

— 'Le Corbusier's Modulor', *New Statesman* 23 Feb. 1952

— 'The Case for a Theory of Modern Architecture', *R.I.B.A.J.* 3rd. series lxiv (1957), 307–13

— 'British Contemporaries of Frank Lloyd Wright', *Studies in Western Art* iv (Acts of the 20th International Congress of the History of Art, Princeton, 1963), 78–87

— 'Sir John Soane and the Furniture of Death', *AR* clxiii (1978), 147–55

Suzuki, H., 'Josiah Conder and England', *Kenchikushi Kenyu* xi (1976–79), 1–15

Tayler, J. E., 'Sir John Soane: Architect and Freemason', *Ars Quatuor Coronatorum* xcv (1982), 194–202

Teyssot, G., 'John Soane and the Birth of Style', *Oppositions* xiv (1978), 67–75

Thompson, G. B., 'Tractarian Aesthetics: Analogy and Reason in Keble and Newman', *Victorian Newsletter* no. lv (1979), 8–10

Thompson, P., 'All Saints, Margaret Street, Reconsidered', *Architectural History* viii (1965), 73–94

Tselos, D., 'Joseph Gandy, Prophet of Modern Architecture', *Magazine of Art* xxxiv (1941), 251 *et seq.*

Unrau, J., 'A Note on Ruskin's Reading of Pugin', *English Studies* Aug. 1967, 335–7

Warren, E., 'The Life and Work of G. F. Bodley', *R.I.B.A.J.* xvii (1910), 305–40

Watkin, D., 'Charles Kelsall: the quintessence of Neo-Classicism', *AR* cxl (1966), 109–12

Webb, I., 'The Bradford Wool Exchange: Industrial Capitalism and the Popularity of Gothic', *Victorian Studies* xx (1976), 45–68

Wiebenson, D. 'Greek, Gothic and Nature, 1750–1820' in *Essays in Honour of W. Friedlander* (*Marsyas*, New York, 1965), 187–94

Williams, R., 'Making Places: Garden – Mastery and English Brown,' *Journal of Garden History* iii (1983), 382–5

Wittkower, R., 'Systems of Proportion', *Architects' Year Book* v (1953), 9–18

— 'Individualism in Art and Artists: a Renaissance Problem', *Journal of the History of Ideas* xxii (1961), 291–302

— 'Genius: Individualism in Art and Artists', *Dictionary of the History of Ideas* ii (New York, 1973), 287–312

Zanten, A. L. Van, 'Form and Society: Cesar Daly', *Oppositions* xiii (1977), 136–45

IV Unpublished Theses

Adams, P., 'Converts to the R.C. Church in England, c. 1830–70' (B. Litt., Oxford, 1977)

Allibone, J., 'Anthony Salvin' (Ph.D., London, 1977)

Bassett, D. J., 'The French Renaissance Revival in British Architecture, 1824–1914' (Ph.D., Edinburgh, 1979)

Bassin, J., 'The Competition System: architectural competitions in 19th century England' (Ph.D., Indiana, 1975)

Becherer, R. J., 'Between Science and Sentiment: César Daly and the Formulation of Modern Architectural Theory' (Ph.D., Cornell, 1980)

Bingham, N., 'Victorian and Edwardian Whitehall' (Ph.D., London, 1985)

Blutman, S., 'English Country Houses, 1780–1815' (M. Phil., London, 1968)

Brandwood, G. K., 'Church Building and Restoration in Leicestershire, 1800–1914' (Ph.D., Leicester, 1984)

Brown, C. V., 'W. R. Lethaby. Architecture as Process' (Ph.D., Carolina, 1974)

Carr, G., 'The Commissioners' Churches of London, 1818–37' (Ph.D., Michigan, Ann Arbor, 1976)

Colley, E. D., 'Thomas Rickman' (M.A., Manchester, 1962)

Darby, M., 'Owen Jones and the Eastern Ideal' (Ph.D., Reading, 1974)

Diestelkamp, E., 'The Iron and Glass Architecture of Richard Turner' (Ph.D., London, 1982)

Dixon, R., 'James Brooks' (Ph.D., London, 1976)

Elgohary, F., 'Wells Coates and the Modern Movement' (Ph.D., London, 1966)

Evinson, D., 'J. A. Hansom' (M.A., London, 1966)

Feinberg, S. G., 'Sir John Soane's Museum' (Ph.D., Michigan; Ann Arbor, 1979)

Fergusson, S. A., 'Victorian and Medieval Sources for the Early Churches of G. F. Bodley' (M.A., Courtauld, 1979)

Grainger, H., 'The Architecture of Sir Ernest George and his Partners, c. 1860–1922' (Ph.D., Leeds, 1985)

Hardman, M., 'The Prose and Ideas of John Ruskin' (Ph.D., Cambridge, 1975)

Lindsay, I. S., 'Dunecht House, Aberdeenshire' (M. A., Edinburgh, 1980)

London, C. W., 'British Architecture in Victorian Bombay' (D.Phil., Oxford, 1986)

Martin, D. S., 'The Architecture of W. R. Lethaby' (M. A., Manchester, 1957)

Mellor, H. D., 'Blore's Country Houses' (M.A., Courtauld, 1975)

Middleton, R., 'Viollet-le-Duc and the Gothic Rational Tradition' (Ph.D., Cambridge, 1959)

O'Donnell, R., 'R. C. Church Architecture in Great Britain and Ireland, 1829–78' (Ph.D., Cambridge, 1983)

Ohman, M. M., 'Latitudinarianism: an architectural theory and its application in England and America, 1840–95' (Ph.D., Missouri, 1973)

Richardson, D. S., 'Gothic Revival Architecture in Ireland' (Ph.D., Yale, 1970)

Rowan, A. J., 'The Castle Style in British Domestic Architecture in the 18th and early 19th century' (Ph.D., Cambridge, 1965)

Simo, M. L., 'Loudon and the Landscape: a study of rural and metropolitan improvements, 1803–43' (Ph.D., Yale, 1976)

Simon, C., 'George Somers Clarke' (M. A., Courtauld, 1983)

Simpson, D., 'Art and Religion in the work of A. W. Pugin' (Ph.D., Keele, 1973)

Spence, T. R., 'Philip Webb' (B. A., Cambridge 1965)

Stamp, G., 'G. G. Scott Jnr.' (Ph.D., Cambridge, 1979)

Stanton, P., 'Welby Pugin and the Gothic Revival' (Ph.D., London, 1950)

Toplis, I. L., 'The Foreign Office: an Architectural History' (Ph.D., Thames Polytechnic, 1980)

Unrau, J., 'Ruskin's Architectural Writings' (D. Phil., Oxford, 1969)

Wainwright, C., 'The Antiquarian Interior in Britain, 1780–1850' (Ph.D., London, 1987)

Index

Bold figures refer to illustration numbers